THIRD EDITION

DATA SYSTEMS AND MANAGEMENT

AN INTRODUCTION TO SYSTEMS ANALYSIS AND DESIGN

ALTON R. KINDRED

Manatee Community College
Bradenton, Florida

Prentice-Hall, Inc., Englewood Cliffs, NJ 07632

Library of Congress Cataloging in Publication Data

Kindred, Alton R., (date)
  Data systems and management.

  Includes index.
  1. Electronic digital computers. 2. System
analysis. 3. System design. I. Title.
QA76.5.K488 1984   001.64′068   84-24785
ISBN 0-13-196189-6

Cover design: Lundgren Graphics, Ltd.
Manufacturing buyer: Ed O'Dougherty

Printed in the United States of America

10 9 8 7 6 5 4 3 2 1

ISBN 0-13-196189-6   01

Prentice-Hall International, Inc., *London*
Prentice-Hall of Australia Pty. Limited, *Sydney*
Editora Prentice-Hall do Brasil, Ltda., *Rio de Janeiro*
Prentice-Hall Canada Inc., *Toronto*
Prentice-Hall Hispanoamericana, S.A., *Mexico*
Prentice-Hall of India Private Limited, *New Delhi*
Prentice-Hall of Japan, Inc., *Tokyo*
Prentice-Hall of Southeast Asia Pte. Ltd., *Singapore*
Whitehall Books Limited, *Wellington, New Zealand*

CONTENTS

PART VI. CASE STUDIES

PREFACE

In just over a quarter century, the electronic computer has reached into almost every business organization and many private homes throughout the world. In business, industry, education, government, and, lately, in recreation, the computer has become the subject of widespread interest and concern.

Programming courses of every description are offered by computer vendors, software houses, schools and colleges, professional organizations, and individuals. Most institutions of higher education offer one or more degrees in computer information systems, data processing, or computer science.

Every properly organized formal curriculum should include at least one course to introduce the fundamental concepts of data systems analysis and design. This book is intended to be a basic text for such a course. Its content covers the suggested outline for course CIS-4, Systems Analysis Methods, in the Model Curriculum for Undergraduate Computer Information Systems Education developed by the Data Processing Management Association-Education Foundation (DPMA-EF).

The text is aimed primarily at second-year students who have had an introductory course in computer information systems and preferably a programming language. However, it can readily be understood by students of business or management or by active line executives who need greater depth of understanding of the electronic computer as a tool for providing information for decision making. The book may have value also as a reference for practicing systems analysts and data processing managers.

The purpose of this book is to show the computer as a valuable tool of the modern business organization, when properly used with all the other resources of the organization. The programming student is led to see that the computer is not an end in itself, but a rapid and tireless servant only when carefully directed and controlled. The business executive finds new avenues of speed, accuracy, and flexibility in providing information for decision making.

While based on sound systems principles, the book uses a practical approach to real-life situations. It retains full coverage of large computer mainframe systems while recognizing the tremendous impact of the microcomputer on the whole of society. It draws on current periodicals and journals for the latest developments in the state of the art to supplement basic principles set forth in conventional texts and references.

This third edition of *Data Systems and Management* has been extensively revised and updated to include many recent developments in the computer industry. New chapters are devoted to the design and control of input and output. Material on management information systems and on verification, control, and auditing has been integrated into the other chapters for better cohesion. A single case study has been carried throughout the entire text. The topics covered in each chapter are applied to the analysis, design, development, implementation, and evaluation of the case study. Three additional case studies are retained for breadth and variety.

Greater emphasis has been placed on the microcomputer and its place in modern data systems. A new section stresses the systems development phase in the systems life cycle. The number of illustrations has been increased to improve visual relationships and patterns.

The text is organized in six parts. Part I consists of two chapters that tell what data systems are and how the systems department is organized. Part II contains three chapters setting forth techniques used in conducting the systems study and analyzing systems to meet the organizational objectives. Part III has four chapters on design and control of data systems. Part IV contains three chapters on development of the hardware and software of the system just designed, with emphasis on data communications. Part V has two chapters telling how to implement the newly developed system, operate and maintain it, and evaluate its effectiveness. Part VI gives three case studies that present both good and bad practices for analysis and discussion.

Each chapter begins with a statement of objectives that the reader should be able to perform upon completion of the chapter. The text material is organized with frequent headings and subheadings to facilitate outlining and understanding of logical relationships. Each chapter concludes with a summary of key points, an application of the continuing case study, a list of terms for review, and questions that provoke discussion or provide activities to sharpen skills used in systems analysis and design.

The text is completely self-contained and needs no additional workbooks, study guides, or other learning resources. It can be adapted to courses ranging from a quarter to a semester to a full academic year. An Instructor's Manual gives teaching suggestions, definitions of the terms for review, answers to the chapter questions, and a bank of true-false and multiple-choice test questions.

Many persons have contributed to the development and review of this textbook. My students and colleagues at Manatee Community College have shown a lively reaction to the first two editions of this text over the past twelve years and have offered many suggestions for this third edition. My wife Joy has provided a haven of comfort and support during the often tedious hours of writing, editing, and proofreading.

The entire manuscript was reviewed by members of the staffs of Sandhills Community College, Bryant College, and Laramie County Community College. They offered many helpful suggestions to improve clarity, cohesion, and completeness.

Finally, I am indebted to the expertise and interest of the editorial and production staffs at Prentice-Hall, Inc., who guided the publication processes to completion.

ALTON R. KINDRED

WHAT ARE
DATA SYSTEMS?

OBJECTIVES

At the end of this chapter, you should be able to:

1. Describe the general characteristics of systems.
2. State the ways in which data systems resemble and differ from systems in general.
3. Identify the components of data systems.
4. Describe the steps in the cycle for developing and operating data systems.
5. Define the major terms used in data systems.
6. Name the three principal types of processing and the characteristics of each.
7. Name and describe the types of personnel related to data systems.
8. Show how control is achieved in data systems.
9. Describe methods of safeguarding the security of data systems.
10. Describe the characteristics of management information systems.

Electronic computers have reached into all phases of business, industry, and government since they were first used commercially in the early 1950s. It has been necessary to change many of the methods by which organizations have processed information, and new careers have evolved to meet the needs of the computer industry.

Computers are more than just machines. They operate only when they are properly instructed through programs stored internally in the memory of the computer. The programs must be designed, written, and tested by programmers to solve specific problems and tasks. The programs require input data captured at some point to furnish details about a transaction or event. The data must be arranged in a form that programmers can specify in their programs. The results of the program are presented in the form of a display or printed report that must have meaning for the recipient. Results may be stored for later use in another processing cycle. Thus we can see that effective use of the computer requires a whole series of related activities.

We prefer to use the term *data systems* rather than *computer systems* because the computer, important though it is, is only a part of the entire process for handling data. Many of the steps occur before data reaches the computer, some are parallel to computer processing, and some happen after the results emerge from the computer. And, of course, much data is processed manually or mechanically without the use of a computer at all.

CHARACTERISTICS OF SYSTEMS

A system may be defined as a group of parts organized to carry out some common function or purpose. But systems are easier to describe than to define precisely. We are all familiar with various types of systems. Some of them are contained within the human body, such as the digestive and nervous systems. Some are the result of ideas, thoughts, or philosophies, such as the judicial system, the democratic system, and language systems. Some provide the means of distributing some useful commodity, such as transportation systems, communications systems, and electric power systems. In business, we refer to accounting, inventory, and marketing systems. Indeed, the entire universe is the most magnificent, complex, and powerful system of all.

Even though their forms are varied and their purposes widely diverse, we can recognize certain characteristics that seem to be common among most if not all systems. First, systems are made up of different parts, or *components.* Second, the parts are *related* and have definite interactions or interdependencies. Third, a change in any of the components is likely to produce some sort of change in other components and in the system as a whole. Fourth, the components all work toward some particular *purpose or function* which is the primary object of the system as a whole. Fifth, the system usually is *complex,* having diverse components such as persons, ideas, materials, forces, procedures, and other factors. Sixth, each system is likely to be a *part of another larger system,* just as it is likely to be *divided into many subsystems.* Further, there seems to be an *infinite number of relationships* possible between systems of all types.

It is not surprising, then, that we have some problem in gaining agreement among writers as to the definition and limitation of the use of the word "systems." The electronics engineer thinks in terms of circuits, electrical components, and connecting lines. The accountant thinks in terms of transactions, books of entry, ledgers, balances, and reports. Production people define systems in terms of time and motion studies, assembly lines, raw materials, and finished products.

All are of course correct. A system is concerned with a function or purpose, and each person thinks in terms of the job he or she is trying to accomplish.

DATA SYSTEMS

Data (used throughout this book as a singular noun, like news) is the lifeblood of modern business. In this book the use of the term "business" normally will imply also industry, government, education, or any other organizational form working to accomplish some particular objective.

It is possible to divide the essential parts of data systems into four categories:

1. The central processing unit of the computer, peripheral equipment, mass storage units, and communication devices. All of this equipment is referred to as *hardware.*
2. Instructions or programs to be executed by the computer, usually called *software.*
3. Personnel to operate and maintain equipment, analyze and set up procedures, prepare instructions, provide input data, utilize reports, review results, and supervise the entire operation.
4. Procedures to tell what data is needed and when, where it is obtained, how it is used, and how it is protected from loss or misuse.

Computer hardware requires certain supplies, called *media,* upon which data is recorded in one form or another. Media include video display screens, punched cards, paper forms, magnetic and paper tapes, and magnetic disks on which data is recorded.

Figure 1-1 shows typical hardware of a modern computer system.

Scope of Data Systems

In view of our earlier observations that data systems mean virtually all things to all people, we must attempt to limit the term as treated in this text. We shall be concerned primarily with those business data systems that

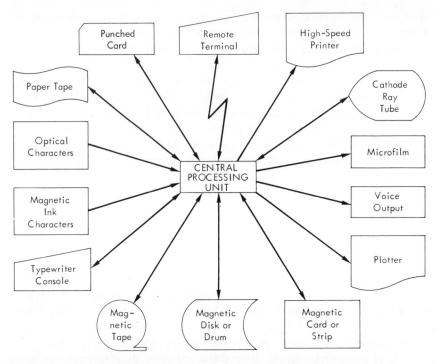

Figure 1-1. Typical hardware of a modern computer system. The central processing unit receives data from input devices and sends the processed information to output devices. Some units may be used for both input and output.

might be applied to a general-purpose digital computer, using one of the typical programming languages, such as BASIC, FORTRAN, COBOL, PL/I, RPG, Pascal, or an assembly language.

Today a multitude of data systems is in use, and a few of these uses are listed below. This list serves to show how the computer permeates almost every segment of our society.

Airline reservations
Bank deposits and clearing house transactions
Text editing
Newspaper type setting
Computer-assisted learning
Credit card purchases and billing
Student registration and grade reporting
Crime prevention and detection networks
Real estate assessment and tax records
Feed and fertilizer blending

Manufacturing bills of materials
Railroad car accounting
Hotel and motel reservations
Sports statistics
Election returns
Indexes of technical journals and abstracts
Home record systems
Computer games

We shall not study those systems requiring highly specialized hardware, analog computers, special interface devices, and so forth. Many such systems are based upon knowledge of electrical engineering, physics, or mathematics far beyond the level of our typical reader. We shall devote our attention to those areas which have been estimated to employ from 75 to 90 percent of all data processing equipment and personnel. The following types of data systems will not be discussed here, but the reader should be aware that they represent valid and important uses of data processing principles:

1. *Process control systems.* These systems regulate production lines and processes to a degree that often becomes largely automatic. The results of manufacturing or blending operations might be fed back through a closed loop to increase or decrease rates, materials, temperatures, and so on, thus regulating later processes.
2. *Scientific systems.* Guidance systems of aircraft, ships, or submarines; measurements of velocities, distances, or physical phenomena; and special data capture devices for rainfall, temperatures, and chemical analysis all involve equipment and techniques so specialized as to be of little value to the typical business-oriented systems analyst.
3. *Medical systems.* Devices that measure or control respiration, heartbeat, functions of internal organs, movement of artificial limbs, vision, hearing, and so forth are beyond the scope of our present study.
4. *Systems programming.* This is the term usually applied to the development and maintenance of software for operating systems. It is really a specialized area of computer programming rather than an application that involves several departments of a business organization. For this reason it is not included in our discussion of data systems.

The Need for Data Systems

In former years the owner of a business was usually the manager and often the only employee. He (or she) knew at first hand each intimate detail of his enterprise. He dealt personally with his customers. He made the purchases, kept the books, swept out the store, made all the decisions, and carried out most of them himself. He decided how he wanted to operate and, with few outside restraints, conducted his business as he chose.

Many of these methods persisted as businesses grew. If the owner had some clerks and assistants, he told them what they should do, watched to be sure that they did as he wanted, corrected them in their mistakes, and rewarded them for good performance on the basis of his personal observation.

Continued growth, however, eventually brought a change in the way of doing things. Businesses spread to different geographical locations. The number of employees became too many for one person to supervise personally. Laborsaving devices began to be employed and standard methods were required for performing various operations. It became necessary to establish uniform methods to assure similar quality and performance among different persons at different locations. The development of the corporation meant that the owners of an enterprise were not necessarily directly involved in its management, and certainly the managers were not directly involved in all aspects of the work.

Early in the twentieth century, Frederick W. Taylor, Frank B. and Lillian M. Gilbreth, and others established basic principles of management which have evolved into fairly well defined systems and procedures. Some of the functions normally carried out under the heading of systems and procedures work are:

Organizational analysis
Systems analysis and design
Office layout
Systems implementation
Forms design and control
Reports analysis and control
Policy, procedure, and bulletin development
Records management
Work measurement
Office equipment selection
Systems research
Management audit

The advent of the electronic computer and its introduction in the last twenty years into almost every aspect of modern business organizations have caused systems work to be more and more concerned with the processing of data by machine. Topics such as office layout and work measurement have declined in importance, while new areas such as file design, access methods, and online real-time information systems have come to the fore.

No longer is it possible for executives having overall responsibility for business enterprises to give their major attention to highly technical questions such as selection of programming languages, comparing performance specifications on highly complex equipment, or writing detailed flowcharts. Thus a whole new group of careers has emerged and new departments are appearing in the organizational structure to reflect the growing need for formal systems activities.

It has been estimated that more than 100,000 persons are now concerned with systems analysis and design, and that this field ranks among the fastest-growing professional occupations. High competition for capable personnel has driven salaries well above those paid for persons in other occupations requiring equivalent education and training.

There is no universally acceptable way of preparing for work in systems analysis. Some employers prefer that a candidate have a college degree as well as experience in mathematics, science, engineering, accounting, or business. Knowledge of computer programming usually is expected, but most important of all is knowledge of the business enterprise itself. The whole field of systems is so broad that analysts tend to concentrate on particular subject matter areas, such as accounting or inventory control, educational administration, planning and forecasting, or research techniques.

Steps in Developing Data Systems

Most larger businesses today have come through a long period of evolution in their business procedures and practices. The transition from the single owner-operator of a business to the large corporation has taken place through a number of gradual steps. But whether the transition takes place gradually over a long period of time or almost immediately, as has happened with many computer service or software firms, data systems still must undergo certain fundamental processes.

1. The general objectives of the business enterprise must be understood and clearly spelled out. Most businesses are organized to earn a profit but governmental or philanthropic organizations have spending as their prime function.
2. The specific areas or applications to be employed in fulfilling these general objectives are then organized and described—for example, selling a new product, offering a service, expanding a plant. In cases where the applications already are being used, the present procedures are analyzed, charted, measured, and otherwise documented. The attempt is to find out as much as possible about the present method of doing things.
3. It is then necessary to explore alternative ways of carrying on these applications. The systems people bring to bear all their knowledge of other equipment and procedures in effect in similar applications elsewhere. They may even attempt to conceive of innovative solutions that have not been tried previously. The most effective overall plan is selected, and detailed design of the new system begins. Occasionally, the system current-

ly in effect is found to be the most effective alternative, so that no new design is made. But even in this case making the study and evaluating the alternatives have been worthwhile, for the knowledge thus gained gives added confidence in the original plan.

4. The next step is to develop the newly designed system. Schedules must be established, detailed programs and procedures written, personnel trained, equipment and materials ordered, and all affected departments consulted and alerted to the impending change.

5. At the agreed time, the new plan is implemented, or put into effect. Sometimes it is desirable to carry on both the new and the old systems in parallel operations for a short while until the transition is complete. This procedure permits a comparison between the two systems and provides control and verification of the results. Because parallel operations cause duplication of resources, they should be limited to the shortest practicable time. The newly implemented system must be constantly reviewed and refined. Every good system must allow some changes to be made without restructuring and redesigning the entire system.

In one way or another, these steps are followed for every application of every enterprise, large or small, manual or electronic. The difference is in the degree of formality, expert analysis, specialized techniques, and documentation that is employed. The modern systems department is intended to bring the highest possible level of expert analysis and design to business activities.

Some Basic Terms Used in Systems

Just as there are, as we have seen already, many different views about the nature of systems, so there are many different definitions of terms and many different opinions as to the relationships between these terms. The following definitions and descriptions are not intended to be exhaustive or authoritative; rather, they are as reasonable and as logical as any others which might be presented.

Data is the set of basic facts about a person, thing, or transaction. It includes such things as date, size, quantity, description, amount, rate, name, or place. Data is often reduced to a coded form for convenience in processing and to save storage space.

Information is produced by comparing, summarizing, grouping, classifying, associating, reducing, or otherwise processing data into a meaningful form. Information necessarily involves the relationship of data with other data. The object of every data processing system is information.

A *data element* is a general class or category of data, such as Social Security number or date of birth. It is usually the smallest piece into which the data is divided logically.

A *data item* is the specific value the data element has at any given time, such as 263-24-1796 or January 8, 1922. Some authorities call the data item an *instance* of the data element.

Data capture refers to the initial recording of data about a transaction. It should normally be in writing or placed directly into a computer system by keying or optical scanning.

Data entry refers to the steps necessary to prepare data for machine processing and to enter it into the computer system. This includes coding, editing, keypunching, verifying, encoding on magnetic tape, or recording at a terminal.

The *data base* is the collection of interrelated data stored so as to serve many applications with minimum duplication.

Data systems employ a combination of hardware, software, personnel, and procedures to process raw data about an enterprise into usable information as a basis for management decisions.

Procedures may be defined as written and oral instructions under which the hardware, software, and personnel operate. They give official sanction and order to the systems and provide for understanding and uniformity in the processing.

Applications are identifiable portions or segments of the larger systems. For example, the keying of data from documents can be considered an application within the larger system of data capture, preparation, and input. Applications are almost always interrelated with other applications, such as the almost unending cycle of activities of requisitioning materials, placing orders, receiving, storing, issuing or selling, requisitioning more materials, and so forth.

The *systems life cycle* involves activities in which the steps are to:

1. Define objectives the system must meet.
2. Analyze the present system as to adequacy in meeting the objectives.
3. Design a new or modified system, considering alternative approaches in terms of effectiveness and cost.
4. Develop the new system.
5. Implement and evaluate the new system, modifying it as necessary.

Figure 1-2 illustrates the systems life cycle. Note that in any of the five steps it is possible to return to any of the preceding steps to make changes to improve the system.

Systems analysis is the formal study and evaluation of activities and procedures. The results of this kind of study form the foundation for managerial decisions and should therefore be presented in formalized and standardized form. Systems analysis implies the examination of each component part of the system, both as a separate entity and in relation to the whole. Systems analysis is elaborated in Part II of the text.

Systems analysis leads logically to *systems design,* which is the creative act of devision or inventing a partially or completely new cheme for pro-

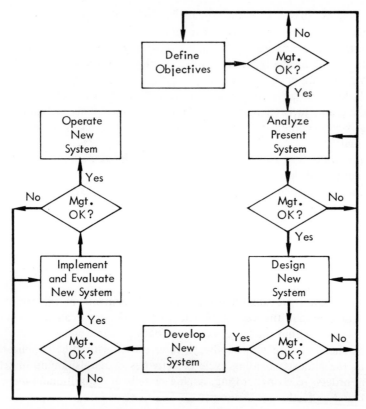

Figure 1-2. The systems life cycle. Management approval is required to
move from each phase to the next. It may be necessary to
return to any prior stage to modify and repeat the cycle.

cessing data. Systems design is expanded in Part III.

Systems development includes all steps necessary to translate the design into a coherent workable whole. Aspects of systems development are
treated in Part IV.

Systems implementation involves those steps necessary to convert from
the old to the new system. The newly implemented system must undergo
continuing *systems evaluation* to see that it meets the objectives for which it
was designed. Systems implementation and evaluation are treated in depth
in Part V.

A *management information system* attempts to integrate the available
information into a whole rather than into separate applications. A central
data base on mass storage devices permits related information to be made
available to all levels and departments of the organization for action and
decision making.

Fundamental Principles of Data Systems

In the relatively short period of about 30 years since electronic computers have come upon the modern scene, a few general principles have evolved. Some have come about by trial and error, some by theoretical application, and some by careful planning. One of the most difficult jobs of the systems person is to differentiate between those things which follow a general principle and those which require individual, specialized treatment.

1. Data about a transaction should be recorded in writing or in electronic form when and where the transaction occurs.
2. At the earliest possible stage in processing, data should be placed in a form which can be read, processed, and stored automatically by machines. Ideally, once data has entered into a data processing system it need not be handled manually again.
3. Every practical method of verifying, balancing, and controlling the data entering the system should be used.
4. Data should be classified so that it can be readily retrieved and associated with other data elements as necessary.
5. Only data which has a reasonable likelihood of being used should be kept permanently in files.
6. Duplication of data among files should be avoided.
7. Reports should focus on information of value in making decisions. This usually means concise summaries rather than voluminous detail. Under the principle of "reporting by exception," only those things that vary from established normal limits are brought to the attention of decision makers.
8. The cost of capturing, processing, and retrieving data must be weighed against the value of having it. Except where required by law, no data should be retained which does not show a "payoff" in value.
9. No system can be devised which is foolproof against personnel who do not know or care enough to make it work properly.

TYPES OF PROCESSING

Data may be processed by computers in two different ways. The method selected is determined by such factors as the type of equipment available, the urgency of the transaction, the volume of work, and the distance involved. In order of historical development, they are (1) sequential batch processing and (2) online real-time processing.

Sequential Batch Processing

Originally, most data processing activity involved accumulating batches of records for processing, and much of it still does today. Files are processed in *sequential,* or *serial,* mode so that each record in turn in the file is examined, processed if necessary or bypassed, before proceeding to the next record. Transactions are sorted into some sequence, listed, and processed to accumulate one or more totals. Then the data is resorted and processed in another way. The output of such a system is usually a large stack of reports that must be searched for significant information.

Sequential batch processing offers advantages of low implementation cost, low operating costs, ease in estimating requirements, concentration on a single application at a time, and standardization of tasks. It has the major disadvantage of not being able to retrieve a desired record without having to search through all preceding records in a file. It is therefore not suited to handling of a large modern data base.

Batches of records may be accumulated and then transmitted over communication lines from the source of the transactions to a central computer some distance away. Such *remote* batch processing eliminates the need for rekeying the data from source documents at the central site and makes the data available for transaction usually on the same day the transaction occurs. It allows data to be transmitted during evening hours when communication rates are lower.

Online Real-Time Processing

Online systems are those in which terminals in many locations may have instant access to the computer and its files. The term *real-time* means that the results of processing are returned quickly enough to allow action to be taken before the transaction is completed.

Online real-time processing allows transactions to be entered into the computer system at the instant the transaction occurs to keep the data base constantly updated. All related records may likewise be promptly updated from transactions occurring in any of the organization's branches.

PERSONNEL IN DATA SYSTEMS

To design, develop, install, and operate systems requires the services of people with many different talents. Their jobs cover a wide range of experience, technical knowledge, responsibility, and opportunity for advancement. Often some of the jobs described here are combined or further subdivided, depending on the size of the installation or the qualifications of the people employed there.

Computer Users

Of the groups who work with computers, the largest are the *users.* Users who are most closely associated with the computer include the workers in organizations—such as offices, factories, and stores—who originate the transactions that create computer data. They may actually enter the data through keyboards or optical scanners at their workstations.

Users are also those who receive information from the computer for analysis and use in performing their regular duties. Such users are found at all levels of the organization and include the top executives, who rely on the computer for information on which to base crucial decisions. Finally, users are the students, writers, investors, hobbyists, homeowners, and other members of the general public whose lives are daily becoming more and more involved with the computer.

Data Entry Operators

The broad term *data entry* generally refers to the origination, recording, classifying, and transcribing of data. Each of these operations requires the services of personnel.

Data *originates* and should be captured when some transaction takes place. Someone places an order, makes a sale, registers for a class, or authorizes an increase in pay. At the time and place the transaction occurs the operator must capture all the data we expect to need.

Ideally, all data about a transaction is *recorded* initially in a form that machines can read. From point-of-sale terminals, operators can enter essential facts about a transaction directly into a computer or place them in machine-readable form on some medium that can later be read into the computer. Other machine-readable forms include optical characters or mark-sensing symbols.

Where it is not practical to record data initially in machine-readable form, a clerk should write the data in a convenient form to be *transcribed* later by keying into a terminal, punched card, magnetic tape, or magnetic disk. Great care should be taken in recording the data, since any missing detail about the transaction may be difficult, if not impossible, to reconstruct at a later time.

The process of determining in what group or class something belongs is called *classifying.* Usually, we assign a code to some class of transactions or data elements. As we will see later in this book, the use of codes saves space, makes data more precise, and speeds processing. Codes may be assigned at the time a transaction occurs or at a later time.

Usually, data entry operators are considered to be clerical employees. Their work is highly important, and they must exercise great care to ensure completeness and accuracy. But they normally do not need a high level of education and training to prepare for this type of work. Manual dexterity, accuracy, and attention to detail are desirable characteristics.

Computer Operators

Other personnel involved in data systems are those who operate the central processing unit and the associated peripheral equipment in the computer center. Computer operators do such jobs as aligning printed forms on the output printers or mounting magnetic tape reels or magnetic disk packs on the tape or disk devices. They may also exercise control over the sequence in which jobs are executed, respond to messages from the computer operating system, and ensure accuracy of information output.

The operator has great responsibility for the smooth functioning of the computer system. On large-scale systems, the operator requires a high level of technical training and experience to produce results on schedule and in good form.

The position of computer operator is often used as an entry point from which to move to a job as computer programmer. The operator usually has completed at least a two-year program from a technical school or community college.

Computer Programmers

Programmers are the people who write the actual instruction that the computer executes in carrying out its functions. Programmers normally work from a general description or detailed specifications of the problem to be solved or the report to be produced. Such specifications are often provided by the systems analyst. In some instances, programmers have responsibility for working out their own logical approaches to the solution of the problem.

Programmers require a thorough understanding of computer capabilities and techniques for storing and manipulating data. In addition, they require a thorough knowledge of the organization for which they work. Programmers are often expected to be competent in more than one programming language and to be able to select the one best suited to a particular problem.

Programmers usually work in one of three general areas:

1. *Business applications*: writing programs such as payroll, billing, accounting, inventory, and educational and government record keeping
2. *Scientific applications*: performing advanced mathematical calculations for science, engineering, and research
3. *Systems programming*: developing programs to improve the power of the computer itself, such as language translators, operating systems, data base management systems, and data communications handlers

Computer programmers normally are expected to have at least a two-year degree or its equivalent from a technical institute to work as application programmers. Scientific applications and systems programming require even higher education and technical competence.

Systems Analysts and Designers

Systems analysts and designers are concerned with the broad aspects of relating the computer system to the total information needs of the organization. Along with knowledge of computer capability, they must be able to communicate freely with users in all departments and at all levels of the organization. They must be able to translate the needs of each department into specific records, files, and programs. They must solve problems of great variety and scope to design and develop effective data systems.

Systems analysts and designers must be proficient in methods of organizing and processing files, safeguarding information, and producing accurate and understandable results. They must be competent in designing and documenting data systems to stay tuned to the needs of management. This entire book is largely devoted to describing their work.

Systems analysts and designers are expected to be broadly educated as well as technically trained and to be able to communicate easily with personnel at all levels within an organization. In addition, experience with computer systems and broad understanding of the organization for which they work are indispensable.

Data Base Administrators

A relatively new position found mainly in larger installations is that of *data base administrator* (DBA). This person is responsible for determining the total information needs of the organization and for defining the form and content of the data base. The DBA determines the most efficient way of organizing the data, sets up standard definitions and names for the various records and fields, and oversees the security system for the data base.

The DBA is responsible for controlling what data elements are placed in the data base, who can have access to it, how it is structured and interrelated, and what items are deleted.

The data base administrator occupies a highly responsible position and requires appropriate education and training.

Computer Center Directors

Overall responsibility for the management of computer services is vested in the *computer center director* or *manager*. In large organizations, this position might well carry the title of vice-president. The director has responsibility for the overall functioning of computer personnel, procedures, and equipment. While familiarity with computer programming, operations, and hardware are desirable, the most important function of the director is to work with personnel to enable them to reach their fullest possible potential.

The work of the computer center is often divided into the four areas of systems, programming, operations, and data entry. Each of these areas might have its own supervisor or manager reporting to the computer center director. The data base administrator might be a part of the computer center staff or might report directly to the general management of the organization.

Other Personnel

There are numerous other jobs related to data systems. Computer vendors employ salespersons, systems personnel, computer designers, and equipment and maintenance technicians. Independent software developers employ systems analysts and both systems and application programmers.

Within the user organization, we sometimes find persons working as *control clerks* or *input/output coordinators*. Their duties involve logging in all work received at the computer center, seeing that it reaches each work station on schedule, and assuring that completed work and reports are distributed to the proper persons.

Many organizations employ a *tape librarian,* who keeps custody of magnetic tapes and makes them available for processing as they are needed.

The *programming librarian* is often found where programmers work in teams. The programming librarian does many of the clerical jobs associated with programming, such as keeping layout forms for files and records, compiling and testing programs, creating and keeping job control procedures, and maintaining documentation.

Figure 1-3 shows a possible organization of a large computer center.

CONTROL IN DATA SYSTEMS

Throughout all systems work every attempt is made to define procedures which will ensure accurate and useful results. *Control* refers to the function by which we attempt to ensure that established procedures are properly followed. *Accuracy* is defined as the degree of exactness of an approximation or measurement. Accuracy normally denotes the quality of computed results. *Precision* refers to the amount of detail used in representing these results. If we have the wrong measurement or value in the first place, we will not make it any more accurate by carrying it to six decimal places.

The Need for Control

Precise control procedures must be spelled out in the following four areas of a data processing system:

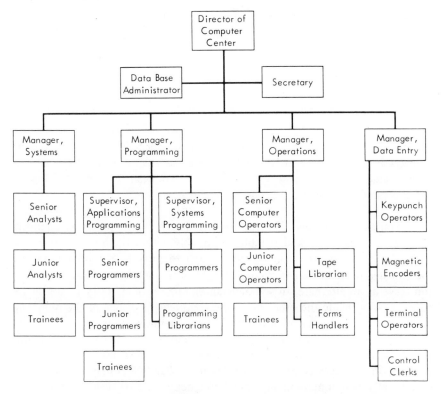

Figure 1-3. Organization of a large computer center. In smaller organizations, systems and programming may be combined into a single unit. Operations and data entry are also sometimes combined.

1. Data capture, preparation, and input
2. Manual and clerical procedures
3. Programming logic and internal computer processing
4. Output and distribution of reports

Figure 1-4 shows application of control functions in this sequence.

Computers are able to handle data at phenomenal rates of speed. They are also quite capable of making errors at the same high rates of speed. Because masses of data are processed in a relatively short period of time, inaccurate data or improper handling techniques will propagate errors throughout a vast number of records very quickly. The more we rely on machines, where numerous steps are performed without the intervention of human judgment, the more we must be very precise in our control techniques.

Incorrect results can arise in at least three different ways: through malfunctions, errors, or mistakes. The term *malfunctions* refers to a failure

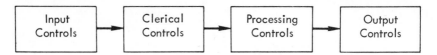

Figure 1-4. Control functions by sequence. Each of the four functions of input, clerical procedures, internal processing, and output requires its own set of controls.

in hardware operation. *Mistakes* are human blunders in recording, coding, transcribing, or interpreting data. *Errors* are incorrect numerical procedures which cause the final result to be different from what it should be. Figure 1-5 shows control functions grouped by category.

Hardware controls. The engineering design of equipment is intended to make it as accurate and reliable as possible within the limits of size and cost. Duplicate circuitry can be constructed to provide a double check on the transfer or the calculation of data. Thus if one circuit fails, the other can serve as an alternate. In some instances one set of circuitry performs an add operation while the other takes the complement of one of the numbers and performs a subtract, with the final results being compared.

The use of a parity bit, so that the number of binary digits in one core location or one data position on disk or tape is either always even or always odd, is a very common control feature. Parity bits may be used both horizontally and longitudinally along magnetic tape or disk to provide a double check on the accuracy of the data that is written or read.

Many devices have duplicate reading stations, so that data read from a card and transferred to storage is reread a second time and compared with the data already in storage. It is also customary to compare data just written on disk records with data in main storage to ensure that no data has been lost.

Hardware can be designed to detect magnetic tape or disk surfaces that are in danger of becoming defective. Some hardware features permit the rereading of information where invalid data has been detected.

Sound operator procedures also can go a long way toward preventing hardware malfunctions. Keeping the machine room free from dust, excessive heat, moisture, and other adverse conditions can help in preventing machine failure.

Microcomputers often have major hardware components in tiny silicon chips that can be easily removed and replaced in event of machine failure.

Arithmetic controls. Even though data may be correctly entered into the system, errors can result from incorrect arithmetic procedures practiced by the programmer. Amounts may be rounded too frequently or not at all. High-order significant digits can be lost if answers are too large for the register or storage location provided. Repeated arithmetic calculations can cause loss of precision if insufficient decimal places are carried in the result. Failure to take into account the sign of a number can completely reverse a result. Dividing in an arithmetic expression before multiplying will reduce accuracy.

Different versions of high-level languages such as FORTRAN can produce different results even when identical statements and data are used. Floating-point hardware or software instructions may produce different answers from fixed-point or integer calculations.

The programmer must be aware of these conditions and must select the technique or formula which best produces the answer he or she seeks.

Control in processing. Even though every effort is made to ensure accuracy during data capture and recording, extensive editing normally is done before or while data is formally entered into the computer. As data is entered into a computer, the programmer may make certain checks to help further prove its accuracy. One such check is that of *reasonableness*. It is not reasonable that a person would work 300 hours per week, just as for most payrolls it is not reasonable that the hourly rate should be greater than $20. Reasonable prices can be established for certain types of commodities and built into editing routines to verify that amounts representing these values do not exceed the reasonable figure.

Programming tests also may be made to determine the class of data: alphabetic, numeric, or mixed. In addition, it is possible to determine that

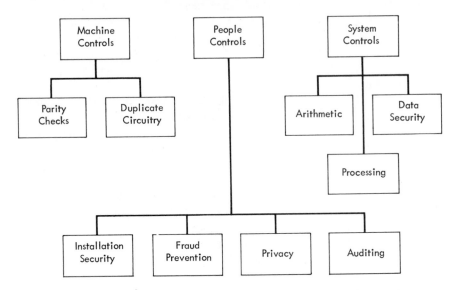

Figure 1-5. Control functions by category. Specific types of controls can generally be grouped into the three broad groups of machine controls, people controls, and system controls.

codes or symbols are those which are allowed for their particular purpose. For example, a college or university can establish a table of allowable grades, and any value appearing in the grade field which does not conform can be rejected.

Security

When considering the security of data systems, we divide our concern into three parts: (1) data security, (2) installation security, and (3) computer fraud.

Data security. There are many physical features to be considered in safeguarding data and equipment in an installation. Operators should be carefully instructed in the proper handling of cards, tapes, disks, and printed reports.

Punched cards should be kept under pressure in properly fitting trays. They should be carefully joggled before being placed in card readers. Paper clips and bands, which can nick the edges of the cards, should not be used. Humidity in the machine room must be regulated to prevent the cards from absorbing moisture. Frequently used punched cards should be duplicated at intervals.

Magnetic tape reels should be handled by the hub of the reel rather than by the flange. The operator should avoid pinching the edges of the tape or allowing it to be twisted or creased. Careful use of interior and exterior labels will help to safeguard tape files. Duplicate copies of master tapes should be retained as backups in case of destruction of the original. Control procedures should also specify when, by whom, and by whose authority tapes are to be copied. Cases have been reported of operators making unauthorized copies of tape files, such as mailing lists, and selling them without authorization.

Disk packs and diskettes also must be protected by careful handling. Packs should be kept under cover on a flat surface when not in use. They should never be dropped or struck at an angle. To remove dust, disk surfaces are brushed automatically by the disk drive when it is started up. Diskettes should be kept in their protective cover and handled only according to directions.

Tape and disk files should be kept in a vault under the control of a librarian. Each tape or disk volume should have its proper place in the library and should be in that place at all times when not actively running.

Online systems have special problems in data security that have previously been mentioned in this chapter. The use of passwords, backup files, and restrictions on who can make changes to the data base are examples. Whenever passwords are keyed in at a terminal, they are normally programmed not to be displayed on the screen so that they cannot be seen by unauthorized persons.

Installation security. The computer installation itself must be protected against accidental or intentional physical damage. Equipment is expensive, and the data base may be almost irreplaceable. Fire, explosion, water damage, or malicious mischief are all real possibilities. Conventional sprinkler systems may do as much damage from water as a small fire itself. Smoke detectors have become common to give early warning of a blaze.

After several recent incidents of flood damage, computer installations are nowadays placed above ground level in buildings. Uninterrupted power supply (UPS) systems are often used to continue operations when commercial power is interrupted for some reason. Air conditioning and humidity control help avoid damage to sensitive electronic components.

Some years ago, the computer center was a point of pride in many organizations. Often it was displayed through large glass windows in public areas. Now, to improve security, many organizations allow limited access to their computer facilities and often keep them out of sight.

Personnel employed in the computer center should be carefully screened as a security precaution.

Computer fraud. Even though many persons contend that the computer has prevented far more fraud than it has encouraged, still the possible misuse of the computer for personal gain is a concern. Unauthorized copying of records and programs is one form of fraud in which operators have reportedly been involved.

Programmers have been said to have doctored programs to their own advantage by establishing their own accounts, altering their college grades, or collecting fractions of cents dropped as amounts are rounded.

In some installations, programmers are not allowed to operate the computer at all. All compiling and testing of programs must be done by operators. Operators are allowed to make no program modifications nor to alter the contents of computer storage through the operator's console. The principle of division of responsibility has long been used in accounting to help prevent fraud.

Opening up the computer to access by terminals and over ordinary long-distance telephone lines extends the possibility of fraud outside the installation itself. The communications system must contain all the safeguards that are feasible to prevent unauthorized intrusion.

Privacy

As data banks grow larger and accessible to more persons through the use of communications terminals, many voices have expressed concern about what appears to be a real and growing threat to individual privacy. Major technological developments have raised new legal problems. The right of individuals to control both the accuracy and the access to information which relates to themselves in data banks is said to be in jeopardy.

In years past, the question of privacy rarely arose. Much of the information available was relatively superficial, decentralized among many different offices and agencies, and difficult to obtain. It normally consisted of only that data necessary for a particular transaction or a small, specialized file.

Now information is collected relating to the most private aspects of a person's life—credit rating, salary, academic record, arrests and convictions, social habits, job applications. Not only factual information but also impressions, rumors, hearsay, and interpretations, which may not always be accurate or fair, are collected. Whenever such personal information may be subject to misinterpretation, loose control, malice, or carelessness, there exists the danger of real damage to a person's reputation, sometimes without his or her knowledge.

Some legislation has already been enacted, and we may expect more to follow. Specific proposals include the following measures to safeguard privacy:

1. Persons should have the right to have access to, to challenge, and to correct information on file that relates to themselves.
2. Access to data banks should be rigidly controlled and granted only to properly identified persons who can show valid reasons for the use of the data.
3. Data made a part of a general information system should be of a statistical type only. Physical, psychiatric, and military information should be excluded.
4. Only statistical information should be transmitted over communication lines to minimize the possibility of wiretapping.
5. Standards for competency for computer programmers should be developed and enforced.
6. Computer operators should be carefully trained and supervised to prevent unauthorized copying, altering, or loss of data from files.
7. The concentration of large data files by federal or state centers must provide safeguards to prevent the possibility of surveillance or monitoring of individual actions by a large, centralized government.

Large, integrated data banks can give valuable management information. But the system designer must be aware of all legal, moral, and ethical considerations in using them.

Auditing Data Systems

For years, the auditing profession as a whole was rather slow to realize that computers were here to stay. Fortunately, the auditors have emerged from their lethargy regarding electronic data processing, and computer training of auditors has increased. Auditing firms now employ and use EDP specialists, and the supply of audit-oriented software has grown as more systems have become more self-controlling and self-auditing.

Some auditing practices include brute-force techniques, such as batch controls on input, making dual entries from terminals, or updating an entire file twice to verify accuracy. More important is a preventive auditing approach, with greater auditor involvement during systems development. The auditor's recommendations for control procedures should be built right into the system from the start.

The *internal auditor* is employed within the organization, or as a consultant, to give continuing checks and reviews to ensure both accuracy of reports and adherence to established procedures. This person might be a permanent member of the systems department, or assigned to the systems study teams as a specialist in ensuring control of data and processing steps.

The *independent auditor* has traditionally been engaged on a periodic basis to express an opinion on financial statements, to evaluate the system of internal control, and to note weaknesses that might be present in the system. This role has been expanded recently beyond financial considerations to include questions of security and efficiency in operations.

MANAGEMENT INFORMATION SYSTEMS

All data processing systems are devoted to recording data, manipulating it in some way, and producing meaningful results, or *information.* Where this information is used by personnel at various levels within the organization as a basis for action and decision making, the term *management information system* has been used.

Characteristics of the Management Information System

The management information system (MIS) has been defined as a combination of people, data processing equipment, input/output devices, and communications facilities to supply timely information for making intelligent management decisions. It employs data both from the outside environment and from within its own data base. It supplies information needed by management at all levels for decision-making functions.

A common thread runs through all the preceding statements: the attempt to involve the computer directly in the decision-making process. No manager can remember all the facts considered in daily and long-range plans. The computer has many facts available about the business as a by-product of its regular applications in making payrolls, billing, inventorying, and budgeting. Other facts may be introduced from other sources. Massive files of data can be accumulated and processed rapidly by computer in such a way that the information extracted meets management needs.

The management information system may have many different forms. Some are simple; some complex. Some are a part of the present data processing system; some are a completely separate entity. Regardless of the form, each MIS requires at least three elements:

1. A method of reporting to management those things that require attention. This is often called *reporting by exception* or *management by exception.* The manager need not wade through mountains of data reporting routine details that demand no special or unusual action.
2. A complete data base that readily provides information of concern in time for action to be taken. The data base may be placed in a single central location or distributed at various points to serve the needs of the entire organization.
3. An expansion of input stations to include data from outside the company as well as from within.

Reporting by exception. The reporting system is based upon the exception principle. Only those items that differ significantly from preestablished standards need be reported. The standards may vary from one management level to another. For example, a report of delinquent accounts going to credit manager might include all those only 10 days past due, whereas a report to the president might be limited to those of large balances more than 30 or 60 days old.

The reporting system should also permit management at appropriate levels to inquire into the status of anything deserving attention. The inquiry system is typically a terminal having either a keyboard, a display screen, or both. Such a terminal is by no means necessary, but the system must respond promptly to management requests for specialized information.

The data base. The data base must be continually collected, summarized, and made available to the proper persons for analysis and action. Much of the data comes from regular processing activities and should be in such detail as is required by management at each particular level within the structure. Supervisors and department heads usually are concerned with full detail—balances of individual accounts, specific quantities on hand, individual pay rates, student grades, or whatever. Each level up the ladder requires data that is more summarized and condensed.

Normal reporting procedures tend to produce this summarization as information flows upward through the organization to its top levels. In addition, top management may have direct access to the data base through terminals.

External data. If the data base is to contain *all* information needed by management to make decisions, it must include many elements not developed from within the company through normal data processing activities. Much information is obtained directly by the manager, through conversations, conferences, newspapers, and journals—even through listening to scuttlebutt and the grapevine. Such external information is often difficult to quantify, code, or relate to internal information in a meaningful way.

Along with an expanded data base goes the notion of an increased number of input stations. Data should be captured as close to its source as possible. Some of the input stations can be used by managers themselves or their secretaries to enter external information that they have gained in some way. This information, like that developed from within the company, can be subjected to analysis or comparison against predetermined standards. For example, stock market quotations, interest rates, wholesale prices, production figures, population trends, election results, and other external factors often have a tremendous effect on managerial decisions. The MIS might well provide normal expectations in such data and report out any deviations from the norm.

Figure 1-6 shows the relationship among the various components of a management information system.

Requirements for a Successful MIS

There is no single structure for MIS that serves all organizations, but there are some considerations that must remain constant regardless of the

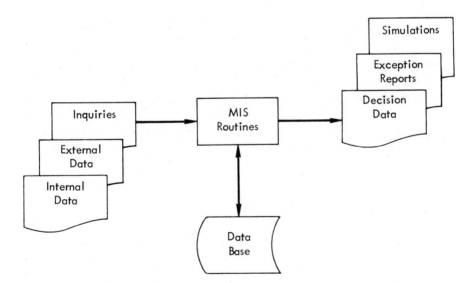

Figure 1-6. Management information system components. The MIS routines receive data from both internal and external sources and make extensive use of a data base to produce information of value for decision making.

structure, complexity, or type of hardware if the system is to function successfully. Here are a few:

1. There must be direction, involvement, and commitment on the part of those administrators who will use the system. People will accept and use their own creation much more readily than one imposed by outsiders.
2. The system must provide an early warning signal about any significant future events. Management must be aware of changes before or as they develop, while there is still time to take action that can have some effect on those changes.
3. The system must be flexible and evolutionary. The number and location of input stations, the data elements within files, and the frequency and content of reports should be able to be changed as needs change.
4. The system should produce meaningful results quickly. This usually means action reports on an interim basis or immediate responses to inquiries. It does not eliminate entirely the traditional historical accounting report, but it does mean that such reports must be supplemented with current, action-oriented reports.
5. Data in the system must describe the external universe as well as the internal operations of the organization. Although some external data may not be placed in the computer, it should nevertheless be a part of the information that must be considered by management. It may be in their files, notes, or merely in someone's head, but it is still part of the system.
6. Computer resources must be consolidated at some level. If separate computers are used in different departments or branches within a company, their output must be collected, summarized, compared, and digested before it is useful for decision making. The more of this process that can be done efficiently by computer, the more the executive is freed for those interpretations and judgments that only the human being can make.

The ideal mangement information system provides the proper balance between the use of the computer for the things it can do best and the use of the manager for those things that only he can do.

SUMMARY

In this chapter we have described and delimited the term *data system* to be the combined use of people, methods, and materials to process raw data about an enterprise into meaningful information in order to provide a basis for decision making. We have concerned ourselves with those applications that are used by the typical business organizations and have dispensed with those of a highly specialized or technical nature.

We have defined or described some of the common terms used in data systems work: data, information, data element, data item, data capture, data entry, data base, procedures, applications, systems analysis, systems department, and total systems concept. More terms will of course be identified and defined in subsequent chapters.

We have seen that three forms of processing are in common usage, batch processing, remote batch processing, and online real-time processing.

We have indicated how the growth in size and complexity of modern business has brought about the need for specialized personnel and techniques for analyzing and designing data systems.

We have shown that a whole new group of careers has grown up around the computer. We have described the nature of these jobs and have pointed out the educational requirements and personal characteristics required for each of them.

The management information system is an attempt to involve the computer directly in the decision-making process. The MIS is intended to combine data produced by normal data processing within the organization with data received from external sources to produce meaningful information for managerial decisions at all levels.

TERMS FOR REVIEW

Application	Information
Batch processing	Management information system
Component	Online real-time processing
Data	Procedures
Data base	Remote batch processing
Data capture	Subsystem
Data element	Systems analysis
Data entry	Systems life cycle
Data item	Systems programmer
Hardware	

QUESTIONS

1. Discuss and give examples of the difference between data and information.
2. How do data systems differ from other types of systems? How are they similar?

3. Describe some specialized types of data systems that are not treated in this text.
4. What conditions and developments have led to the use of systems personnel in modern business organizations?
5. Describe the steps necessary to develop modern data systems.
6. What operations are involved in data entry? Identify some of the personnel who perform these operations.
7. Into what four areas is the work of a computer center often divided? Describe the nature of the work in each area.
8. Distinguish between applications programming and systems programming. What education, training, and personal characteristics are necessary for programmers in each field?
9. Distinguish between batch processing and online real-time processing. What are the advantages and disadvantages of each?
10. List characteristics of the management information system.
11. What are some of the requirements for a successful management information system?

CASE STUDY
SUNCOAST COMMUNITY COLLEGE

Suncoast Community College is one of 28 publicly supported community colleges in Florida. It is situated on the Gulf of Mexico with its original North Campus in Sun County and a new South Campus in Coast County. The two counties, with a population of 350,000, make up its official district and supply 90 percent of its students. Five percent of the students come from other Florida counties, and 5 percent from out of state.

Suncoast was established 25 years ago as a part of a program designed to place a community college within commuting distance of 95 percent of the population of Florida. It serves about 30,000 students annually, of whom approximately one-third take courses for credit and two-thirds for noncredit. In keeping with national trends, more than half of its credit students are women and more than half are enrolled part-time. According to a prescribed state formula, enrollments are converted to full-time student-equivalents (FTE) by dividing total semester hours by 40. The current FTE is 4500 per year for funding and reporting purposes.

By state law, Suncoast offers instructional programs in three categories:

1. University parallel courses for students who wish to transfer to other colleges and universities.
2. Occupational and technical courses for those students who wish to enter employment at the end of one or two years of college work.
3. Continuing education (normally on a noncredit basis) with courses classified as citizenship, vocational, and avocational.

Approximately two-thirds of the credit students are in university parallel courses and one-third in occupational and technical courses. The university parallel courses, which lead to the Associate in Arts degree, are classified into 14 disciplines, such as Business, Fine Arts, Biological Science, Physical Science, Communications, and so forth. Occupational and technical courses fall into seven broad areas: Agriculture, Business, Distributive Education, Health, Home Economics, Industrial and Engineering, and Public Service. There are 40 separate occupational programs leading to the two-year Associate in Science degree, and 13 leading to one-year certificates.

COLLEGE ORGANIZATION STRUCTURE

The college is governed by five trustees appointed by the Governor of Florida and is under the general direction and coordination of the Division of Community Colleges, one of four divisions of the Florida Department of Education. It receives 62 percent of its operating funds from the state by appropriation from the legislature, 30 percent from student fees, and 8 percent from federal grants and private contributions.

The President of the college, Kort Stevens, chief executive officer of the institution, is charged by law with responsibility for carrying out the policies of the Board of Trustees. He is also Executive Secretary of the Board. There are three Vice-Presidents: Ray Rainey for Academic Affairs; Bert Amana for Student Affairs; and Ballard Roberts for Administration.

Reporting to the Vice-President for Academic Affairs are Rance Wallace, Dean of Liberal Arts; Till Binsley, Dean of Occupational Education; Dennis Douglas, Dean of Continuing Education; Dale Jackson, Dean of the South Campus; and Karl Chauder, Dean of Libraries.

Immediately responsible to the Vice-President for Student Affairs are Chris Wells, Dean of Student Counseling; Neal McGill, Dean of Admissions and Records; Lucy Lindell, Dean of Financial Aid; and Carol Fischer, Dean of Student Activities.

Reporting to the Vice-President for Administration are Mack

Cordron, Dean of Data Systems; Richard Allison, Dean of Business Services; and Bray Sing Ton, Dean of Physical Plant.

The Directors of Information Services and of Institutional Advancement report directly to the President in staff capacities.

Figure 1–7 shows the overall structure of the college and the functions and services under each dean and director.

COMPUTER HARDWARE

For the past three years, the college has used an **IBM 4341** computer system with 2 million bytes of storage currently supporting 66 online terminals. The terminals are located on both campuses and in Sun County public schools. The system has two line printers rated at 1100 lines per minute; two card readers, one with punch unit; three disk drives with 1.2 billion bytes of storage; and three tape drives storing 1600 bits per inch. The computer is used for both administrative and instructional applications. In addition to the mainframe network, the college has about 40 microcomputers used exclusively for student programming instruction.

ADMINISTRATIVE APPLICATIONS

There are three major areas of administrative applications: registration, student records, and accounting. All are now online, following a major systems project lasting several years. Most data entry is through terminals located in the respective administrative offices. Information retrieval is available through display screens, but many printed reports and summaries are produced in batch mode.

Registration

All registration is done in online real-time mode. About midway through each semester, students may register for the next semester, following consultation with their academic advisors. Students are assigned priorities according to the number of credit hours they have earned, so that those nearing graduation may choose their class sections before classes are filled, Courses may dropped or added from the time of registration until the end of the first week after classes begin. The advance registration assures students well before the semester begins that they will have the classes they need. It also permits the college administration to add or delete classes as needed well in advance of the opening of the term. Students may register at any of several terminals located on both campuses.

Student Records

Student records are the responsibility of the Dean of Admissions and Records. Through terminals located in the office, student records are created from the application form and updated during the admissions process as additional documents are received. Registration records are incorporated into student records after registration is completed, and grades are recorded at the end of the semester in batch mode.

Entries to assign the student to an academic advisor and a program of study, designate a major, and approve overloads and special requests are made by the Director of Counseling. Student scholarships, loans, and work assignments are entered by the Financial Aid Office. Entries on assessment and payment of fees come from the Business Office. The office that originates each type of data is responsible for updating and verifying the accuracy of that data.

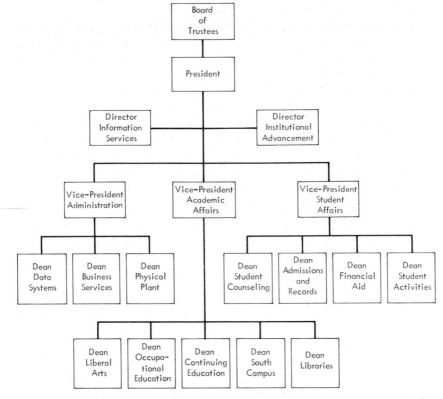

Figure 1-7. Organization chart of Suncoast Community College. The president is ultimately responsible to the Board of Trustees for operation of the college. Assisting him are three vice-presidents, each with deans of specific areas.

Accounting

Accounting transactions are processed daily at online terminals in the Business Office. Transaction files and master records are available for inspection at any time on the terminals. Some journals and registers are run daily, others several times per week, and some weekly. Budget reports, the general ledger, and financial summaries are run monthly. The accounting system permits close control of budgets and current information as to the status of all accounts.

QUESTIONS AND EXERCISES

1. Make a list of computer hardware at your college, university, or business organization and compare it with that at Suncoast.
2. What advantages do you see in allowing students to have advance online registration for courses? What disadvantages, if any?
3. Do you believe Suncoast has a management information system as the term is used in this chapter? Why or why not?
4. Draw an organization chart of the top level of the institution you attend or the organization for which you work. Compare the structure with that of Suncoast.

2

ORGANIZATION OF THE SYSTEMS DEPARTMENT

OBJECTIVES

At the end of this chapter, you should be able to:

1. Identify developments in modern business that led to the need for separate systems departments.
2. State advantages and disadvantages of centralized versus decentralized systems organization.
3. Distinguish between line and staff positions in an organization.
4. Demonstrate the relationship between the systems department and the data processing center.
5. Explain how projects are conducted in performing the work of the systems department.
6. Cite reasons for the use of consultants.
7. State personal characteristics important to systems personnel.
8. Prescribe a desirable education and training program for systems personnel.
9. Describe physical facilities that enhance the work of the systems department.

We have seen in the first chapter some of the reasons why separate departments concerned with systems work have been set up in many organizations. In this chapter we shall examine the placement of the systems department within the structure, the relationships between this department and others, some of the characteristics of systems personnel, and methods of developing and training people for systems work.

SYSTEMS FUNCTIONS OF MANAGEMENT

As we have noted already, in the past each manager did his or her own systems work, although managers undoubtedly did not think of their role in these terms. In many respects modern managers still personally perform many of the systems functions. They must be responsible for setting goals and objectives, must figure out detailed plans for reaching these goals, must consider all reasonable alternatives, evaluate probable cost and time factors, select the most likely plan, employ and train staff, instruct them in the necessary procedures, provide equipment and supplies, and implement the system. They must then watch closely to see that it is functioning properly and make changes where indicated.

Managers cannot avoid their responsibility for these functions. It is the reason they are managers.

When the size of the organization reaches the point that managers can no longer attend to these functions personally, they must arrange for help. The first step as the organization grows is usually to hire an assistant, to whom is delegated some of the administrative details. Later, additional assistants may be required, and finally the needs become such that management sets up a complete department to be concerned specifically with systems analysis and planning, just as in other areas of the firm there are departments for purchasing, accounting, advertising, and other necessary functions.

ORGANIZATION FORMS

Business organizations employ almost as many different forms and structures as they produce products and services. Some may choose a rather autocratic structure, where the reins are closely held by single individual who delegates little real decision-making authority even to his or her subordinates who hold impressive titles. Others function as a loose assembly of teams or groups who go their separate ways to the extent that it is hard to tell who is in charge. And between these extremes we can find a full spectrum of subtle variations.

Regardless of the formal organization structure, duties and responsibilities inevitably shift somewhat according to the talents and preferences of the persons who occupy the positions on the chart. The chief executive in one instance may have come up through the ranks of public relations, marketing, or advertising and have little taste for finance and administration. His (or her) successor may come up through quite another track. Each is likely to direct personal attention to those areas he prefers and to delegate more latitude and authority where his interest is less.

Line and Staff Relationships

It is vital that the difference between line and staff functions in an organization be kept clearly in mind. Authority flows downward and responsibility flows upward through the *line*. Various individuals in the organization are charged by the board of directors or the corporation charter with responsibility for some aspect of the business and are given necessary authority to act within the scope of their responsibility. The line structure might involve a number of levels, from the chief executive down through division heads, then department heads, then supervisors, then seniors, juniors, and trainees. The exact relationship of this hierarchy may be shown on an organization chart such as Figure 2-1. The line provides the chain of command through which the normal flow of directives, orders, reports, grievances, and other communications pass.

At any level of management, line personnel may be assisted in their duties by *staff* members. Top-level executives have attorneys and public relations advisors working in a staff capacity; such personnel may appear high in the organizational chart but they do not have any line authority over personnel in other departments.

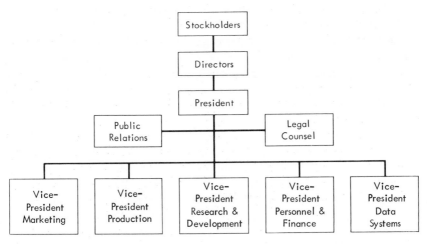

Figure 2-1. Organization chart. The five vice-presidents are line executives responsible to the president. The public relations officer and legal counsel are staff personnel.

Systems work is a staff function. The systems person normally has no direct authority over any other department. He or she can only make recommendations and suggestions to the line executive, who will adopt or reject them on their merits. Systems work can be successful, then, only to the extent that it produces the results that the executive wants, and only so far as that executive can be persuaded to adopt the recommendations submitted.

In doing its work the systems department must cross departmental lines, both vertically and horizontally within the organization. It has no authority to compel the cooperation of any other department. It must rely on the authority of the line executive to gain access to records, files, and the time of persons in other departments. Most important, it must depend upon persuasion and good will to reach an amicable working relationship throughout the departments.

Personnel in many departments will feel understandably threatened when "outsiders" from the systems department come in to analyze their operations in minute detail. People don't cherish the thought of being replaced by a machine and never quite feel that anyone else fully understands the demands and complexities of their position. So-called "efficiency experts" are unwelcome in many quarters where they come to poke, prod, measure, and criticize the real or imagined inadequacies of the work force. Systems people need real tact and understanding to allay these fears and suspicions, to enlist the support and cooperation of those with whom they have to deal, and to gain their acceptance and approval of suggested changes.

Centralized versus Decentralized Organization

Two major approaches can be employed in setting up the systems department. The first is the *centralized* arrangement. Under this plan, a single department is set up for the entire organization. A full-time systems director is in charge, assisted by a staff of senior and junior analysts, aided by typists, clerks, and perhaps draftsmen and other aides. Typically, members of the systems staff are specialists in different areas, one concentrating on accounting, another on production, another on marketing, another on engineering, and so on through the various activities of the organization.

The centralized department frequently is assigned to make specific studies of problems that require attention in various departments. This project team might be supplemented on a temporary basis by personnel from the department under study, but the responsibility for directing each project, for staffing the teams, for reporting results, and for making recommendations rests within the centralized systems department (see Figure 2–2).

Under, the decentralized plan, one or more systems specialists may be attached to each of the departments. If there is a systems coordinator for the organization as a whole, he or she would have no line authority over

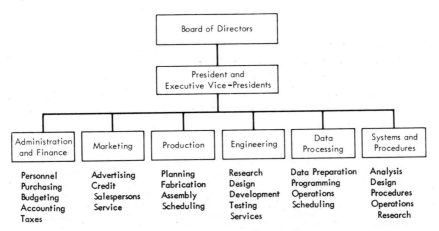

Figure 2-2. Centralized systems organization. All systems personnel are gathered into a single department, from which they can be assigned to specific projects anywhere in the organization.

other systems personnel, who would be responsible directly to the manager of the department they serve (see Figure 2–3).

Advantages of the centralized plan are:

1. Systems effort is pooled so that it may be concentrated in areas of greatest need.
2. A greater variety of talents probably will be available.
3. Responsibility for systems activities can better be pinpointed.
4. Personnel are less likely to be diverted into activities not related to systems.

Advantages of the decentralized plan are:

1. The systems person probably will be in closer touch with the immediate problems of the department to which he or she is attached.
2. The review and maintenance of procedures and documentation within the department will be more constant and current.
3. The systems person will be in constant touch with both the department manager and operating staff and presumably should have better rapport with them than "outsiders" would.

Relationship between Systems Department and Data Processing Center

The systems department in some organizations is one of the sections under the director of the data processing center, who is also responsible for

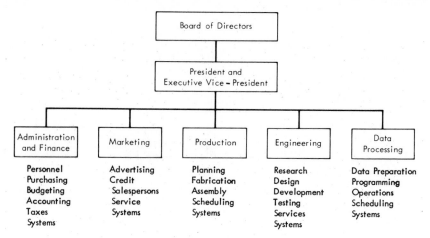

Figure 2-3. Decentralized systems organization. Some systems personnel are regularly assigned to each department. Their activities are more loosely coordinated than they are under a
centralized systems organization.

programming and machine operations. In other organizations, particularly
those where the establishment of the systems and procedures department
preceded the use of a computer, this department is separate.

Figure 2–4 shows an arrangement with the systems department under
the director of the data processing center. Note that where this structure is
used, the procedures function will probably be combined with the systems
analysis and design functions.

A second approach (Figure 2–5) is to have the manager of systems
and procedures report to an executive outside the data processing center.
Under this plan, the systems analysis and design function would remain un-

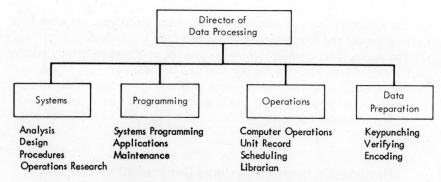

Figure 2-4. Systems responsible to director of computer center. Most of
the systems work under this organization would be related
primarily to the needs of the computer center itself.

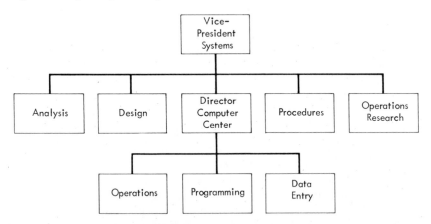

Figure 2-5. Director of computer center responsible to vice-president for systems. This organization stresses the importance of the systems function and suggests that the computer is merely a tool for providing information needs.

der the director of the data processing center and would tend to be directed more specifically toward problem definition and systems within the center than for the entire company.

Smaller organizations, which cannot afford so elaborate a structure, often have to depend upon the director of the DP center to perform the systems functions and to use other departments and the programmers to perform duties such as flowcharting, detailed analyses of work volumes, or procedure writing.

Project Assignments

Although it is hoped that the systems department will not limit its activities solely to the "firefighting" approach to problems that arise, much of the systems work inevitably takes the form of special assignments and special study groups to look into trouble spots in the organization. When such a project is initiated, for whatever reason, the team may be made up of any of the following in many possible combinations:

1. Regular systems personnel (headed by a team chief) and as many regular assistants as necessary normally will be the backbone of the team. A specialist in the area under study certainly would be one of the persons to be put on the team.
2. One or more representatives from the department under study normally would be included. This procedure provides a closer working relationship and should save considerable time and effort in familiarizing the team with internal details of the user department.

3. Outside consultants might be engaged where appropriate. In cases where the systems department is very small or relatively new and perhaps lacking in experience, the use of consultants is especially indicated.

There are a number of reasons for using outside consultants, among which the following are prominent:

1. *Unique area of expertise.* Consultants can afford to specialize to a degree not practical in a typical systems department.
2. *Limited or one-time use of specialized skills.* Often the need for a special body of knowledge is limited to a very small phase of the systems study. The outside consultant can provide this in such areas as computer software, data communications, market planning, and so forth.
3. *Company wage scale.* Often a firm can justify a high-priced person on a short-term basis where it is not at all feasible to bring in a regular employee at such a salary.
4. *Unavailability of skills in the present market.* Consultants may be able to devote their specialized talents over the entire country or a large section of the country, thus bringing expertise to many users who might not be able to find such skills as a part of their permanent staff.
5. *Objectivity.* Outside consultants presumably will bring a less biased viewpoint to their study of an organization than company people who are working among their close friends and personal acquaintances.
6. *Access to outside sources.* Consultants may themselves often employ other consultants where they need additional support and professional knowledge.
7. *Multiple exposure to alternate solutions.* The outside consultants presumably have met many times before the problems that are being faced in the organization which has retained them. They should be able to propose solutions that have been applied successfully in other institutions.
8. *Respect of top management.* It is sometimes unfortunate but nevertheless true that outsiders have easier access to the ear, as well as the respect, of top management. A person away from home becomes an expert. Recommendations coming from a consultant frequently carry more weight than equally good recommendations coming from a member of the organization's own staff.
9. *Availability of executive time.* Even where the company executives have the knowledge and ability to devise systems and procedures for new applications, they often do not have the time to do so because of the press of their other duties. They might therefore bring in consultants to tackle specific jobs on a short-term basis.
10. *Management training and education.* Because consultants must deal with a wide variety of clients, many of whom have similar problems, the consulting firm is likely to have well-established techniques, good

documentation, adequate staff for charting, coding, and writing procedures, as well as methods of training the customer's personnel. It would be an extremely well-organized, well-funded systems department that would be able to perform all of these functions within a single organization.

QUALIFICATIONS OF SYSTEMS PERSONNEL

Systems work demands a wide variety of talents which are not often found in a single individual. Systems people must be able to work well with others, suggesting an outgoing, gregarious nature. At the same time they must be masters of detail, planning, and documentation—qualities usually associated with the introvert. They must be problem solvers of great ingenuity, patience, and persistence. They must be able to converse intelligibly with people at many occupational levels, but also must know and use specific technical terms. They must be technicians in their knowledge of hardware, programming methods, flowcharting, and use of statistics, but they must be generalists who can understand and appreciate the broad scope and interrelated activities of the organization.

Perhaps the most important qualifiation of all is experience. No matter how thorough the preparation and technical training the systems people might have, they are fully valuable to their organization only when they are thoroughly familiar with the personalities of its members, the strengths and weaknesses of its operations, and the informal as well as the formal power structure at work in the organization.

Personal Traits

Numerous authorities have cited the importance of personal qualifications quite outside the experience and formal training which systems people must have. Lack of the following traits can hinder or destroy the effectiveness of otherwise qualified individuals:

1. *Initiative.* Systems people must be constantly alert for problems before they become severe, They are often given great latitude in undertaking a systems study, and must be quick to seize upon the direction of greatest potential benefit.
2. *Cooperation.* Systems people have no line authority outside their own department. All the results they can get depend upon the cooperation they elicit from those with whom they work.
3. *Ability to communicate.* Systems people must be able to interview others in the company from the highest to the lowest organizational level, to understand their needs and wants, and to make their own thoughts

clear. Their reports must clearly show management what their proposals will involve. Their procedures must translate into effective action.

4. *Alertness.* Systems people work in a constantly changing environment where new products, techniques, and personnel combine into an infinite series of shifting relationships. They must be sensitive to gradual changes as well as prepared for rapid changes. They must keep informed about changing technology. They must do as much reading in the advertising pages of trade journals as in textbooks and articles.

5. *Imagination.* They must be able to perceive possible solutions to problems that have never been tried before. They must be able to visualize the possible effect of any anticipated course of action.

6. *Understanding of human nature.* Systems people will encounter the whole gamut of human emotions in the course of a day's work. They must maintain a sense of humor and perspective. They must be sensitive to the fears, suspicions, ambitions, and needs of others, but they must be relatively thick-skinned about resistance and criticism.

7. *Loyalty.* Given the opportunity to probe into the most intimate details of many departments across the organization, systems people must be fully trustworthy. They must have a genuine interest in and concern for their employer. They must make the good of the total organization their chief concern.

8. *Respect for role.* There is a danger that systems people in analyzing, specifying procedures, and informing personnel of their place in some particular process, will think of themselves as authorities. Systems people should not and cannot usurp the role of management in decision making. They can recommend, persuade, suggest, and urge, but they must remember that management makes the final choice.

Some analysts have been accused of insolence, procrastination, attempts at empire building, obscure writing, and isolation from the users they are supposed to serve. Generally, such attitudes do not pay off, for there is a real need for a close working relationship between the systems analyst and users in other departments. The combined efforts of the systems technician and the user who is knowledgeable in application areas can result in the development of a unique system. Figure 2–6 shows a job description for the systems analyst.

Education and Training of Systems Personnel

We can see that the systems analyst requires not only unique personal characteristics, a wide variety of talents, and a broad, well-balanced education, but also a great deal of specific training in order to be effective in the job.

What are the most likely sources for recruiting and training effective systems personnel? What career paths are open to permit promising sys-

JOB TITLE: Systems Analyst

RESPONSIBLE TO: Systems Manager

GENERAL DESCRIPTION:

Collects and analyzes data for present or proposed data systems. Designs new or modified systems, sets their specifications, and oversees their development and implementation. Evaluates systems in operation and recommends improvements. Prepares system documents and makes oral and written reports of results and recommendations of study.

RESPONSIBILITIES:

1. Defining objectives data systems must meet.
2. Ensuring that recommendations are cost-effective.
3. Working as leader or member of systems study team.
4. Providing control and security of data and other resources.
5. Conducting adequate testing that systems meet specifications.

DUTIES:

1. Estimate systems costs in terms of money, time, and personnel.
2. Develop and review proposed systems solutions.
3. Plan and schedule use of all systems resources.
4. Develop and enforce standard operational procedures.
5. Evaluate and report on performance of systems personnel.
6. Plan and carry out training for personnel at all levels.
7. Assist in acquiring, training, and developing systems personnel.
8. Follow current standards in developing systems documentation.
9. Conduct interviews, administer questionnaires, and use other data gathering techniques.
10. Evaluate and set specifications for appropriate hardware for data systems.
11. Ensure security and control in systems design, development, and operation.
12. Develop data base structure and processing methods.
13. Design display screens, forms, and reports.
14. Prepare detailed specifications for programmers and procedure writers.
15. Prepare and present written and oral reports.

EDUCATION AND EXPERIENCE:

1. Bachelor's degree (preferably in computer science or related discipline) or equivalent. Advanced degree is desirable.
2. Training in management, supervision, systems analysis and design, and quantitative methods.
3. Five or more years of data systems experience in programming, operations management, or analysis and design of specific applications areas.
4. Thorough knowledge of information needs of the organization, computer capabilities, and oral and written communications.

Figure 2-6. Job description of systems analyst. Broad general knowledge of systems methods and of the business organization itself are more important than specific programming ability.

tems people to be developed both from within and outside the organization?

The following devices all aid in the difficult but vital matter of locating, identifying, educating, training, and updating systems personnel:

1. Aptitude tests
2. College and university computer curricula
3. Courses by manufacturers and software companies
4. Short courses, institutes, and seminars
5. On-the-job training
6. Self-evaluation tests

Let us examine each of these topics in more detail.

Aptitude tests.   Knowledge of computer programming is frequently required of a potential systems person. Although well-recognized aptitude tests for systems work are not common, the programmer aptitude test has been employed for many years to measure attention to detail, mathematical facility, and ability to do logical problem definition. The programmer aptitude test, then, might be at least one index of a person's potential as a systems analyst. In many organizations a career path is open into systems work from the position of computer programmer.

College and university computer curricula.   Many, if not most, colleges and universities now offer courses related to computers. Although it is not an absolute requisite that a systems analyst should have a four-year degree, the value of a broad liberal education cannot be minimized. Many large organizations require a four-year degree for their management positions, and it is a rare exception when a person without college training reaches a position of executive responsibility.

In community colleges and technical institutes, most data processing instruction is intended to prepare computer programmers. Such programs typically include one or two courses in systems analysis and design. This textbook is intended for such courses. But very few students leave these programs to enter directly into a position as systems analyst. They often can move from programming positions into systems work after two or three years of experience.

Liberal arts colleges and universities typically offer courses in computer science. These courses usually place more emphasis on computer architecture and systems programming than on business data systems. A study at Northeastern University rated computer science curricula as being very effective in preparing computer designers and systems programmers, but far less effective in preparing business application programmers and systems analysts. Thus additional courses in business and management, as well as experience and training on the job, are usually needed to supplement the bachelor's degree in computer science.

Graduate degrees in computer science are offered in many universities. In addition, the Master's in Business Administration (MBA), so highly prized in many business organizations, usually places fairly strong emphasis on the use of computers. The holder of the master's degree or the doctorate from such programs is a good candidate for work as a systems analyst. However, experience with a firm is essential to gain knowledge of that particular organization.

Courses by manufacturers and software companies. For years, International Business Machines Corporation, Control Data, and other computer manufacturers have offered courses for their customers. Most of these have been concerned with machine operations and computer programming. Recently, very sophisticated, high-cost, and lengthy courses have been offered in many areas of systems analysis and design. Certainly a person attending one of these courses receives both broad and intensive training in data systems.

The "unbundling" announcement of 1969, by which some manufacturers separated charges for hardware from charges for software services, has led to the marketing of many new courses dealing with data systems and management. Many major firms are finding education to be as lucrative as software development or consulting services.

Courses may be conducted on or off the customer's own premises. It is not uncommon to send employees to regional education centers in various parts of the country where manufacturers offer such courses. Special education programs may also be brought to the customer's own facilities. There it is possible to reach more persons at less cost than it would take to send them away, and they also will have the advantage of being in their normal working environment.

Short courses, institutes, and seminars. Short courses of from one to five days are frequently conducted by professional groups such as the American Management Association, the Data Processing Management Association, the Association for Computing Machinery, the Association for Systems Management, and others. Workshops are also held by colleges and universities, by private consulting firms, and by manufacturers. Each institute or seminar usually is devoted to a single specialized topic. These short courses often provide a way of meeting immediate needs and of learning about the most current developments in the state of the art. The institutes and seminars are valuable not only in the initial training of systems personnel but also for keeping them up to date throughout their working careers.

On-the-job training. In large systems departments it is not at all uncommon to have a section devoted entirely to training. This group can be used for internal training of systems personnel as well as for training the users in other departments in special techniques and procedures for carrying out whatever systems are devised. Of course, each hour spent in training a systems person requires an hour away from systems development and design. Not all departments can afford this amount of time.

The most logical person to do the training would seem to be the senior systems analyst with the most experience, but he or she is also the most expensive employee, whose talents are needed in areas of supervision and guidance for the ongoing work of the department.

The senior person is not necessarily the best communicator, nor the most patient or effective with the new employee. Some other analyst may therefore be designated to conduct or oversee on-the-job training.

Many organizations are able to make use of self-study materials for various phases of systems work. These materials may be used repeatedly and often require only minimum attention from experienced personnel in the department to oversee the instruction. Review of documentation of existing systems provides excellent orientation for the beginning analyst.

However it is organized, some form of in-house training program should be constantly under way. The team approach used in most systems departments provides an excellent means for training. The trainee or clerical assistant is assigned to a junior systems analyst, who in turn works under the supervision of a senior analyst. Each level assists the next to become familiar with the requirements of the next higher position and helps to broaden the abilities of its charges and to prepare them for responsibilities they will assume later.

Some of the features that might be included in a training program within a systems department are:

1. Basic training in use of company hardware
2. Fundamentals of systems analysis and design
3. Training in the use of new systems hardware, software, and operating procedures
4. Development of professional skills, such as special-purpose programming languages, systems management subjects, public speaking, or general business skills such as accounting or management.
5. Principles of structured programming and structured systems design
6. Data base organization and processing
7. Data communications systems

As mentioned earlier in the text, consultants can be helpful in the training of the customer's personnel. The same advantages of using consultants apply to training programs within the systems department. A highly competent consultant might be brought in for a period of several days or even weeks to work with personnel of the systems department in order to teach them basic skills or special techniques useful in their work. Many consultants have special training manuals, audiovisual presentations, sample studies, or other well-designed means of aiding systems people in preparing for their careers.

Self-evaluation tests. The Association for Computing Machinery has spearheaded a program of self-evaluation for professionals in different areas of computer work. The tests cover a broad spectrum of subjects in considerable depth. They are intended to measure familiarity with current topics of concern in programming and systems. The relative score on the test will indicate areas in which the student may need further study or a refresher course.

Self-evaluation is particularly valuable as it offers no threat from one's peers or superiors, as might be felt in other forms of tests. This form of evaluation might be used to set up a program of initial training for the new employee or to suggest areas in which more experienced employees need updating.

PHYSICAL FACILITIES OF THE SYSTEMS DEPARTMENT

Like any other department, the systems department must be housed in congenial surroundings if it is to function efficiently. The office arrangement should be well designed and well lighted, should have available sufficient equipment, adequate desk space, adequate files and references, and clerical assistance for the technical personnel.

Some business organizations have provided magnificent, air-conditioned, well-lighted, dust-free sites for their computer center, but have relegated their programming and systems staffs to a dimly lit, crowded back corner of an old warehouse. Personnel are entitled to even more consideration than equipment. Those who are expected to be creative, to work at a professional level, and to look at the broad aspects of a business are entitled to certain creature comforts that will permit them to work at peak efficiency. Indeed, one principal function of the systems and procedures department traditionally has been office layout. The placement of the desks and files, the relationship of one station to another, the convenience of the workers to their reference materials, the amount of motion necessary to communicate with other departments, access to telephones—all of these features are a part of the systems person's stock in trade. It is the responsibility of top management to provide sufficient resources so that systems people can do their work. It is the responsibility of the systems department to arrange the resources in the most practical way to permit maximum efficiency.

The systems department will be a poor recommendation to others if it does not have its own working area well organized and its own procedures documented and functioning in an exemplary way.

SUMMARY

In this chapter we have looked at the organization of the systems department. We have seen that management has always had responsibility for the functions of systems work—planning, organizing, providing instructions, evaluating effectiveness. In recent years the growth in the size and complexity of business organizations has led to the establishment of special departments to assist managers with the technical details of their systems planning. It has been shown that the manager retains the line authority and that the systems department works in a staff relationship. Systems people must rely upon persuasion and cooperation to bring about the desired result. They have no authority to direct, order, or compel other personnel or departments to make the changes they recommend.

We have analyzed the possible ways of organizing a systems department, contrasting the centralized approach with the decentralized approach. We also have looked at the possibility of placing the systems department under the director of the data processing center or as a separate department responsible to some other executive.

We have seen that the systems department, in order to reach effectively into all parts of the organization, should be responsible to an executive high in the organizational structure. Only such an executive can require the cooperation of the other user departments and can issue the necessary directives to implement the system and to cause it to be carried out.

We have examined the personal traits that make a good systems person, stressing the ability to work with other people, to understand their problems, and to recognize his or her own role as a staff and resource person rather than as an authoritarian dictator.

We have looked at the professional qualifications of the systems person, stressing ability to communicate, knowledge of data processing equipment, knowledge of programming, and knowledge of the organization for which he or she works—both through the formal structure and through the informal structure which evolves as a result of the particular powers and talents of the individuals in the organization. We have seen that of all the characteristics, experience is the most valuable for the systems person.

We have looked at the methods of recruiting and training systems persons and have noted that the use of the programmer aptitude test might reveal promising candidates. Two- and four-year college courses provide the fundamental academic and technical subject matter on which to base a systems career. Courses offered by manufacturers both as formal full-term courses and as short courses and seminars provide an excellent way of keeping systems up to date with the current technical developments of the art. The short courses may be offered at regional training centers or on the customer's own premises on a contract basis. We have seen that on-the-job training, possibly utilizing outside consultants, should be provided for continued growth within each systems department. The use of self-evaluation tests permits both trainees and experienced analysts to find areas in which they need additional training without feeling threatened.

Finally, we have seen that the physical facilities should be conducive to the most efficient output on the part of the systems people. Good lighting, pleasant surroundings, a noise-free environment, and other features of good office planning should be most apparent in the offices of those who prescribe these for other departments.

TERMS FOR REVIEW

Centralized organization	Line
Computer science	Programmer aptitude test
Consultant	Self-evaluation test
Decentralized organization	Staff
In-house training	Unbundling

QUESTIONS

1. What developments in modern business led to the need for separate systems departments?
2. Contrast the advantages and disadvantages of centralized versus decentralized systems organization.
3. How do you rank the relative importance of knowledge of the organization as compared with specialized technical skills for a systems analyst? Why?
4. You have just been employed to head up the newly established systems department for an established manufacturing firm that is just acquiring its first computer. Write a recommendation regarding the placement of your department in the organization chart and your plan for staffing and training your department.
5. Give some of the pros and cons on the use of outside consultants in systems work.
6. As systems manager, you have a senior analyst who is technically proficient but who antagonizes everyone with his dictatorial ways. How would you cope with the problem?
7. Do you see any conflict in the fact that systems work must be creative and adaptive and at the same time must function through prescribed, orderly procedures? Can creative people be systematic?

8. What is meant by the "informal power structure" of an organization? How must the systems department recognize and work through it?
9. You, as head of the systems department, are in need of an additional junior analyst. The personnel department will screen applicants for you, but it has asked you to state just what duties you expect the analyst to perform. Write a job description for the position of junior systems analyst.
10. Outline an orientation and training program for a newly employed junior systems analyst.
11. Draw a layout of an office to house five systems people and two secretaries.

CASE STUDY
SUNCOAST COMMUNITY COLLEGE

Since its founding, Suncoast Community College has shared data processing facilities with the School Board of Sun County. Each entity has its own data processing manager, programmers, and operators. School personnel use the computer system weekdays from 4:00 A.M. until noon, and college personnel from noon until midnight. The work load requires some weekend operations.

DATA SYSTEMS ORGANIZATION

Mack Cordron, Dean of Data Systems, serves as data processing manager and oversees four sections, each having a director. Rick Jagsby is Director of Systems Development; Saundra Dean heads Programming; Jewel Webly is in charge of Computer Operations and Data Entry; and Bob Eberlino is Director of Institutional Research. All directors are well qualified for their positions and have been at Suncoast for more than five years. The center also has a secretary-receptionist (see Figure 2-7).

The systems area is basically decentralized. Each administrative office and instructional department does its own systems work, designs and produces (or acquires) its own forms, and writes its own procedures under the supervision of its regular line administrator. Only where the office requires computer service does it coordinate through the Director of Systems Development with other Computer Center personnel. Rick Jagsby, Director of Systems Development, has responsibility not only for the analysis and design of computer appli-

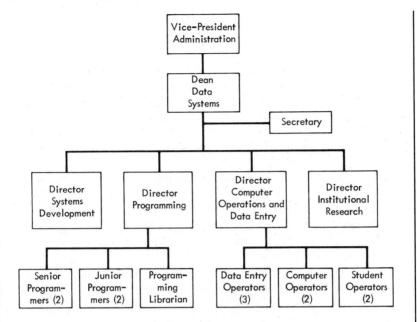

Figure 2-7. Organization chart of Suncoast data systems. As compared with Figure 1-3, the operations and data entry functions are combined and institutional research is an added function.

cations, but also for systems programming and for administration of the data base. He also serves as Acting Dean of Data Systems in the absence of the dean.

The lack of overall college-wide systems direction and coordination tends to cause some inconsistency in the names of data elements, use of codes, and the form in which data is captured. There are also some overlapping functions and some gaps where no one has assumed responsibility.

Reporting to Saundra Dean, Director of Programming, are two senior programmers, two junior programmers, and a programming librarian. ANS COBOL is used for about 90 percent of the programs. Most application programs have been written in-house, but recently some software has been purchased or leased. It is expected that acquisition of software from outside sources will increase.

Jewel Webly, Director of Computer Operations and Data Entry, oversees the work of three data entry operators, two full-time-computer operators, and two part-time student operators. Most data is entered through terminals in various administrative offices. Operators in the Computer Center use keypunches for those applications that require punched cards. They work from 8:00 A.M. until 4:30 P.M., with an hour lunch break. Overtime is sometimes necessary during peak periods of registration, grade reporting, running payrolls, and financial reporting. As mentioned earlier, the computer is used by the School Board of Sun County from 4:00 A.M. until noon. The School Board has its own systems, programming, data entry, and operations personnel. The Suncoast computer operators take over at noon. One operator is on duty from noon until around 8:00 P.M., while the other works from 5:00 P.M. until midnight or later, depending upon work requirements. Student operators divide their time between afternoon and evening hours, and fill in for full-time operators in case of absence.

The Director of Institutional Research, Bob Eberlino, has been made responsible to the Dean of Data Systems because of his strong dependence on the computer data base for producing required state and federal reports. A major portion of his time is required for external reports, but he also produces comparative studies of student aptitude test results to predict the probability of their success in college. He also works closely with deans and directors of other offices to coordinate reports that they prepare and ensure that all are submitted promptly and in good form.

EDUCATION AND TRAINING

The Dean of Data Systems is a strong believer in continuous upgrading and improvement of personnel. Members of the programming and systems staff are encouraged and assisted financially to take active roles in professional organizations such as the Data Processing Management Association, Association for Systems Management, and Association of Educational Data systems. Computer Center personnel attend conferences and conventions of the professional organizations and frequent short workshops on such topics as structured programming, data base management, computer center management, and specialized software. Persons returning from outside meetings hold briefing sessions to share their findings with other personnel. Outside vendors are invited to present new hardware and software products to the entire staff.

PHYSICAL FACILITIES

The physical facilities of the Computer Center are now fairly adequate. Three years ago, because the space used then was becoming crowded, half of the former library building was remodeled into a new computer facility. Each programmer now has a separate office cubicle along the east side of the building with a terminal for online program development. The programming librarian's office in this section houses files and documentation for all programs. Offices of the Dean of Data Systems and the Director of Systems Development are between the programming offices and the computer room, which houses the IBM 4341 central processing unit and all peripheral equipment except the terminals. A student lab on the south side of the computer room contains worktables, 16 terminals for student programming, an enclosed office for the professional lab assistant, a desk for student assistants, file cabinets, and book racks. The student lab facilities and personnel are supervised by the Chairman of the Data Processing instructional department. A large storeroom for cards, forms, paper handling equipment, and old reports is on the north side of the computer room. Offices of School Board personnel are housed east of the storeroom and north of the programmers' offices.

QUESTIONS AND EXERCISES

1. What advantages do you see in Suncoast's decentralized systems organization? What disadvantages, if any?
2. What is your reaction to having the Director of Institutional Research report to the Dean of Data Systems? Would it be logical to make data systems report to the research function?
3. Evaluate the education and training program for data systems personnel at Suncoast.
4. Draw an office layout form for the physical facilities of the Computer Center and offices.

3

THE SYSTEMS
STUDY

OBJECTIVES

At the end of this chapter, you should be able to:

1. Give reasons for requesting a systems study and state who does it and how.
2. Describe the conduct of a preliminary study, indicating its purpose and who participates in it.
3. Present an overall description of the activities involved in the detailed systems study.
4. Identify and describe each of the major duties of the systems team in conducting the systems study.
5. Cite effective interviewing practices by systems personnel.
6. List and describe documents used in gathering data on work measurement.
7. Identify three classes of work flow and show how they are related to office layout.
8. Describe charts that may be used in planning and conducting the systems study.
9. Define structured design and show how it is used in the systems study.
10. Name the reports produced in the course of the systems study and describe their content.

Everyone in a business organization is concerned with systems. The manager is responsible for overall planning, organizing, staffing, directing, and controlling. Other personnel are concerned with carrying out policies, performing their duties according to specific procedures, and recording and analyzing the facts about the various transactions that occur. Only the systems department, however, has the analysis, design, evaluation, and implementation of systems as its *major* concern.

One of the principal ways in which the systems department does its work is through the systems study, or project. In simplest terms, a systems study is a detailed analysis of the way of doing something to see if the method should be continued as is, modified slightly, or completely revised.

In this chapter, we shall examine some of the following questions:

Who requests a systems study and why?
Who carries it out?
What steps are taken?
What forms or documents are used?
What kinds of reports or recommendations are produced?
Who decides what to do about the recommendations?

REQUESTING THE STUDY

The systems department will have some regular, continuing duties that proceed from day to day with little variation, but its main contribution to the organization normally will be made through projects involving detailed study of some particular aspect of the business. To assign priorities, establish control, and marshal the resources of the department, each study should be made only after a formal, written request has been evaluated and approved by the appropriate authorities.

Reasons for Requesting the Study

Normally, a systems study is requested when there is some dissatisfaction with the present or expected performance of the systems. Perhaps input or output information may contain too many errors; reports may be late or inadequate; or customers may be complaining about the quality or timeliness of service. Or perhaps management may see that, although the system is functioning smoothly at present, it will not be able to meet the demands placed on it in the future as a result of growth, reorganization, or new technology. New methods of handling or transmitting data might render present methods obsolete, or new equipment might perform more accurately, faster, and at less cost than equipment now being used.

To take care of present or projected needs, a systems study is requested so that necessary changes can be made before the situation becomes an emergency.

Origin of the Project Request

Almost anyone in an organization might initiate a request for a systems investigation. Top management, with a view of and responsibility for the overall functioning of the organization, should detect trouble spots quickly. Often, members of the systems department, in the course of making one study, will uncover another problem area that merits attention. Workers at any level within a user department might call the attention of their supervisors to a situation which could result in a request being made for a systems study.

A project request always should be in writing and should flow through the normal line organization channels to the systems department. The written request might be similar to the one shown in Figure 3–1. It should state briefly the department involved, the nature of the problem, previous studies that have been made, the number of persons involved, the possible size and scope of the study, and the person to contact for further information.

The systems manager, in consultation with his or her immediate superior and executives of the requesting department, then schedules a preliminary study to see what further action might be indicated.

THE PRELIMINARY STUDY

Once the project request has been accepted, the systems manager appoints the project leader or manager and offers help, if necessary, in the selection of the study team. The number of persons on the team varies according to the size and complexity of the study. The team should represent the different departments involved in the preliminary study and provide varied talents for the task.

The *preliminary study*, often called the *feasibility study*, is not intended primarily to come up with a solution to the problem. Its main purpose is to define the problem clearly, to establish a plan of attack on it, or recommend whether further detailed study is necessary or desirable, and, if so, to estimate the time, personnel, and other resources required for conducting a detailed study.

The length of time required for a feasibility study normally ranges from several weeks to several months. During this time, the team members interview personnel and go through all the steps of a formal study, but on a smaller scale and in a more generalized way. What is being sought at this time is not the answer, but a clear understanding of the problem and an idea of how to get at the answer.

The project leader should provide interim reports perhaps once or twice a month to keep superiors and other concerned individuals informed on the progress being made. The fact that frequent reports are required ensures that the team moves ahead, crystallizes its analysis and observations

REQUEST FOR SYSTEMS INVESTIGATION

From: Morgan Childs   Department: Engineering   Date: 2/11/XX

Reason for Request (Limit remarks to scope and boundaries of problem)

    Request feasibility study for conversion to computer-aided design and drafting. Present manual methods of revising working sketches and drawings are slow and tedious. Terminals are presently in place in Engineering Department for use with parts inventory. Can present equipment be adapted to handle design and drafting?

Previous Studies of System: Yes (X) No (   )

If yes, give date: 7/14/XX

    Procedure number or title: ENGR-INV

    Revisions: None

    Remarks: ENGR-INV was study that implemented online inventory system.

Personnel Affected: (Give number of persons by job title)

    Department Heads: 1
    Supervisors: 3
    Others: (Drafters) 12

For further information, contact:

Name: Morgan Childs   Title: Engineering Manager

Place: Room 227   Date: 2/20/XX   Time: 9:00–12:00

Requested by: *Morgan Childs*
Signature & Title

ACKNOWLEDGMENT AND ACTION

Request Approved (✓) Denied (   )   Project No. ENGR-DRFT-01

Analyst Assigned: Michael Wright

Gerald Phipps
Systems Manager

Figure 3-1. Request for systems study form. The request may originate in any department and is forwarded through channels to the systems department.

into something specific, and advises the relevant parties of any new or unanticipated developments.

The final report of the preliminary study will contain one of three possible recommendations:

1. *No further action necessary.* Sometimes the problem cures itself during the course of the preliminary study. The mere fact that a study is being made may give workers in the problem department some additional insight or may increase their concern. Or perhaps the preliminary study may turn up some fairly obvious difficulties. It has been said—not completely in jest—that the best thing that can happen to an organization is to make a feasibility study and then not buy any new equipment.
2. *Minor revisions necessary.* The team may recommend a more detailed study of some limited application or procedure, but not general overhaul of the entire system.
3. *Major revision of new system needed.* Where this recommendation is made, estimates should be furnished of the time, personnel, and cost requirement for the detailed study. Several alternative plans of attack might be suggested. Any new facts uncovered during the preliminary study should be set forth.

Depending upon the size of the proposed system to be installed or modified, the preliminary study report may be only a few pages or a sizeable document. The systems manager reviews it and, after consulting with other top executives, makes the decision (or receives it from other higher authority) whether a further detailed systems study should be made.

THE DETAILED SYSTEMS STUDY

When it is determined that a detailed study is warranted, the systems manager appoints a project leader, or manager, who may or may not be the leader of the preliminary study. The duties of the project leader are to assemble the team and oversee its work through the following steps:

1. Determine the scope and objectives of the study.
2. Analyze the present system in minute detail.
3. Project future requirements of the system.
4. Explore alternative solutions to meet present and anticipated requirements.
5. Submit a final recommendation to management.

Many steps are involved between the original realization that a need exists and the systematic review of operations after the new system is fully implemented. We consider each of these steps now in greater detail.

Scope and Objectives of the Study

The project leader's first duty is to review thoroughly the preliminary report. From it she (or he) should be able to make a reasonable estimate as to the time, cost, and numbers of persons to be involved in the study. She may prepare a Gantt chart such as Figure 3–2 showing the time require-

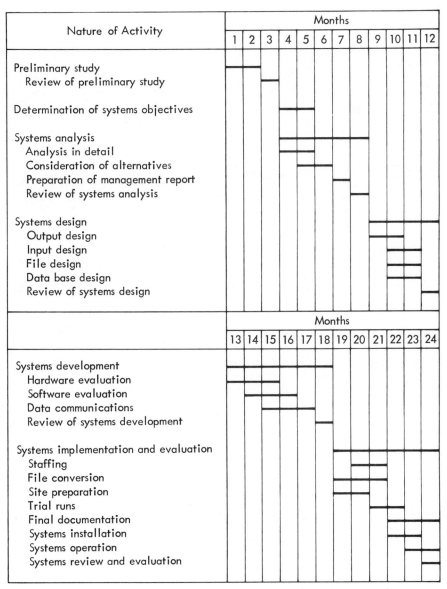

Figure 3-2. Gantt chart showing time requirements for a systems study. This type of chart shows clearly which activities may overlap and which are completed before others begin.

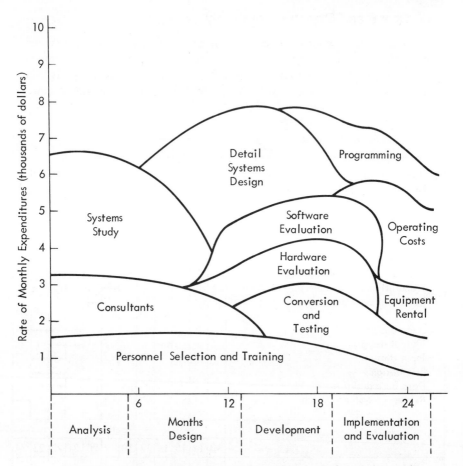

Figure 3-3. Implementation plan cost summary, by task and time period. Expenditures for the different activities vary widely through the different phases of the systems project.

ments of the various activities in terms of months and personnel. She also may chart financial data as in Figure 3–3. She next proceeds to assemble her project team.

Composition of the team. At least some of the team members who did the preliminary study should be included in the detailed study. They will be familiar with the basic problem and the steps taken to date. They will be able to brief new members of the team and to help expedite the entire project. They must, however, clear their minds of any preconceived notions of the solution until they have examined all the facts and explored all the alternatives.

It is usually preferable to have a smaller team of people working full time on the project than to have a larger number of people on a rotating, short-term basis. This principle applies primarily to staff personnel and in no way precludes calling in additional persons, particularly those of special talents or experience, for a short period.

Use of consultants. There is a growing tendency to turn an entire systems study over to a consulting firm, assigning certain persons within the organization to work as liaison with them.

Consultants may offer many positive benefits described earlier in the chapter. Among them are high level of expertise, objectivity, access to outside sources of information, respect of top management, and proven methods.

On the other hand, when consultants are employed, certain problems may be encountered:

1. Management should realize that using consultants probably will require a larger direct expenditure than would using in-house personnel.
2. The consultants will require more time than local people to become familiar with the organization, its personnel, and its functions.
3. There may be a tendency for an outside consultant to try to apply a package developed for some other situation that does not fit the present one.
4. Consultants usually are not around to have to live with the deficiencies that might crop up after their systems have been implemented.

Analysis of the Present System

All the resources of the project team are brought to bear on the detailed analysis of the present system. The major duties of the systems team fall under the following categories:

1. *Interviewing.* Perhaps the most important source of information is in discussion with persons involved with the system, from managers and supervisors down through the working ranks.
2. *Work measurement.* A wide variety of reports and forms are examined to produce as many statistics as possible about volume of transactions, time required for each operation, distribution of time by each employee, cost to each department of performing essential functions, and so forth.
3. *Review of documents.* A sample of each document used is collected. A forms analysis chart can be prepared to show items of information that are common to different forms.
4. *Observation of the actual procedure.* Watching the procedure in progress furnishes information to the analyst that might not be indicated from the written procedure or from interviews.
5. *Review of office layout and data flow.* Charts showing flow of traffic and data through the various workstations can reveal waste motion or gaps in processing steps.

6. *Preparation of interim reports.* It is vital to keep management informed of the progress of the study, especially if it appears that the length, cost, or objectives of the study are to be changed.

Interviewing. Many people believe that the most important and effective means of gathering facts is the systems interview. A good interviewer can make people feel at ease, People are more apt to talk about a topic than to put their thinking about it into concise written form. The analyst must approach the interviewee in a friendly attitude, not as an accuser or critic. She asks questions about the person's job, what he likes about it, what he would like to do to make it easier or better. Excellent suggestions, as well as facts, can be brought forth through skilled interviewing.

The analyst must be at home with people of all levels through the organization, those of high education as well as the relatively untutored, those of broad powers and those who do rather menial tasks. She should not force or press or hurry the interview. She should not be embarrassed by an occasional period of silence.

To reduce the chance of introducing bias into the interview, the analyst would do well to observe the following pointers:

1. Plan carefully with a list of questions to be covered during the interview (see Figure 3–4).
2. Use open-ended questions which draw out the respondent's own opinions, attitudes, and suggestions rather than direct or leading questions calling for yes or no answers.
3. Be alert to nonverbal responses such as facial expressions, tone of voice, gestures, and body orientation.
4. Put interviewee at ease. Take plenty of time. Hold the interview at his workstation, if sufficient privacy is available there, rather than in the systems office.
5. Set the tone of a friendly conversation rather than that of an investigation or inquisition.
6. Maintain an eye-level body orientation. Sit if the other person sits; stand if he has to stand. Keep a suitable physical distance, neither too remote nor uncomfortably close.
7. Keep the interview moving. Keep to the subject. End it on a positive note. Thank the person interviewed for his cooperation.

If the interviewer takes notes during the conversation, she should do it unobtrusively so as not to distract her from what the person is saying. Especially if she does not take notes during the interview, but even if she does, she must carefully record all the essential facts as soon as possible after the interview is concluded. The record of the interview then becomes an important part of the system working papers and documentation. A tape

DATA SYSTEMS DEPARTMENT
INTERVIEW GUIDE

Name of project: Computer-aided design and drafting   No. ENGR-DRFT-01
Name of person interviewed: Benito Martinez
Job title: Drafting Supervisor
Department: Engineering
Date of interview: Tuesday, March 10   Time: 10:30 a.m.
Place: Room 238
Special arrangements: Check that inventory terminal is available

Questions:

1. Are you familiar with computer-aided design and drafting?
2. How many drafters in the department have ever used CADD?
3. Do you have a favorite CADD software package?
4. Are any drafters familiar with terminal operation for inventory application?
5. Give a brief description of the present manual method for originating and modifying drawings.
6. What do you consider to be the most severe problems with the present manual system?
7. Can they be corrected without CADD?
8. Are drafters receptive to change in technique?
9. Can we perform parallel operations if new system is implemented?

Figure 3-4. Interview guide. Careful planning enables the analyst to ensure that pertinent points are covered.

recorder may be a more reliable and less obvious tool than written notes for capturing the essence of the interview.

Work measurement. The systems analyst should have very thorough documentation of her study, just as an auditor prepares and retains detailed working papers and schedules in conducting an examination of financial records. The entire project is a team effort, and the findings must be accessible to all analysts in written form. (Copying equipment is helpful to the systems team in providing copies of a document to any members who require them.) Information from various sources can better be correlated and compared when there is good documentation.

Some essential facts to be recorded are:

Workplace and its layout
Personnel
Organizational arrangement
Duties of each job
Frequency of occurrence
Time required

Some of the titles of documents used for data gathering are:

Organization chart
Position chart
Personnel chart
Machine utilization report
Activity sheet
Operation sheet
Resource usage sheet
Procedure analysis worksheet
Work distribution chart
Task list
Forms analysis chart
Frequency distribution chart
Office layout and traffic flowchart

There is no single, standard form used for these documents, nor even any uniformly recognized name. By whatever name it is called, a document should convey information in meaningful classifications, appropriately headed columns, and specific quantities or units of measure.

Figures involving work measurement should be verified so far as possible by the department manager or supervisor. Errors resulting from figures entered hastily or without verification might tend later to discredit the entire report.

Review of documents. The number of different forms used in a department is sometimes astonishing. Many of them have been hastily devised for a temporary purpose and never have been subjected to critical analysis. By gathering a copy of each form used, the analyst can make a systematic tally of the items of information that appear on each. She can check for redundancy of data. She may spot forms that are so similar that one can be eliminated. She may find it is possible to combine several forms into a single one that will do several jobs. She will be able to suggest rearrangement of format to make the form better serve its purpose. (In Chapter 6 we shall look in depth at the principles of good form design and control.)

Observation of the actual procedure. By watching the system in actual operation, the analyst may discover waste motion, incorrect procedures, unnecessary steps, and other problems not apparent from the formal procedures or records. On the other hand, she may find that someone has developed individual innovations and improvements which should be adopted as standard practice.

A registration procedure in a college or university is a good example of an activity which is likely to deviate widely from the established procedure. Many assistants are drafted—temporarily and probably unwillingly

—to hand out cards, check schedules, issue directives, search lists, take photographs, collect money, and perform myriad other tasks. They often have little or no briefing, receive no written instructions, and stand against the onslaught of thousands of students whose chief thought is to get finished and get home. Fortunately, the registration is finally completed, but all the good resolves and formal procedures adopted when it is over never seem to prevent the same situation from occurring next semester.

Most business systems are more regularized. A bank teller or grocery bagger normally is familiar with the duties of his or her job, and performs them in a similar manner from day to day under some degree of supervision and in conformity to established policy and procedure.

Questionnaires. At times, the pressure of work may not permit extensive personal interviews or direct observation of the actual procedures. Sometimes the systems study involves widespread geographic sites or branches, not all of which can be visited personally.

In such cases questionnaires may be employed to obtain valuable information to supplement other sources available to the analyst. Questionnaires should be short and specific, using checkoff answers or multiple-choice responses where feasible. Space may be allowed for additional comments or criticisms (see Figure 3–5).

TASK ANALYSIS QUESTIONNAIRE

Employee Name		Instructions:						
Dept.		1. Write or print clearly.						
Job Title		2. Number each task. 3. List most important tasks first.						
Supervisor		4. Describe each task.						
Date Approved by		5. Report time to nearest 1/10 hour.						

Task No.	Listing of Tasks	Frequency					Quantity	Time
		Day	Wk.	Mo.	Yr.	Other		

Figure 3-5. Task analysis questionnaire. This type of questionnaire enables the employee to compare tasks actually performed with those stipulated in the job description.

BEFORE. This Flow Diagram revealed wasted steps...
wasted time...wasted energy...wasted money. Solid lines
show how each order once traveled 162 ft. Broken lines indicated how auxiliary forms once traveled 80 ft.

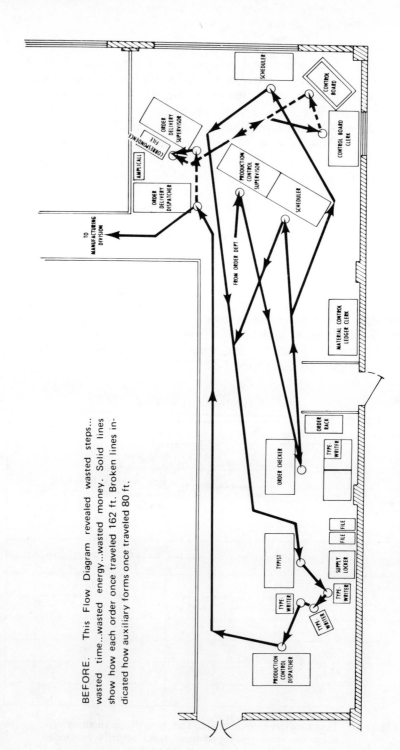

Figure 3-6. Office layout and data flow diagram. (Courtesy of The Standard Register Company.)

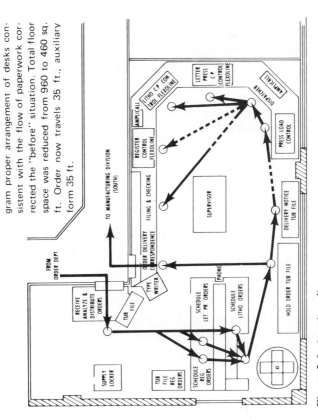

AFTER. As shown in this Flow Diagram proper arrangement of desks consistent with the flow of paperwork corrected the "before" situation. Total floor space was reduced from 960 to 460 sq. ft. Order now travels 35 ft., auxiliary form 35 ft.

Figure 3-6 *(continued)*

67

In most instances, it is desirable to know who completed the questionnaire so that any matters not clear can be followed up. But unsigned questionnaires may be used where disclosure of the person answering might cause embarrassment or prevent full and frank response.

Provision should be made for follow-up by telephone or mail where questionnaires are not returned within the time requested. Often a second copy of the questionnaire is mailed in case the first has been mislaid.

Review of office layout and data flow. As ways of communication become more sophisticated, more information might be transmitted by telephone, telegraph, or visual display. The physical movement of paper work and personal traffic tend to be reduced. But there is an irreducible minimum that cannot be eliminated. A chart showing the position of the various desks and work stations can be superimposed with lines showing the movement of data as the various processing steps are performed. Often rearranging desks, files, or other facilities will greatly reduce confusion and make for smoother work flow (see Figure 3–6).

Several fundamental principles of data capture and data flow can be stated here:

1. Record essential facts about a transaction at the source.
2. As early as possible, convert the data into machine-processable form.
3. Keep manual recopying of data to an absolute minimum. Let machines make the copies.
4. Make information available to all users from the same source data either by making multiple copies of output or by providing inquiry stations.

Work flow is sometimes classified under three headings:

1. *The serial or assembly line plan,* in which work flows through a single channel, where each employee performs a particular, specialized task. This method is highly efficient when handling large amounts of material.
2. *The parallel or concurrent handling plan,* in which work is divided among two or more persons or groups, each of whom does all the tasks necessary to complete the job. This method may offer greater variety and interest to the worker than the serial plan, but it requires more training and higher comprehension.
3. *The unit assembly or simultaneous handling plan,* in which multiple copies of paperwork are made, with a separate copy going to each of several clerks, who then simultaneously perform a separate, single task. The forms are then reassembled and consolidated.

Work-handling schemes often will combine several of these plans, or use different plans for different forms of production. Figure 3-7 shows a comparison of the plans.

Preparation of interim reports. As the study unfolds, progress reports should be provided by the project manager at regular intervals, probably monthly. They should not be voluminous, but should focus attention on any exceptional situations that have or might be developed. They should be distributed by the systems manager to the line executives in and above the department being studied. Figure 3-8 shows a typical interim report.

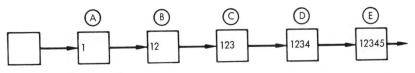

Serial or Assembly Line Plan.

A, B, C, D, E = Work stations

1, 2, 3, 4, 5 = Operations

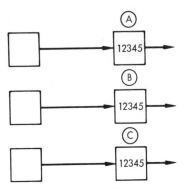

Parallel or Concurrent Handling Plan.

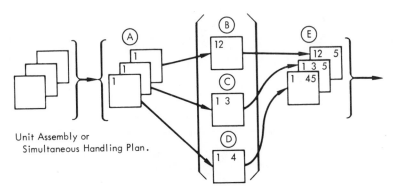

Unit Assembly or
Simultaneous Handling Plan.

Figure 3-7. Three types of work flow. Under the serial plan each employee or station performs a single task. Under the parallel plan an entire unit is completed at each station. The unit assembly plan is often used with paperwork such as purchase orders and receiving reports.

DATA SYSTEMS INTERIM REPORT

To: Gerald Phipps, Systems Manager

From: Michael Wright, Project Manager

Project No.: ENGR-DRFT-01   Date: 4/10/XX

Description of Project:

   This study investigates conversion to computer-aided design and drafting with possible use of terminals presently handling parts inventory in Engineering Department.

Progress to Date:

1. Present terminals lack graphics capability for CAD.
2. Drafting personnel have little involvement with parts inventory system.
3. Study team has reviewed three CAD software packages with Engineering Manager.
4. Meeting with CAD consultant is scheduled for April 15 to consider suitable CAD terminals.
5. Two drafters have limited prior experience with CAD.

Problem Areas Encountered:

1. Need for separate CAD terminals will increase cost of project approximately $18,000.
2. CAD training materials are generally poor and expensive.

Recommendations:

1. Continue with project considering separate terminals. Annual savings after first year are estimated at $14,500.
2. Continue search for effective training materials.
3. Evaluate three different CAD terminals compatible with present mainframe.

Report Accepted and Distributed (✓)   Returned for Revision (   )

Gerald Phipps
Systems Manager

Figure 3-8. Interim report. Periodic reports enable the systems team to keep management informed as the study progresses.

Projection of Future Requirements

   Once the project team has learned as much as it can about the existing system, it should attempt to determine the demands that will be placed upon the system in the future. It is futile to design a system that will meet today's needs but will be inadequate tomorrow. It is equally futile to try to design a system for eternity. A system that will meet the present requirements and allow for the expected growth of the next five years or so is probably a reasonable goal.

One important technique for meeting future needs is to design a modular system—that is, one to which additional components can be added as the system grows. Most modern computer systems are designed to permit the addition of terminals, installation of faster or larger-capacity disk or tape files, replacement of slower printers with faster ones, expansion of main storage, and even linking to other CPUs without exchanging or replacing the entire configuration of equipment.

The team must examine and consider not only the facts about the existing system, but virtually all information it can obtain from other sources to try to plan for the future. Long-range policies of the organization's top management certainly must be known. Economic trends, international relations, styles and fads, inventions, taxes, pollution control laws—all these may have a profound impact upon the future operations of the business. Systems analysts cannot control many, if any, of these factors, but as far as possible they should consider them in their plans.

Exploring Alternative Solutions

System design is as creative an activity as writing a poem, painting, or composing music. But systems designers must couple with their creativity a practical, hardheaded sense of reality not often found in the arts. They also need a thorough knowledge of equipment, people, and methods in their infinite combinations.

Out of the almost unlimited possibilities that may exist for carrying out the system under study, the designer has to be able to discard fairly quickly those of least value. Usually, the choices will boil down to one or two most likely methods, with several options for each. For example, even after a definite decision to install a computer still there are options between online and batch processing; tape or disk files; card, keytape, or optical input; high-speed printer or visual display of output; and other choices.

The alternatives available seem to multiply daily as new technical milestones are reached involving laser memories, microfilm storage of data, voice response, data communications networks, and other modern phenomena. In spite of all these advanced choices, though, the analyst must still consider the same basic factors:

1. Will the system do what needs to be done?
2. Is it as simple as practicable?
3. Is it the least expensive way consistent with good results?
4. Is it flexible enough to adapt to changing conditions?
5. Can we persuade management to adopt it and the employees to use it properly?

The Management Presentation

The end product of the systems study is the report of the study to management. It will contain all or most of the following sections.

1. *Title page.*
2. *Table of contents.*
3. *Statement of the problem.* This is a restatement of the problem that was the object of the detailed study, or a new definition of the condition that prompted the original feasibility study.
4. *Summary or abstract.* This section should be limited to a page or two giving a concise statement of the main findings and recommendations. It should focus on costs, people, and time required to develop, implement, and check out the new system.
5. *Main body of the report.* This is a more detailed statement to support the findings and recommendations.
6. *Credits.* This would recognize the participants in the study and various other persons who contributed to or supported it.
7. *Appendix.* Here might appear the detailed procedures, manufacturer's literature, tables, and charts developed during the course of the study.

The best possible system on paper is still valueless until it is properly installed and functioning. Sometimes management is fully aware of the new system being recommended and is completely sold upon its merit; in other cases the analyst must make a specific presentation to management to try to persuade the adoption of the new system. The technique to be used in making the presentation to management depends in part upon the time available for presentation, and in part upon whether a "hard sell" or "soft sell" is required. The presentation also may be shaped by the degree to which management is already familiar with the result of the systems study. If time for preparing the presentation is short, the analyst may be able to give only an oral report, with blackboard illustration. With an extra day or two, she (or he) might prepare a flipchart or posters. With one week or more to prepare, she may use slides or transparencies. For a major hard-sell pitch with considerable preparation time, she might even use professionally prepared motion pictures.

The analyst should be sensitive to the responsibility of the person to whom she is making the presentation. For example, accounting personnel are particularly affected by their schedule for preparing reports. It would indicate poor planning to schedule a presentation to accounting personnel during the first five days of a new year, when they would be submerged in the preparation of year-end reports.

The analyst should pace her presentation so that each point can be fully comprehended before moving on to the next point. If she glibly tosses out many facts and figures which are not fully comprehended, management may be impressed with her knowledge but it will not be sold on the new system.

The selling of a system is a composite of many things, of which the final presentation to management is only one. If all phases of the systems study, analysis, and design have been well done, selling will be much simpler. If the department has established a tradition of effective, sensible, and economic design, management will have confidence in its product. If effective progress reports have been made as the systems study proceeds, management will be more receptive toward the final recommendation and report. Finally, good documentation will provide the backup to justify the final conclusions which have been reached by the study team.

PROJECT APPROVAL

Approval and acceptance of the report and recommendations are the responsibility of top line management, which may adopt the plan in whole or in part, for immediate or later implementation. Or it may reject the plan outright and order a new study. Such an action would indicate a drastic failure on the part of the systems team. If it had properly kept management informed of its progress, it should have been able to adjust its approach and to produce an acceptable system.

PHASES FOLLOWING PROJECT APPROVAL

If top-line management approves the systems project, the remaining steps of the systems cycle are carried out. We will recall that the three steps following systems analysis are (1) systems design and control, (2) systems development, and (3) systems implementation and evaluation.

Systems Design and Control

The systems team uses *structured design,* sometimes called *top-down design,* to build the system by describing first the broad functions the system is to serve. Then each of the functions is divided, or *decomposed,* into smaller segments at a lower level and refined in greater detail. The design phase usually begins with the desired output. Then the input necessary to produce that output is designed. Finally, the data base and processing techniques are designed.

Systems designers prepare a report specifying details of the system *to be built.* The *design report* is reviewed by the various user departments and by top management. If the design is approved, the systems development phase begins. Part III examines systems design and control in detail.

Systems Development

Where systems design has called for new or additional hardware, there is a wide—sometimes frustratingly wide—choice of equipment from which to select. Microcomputers may be used as stand-alone units or attached as terminals to larger mainframes. Equipment may be leased or purchased from the original manufacturer, leased from a third party, or purchased from a previous user or a broker. Hardware prices may include full, limited, or no software, services, and support. During the development phase, any new or additional hardware must be selected, ordered, installed, and tested.

The problem of writing or selecting software which operates and controls the equipment is even more complex than choosing the hardware. Measures of software effectiveness are far less precise than measures of hardware speed or capacity. The analyst must considered various languages and packages, in-house versus contract programming, standardization, and many other factors.

Most modern systems involve a network of some type to permit data to be gathered from various sources and display the resulting information where it is most needed. Data communications networks require additional levels of sophisticated software to service the demands of many terminal users and the technical details of data transmission over communication lines.

The systems development report describes the system *as built.* It is reviewed by user department personnel as part of their orientation to the new system. Systems development is treated in detail in Part IV of the text.

Systems Implementation and Evaluation

Putting the newly developed system into effect normally is not the duty of the entire project team. Many of the details will fall to line management, while the systems department will be responsible for briefing management and training operating personnel. The problem of implementing and evaluating the performance of the system will be covered fully in Part V.

SUMMARY

Whenever a system runs into problems—such as inaccurate or late information, customer complaints, lack of capacity, or obsolete equipment—a request for systems investigation may be made. Such a request may originate from top management, from the systems department itself, or from the user department.

A preliminary study is made by a team selected by the systems manager to define the problem precisely, formulate a plan of attack, and determine the scope and objectives of the detailed study. The report resulting from the preliminary study helps management decide whether to make a detailed systems study.

The detailed study requires the efforts of a team made up of people with many talents. First, it examines in detail the present system by using the methods of interview, work measurement, document review, survey of actual procedures, analysis of office layout and data flow, and interim reports.

Next, the team estimates future requirements of the system, explores alternative solutions, and prepares its findings and recommendations in a final report to management.

If the system is approved, the systems department starts up the next phase of detailed systems design. Later, if the design is also approved, systems personnel conduct the systems development phase and, finally, the system implementation and evaluation.

TERMS FOR REVIEW

Assembly line plan
Concurrent handling plan
Data flow
Document
Feasibility study
Hardware
Interim reports
Preliminary study

Project leader
Project request
Simultaneous handling plan
Software
Structured design
Systems study
Top-down design

QUESTIONS

1. What are some conditions that might prompt a request for systems study?
2. What are the main objectives of the preliminary study?
3. What are the advantages of having the same person on both the preliminary study team and the detailed study team?
4. Name the principal steps involved in the detailed study.
5. Describe the characteristics of a good interviewer.
6. What are some of the documents used in work measurement?
7. What are the duties of the project manager? How is he or she selected?
8. What features are included in the final systems report and recommendations?
9. As systems manager, you receive a request for systems investigation from your billing department stating that invoices are being delayed

three to five days and monthly statements up to 10 days. What qualifications would you look for in the systems department personnel you appoint to the project team to study the complaint? Who, if anyone, would you appoint from the rest of the organization? What suggestions would you give the members?

10. An office is staffed by *B, C,* and *D* under the supervision of *A.* These people process forms 1, 2, 3, 4, and 5. Forms 2 and 4 are filed after processing; the rest are routed to other offices. *B* works on forms 1, 2, and 5. *C* works on 3, 4, and 5. *D* works on 1, 2, 3, and 4. *A* supervises the others and inspects all finished forms. Forms 3, 4, and 5 are partially processed by machine *Z.* Design an office layout showing the position of machine *Z* and the desks of *A, B, C,* and *D.* Indicate the paths taken by the five forms.

11. Describe the process of top-down design. What are its advantages?

12. Who makes the final decision on whether or not a proposed system shall be adopted and implemented?

13. Describe and distinguish between the three classes of work flow described in this chapter.

CASE STUDY
SUNCOAST COMMUNITY COLLEGE

For a number of years, Suncoast Community College has used its computer system in instruction as well as for administrative purposes. The Data Processing Department offers the Associate in Science Degree preparing students for entry-level positions as computer programmers. It also has offered two tracks leading to the Associate in Arts Degree for transfer to four-year institutions. The Computer Systems track emphasizes the use of computers in business, accounting, and management, while the Computer Science track concentrates on math, science, and engineering applications. The computer has also been used extensively for scoring and analyzing tests, with an optical mark reader to sense answers marked by the students on multiple-choice tests.

Most administrative applications are now online. Student records, registration, grade reporting, and financial aid are the applications relating mainly to students. Payroll, accounting, and property records are the principal business applications. The file management system was written in-house, but embodies many sophisticated features found in commercial data base management systems.

As a public institution receiving most of its funds from state appropriations, Suncoast Community College has not had a major program to attract private donations. However, for several years state appropriations have not kept pace with increased costs of operation. President Stevens has recently appointed Marilyn Woods as Director of Institutional Advancement with two major responsibilities:

1. Activate and promote the dormant Suncoast Foundation, a non-profit organization to receive grants and donations for the benefit of the college.
2. Enlarge and increase activities of the Suncoast Alumni Association.

REQUEST FOR SYSTEMS STUDY

Dr. Woods decides first to concentrate on the Alumni Association, since most of the records needed for graduates and former students are already available in the student files. On March 1 she sends a Request for Systems Study (Figure 3-9) to Mack Cordron, Dean of Data Systems. He refers the request to Rick Jagsby, Director of Systems Development, who assigns Gerald Phipps, Senior Systems Analyst, as project manager to make a preliminary study.

Phipps asks three persons to join him in making the preliminary study: Marilyn Woods, Director of Institutional Advancement; Chris Wells, Director of Student Counseling; and Neal McGill, Director of Admissions and Records.

They determine that the student master file contains more than 100,000 records of students who have taken one or more courses for credit and therefore might be considered alumni of the institution. Approximately 12,000 students have actually received degrees, with the number growing at about 800 per year. They propose to make a separate alumni file of graduates from the present master file. It can be used for mailing labels, lists of students by years, and statistical tabulations.

In addition, they plan to create a donor file yearly with a separate record for each alumnus who contributes to the college. Later, other small files might be created with records of officers of the association, regional directors, and various activities other than contributions.

PRELIMINARY STUDY REPORT

Because the alumni application will utilize existing files and equipment to a large degree, the preliminary study team believes that the detailed study can be completed within a few months. They recognize that some personnel involved will be unable to devote full time to the

REQUEST FOR SYSTEMS INVESTIGATION

From: Marilyn Woods   Department: Inst. Advancement   Date: 3/1/XX

Reason for Request (Limit remarks to scope and boundaries of problem)

   Request study on feasibility of developing online alumni record system. It should provide mailing lists and labels arranged by class, major, or alphabetical order. Detailed donor records should be kept for each alumni member making a contribution to the college. We wish to enter transactions from terminal in the office of Institutional Advancement.

Previous Studies of System: Yes (   )   No (X)

If yes, give date:

   Procedure number or title:
   Revisions:
   Remarks:

Personnel Affected: (Give number of persons by job title)

   Department Heads: 2
   Supervisors: 3
   Others:

For further information, contact:

Name: Marilyn Woods   Title: Director of Inst. Advancement

Place: Room 135   Date: 3/8/XX   Time: 2:00–3:00 p.m.

                                   Requested by: *M Woods*
                                                  _____
                                                   Signature

ACKNOWLEDGMENT AND ACTION

Request Approved (✓)   Denied (   )   Project No. ALUM-01

Analyst Assigned: Gerald Phipps
                                          Rick Jagsky
                                          Dir., Sys. Development

Figure 3-9. Request for alumni systems study. If the request is approved, the feasibility study team will be appointed and the study will begin.

alumni application and must continue with other regular duties. On April 5 they prepare a report to Rick Jagsby estimating the following schedule for the detailed systems study:

Define system objectives	1 week
Design alumni master file	1 week
Design donor file	1 week
Design forms and screens	1 week
Order forms	1 week
Design programs	2 weeks
Develop programs	5 weeks
Test programs	3 weeks
Test system	2 weeks
Implement system	1 week

The preliminary study team recommends that the college administration authorize a detailed systems study, using regular college personnel to proceed as expeditiously as possible without disrupting ongoing activities.

MANAGEMENT APPROVAL

Rick Jagsby forwards the preliminary study report via Mack Cordron to the Administrative Council, recommending approval. The Administrative Council is made up of the president with his three vice-presidents. They meet regularly each week and by special call as necessary. At their next regular meeting on April 10 they approve the preliminary study report and return it to Jagsby for further action.

DETAILED SYSTEMS STUDY

Jagsby appoints Gerald Phipps, Senior Systems Analyst, as project manager for the detailed systems study. Phipps selects the remaining members of the team:

Marilyn Woods, Director of Institutional Advancement
Werk Dunn, President of Alumni Association
John Shirley, Senior Programmer
Sally Waters, Data Entry Operator
Richard Allison, Dean of Business Services

The team agrees that Phipps and Shirley will do the detailed systems and programming work and call on the other team members regularly as consultants and periodically for special services or projects. Arnold Strong, a state auditor who is expected to be on campus during much of the systems study, is asked to serve as a consultant with emphasis on security and control features.

QUESTIONS AND EXERCISES

1. Can you suggest any other persons who might have been included on the preliminary study team? On the detailed study team? Why?
2. Were proper channels followed in submitting and approving the request for systems study? Justify your answer.
3. What adjustments, if any, would you suggest to the schedule adopted for the detailed systems study?
4. Draw a Gantt chart to schedule the systems project.

SYSTEMS FLOWCHARTING

OBJECTIVES

At the end of this chapter, you should be able to:

1. Name the four major uses for charts in systems work.
2. List tools typically found in a systems department.
3. Name the groups that have led in standardizing flowcharting symbols and conventions.
4. Identify and give the purpose for each of five different classes of flowcharts.
5. Draw simple flowcharts of each of the classes described in the chapter.
6. Identify the parts and cite the uses of decision tables.
7. Distinguish between charts used for conventional programs and for structured programs.
8. Describe the three basic logical forms used in structured programming.
9. Name and describe the two principal types of scheduling charts.

Many areas of study besides systems have utilized charts, graphs, tables, and other methods of displaying information in pictorial form. Charts provide a language of abbreviation that enable one to see relationships, flows of information, relative magnitudes, and many other useful facts in a convenient and compact way.

Flowcharting is by no means unique to systems work, but it takes on an unusual amount of importance to the systems analyst or designer. Charting has been called "the mainstream of system technique." The use of pictorial figures, graphics, and symbols is one main difference between the systems person and the supervisor. Both are concerned with the design and implementation of good systems procedure, but the systems specialist is far more concerned with the use of charts to display the information he or she needs to convey to all personnel from top management to those in operations.

USES OF CHARTING

Systems analysts will find four major uses for charts:

1. In the survey, or systems study
2. In design of new systems
3. In presentation of the system, both to management for adoption and to other employees for implementation
4. In actual installation of the new system

Charting in Analysis

In making the survey, or systems study, analysts are concerned with investigating the present method of performing the job. They assemble data from many sources by interviewing personnel, tabulating existing records, making personal observations, and preparing schedules and analyses. All this information must be digested and put together into some logical, coordinated whole. By preparing flowcharts, analysts demonstrate their comprehension of the techniques now in use. At this state, it is not essential to produce a finished copy. Even a very rough draft of a chart can indicate the proper flow and relationship between elements of the present procedure. The chart developed in the systems study has value even if it is not retained permanently. Its main value is to provide a means by which the analysts crystallize the multitude of details they have assembled into a form from which both they and others can see the pattern that has emerged.

The chart as developed in the survey also can be helpful in confirming the procedure with personnel of the department being studied. The practice of reviewing the chart with the appropriate department gives opportunity to correct errors that might occur in collecting the original data, recording the interviews, or preparing the chart itself.

Charting in Design

Building upon the chart developed in making the systems study, the analysts are now in position to eliminate duplications, awkward procedures, and loose ends that appeared in the original procedure. The chart becomes a model of the system they are attempting to design, and gives them the opportunity to explore alternatives and to rearrange the flow of data, personnel, or equipment. Thus in a relatively inexpensive way the analysts may consider the ultimate demands of the system they are designing.

Charting in Presentation

Through the effective use of charts, analysts can demonstrate clearly to management how the old system works and how and why it should be improved. Charts can simplify and shorten the explanation of the new system being proposed.

Many different types of charts may be used in presenting a new system. The particular merit of the chart at this point is its capacity to compress a large amount of information into a relatively small space and to show rather complex relationships more clearly than paragraphs or even pages of narrative explanation.

Charting in Installation

Final systems documentation almost always will include charts. Charts used by operating personnel should be simple, free from unusual terms or highly complex technical symbols, and limited to the particular job to be explained. Various levels of charts may be prepared—some showing overall procedure for high-level executives, others showing the smallest operating details for line workers.

One effective way to use charts for installation is to tie a narrative description of the procedure to the chart itself by means of numbered keys.

TOOLS USED IN CHARTING

Charts may be very simple or elaborate, depending upon their intended use. The size of the systems department and the organization tends to determine the number of personnel available and the diversity of their talents. Every systems analyst should be adept with general charting tools and should understand the fundamentals of charting technique. In more elaborate departments, or for special presentations to management, the services of professional draftspeople or commercial artists might be used. There are occasions where drawings using multiple colors, varied type sizes, and elaborate symbols are appropriate.

All or some of the following tools are found in a typical systems department:

1. Drawing or lettering instruments
2. Drafting pens of different sharpnesses and widths
3. Felt-tip pens for broad lettering, filling in blocks, and shading
4. Plastic or metal templates and rulers for drawing the various figures used in charting
5. Scissors, tweezers, paste, transparent tape, and other supplies
6. A professional drawing board with horizontal or vertical guides
7. Colored pencils, inks, or paints
8. Pictographic symbols or cutouts, such as people, computers, telephones, desks
9. Layout planning charts

In recent years, many devices and media have been made available to simplify and enhance the charting process: adhesive-backed tapes; overlays; headings with numbers, letter, or months of the year in different sizes; grids; and special forms. Where colored inks and paints are used, it is important that they be washable. It is inevitable that some accidents will occur, and the paint or ink should be removable from clothes, paper, or furniture. White paint is useful to make corrections or clean up a chart by applying it directly over other lines or figures.

Reproducing Charts

Making charts available to all members of the study team as the study progresses helps keep them informed as to progress being made. Then, in the complete report, a set of charts is needed for each copy of the documentation. For these reasons some means of reproducing charts is a prime requirement in the systems department. Reproducing charts in color is very expensive and may not be economically feasible. The fact that certain colors of blue do not reproduce with photocopying methods often can be usefully applied. For example, the background grid which is used as a guide in making flowcharts may be printed in blue ink, which will disappear in the photocopy, leaving only the symbols, arrows, and connectors that have been drawn.

It is helpful to be able to enlarge or reduce charts to a uniform size. The standard 8½-by-11-inch page is most convenient to handle and file, but often larger sheets are better for the original drawing. When copies are enlarged, any imperfections are magnified; similarly, when copies are reduced, small flaws tend to disappear. It is not possible to reproduce delicate shading. Most charts therefore should show sharp contrast and avoid large blocks of solid dark colors.

Charting Conventions

Efforts have been made over the years to arrive at some form of standardization in charting. Figure 4-1 shows the most recent symbols approved by the U.S.A. Standards Institute (now American National

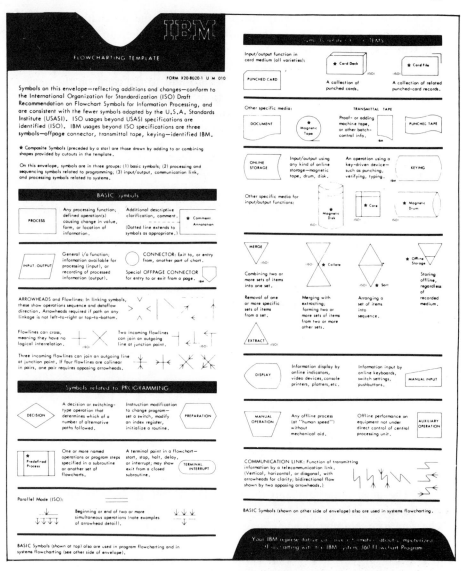

Figure 4-1. Flowcharting template. Basic symbols may be used in either systems flowcharts or program flowcharts. Certain symbols as shown may be used in one type only. (Courtesy of International Business Machines Corporation.)

Standards Institute), additional symbols adopted by the International Organization for Standardization, and still additional usages by International Business Machines Corporation.

The illustration shows basic symbols used in both program flowcharts and systems flowcharts, four additional symbols used primarily in programming, and 21 symbols related to systems. Many of the symbols can be drawn directly from the template provided with the instructions shown here. Composite symbols are those which require adding to or combining the symbols on the template.

Flowcharts may be drawn vertically or horizontally. In either case, the primary directions of flow are downward and to the right on the page. When the flow lines are in these directions, arrowheads are not required, but they may be used if preferred. Any flow lines upward or to the left should always have arrowheads to show the direction of flow.

TYPES OF CHARTS

There appear to be no limits to the variety of charts that prove useful from time to time in systems work. Charts may be used to depict the sequence of operations, to show architectural features, to delineate personnel relationships such as organization charts, or to display statistical summaries of numerical or logical relationships.

We shall consider the following five major types of charts and then look at several of the important subclassifications of each.

1. Flowcharts. These may show the flow of operations, the flow of data through a complete data system, the flow of paperwork, or the logic flow used in computer programs.
2. Computer-written flowcharts.
3. Decision tables.
4. Scheduling charts.
5. Other miscellaneous charts.

Flowcharts

The most important and most widely used of all systems charts are the flowcharts. They appear in a variety of forms, but have one common characteristic. No matter what symbols, format, or titles are used, they give a symbolic or pictorial representation of a procedure.

In this section we shall illustrate in some detail each of the following classes of flowcharts:

1. Data flow diagram
2. Process flowchart
3. Program logic flowchart
4. HIPO chart
5. Pseudocode
6. Systems flowchart
7. Forms distribution chart
8. Layout flowchart

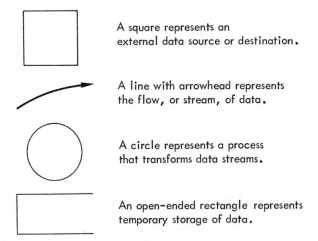

Figure 4-2. Data flow diagram symbols. The limited number of symbols makes data flow diagrams easy to draw and to understand.

Data flow diagram. A data flow diagram describes the flow of data through a system and the processes that change, or transform, the data. The four basic symbols used in data flow diagrams are shown in Figure 4-2. The square represents a data source or destination. A line with an arrowhead shows the flow of the stream of data. A circle represents a process

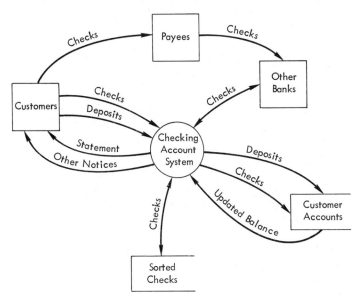

Figure 4-3. Context diagram for checking account system. The context diagram shows the entire process as a single circle, with its major data sources and destinations.

that transforms incoming data into outgoing information. An open-ended rectangle represents temporary data storage.

Data flow diagrams may be drawn at various levels. The highest level, called a *context diagram,* defines the context or scope of the system. At this level all the external data flowing into the system and the processed data flowing out of the system are shown. The entire processing of the system might be represented by a single circle (see Figure 4-3).

At the next level, the process symbol is *exploded,* or *decomposed* to show specific data flows being transformed at a more detailed level. The three principal methods of transformation are combining, splitting, and modifying data streams.

The decomposition continues until a data flow diagram has been prepared showing the transformation of every data element within the system. Figure 4-4 shows a more detailed level of processing.

Process flowchart. Figure 4-5 illustrates a process flowchart. It is the simplest of all the charts to draw because it needs no special layout, templates, or other drawing materials. Each line has the five special symbols,

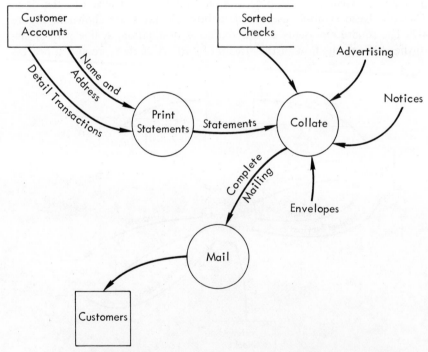

Figure 4-4. Low-level data flow diagram. At successively lower levels, each process circle is decomposed into smaller processes with their own data flow sources and destinations until every data element has been processed.

Summary	Present No. Times	Proposed No. Times	Difference No. Times
○ Operations	7		
⟢ Transportation	4		
□ Inspections	2		
D Delays	2		
▽ Storages	1		
Distance Traveled	540 Ft.	Ft.	Ft.

PROCESS FLOWCHART

Job ___ Requisition of supplies

□ Man or □ Material ___

Chart Begins ___
Chart Ends ___
Charted By ___ A. R. K.

Dated ___ September 8, 19xx

Details of (Present) (Proposed) Method	Operation / Transportation / Inspection / Delay / Storage	Distance in Feet	Quantity	Time	Notes
Requisition made out	●⟢□D▽				
Put in outgoing mail basket	○⟢□●▽		60		
To mail room	○◆□D▽	250			
Sorted	●⟢□D▽				
To supply room	○◆□D▽	20			
Supplies pulled from shelves	●⟢□D▽				
Supplies checked against requisition	○⟢■D▽				
Quantity issued is recorded	●⟢□D▽				
Supplies are boxed	●⟢□D▽				
Put in outgoing mail basket	○⟢□●▽		60		
To mail room	○◆□D▽	20			
Sorted	●⟢□D▽				
Carried to department	○◆□D▽	250			
Supplies checked against requisition	○⟢■D▽				
Receipt is signed	●⟢□D▽				
Supplies stored in drawer	○⟢□D▼				
	○⟢□D▽				
	○⟢□D▽				
	○⟢□D▽				
	○⟢□D▽				
	○⟢□D▽				

Figure 4-5. Process flowchart. Each process is analyzed into five steps of operation, transportation, inspection, delay, and storage. Total distance traveled and total delay time can be shown.

representing operation, transport, inspection, delay, and storage. Each step in the procedure being studied is entered and described briefly on a separate line. The symbol for the type of operation performed in that step is filled in, and a line is drawn to connect each of the filled-in blocks. Additional columns give distance in feet, the quantity of items, and the time elapsed for the job step. Summaries are provided for the totals of all steps in the procedure to shown the total distance traveled, total quantities handled, and total time elapsed.

When a new system is recommended, one process flowchart is made for the old procedure and another for the new. The summary figures of the two will show clearly the savings in time or distance between the two methods.

Detailed explanations of the five operating symbols, as well as examples of their use, are shown in Figure 4-6.

Program logic flowchart. The most common type of chart used by a computer programmer is the program logic flowchart. It is concerned with the internal logic used in solving a particular computer problem. The various input/output steps, detailed decisions, processing steps, branches, switch settings, and address modifications are all included in the program logic flowchart.

Systems analysts are especially concerned with this type of chart when they work closely with the data processing department. In many installations the analysts serve also as programmers. One of their duties is to draw detailed program logic flowcharts, from which junior programmers code specific computer instructions. In other installations, program flowcharts are drawn by the programmers themselves, who work under broad guidelines and specifications supplied by the analysts.

The widespread move toward structured, or top-down, programming since 1970 has created several different forms of charting that are commonly seen. Corrado Bohm and Giuseppe Jacopini proposed in 1966 that any proper program can be constructed from three basic structures known as:

1. *Sequence structure.* This is a series of processing blocks in the order steps are taken.
2. *IF-THEN-ELSE structure, or selection.* If a condition is true, one logical path is taken. If the condition is not true, a different path is taken.
3. *DO-WHILE structure, or repetition.* If a condition is true, one or more steps are executed and the condition is tested again. When the condition is not true, the steps are not executed. This structure is often called a *loop.*

These structures are illustrated in Figure 4-7.

Figure 4-8 is an example of a structured program logic flowchart. This type of chart helps to avoid a number of poor programming practices, such as excessive branching from one section of the program to another.

OPERATION ◯	Wrapping Part	Drill Hole	Typing Letter
	An operation represents the main steps in the process. Something is created, changed, or added to. Usually transportations, inspections, delays, and storages are more or less auxiliary elements. Operations involve activities such as forming, shaping, assembling, and disassembling.		
TRANSPORTATION ⇨	Move Material by Truck	Persons Moving Between Locations	Move Material by Carrying (messenger)
	Transportation is the movement of the material or man being studied from one position or location to another. When materials are stored beside or within two or three feet of a bench or machine on which the operation is to be performed, the movement used in obtaining the material preceding the operation and putting it down after operation are considered part of operation.		
INSPECTION ▢	Examine for Quality & Quantity	Review for Accuracy	Checking for Information
	Inspection occurs when an item or items are checked, verified, reviewed, or examined for quality or quantity and not changed.		
DELAY D	Material Waiting in "in" Basket	Person Waiting in Line	Waiting for Signature
	A delay occurs when conditions do not permit or require immediate performance of the next planned action.		
STORAGE △	Suspense Copy on File	Material in Warehouse	Filed for Permanent Record
	Storage occurs when something remains in one place, not being worked on in a regular process, awaiting further action at a later date, permanent storage or disposal.		

Figure 4-6. Examples of process flowchart symbols. An explanation and three examples are shown for each of the five steps.

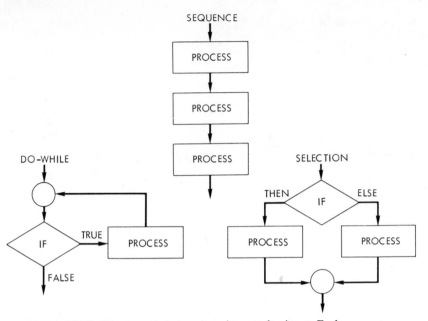

Figure 4-7. Basic structured programming mechanisms. Each process block in **DO-WHILE** or **IF-THEN-ELSE** structures may be decomposed into any one or more of the three basic structures.

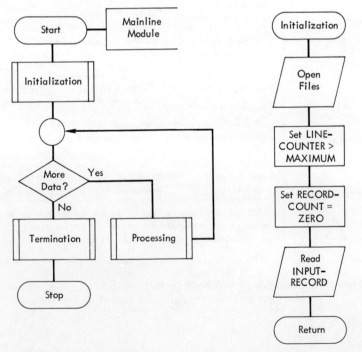

Figure 4-8. Program logic flowchart. The mainline module at the top shows overall program logic. Then each module is further expanded into detail steps.

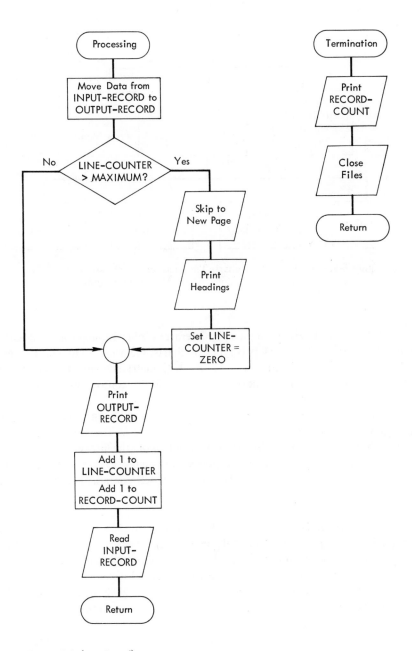

Figure 4-8 (*continued*)

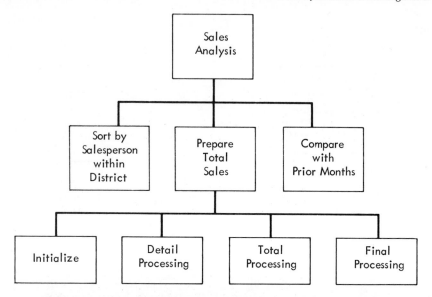

Figure 4-9. HIPO hierarchy chart. The hierarchy chart shows the relationship of the modules within the entire program.

HIPO chart. HIPO stands for Hierarchy plus Input-Processing-Output. The HIPO system uses two types of charts: (1) a hierarchy chart showing each processing module, and (2) an IPO chart showing the details of each module. The HIPO charts may be used in conjunction with other charts in systems analysis and design.

The hierarchy chart (Figure 4-9) is useful in showing the level of each function or module and its relation to other modules. The IPO chart shows each function separately with its own input data, the processing steps for transforming the data, and the output requirements. Figure 4-10 shows an example of an IPO chart. The IPO chart is self-contained and does not show hierarchy.

Pseudocode. Another graphic form of presentation used in structured programming is pseudocode. It will be apparent from Figure 4-11 that this is not really a chart, but it is included in this section because it provides a definite structured form to help to clarify program logic.

Pseudocode consists of the use of regular English words to describe the various processing steps to be performed. The programmer or analyst in working with pseudocode is concerned solely with logic and need not worry about the detailed rules of a particular programming language. Once the logic has been developed and carefully examined, then each statement in pseudocode is translated into the language to be used, such as COBOL, PL/I, or FORTRAN.

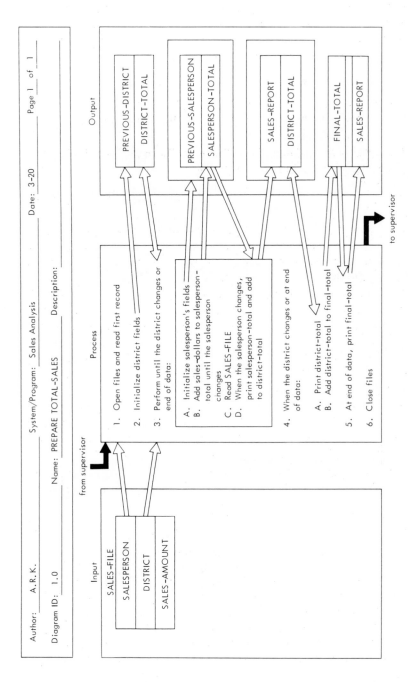

Figure 4-10. IPO chart. Each block on the HIPO hierarchy chart is decomposed into its own inputs, processes, and outputs.

```
Open files
Read a sales record; at end-of-file set no-more-data switch
Clear final total
DO-WHILE there is more data
    Clear district total
    Set PREVIOUS-DISTRICT = DISTRICT
    DO-WHILE  DISTRICT = PREVIOUS-DISTRICT  and there is more data
        Clear salesperson total
        Set PREVIOUS-SALESPERSON = SALESPERSON
        DO-WHILE  DISTRICT = PREVIOUS-DISTRICT
            and SALESPERSON = PREVIOUS-SALESPERSON
            and there is more data
                Add sales amount to salesperson's total
                Read a sales record; at end-of-file set no-more-data
                switch
        END-DO
        Print salesperson's total
        Add salesperson's total to district total
    END-DO
    Print district total
    Add district total to final total
END-DO
Print final total
Close files
```

Figure 4-11. Pseudocode is made up of ordinary English with a few
keywords and indentation to show program logic. The analyst need not be concerned with detailed rules for a specific programming language.

Systems flowchart. The systems flowchart describes the flow of data
through all parts of a system. In contrast to the program flowchart, the
system flowchart normally shows an entire program run, or phase, in a single processing block, with the appropriate input/output blocks showing the
type of the device used.

Normally, more flexibility is permitted in constructing a systems flowchart than is customary with a program flowchart. Figure 4-12 shows in
skeleton form a rather elaborate university system from the original application of the student for admission to his or her transfer to alumni/ae sta-

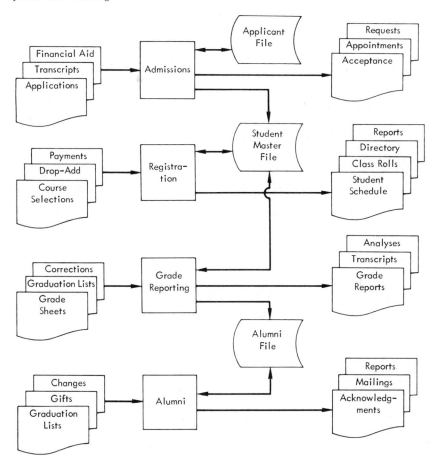

Figure 4-12. University student system flowchart. This chart shows the major flow of data from receipt of the student's application for admission to alumni activities after graduation.

tus. This overall view of the large, long-term system can be broken down into numerous subsystems, giving more specific details as to the methods of handling the smaller units.

Sometimes a systems flowchart combines pictorial symbols on the left side of the page with a narrative describing the procedure more fully on the right half of the page. This technique is particularly appropriate for those operations flowcharts describing specific smaller job steps, so that operators can see precisely what they are to do. The narrative permits a greater amount of detail to be spelled out than can be placed within the limits of the flowchart blocks.

There are four basic symbols often used in paper work flow. They are: square, triangle, large circle, and small circle. These symbols often appear on a ruler or charting template. They may be used alone or in combination to produce the following symbols.

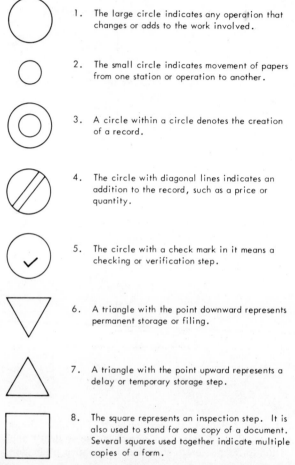

1. The large circle indicates any operation that changes or adds to the work involved.

2. The small circle indicates movement of papers from one station or operation to another.

3. A circle within a circle denotes the creation of a record.

4. The circle with diagonal lines indicates an addition to the record, such as a price or quantity.

5. The circle with a check mark in it means a checking or verification step.

6. A triangle with the point downward represents permanent storage or filing.

7. A triangle with the point upward represents a delay or temporary storage step.

8. The square represents an inspection step. It is also used to stand for one copy of a document. Several squares used together indicate multiple copies of a form.

Figure 4-13. Charting symbols for paperwork flow. There are four basic symbols often used in paperwork flow. They are the square, triangle, large circle, and small circle. These symbols often appear on a ruler or charting template. They may be used alone or in combination to produce the following symbols.

Forms distribution chart. The forms distribution chart is another widely used type of chart showing the distribution of each of the copies of multiple-part forms. Figure 4-13 shows the basic symbols used in describing the flow of paperwork and also the composite symbols made by combining basic symbols with additional lines or marks.

This type of chart does not include activities unrelated to paperwork. Its major value is to show the reason why the specific number of copies is produced for each type of form. It should pinpoint any excess in the number of copies prepared at any station.

Figure 4-14 shows the distribution of forms in the procedure for receiving materials. Where several processing steps occur at one station, their symbols are enclosed in a long vertical rectangular frame. Notice that each part of a form is numbered to show clearly how that part goes through its processing cycle. In practice, different copies of a form often are of different colors, to help prevent errors in distribution and to make it easier to identify those that belong together.

Layout flowchart. A layout flowchart is useful in planning the physical arrangement of an office or work station. A special planning guide is often used which provides a ruled grid along with cutouts to scale showing the various pieces of furniture or equipment to be used. A common scale for the grid is $1/10$ inch to 1 foot of floor space.

Figure 4-15 shows the layout of a computer installation. The cutouts may be positioned in various places on the grid as a way of examining various arrangements for operator actions, flow of work, access to storage devices, servicing requirements, and other details in normal office functions. When the best arrangement has been found, the cutouts may be pasted or taped into position and a photocopy made of the final layout.

This type of chart may also be used with curved lines and arrows indicating the direction and frequency of traffic flow for different types of procedures within the area, as in Figure 3-6.

Computer-Written Flowcharts

The development of computer programs to produce flowcharts directly from source statements in various programming languages, such as FORTRAN, COBOL, or assembler language, is a technological advance of tremendous importance.

The computer-written flowchart overcomes one major difficulty in charting—that of making revisions. Any manual change in program logic or processing method required many hours of chart revision, and often meant redrawing the entire chart. Through use of the computer, a completely new flowchart incorporating any changes in the source statements can be produced in a few minutes. Thus it is possible to have charts up to date with the latest revision of each program.

Such software is expensive, but it may pay for itself in the time saved for analysts and programmers. Figure 4-16 shows a portion of a chart produced from a COBOL source program.

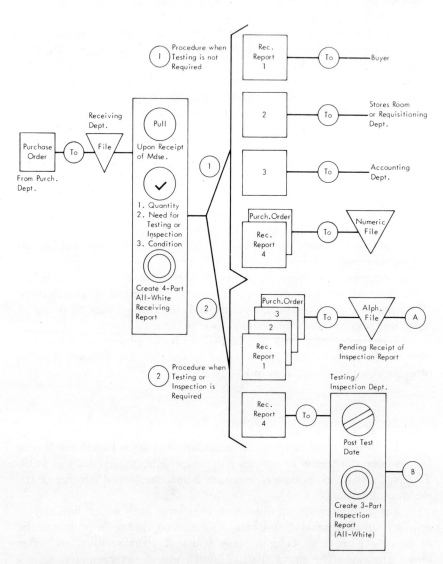

Figure 4-14. Forms distribution chart. This chart shows origination of each paper document and the distribution and ultimate disposition of each copy.

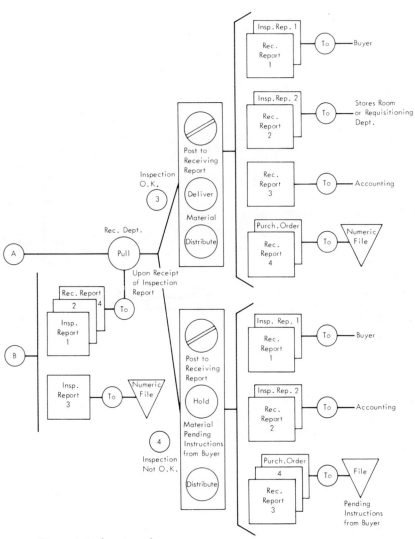

Figure 4-14 (*continued*)

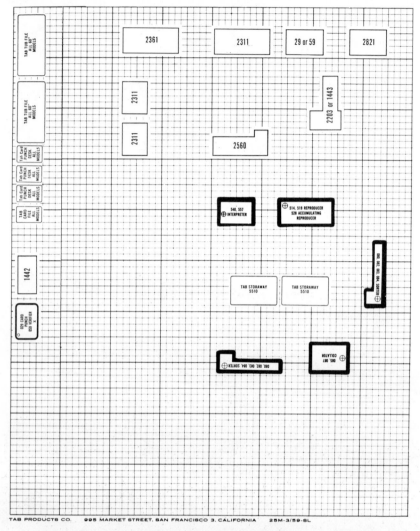

Figure 4-15. Office layout planning chart. This chart permits equipment and furniture to be arranged to permit the best possible access by operators and repair technicians.

Decision Tables

Decision tables are a means of bringing together and presenting related information to express complex decision logic in a way that is easy to visualize and follow. By presenting logical alternative courses of action under
various combinations of conditions, decision tables enable the analyst to
think through a problem and present its solution effectively.

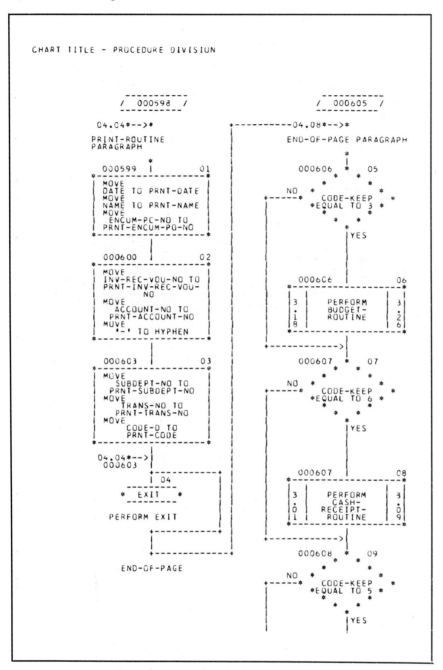

Figure 4-16. Computer-written flowchart. A special computer program produces this type of chart directly from program source statements. A new updated chart can be readily produced whenever the program is changed.

The decision table is independent of equipment and in fact may be used by people with little knowledge of equipment. The principal value of the decision table is its ability to present a complex condition based on many variables in a relatively small amount of space. Frequently, a decision table occupying a single page can show all the possible conditions that would require four or five pages on a conventional flowchart, with its multiple decision blocks.

There are four basic elements that make up a decision table. The upper half of the table refers to the *conditions* and the lower half to the *actions* to be taken. The left half of the form is called the *stub*, and the right half the *entries*. The general logic of the table is "IF (CONDITION), THEN (ACTION)." The upper-left quarter then becomes the condition stub, the upper-right portion the condition entries, the lower-left portion the action stub, and the lower-right portion the action entries.

Figure 4-17 illustrates a decision table. There are two types of entries, called *limited* or *extended entries*. Limited condition entries are restricted to the letters Y or N standing for *yes* if the condition is true and *no* if it is false. The entry is left blank or filled with a hyphen if not applicable. Limited action entries consist of an X, indicating that the action is to be taken,

Stub	Body								
				Rule Number					
Condition	1	2	3	4	5	6	7	8	9
Start?	Y	–	–	–	–	–	–		
File 1 key < file 2 key?	–	Y	N	N	N	N	N		
File 1 key = file 2 key?	–	N	Y	N	N	N	N		
File 1 key > file 2 key?	–	N	N	Y	N	N	N		
End of file 1?	–	N	N	N	Y	N	Y		
End of file 2?	–	N	N	N	N	Y	Y		
Action									
Open file 1 and file 2	X								
Write from file 1		X	X			X			
Write from file 2				X	X				
Read file 1	X	X	X			X			
Read file 2	X			X	X				
Write end of file record							X		
Close file 1 and file 2							X		

Figure 4-17. Decision table. Each vertical column represents a rule showing actions to be taken based on each combination of conditions that may occur.

or blank, indicating that the action is not performed. Figure 4-14 consists entirely of limited entries.

Extended entries permit a larger set of choices. For example, the condition stub might ask "Grade earned?" for which extended entries in different columns might be A, B, C, D, F, or other. In the corresponding columns, the action stub might indicate "Grade points awarded" with extended entries of 4, 3, 2, 1, 0, and 0, respectively. Limited and extended entries may both appear on the same chart, but they may not be mixed on a single line.

All the conditions to be considered before a certain action can be taken are called a *rule*. The rules appear in vertical columns on the entry side of the table numbered from 1 to 14 in the example shown. Each rule must be a unique combination of conditions.

After all applicable conditions have been considered, any other conditions that might occur are grouped together under an *else rule*. This grouping eliminates the need for a separate statement of each of the many possible combinations of conditions where all result in the same action.

Actions should be listed in the order they are to be performed. An action checked will be performed only if *every* one of the conditions stated in the applicable rule has been met.

Scheduling Charts

Charts are widely used in systems work for setting schedules of activities to be performed over a period of time and to keep track of progress toward meeting that schedule. There are two principal forms of scheduling charts: The Gantt chart and the PERT chart.

Gantt chart. The Gantt chart was first formulated by Henry L. Gantt in 1917 as a means of controlling the production of war material. It is now used in many systems applications for scheduling the installation of machines, the phases of a systems study, or production tasks. The horizontal axis is used to depict time, with activities, items, or personnel listed vertically in the left-hand column.

Sometimes the chart is used to compare actual performance with planned performance. When using a Gantt chart for this purpose, the planned schedule appears in one color and the actual times achieved are filled in with another color as the various activities are accomplished. The Gantt chart is shown in Figure 3-2.

PERT chart. PERT (Program Evaluation and Review Technique) was first used in 1957 by the navy in connection with the Polaris missile project. It combines network charting techniques with a relatively simple mathematical formula. PERT networks center on *events,* which are points in time at which tasks are completed, and *activities,* which are stated in terms of time required to accomplish the events.

The network is constructed as a form of modified bar chart, which is used to show how the various parts of a project depend on each other and how certain tasks must be finished before others can be started.

Concurrently, CPM (Critical Path Method), a somewhat similar technique, was being applied to project planning in civilian business and industry. During the years, the distinctions between the two plans have tended to disappear, and today they are generally called PERT/CPM.

Three separate steps are used to apply PERT/CPM to a project: (1) planning, (2) scheduling, and (3) monitoring and control.

1. *Planning.* The network is developed during the planning process. First, each activity associated with the project is listed and may be assigned an arbitrary number for identification. Like flowcharts, PERT/CPM networks may vary in the amount of detail they represent. Thus the same project can be represented by a few dozen activities or many hundred. An activity is anything which represents the expenditure of manpower, time, or materials.

On the chart, each activity is represented by an arrow. An event, which usually indicates the beginning or the end of an activity, is represented by a circle, or node.

In constructing the network, it usually is best to begin with the final activity and work backward by deciding what activities must be completed before a given activity can begin. Of vital importance is the question of overlap. Some activities are not directly related to others, and can proceed concurrently or in parallel. Other activities are dependent upon the completion of previous activities and must proceed in a serial fashion.

Sometimes activities that are completely independent of one another must be completed before another activity can begin. In this case, a dummy activity, represented by a dotted line, can be entered into the network. For example, in building a house, the installation of wiring does not depend upon plumbing fixtures being available, but neither the wiring nor the plumbing can be done until the shell is erected. Therefore, from the end event of erecting the shell one dummy activity line is drawn to the beginning event of installing the wiring and another is drawn to the beginning event of installing the plumbing. The dummy activity involves no expenditure of manpower, time, or materials but only reflects time dependence.

2 *Scheduling.* Once all the activities have been listed and the network has been drawn to show the relationship of the activities and events, it is then necessary to obtain time estimates for each activity. Normally, three estimates are made: the most optimistic—that is, the shortest time required if everything goes well and no mishaps occur; the most likely time; and the most pessimistic, or longest time barring a complete catastrophe.

On some charts all three times are shown in the form 8–10–15, where 8 is the most optimistic, 10 the most likely, and 15 the most pessimistic time. On other charts, a single time figure is calculated using the formula

$$T = \frac{T_0 + 4T_1 + T_p}{6}$$

where T_0 is the most optimistic, T_1 is most likely, and T_p is the most pessimistic time. The single time calculated from 8–10–15 above is 10.5.

Sometimes the variance is also included, computed by means of the formula

$$V = \frac{(T_0 - T_p)^2}{6}$$

The variance on the times of 8–10–15 is 1.4.

After recording times for each activity on the chart, the next step is to calculate the earliest expected time for each event. This is calculated by adding up the expected times of all activities that precede the event and using the sum of the longest time path. For example, if one path to an event has a single activity with time of 20 days, and another path has two activities of 10 and 15 days, then the earliest expected time of arrival for that event is 25 days. The earliest expected time is calculated by working forward through the network from the start along each path until the conclusion.

The critical path is the one for which the sum of times of the activities is the largest in the network. The critical path determines the overall estimated time for the project.

The latest allowable times are then calculated by working backward through the network from the final event and subtracting the longest time path from the event being considered to the end event. For example, if the total completion time of a project is 75 weeks, and two paths lead from event X to the final event, one having a total time of 17 weeks and one of 22 weeks, the latest allowable time for event X is 75–22, or 53 weeks. The latest allowable time is the latest possible time an event can occur without extending the total project time.

Along the critical path, the earliest possible time and the latest allowable time will be identical. Along all other paths, there will be a certain amount of slack for each event. Slack is the amount of delay permitted for an event without extending the total project time.

The ways of recording the various times in PERT/CPM are not standardized. Sometimes they appear above or below the event circles in blocks and sometimes in the quadrants of the circles themselves. In Figure 4-18, we shall use the event number in the upper quadrant, the earliest possible time in the left-hand quadrant, and the latest allowable time in the right-hand quadrant. The time for each activity appears below the arrow, and the description and number of each activity appear above the arrow.

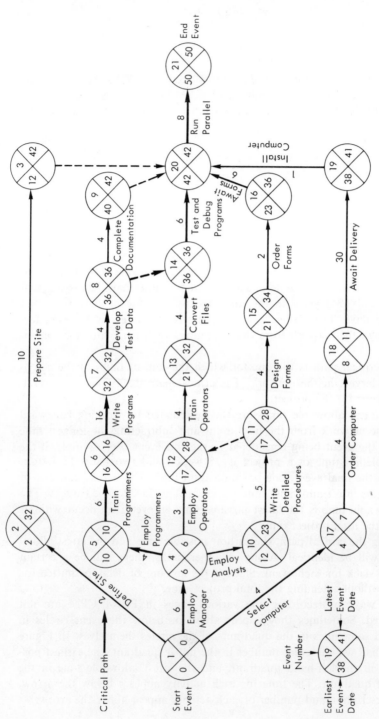

Figure 4-18. PERT/CPM chart. Lines represent activities with their estimated time. Circles represent events showing completion of activities. The difference between the earliest possible time and the latest allowable time of each event is called float, or slack time.

3 *Monitoring and control.* As the project proceeds, it is necessary to keep careful watch on its progress and to note any deviation from schedule. Delays along the critical path are especially notable because each delay here directly delays the entire project. It is also true that the critical path may change from time as the project progresses, if delays beyond the latest allowable time are encountered on some noncritical path.

The computer is widely used to assist in monitoring and producing progress reports. It is customary to calculate the amount of spare time, called *float,* for each activity. One or more types of float may be used to show meaningful relationships between each activity and those immediately before or after it.

There is no float along the critical path. However, on Figure 4-18 notice the activity to prepare site between events 2 and 3 at the top of the chart. If we reach event 2 by the second week and need not finish event 3 until the forty-second week, we have the possible elapsed time of 40 weeks. After deducting the 10 weeks required to prepare the site, we have a possible float of 30 weeks for this activity.

Other Miscellaneous Charts

Some other common charts not falling into any of the categories covered in the foregoing discussion are organization charts, graphs, and a variety of tables.

Organization charts were described and illustrated in Chapter 2. A wide variety of tables, usually arranged in columns and rows for organizing and comparing various measurements, also can be classified as charts. Some of these were described in preceding chapters, while others will appear later in the book.

SUMMARY

We have seen in this chapter that charting is the mainstream of systems technique. The use of pictures, symbols, and other graphic means of representing data greatly aids the analyst in understanding the procedure. It also makes clear to the user the relationship between the various jobs, forms, and operations. Charts are important in survey, design, presentation, and implementation.

Systems charting tools range from relatively simple to highly elaborate, depending upon the demands of the installation. Tools used include drawing and lettering sets, drafting pens in a variety of widths, felt tip pens, rulers and templates, scissors, tweezers, transparent tape, drawing boards, colored inks and paints, pictographic symbols, and office layout forms.

Charts may be arranged horizontally or vertically. They may be highly formal and artistic, or they may be relatively simple. One may use either conventional symbols which appear on the template or symbols especially prescribed for the installation.

The principal types of charts are flowcharts, computer-written flowcharts, decision tables, and scheduling charts. Other miscellaneous charts are also important. Flowcharts are subdivided into process flowcharts, program logic flowcharts, systems flowcharts, forms distribution charts, and layout flowcharts. Program logic flowcharts are further subdivided into conventional flowcharts, structured flowcharts, HIPO charts, and pseudocode. Examples of scheduling charts are Gantt charts and PERT charts.

TERMS FOR REVIEW

Action entry	HIPO chart
Activities	Layout flowchart
Body	Limited entry
Condition entry	PERT chart
Data flow diagram	Process flowchart
Decision table	Program logic flowchart
Else rule	Pseudocode
Events	Scheduling chart
Extended entry	Structured flowchart
Float	Stub
Forms distribution chart	Systems flowchart
Gantt chart	Template

QUESTIONS

1. Why is charting so important in systems work?
2. How are the purposes of charting for survey different from those of charting for presentation?
3. Describe how the features of a process flowchart differ from those of a systems flowchart.
4. Draw a process flowchart to show the necessary steps for formulating dictating, typing, verifying, signing, and mailing a letter.

5. Point out the differences between the systems flowchart and the forms distribution chart in terms of the symbols used and the intent of the charts.

6. Name and distinguish between the classes of flowcharts described in this chapter.

7. Differentiate between limited entries and extended entries on a decision table. Give examples of each.

8. What is the source of data used for making computer-written flowcharts? What is a major advantage of using them?

9. Slick Oil Company uses the following credit card procedure. The customer presents a credit card to the service station attendant, who completes the invoice, giving one copy to the customer. Weekly, the station manager batches the accumulated invoices, together with an adding machine tape, and sends them to the company's regional office. The company verifies the amounts, credits the station's account with the amount of the batch, and holds the invoices until the end of the month.

At the end of the month, the company sorts the invoices by customer number, microfilms them, adds the invoices to the customer account tape file, prints the monthly statement, and mails it to the customer together with the invoices. Upon receipt of the payment, the company verifies the amount of the check against the payment stub, sorts the daily batch of stubs by customer number, and subtracts the payment from the customer account on the tape file.

Draw a systems flowchart to reflect these procedures.

10. Draw a decision table showing the possible outcomes of the seven-game World Series. The series ends when one team has won four games.

11. Midstate College uses the following procedure when a student wishes to drop a course. The student requests permission from his advisor to drop the course, and if granted approval, she prepares a five-part form. The student takes parts 4 and 5 to the business office. If a refund is due, the bursar issues a check, gives it to the student with copy 5, and files copy 4. If no refund is due, copy 5 is stamped "No Refund," returned to the student, and copy 4 is filed. The advisor sends copy 1 to the registrar, sends copy 3 to the instructor whose course is dropped, and files copy 2. The registrar cancels the course from the student's schedule card and subtracts the hours dropped from the student's total hours carried. The instructor records a grade of "W" next to the student's name on the class roll.

Draw a forms distribution chart to reflect this procedure.

12. Draw and describe the three basic symbols used in structured programming.

13. List the steps necessary to prepare a PERT chart.

14. What is meant by float in connection with a PERT chart? How much float is there along the critical path?

15. Write in pseudocode the following procedure used by Southeastern Air

Lines in selling tickets. There are 100 tickets available on the next flight, 50 in first class and 50 in tourist class. Once a class is full, the airline will inquire as to whether or not the remaining class is acceptable to the purchaser before rejecting his or her request. Processing stops when all tickets are sold.

CASE STUDY
SUNCOAST COMMUNITY COLLEGE

Gerald Phipps and the other team members first determine the scope and objectives of the detailed systems study. They accept the timetable proposed by the preliminary study team as reasonable. They decide to consider the present systems study as phase I of a possible longer-term project that will ultimately link the alumni application with the Suncoast Foundation's major fund-raising effort. Other proposed expansion features might include alumni placement, recruitment of alumni children as prospective students, and extended word processing features.

The scope of phase I is limited to:

1. Determining the data elements currently in the student master file that will be extracted for most value to the alumni master file.
2. Designing an annual donor file that can be related by student Social Security number to the descriptive data in the student master file.
3. Designing display screens and report forms.
4. Designing, writing, testing, and implementing programs to produce the desired records and reports.

OBJECTIVES OF THE SYSTEM

Marilyn Woods proposes specific objectives which the team accepts. She suggests that the system should be able to:

1. Produce listings sorted in any of the following sequences:
   a. Alphabetic
   b. Year of graduation
   c. Degree earned
   d. Major field of study
   e. Amount of annual contribution
   f. Age (or age group)

2. Produce listings of selected records from any of these groups:
   a. Graduates only
   b. Specific year or years of graduation only
   c. Specific major
   d. Donors only
   e. Nondonors only
   f. Specific age group
3. Print mailing labels for any category mentioned above
4. Provide online data entry of contributions
5. Display any selected alumni record on terminal screen
6. Maintain records of pledges for regular or special projects and provide for follow-up notices and status reports

ANALYSIS OF SYSTEM

There is no present alumni application system at Suncoast. The only alumni activities have been several reunions arranged by individual class members and an annual exhibition baseball game between the varsity team and alumni who were formerly on the varsity. Marilyn Woods arranges interviews with alumni directors in five nearby institutions—three state universities and two private liberal arts colleges. She develops a questionnaire to be sent to a sampling of alumni asking suggestions for the formation of an Alumni Association. She also arranges interviews with faculty members who are alumni of Suncoast and with students who expect to graduate during the current semester.

FLOWCHARTING

Meanwhile, Gerald Phipps draws an overall systems flowchart (Figure 4-19). He begins work on design of the donor record and the display screens to be used for data entry and information retrieval. He begins structured design of the programs that will be needed. He determines that no changes in office layout will be required in phase I other than to install a terminal in the Institutional Advancement office.

John Shirley draws a record layout form consisting of those data elements extracted from the student master file that will be most useful for alumni applications. In consultation with Phipps, he determines that rather than process the entire student master file for alumni purposes, it will be more efficient to create a separate file made up of fewer data elements. The alumni file, or records selected from it in the desired categories, will then be sorted into the proper sequence to produce the needed reports.

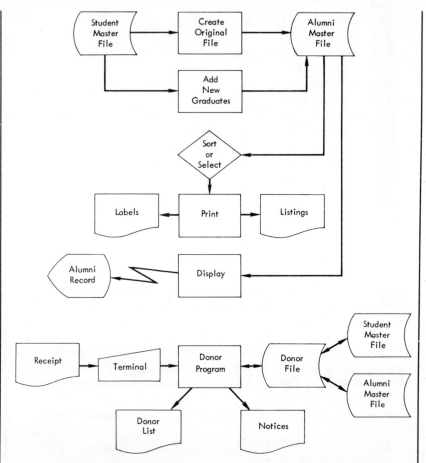

Figure 4-19. Overall systems flowchart of alumni application. Square
symbols represent programs that receive their inputs from
master files or the terminal keyboard to produce reports
or updated files.

QUESTIONS AND EXERCISES

1. What additional objectives, if any, would you have set if you had
   been on the detailed study team?
2. Make an outline of questions and topics for the interviews with the
   alumni directors in the five nearby institutions.
3. Draw the schedule for the detailed systems study in the form of a
   PERT chart. Calculate the earliest and latest time for each event.

5

DOCUMENTATION AND WORD PROCESSING

OBJECTIVES

At the end of this chapter, you should be able to:

1. Name and describe the principal types of manuals used by a business organization.
2. Distinguish among four classifications of procedure manuals used in systems work.
3. List elements contained in each of the four classifications of procedure manuals.
4. Define and describe the content and purpose of data element dictionaries
5. Name some common techniques and practices described as installation standards.
6. Give reasons why documentation is needed.
7. Describe the steps followed in producing documentation.
8. Name and describe the principal aids to documentation that are available to the systems department.
9. Tell how computers may be used to aid in documentation.
10. Define word processing and tell how it can be used in improving documentation.

We have seen in earlier chapters the important role played by various forms of paperwork throughout a business enterprise. Printed forms, punched cards, flowcharts, narrative descriptions, and other forms all play important roles in communicating the policies and procedures that management wishes to have carried out.

Documentation is defined as the process by which the various papers are assembled into a manual to describe a particular organization, policy, or procedure.

The well-written manual, properly kept up to date, is a valuable tool of communication. There appear to be, however, certain areas with a company where manuals are more effective than in others. Manuals permit communication downward but not upward through the organization. They are accepted and used extensively in the form of production and engineering manuals for plant operation. They also have been successfully used to ensure understanding of financial responsibilities at all levels of management. Sales executives often employ sales policy and training manuals.

In a decentralized organization, manuals provide an important way of informing branch executives of established policies and procedures which must be consistent with home office managment.

TYPES OF MANUALS

There are five major classifications of manuals discussed in this chapter. The structure, the amount of detail, and the type of employees for whom the manual is intended vary with each class. The extent of involvement of the systems department in each manual likewise varies. The principal classes of manuals are:

1. Organization manuals
2. Policy manuals
3. Procedure manuals
4. Data element dictionaries
5. Installation standards

Organization Manuals

In some companies the organization manual consists only of organization charts. In others it includes such features as corporate objectives, the difference between lines of organization and lines of communication, relationships between line and staff, and the specific duties and responsibilities of managerial personnel. Some manuals include a lengthy preface made up largely of "pep talk" material. Others give summarized job descriptions for every member of the management team.

The organization manual normally is reissued only when changes in the organizational structure occur. Routine changes in personnel may be announced by bulletin. Every member of the management team, from the board of directors to the first level of supervision, should receive a copy of the entire organization manual.

Good organization manuals are vital for depicting lines of authority and responsibility and for clarifying the relationships between departments. Management problems can be minimized by showing line personnel clearly their respective roles. The organization manual also serves to show the systems department the proper framework and authority for developing specific procedures.

Policy Manuals

Written statements of policy are an important means of transmitting management attitudes. They establish guidelines, a framework within which managerial personnel may operate, and uniform objectives based on local conditions.

Because policies often are developed in terms of specific functions, such as finance, sales, manufacturing, purchasing, and personnel, it is natural that policy suggestions frequently come from line personnel. Nevertheless, the responsibility for the adoption of policies and their formal statement in the policy manual rests with the chief executive and the board of directors.

Procedure Manuals

The tasks of preparing and updating procedure manuals occupies the major effort of the systems department. These manuals may show a rather broad picture of the flow of data across departmental lines, or they may show in complete detail each processing step to be performed by an individual worker at a single station. Procedure manuals are intended to give careful guidance at every stage of data handling to ensure that uniform methods are followed.

Part of the documentation for procedure manuals is developed by the systems analyst, and other parts by the programmer. The documentation might well be suggested and later reviewed by clerical, operating, and supervisory personnel who are involved in the procedures, but the prime responsibility for producing the documentation rests with the systems analyst and the programmer.

For computer systems, procedure manuals often are divided into the following four classifications:

1. System manuals
2. Clerical and control procedures manuals
3. Program manuals
4. Operator's run manuals

Figure 5-1 shows 25 distinct elements that may be required in some applications. Each of the elements may be produced in a standard format. Preprinted forms are used wherever possible to reduce preparation time and promote consistency. Where the same element appears in more than one type of manual, photocopies may be provided. The 25 items can serve as a checklist to ensure that each manual is complete.

Element	Originator	System Manual	Proc. Manual	Prog. Manual	Oper. Manual
1. Title and cover page	S P	X	X	X	X
2. Table of contents	S P	X	X	X	X
3. Revisions	S P	X	X	X	X
4. Previous system description	S	X			
5. New system description	S	X	X	X	
6. New system flowcharts	S	X		X	
7. Hardware requirements	S	X		X	X
8. Software requirements	S	X		X	X
9. Source documents	S	X	X		
10. Clerical procedures and controls	S	X	X		
11. Data entry procedures and controls	S	X	X		X
12. Glossary	S	X	X		X
13. List of programs	S	X		X	X
14. Program description	P	X		X	X
15. Input record layouts	S	X		X	X
16. Output report layouts and samples	S	X	X	X	X
17. Screen design layouts	S	X	X	X	X
18. File and record layouts	S	X		X	
19. Processing specifications	S	X		X	
20. Program logic charts	S P	X		X	
21. Timing criteria	S	X		X	X
22. Operating instructions	P			X	X
23. Messages and error handling	P			X	X
24. Program listings	P			X	
25. Test output results	P	X	X	X	X

S—Normally originated by systems analyst
P—Normally originated by programmer

Figure 5-1. Typical data system documentation. Certain elements of the documentation may appear in all four major manuals, while others may appear in only one or two.

It will be seen from Figure 5-1 that many elements of information are common to several manuals. In general, the *system manual* is the primary documentation of the entire application. It defines the design by using narrative summaries in nontechnical language of the important aspects of the system. It records important decisions and agreements reached during the system design. Flowcharts describe the flow of data through the system and show the relationship of the various steps. The manual gives detailed clerical, control, and keypunch procedures and defines terms that may not be familiar to people other than data processing personnel. The system manual includes, in summary form, a description of each program used within the system, together with its purpose, frequency, inputs and outputs, options, and processing specification.

The *clerical and control procedures manual* describes the sequence of processing steps to be performed by all personnel, both inside and outside of the computer center. Well-written procedures should reflect the "six Cs": they will be complete, clear, concise, consistent, coordinated, and current. An effective form for writing procedures is the *Playscript format* in which the left-hand column of the page names the responsible person and the right-hand portion of the page describes the action to be taken using numbered steps. This format is similar to that used in recording the dialogue and stage "business" in a drama. A typical procedure written in Playscript format might be:

> *Sales Department:* Receive purchase order from customer. Prepare three-part sales order. Forward to credit department.
>
> *Credit Department:* Review customer credit record. If rejected, return to sales department. If OK, forward to office supervisor.
>
> *Office Supervisor:* Approve sales order. Sort whether to be filled from stock or from supplier. Send stock orders to warehouse and supplier orders to purchasing department.
>
> *Warehouse:* Select merchandise. Sort by delivery area and mode of transportation: parcel post, railroad, or truck.
>
> *Packer:* Put merchandise into proper container. Weigh. Affix shipping labels.
>
> *Shipping Clerk:* Parcel post: record date and affix postage. Railroad: prepare three-part bill of lading. Truck: prepare two-part dray slip.

Clerical procedures refer to the preparation of all source documents, their flow through the various departments, and eventually the distribution of the output reports. At each step control procedures and audit trails are used to ensure that all documents are properly accounted for. Sample documents, completely filled in and having detailed instructions for their use and completion, are a part of each procedure.

The *program manual* compiles all information needed to understand, maintain, and modify the application and the individual programs which make it up. One section is devoted to the system description, which shows the relationship of this particular program to every other program in the system. The program manual contains operating instructions for the computer room personnel, including error conditions, special setup instructions, and proper disposition of files. It includes detailed storage layouts, input and output formats, and detailed program flowcharts. Documentation of the program manual is completed by using the program listing, test data and criteria, test output results, and test timing results.

The *operator's run manual* normally is made up entirely of extracts from the program manual, so that it requires little additional effort to produce. In many installations the operator actually uses the program manual itself for guidance, but in the larger installations he or she has a separate run book or manual which omits such items as storage layout, the detailed program flowchart, compiler output, and test data.

Data Element Dictionaries

The rapid growth of data base management systems has brought the need for standard data definitions to be used by all applications programmers. The data element dictionary is a manual that typically devotes one page to each data element required in the organization's information system.

The dictionary may contain such entries as:

1. Complete name of data element
2. Name to be used in COBOL or FORTRAN programs
3. Length and size of the element
4. Type (whether alphabetic, alphanumeric, or numeric)
5. Minimum and maximum values the data can take
6. Source of the data
7. List of files in which the data element appears
8. Editing pattern for numeric data
9. List of allowable codes, where codes are used

The data element dictionary is the responsibility of the data base administrator, where one is employed. Otherwise, it is usually compiled and maintained by the systems or programming staff. Every data element used in every file should be included, and no records should have fields added or deleted without a corresponding change to the dictionary.

Figure 5-2 shows a page from a data element dictionary. Software packages have been developed for creating and maintaining dictionaries in connection with data base management systems. Usually, they are separate from the rest of the DBMS software, but in the future it is likely that they will be integrated into the entire DBMS software system.

```
                         MANATEE JUNIOR COLLEGE              PAGE  41
                         DATA ELEMENT DICTIONARY             08/17/

SYSTEM:            STUDENT RECORD


ELEMENT_TITLE:     COURSE FINAL GRADE
                   CALCULATED GRADE


DEFINITION:

    A LITERAL GRADE ISSUED A STUDENT AT THE END OF THE TERM FOR THE
SPECIFIC COURSE ENROLLED.


CODES,_CATEGORIES,_AND_COMMENTS:

    A ONE CHARACTER ALPHA-NUMERIC ELEMENT.

    CODE      CATEGORY
     A        A   EXCELLENT (4 QUALITY OR GRADE POINTS)
     B        B   GOOD (3 QUALITY OR GRADE POINTS)
     C        C   AVERAGE (2 QUALITY OR GRADE POINTS
     D        D   POOR (1 QUALITY OR GRADE POINTS)
     F        F   FAILURE (0 QUALITY OR GRADE POINTS)
     1        IF  INCOMPLETE FAILING (0 QUALITY OR GRADE POINTS)

    ONLY THE ABOVE GRADES ARE CALCULATED IN THE GPA

     W        W   WITHDREW
     X        X   AUDIT
     S        S   SATISFACTORY
     N        N   NO CREDIT
     2        NC  NO CREDIT COURSE
     3        NR  GRADE NOT REPORTED
     I        I   INCOMPLETE

    THE ABOVE CODES WILL BE CONVERTED TO THE LITERAL GRADE UNDER
CATEGORY THE USER WILL ENTER THE LITERAL GRADE DESIRED AND THE
COMPUTER WILL MAKE THE CONVERSION TO THE FILE.


TYPE_OF_STUDENT:

    ALL STUDENTS


UPDATE_OFFICE:

    RECORDS OFFICE


DOCUMENT:

    INSTRUCTOR'S GRADE ROLLS


DATE_DEFINED:

APRIL 5, 19
```

Figure 5-2. Page from a data element dictionary. The dictionary may
appear in a loose-leaf binder, or in more complex systems,
in elaborate disk files.

Installation Standards

Many data processing installations maintain a manual setting forth conventions and standards to be employed by all personnel. It may cover such topics as flowcharting techniques, programming languages to be used for various applications, organization of programs, rules for page headings and number of lines, and many other subjects.

As structured programming techniques become more widespread, the need for standards for program design becomes more crucial. The installation standards manual may spell out such details as:

1. Skipping to new pages and spacing between sections of source programs for clarity
2. File- and record-naming conventions within programs
3. Grouping of data elements in the working-storage section of programs
4. Naming paragraphs with a numerical sequence identifier to aid in locating the paragraph within long programs
5. Indentation within record descriptions to show fields that are subordinate to others
6. Indentation of IF and ELSE statements to show proper dependence of conditional statements
7. Position of identifying codes on page headings and visual display screens
8. Conventions for error messages and notices to operator
9. Use of indexes rather than subscripts to speed table searches
10. Handling of initialization and end-of-data routines

The standards might also specify procedure to be followed for modifying programs, as well as for compiling and testing them. Some installations do not allow programmers to operate equipment for security reasons, while others permit programmers to do their own testing. The standards might also provide procedures for obtaining final approval for and adoption of completed programs.

THE VALUE OF DOCUMENTATION

The amount and quality of documentation in a data processing center give a quick and accurate measure of its effectiveness. Despite its importance, so many managers are vulnerable to the charge of neglecting documentation that it has been called the "Achilles' heel" of the computer installation.

The Need for Documentation

Systems analysts and programmers occasionally have been criticized for failing to use their particular talents in their own internal environment. Here are some of the reasons why good documentation is so critical:

1. *Rapid job turnover.* The person who designed the procedure or wrote the program may not be available to make necessary modifications or corrections.
2. *High volume of output.* Even though the original analyst or programmer is still on hand, he (or she) is likely to forget many of the vital details over a period of some months. Without good documentation he will spend an excessive amount of time refamiliarizing himself with his original plans.
3. *Diversity and complexity of third generation computers.* Modern operating systems require a large amount of detail regarding files, labels, communication messages, device assignments, and many other matters which must be consistently handled.
4. *Equipment conversions.* Sooner or later even the most frequently run jobs will be converted to new machines. When equipment is replaced or upgraded, some if not all of the programs will have to be redesigned, rewritten, or converted in some manner. Good documentation greatly facilitates this conversion.
5. *Long-term updating.* Changes in federal laws, tax rates, record structure, or other elements of data are inevitable over a period of time. Good documentation greatly speeds the process of making the necessary corrections and revisions in programs.

Good documentation improves communication of systems specifications from analysts to programmers. It properly conveys the programmer's intention to the operator and provides complete and formalized instruction at each step in the processing cycle. A good record of the work performed by the entire EDP group keeps management aware of the group's contribution to the organization. Good documentation helps to keep the users of the systems and programs informed, and guards against charges that the systems and data processing staff lives in an ivory tower.

Documentation for Applications Programming

In each computer installation, most of the work load consists of applications programs. Much of the programming for applications will be done in-house even though some applications packages may be purchased, leased, or acquired gratis. The major responsibility for all programming done in-house falls upon the local personnel, principally the analysts and programmers. In spite of the fact that higher-level languages such as COBOL are intended to be largely self-documenting, the programs themselves are woefully inadequate when considered in terms of the documentation needed for daily operations.

Applications programming needs to be well documented both in its initial development and in the modifications that inevitably occur through the passage of time. Four basic areas have been defined for applications programming:

1. Requirements documentation
2. Programming documentation
3. Operations documentation
4. Modification documentation

Figure 5-3 describes some of the content material to be included under each classification. Note that requirements documentation as here described contains some of the same material that might normally appear in
the final report of a system study. The programming documentation is similar in content to the program manual depicted in Figure 5-1. The operations documentation groups together much of the material that appeared in
Figure 5-1 under the three separate headings of system manual, procedures
manual, and operator's manual.

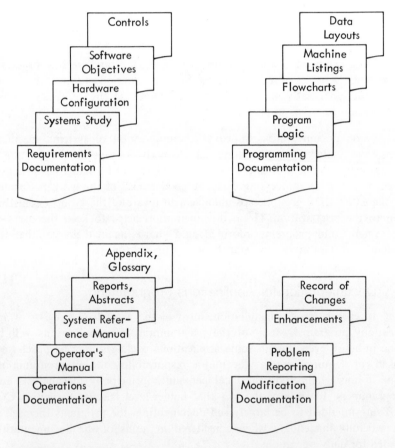

Figure 5-3. Applications programming documentation. The four categories cover requirements of the entire system, each specific
program, operating instructions, and authorization for program changes.

Modification documentation is concerned entirely with changes made after the original application is in effect. Programs are changed for a number of reasons:

1. Because of errors that crop up after adoption in spite of extensive testing
2. Because of changes in basic classifications, tax rates, union agreements, acquisitions, mergers, or other internal or external forces
3. Because of changes in basic equipment or peripheral devices
4. Because of programming enhancement, including consolidation of steps, improved data organization, and other techniques that improve efficiency

Proposals for changes in programs should be described in narrative form and approved in writing. Changes then should be fully documented, giving the authority, name of the person making the change, nature of the change, and effect upon the application. Care must be taken that all documentation affected by the change is revised and updated.

Additional material concerning program maintenance and modification appears in Chapter 14.

Reasons for Poor Documentation

There seem to be three principal reasons why good documentation is not produced:

1. *The press of everyday business.* Systems and programming personnel are constantly under time pressure created by new developments. They often complain that they do not have time to go back and document what has been done.
2. *The unglamorous nature of documentation.* Analysts and programmers usually prefer the challenge of new pursuits. Concerned with solving the problems of system design, development, and implementation, they tend to feel that producing the necessary supporting paperwork is a waste of their time and talents.
3. *Lack of uniform documentation standards.* Often management provides few specific guidelines as to required documentation. Programmers, like other human beings, react poorly to vaguely defined specifications.

STEPS IN PRODUCING DOCUMENTATION

There are well-defined steps which may be followed in the largest as well as in the smallest organization to produce documentation. In some firms there will be a separate staff for each of the steps, whereas in others one individual may have to perform several if not all of the steps. These steps include:

1. Reviewing concepts and data
2. Writing the initial draft
3. Editing for clarity, style, and format
4. Document production
5. Quality control, or editing of the finished masters
6. Publication
7. Distribution

The person doing the writing may be the one who has been involved with the initial design, interviewing, record layout, and program logic. If so, he (or she) is already familiar with the basic concepts and data; if not, he must study the concepts and data of the system and confer with those who have been involved all along. Writing the first draft of the document places something tangible on paper. Once there, its impact can be determined, the style and approach assessed, and length and complexity determined. Some rewriting normally is indicated at this stage.

Editing may be done by the writer himself, but ideally at least one other person should read the document to offer comments and suggestions. The writer manufactures the content of the document whereas the editor manufactures its format.

Production involves typing, illustrating, reproducing, and proofreading the document. For most in-house production this involves the preparation of masters from which copies of the document ultimately will be run.

Quality control involves the final editing of the finished masters. They should be reviewed at this stage by senior persons within the data processing systems department, and in some cases also by higher management executives.

Publication involves the actual printing, binding, titling, and other related steps. Here the overall quality and impression of the document are finally realized.

There should be a well-defined distribution list for each type of document produced within an organization. Organization charts and policy manuals are distributed only to top-level management and supervisors. Systems manuals are distributed within the systems department and within user groups. Clerical and control procedures manuals are distributed to those who use them in the normal course of their daily work. Program and operator's run manuals are retained primarily within the data processing department.

Some organizations provide for a documentation librarian who has the responsibility of controlling requests for changes in programs. He or she maintains the security of all documents, keeps track of all documents withdrawn from the library, and notes when they are returned to the files. The documentation librarian also maintains manufacturers' technical manuals, inserting new editions and updated pages as they are received.

Aids to Documentation

At least four methods are available to help to improve the quality of documentation:

1. Use of the technical writer
2. Use of tape recordings
3. Use of computer-written flowcharts
4. Use of the programming secretary or librarian

Where budget and staffing will permit, a technical writer can be assigned to work directly with a programmer or analyst beginning with the design phase of a project. The technical writer need not be skilled in programming but should be able to organize and present information. He (or she) needs a basic technical understanding and should be able to comprehend information and ideas which are given to him by the programmer or analyst without undue repetition. He should be skilled in the use of the English language and capable of tailoring his presentation toward the educational level and understanding of his audience. He should use standardized nomenclature and terminology and be alert to ambiguities, vague references, and indefinite statements. The technical writer should concentrate on the narrative presentation, freeing the analyst and programmer for the more technical details of their job.

It is a great convenience for programmers or analysts to have at their disposal a tape recorder into which they can speak any comments or notes that they wish to make as they proceed to design or program the system. Any oral discussion of the particular logic that they have in mind, the relationship between certain program segments, or the meaning of certain switch settings or codes can be captured readily by using the tape recorder. The recording later can be transcribed and edited to supply narrative descriptions to accompany the flowcharts and program listings.

A third valuable aid—one which was illustrated in Chapter 4—is the computer-produced flowchart. Where source program statements can produce up-to-date flowcharts, the programmer is relieved of a great deal of tedious drawing and redrawing when program revisions are necessary.

The programming secretary or librarian came into being with the evolution of programming teams for large structured programming projects. The secretary is assigned to the team to take care of many clerical and procedural details to free the programmers to concentrate on program design, coding, and testing. The secretary sometimes keypunches source programs or enters them into terminals, but is nearly always responsible for delivering the source programs to the computer operators for compiling. The secretary maintains the latest version of programs during the testing cycle and the official version upon completion and acceptance. The secretary may prepare or assemble record layout forms, flowcharts, compiler output, test data, and sample reports. In addition to collecting, organizing, and maintaining documentation for individual programs, the programming secretary may maintain the index of all programs available under a variety of classifications.

Updating Documentation

Almost as bad as inadequate documentation is outdated documentation. When a program is first designed and installed, the documentation is likely to be good. All too frequently, changes are made later in programs without being recorded in the program listings and the supporting documents.

Changes are made in programs for at least three reasons. The first is to enhance or improve the program. We must strike a reasonable balance between the desire to make constant improvement and the practical need to have something complete and operating. Sooner or later it is necessary to decide that a program or procedure is as good as we can make it at the time and put it into effect.

A second reason for changing or updating programs is because of problems which arise. Inevitably some errors will crop up, some exceptions will have been overlooked, or some other unforeseen problems will appear. Of course these must be corrected and the documentation must be brought up to date.

The third type of updating is emergency programming documentation. Sometimes a critical problem dictates that a "patch" or "fix" be made immediately without waiting for the normal program development and documentation processes. When this is necessary, all previously developed documentation should be updated within a reasonable period.

There are three principal ways of updating documents:

1. Errata and addenda sheets
2. Updated pages
3. New manuals

The errata and addenda sheets list by page and line number any corrections or additions that need to be made within the document. Handwritten entries are then made on the original document and the errata and addenda sheets are filed in the front for reference.

Where corrected pages are distributed, they should show the date of the revision and indicate the portion of the page which has been changed. A common practice is to draw a black line down the left margin opposite the line or lines that have been changed. The corrected pages are inserted directly into the manual and the superseded pages are removed.

When a large number of changes have accumulated, or when a major change is made at one time, it may be practical to reissue the entire corrected manual. A common practice is to use a coded suffix to identify each version of the manual. For example, manual 1395–0 would be the original issue of one particular manual, and 1395–1 would represent the first revision of the entire manual.

THE USE OF COMPUTERS IN DOCUMENTATION

A readily available aid to documentation is the use of the tools we already have—online terminal or keypunch, magnetic disk, computer, and printer. Using the same techniques that are common in file maintenance and updating, we can keep our documentation on magnetic disk. Input and alterations to the system may be keyed into a terminal or handwritten by the analyst, keypunched, and verified by the data entry section. Such changes are then run against the master file using regular add, delete, and replace functions.

By using page and line numbers as keys to the documentation, it is possible to input only the lines which are to be changed and to output only the pages which are to be changed. Upon request, any or all of the document pages can be printed, copied, and distributed.

This system takes maximum advantage of the facilities already available. Keypunching and verification provide about the only additional cost. Trained keypunch personnel give better accuracy than the average typist. Computer printed output may be placed directly upon masters for duplication, or it may be printed on a full page and photographically reduced to 8½-by-11-inch size for convenience in binding and filing. A very short turnaround time is required, and the resulting document gives a professional appearance.

Figures, charts, and graphs, which normally cannot be stored readily on magnetic tape, can be handled separately from the text. This is not a major problem, however, inasmuch as the bulk of the document often consists of narrative, which is easily handled as described in this section.

The source statement library of the computer operating system offers another approach to documentation. Just as program statements may be stored in this library and copied into other programs as needed, so can the text of manuals, reports, and other documents be stored and retrieved. Standard operating system software permits statements to be cataloged into the library, modified and updated, and printed out as required. Software packages, such as DOKUMENTR, are available that will supply headings, page numbering, and indexes as requested.

Software that handles terminals often provides for text editing. This permits the operator to key in sentences or paragraphs, insert or correct individual words, and store the data for later recall and printing on high-speed devices.

WORD PROCESSING IN DOCUMENTATION

Word processing is a term used to describe equipment and systems that facilitate the handling of words or text. It originally was used to centralize the transcription of correspondence dictated by business executives. The central pool of typists would receive cassettes, tapes, or belts containing the dictated material. In typing it, the typist would create a paper tape or magnetic card. The tape or card could then be replayed on automatic typewriters to create as many copies of the letter as necessary automatically at high rates of speed.

Word processing is now used in many applications from handling correspondence to producing large manuals. Although early word processing systems used paper tape, virtually all present systems involve recording the text on magnetic media as the document is being typed. The text thus recorded can be updated and edited as desired and then printed out automatically at high rates of speed with no operator intervention. For some applications standard paragraphs can be stored on magnetic cartridges or cassettes and later brought together in the proper sequence to create the desired document.

Figure 5–4 shows some of the common features of many word processing programs.

Types of Word Processing Systems

Word processing systems may be found in at least three different configurations: (1) keyboard stand-alone systems, (2) keyboard display stand-alone stations, and (3) micro- or minicomputer systems.

Keyboard stand-alone systems normally use a mechanical or electromechanical keyboard. Twelve to forty pages of material may be contained on magnetic cassette or cartridge, while only one or two pages may be contained on magnetic cards. Limited-to-moderate editing may be done, and output may typically be printed at speeds of 15 to 30 characters per second. Sometimes optional high-speed printers are available at up to 300 lines per minute.

Keyboard display stand-alone stations may provide one master station and several slaves. The text is displayed on a visual screen, or cathode ray tube (CRT). Magnetic storage is usually on cassette or floppy disk, capable of holding 60 to 140 pages of text. Some systems may be programmed, and include such features as automatic indexing, formatting and pagination, and the ability to change specified words anywhere throughout the text.

The most flexible form of word processing systems involves *micro- or minicomputer systems* with shared logic. Thirty or more input stations may be used on a single system. Magnetic cartridge will store 100 to 150 pages of text, while floppy or hard disk might provide from 1000 to 5000 pages. Efficient editing allows easy movement or changes in any part of the docu-

Create Text:

    Set margins, tabs, and spacing
    Use buffered keystrokes
    Place words automatically at end of line
    Jump cursor rapidly to start or end of line or text
    Overstrike previous text
    Create headers and footers
    Save text on disk
    Modify screen width
    Request present line number, document length, or available memory

Modify Text:

    Delete character, word, line, paragraph, block, or all remaining text
    Insert character or line
    Overstrike previous text
    Exchange words, paragraphs, or blocks
    Search for specific text and replace
    Change margins and tabs
    Hyphenate words at end of lines
    Load from disk
    Chain disk files together
    Resave on disk

Print Text:

    Print continuous forms or single sheets
    Center horizontally or vertically
    Number pages automatically
    Print headers or footers at top or bottom of every page or alternate pages
    Print only designated parts of text
    Justify margins left or right
    Hyphenate words at end of lines

Figure 5-4. Word processing features. The typical word processing program provides many features that assist the writer in creating text, revising it, and printing it out at high rates of speed.

ment almost instantaneously. Paragraphs, subparagraphs, and pages may be renumbered. Automatic indexing and hyphenation are often available, and document assembly may be totally automatic. Printout speeds range from 15 characters per second to 600 lines per minute. Both right and left margins may be justified, and on some printers the characters may be spaced so that no hyphenation at the end of a line is ever required. Some word processing programs check spelling of each word against a list of thousands of common words. Any word not found on the list is flagged as a possible error.

Cost Savings

Several studies have shown the value of word processing equipment in reducing the cost of producing documentation. The cost of producing a document involves the originator's time, the secretary's time, and material cost. Studies have shown that the originator can dictate to a machine faster than to a secretary taking shorthand, and much faster than writing a draft in longhand.

The conventional office secretary is frequently interrupted in transcription by the telephone, visitors, and other duties. The word processing secretary is freed from these duties and consequently can transcribe from a machine much faster than from shorthand or from reading longhand. The secretary also is relieved from the time spent in taking the original dictation in shorthand. Finally, the secretary saves time in never again having to retype the entire document. After reviewing the text on the screen, the secretary types only material that needs to be changed. Typing of the final edited version of the document is entirely automatic.

Material cost includes paper used for the initial draft, final copy paper, recording media, and machine cost. The cost of the word processing equipment is at least partially offset over time by the reduction in quantity of paper used.

In each case studied, the saving of secretarial time alone is enough to justify the investment in word processing equipment.

Cycles in Word Processing

There are three cycles in producing documentation, and each cycle may be divided into four separate steps. The cycles are (1) origination, (2) production, and (3) utilization.

Origination of the data involves the following four steps:

1. *Research*: locating and compiling relevant information, study, and review
2. *Composition*: organization of thoughts into words, sentences, and paragraphs on some form of media
3. *Conversion*: transcription of recorded thought into some readable and editable form
4. *Revision*: review and editing by the author

The production of documentation involves the following four steps:

1. *Preparation*: arranging in the proper format, composition, photographic processes, or providing for variety between reproductions such as form letters
2. *Reproduction*: preparation of multiple copies by automatic typing, photocopy, offset press, or audio rerecording

3. *Bundling*: preparation for distribution such as collating, stuffing envelopes, affixing postage
4. *Distribution*: transportation of the bundled documents to the proper destinations

The utilization of documentation involves the following four steps:

1. *Reception*: receipt of information mentally and physically by the addressee
2. *Response*: action taken on information by the recipient, such as routing, making additional copies, or giving instructions for filing or destroying the information
3. *Transcribing*: changing the document to another medium for storage
4. *Storage*: indexing and filing the document for later access

Figure 5–5 shows the way in which each of these functions and steps might be aided through the various kinds of word processing equipment.

Word processing offers many ways to simplify and improve documentation. Dictating equipment makes it easy for the systems person or line executive to originate raw material for documentation. Transcription can be centralized with skilled operators. Text editing programs offer a quick, flexible way to correct and review the first drafts of the material. Magnetic storage holds the text as long as needed in a compact, readily accessible form. Finally, when desired, the text can be printed out at high rates of speed automatically without typing errors.

Cycle Function	Cycle Steps	Dictation Equipment	Electric Typewriters	Automatic Typewriters	Graphic Machines	Copying Machines	Facsimile	Microfilm	Supplies
	Research	x		x		x		x	x
Origination	Composition	x	x						x
	Conversion		x	x					x
	Revision		x						x
	Preparation	x	x	x				x	x
Production	Reproduction		x			x		x	x
	Bundling					x			
	Distribution		x				x	x	x
	Reception		x				x	x	x
Utilization	Response								
	Transcribing							x	
	Storage							x	

Figure 5-5. Word processing equipment used in functions and steps. Many types of equipment may be used, as shown in the 12 cycle steps that make up the four major cycle functions.

SUMMARY

Manuals play a vital role in the smooth functioning of an enterprise. The organization manual is made up of charts and narrative to show lines of authority and communication, relationships between line and staff, and specific duties and responsibilities of managerial personnel. The policy manual provides guidelines and objectives for the various departments and the organization as a whole.

Data element dictionaries give complete definitions of data used in each record and file through the entire organization. They help to ensure consistency among programs and manuals by using uniform names, sizes, and formats for the various data elements. Installations standards and conventions are also summarized in manuals for the guidance and direction of programmers and users.

Procedure manuals are often divided into four subclassifications: (1) systems manuals, (2) clerical and control procedures manuals, (3) program manuals, (4) operator's run manuals. The systems manual describes in summary form the overall flow of data and the responsibilities of each section that handles it. The clerical and control procedures manual describes the preparation of source documents, the control of input to the data processing system, and the distribution of output reports. The program manual includes detailed logic, record layouts, source program, and compiler output, along with test data and instructions to the operator. The operator's run manual duplicates that part of the program manual which tells precisely how to run the program.

Good documentation protects against loss due to high personnel turnover. It is vital when programs must be revised, corrected, or updated, or when new equipment or procedures are being introduced. It ensures communication between management and analyst, analyst and programmer, and programmer and operator.

Poor documentation is often attributed to the press of everyday business, to programmer resistance, and to lack of uniform standards. It is often felt that documentation is "catching up" with work already done and is less glamorous than the excitement of system design and programming.

The technical writer may perform a helpful role in producing clear narrative descriptions, thereby allowing analysts and programmers to concentrate upon other technical aspects of their jobs. The use of a tape recorder to capture programmers' ideas as they work on a project simplifies their task and guides the narrative writer later. Computer-written flowcharts, which can be updated as often as source statements are changed, help to keep documentation up to date.

The steps in producing documents are review of concepts and data, writing, editing, production, quality control, publication, and distribution. Each step should be reviewed by a responsible leader or executive.

Documents may be controlled by a librarian to ensure prompt

updating, ready retrieval, and protection against unauthorized changes. Updating may take the form of errata and addenda sheets, updated pages, or completely new manuals.

Data processing facilities may be used to keep documentation up to date, just as they keep master files current by recording transactions as they occur and reporting those records that change.

Word processing systems permit the text of manuals to be dictated into machines, transcribed onto magnetic media for easy correction and editing, and written out automatically on high-speed printers when desired. They not only speed up the documentation process and make it more accurate, but can also save money. Work processing cycles include origination, production, and utilization, and each cycle may be broken into four separate steps.

TERMS FOR REVIEW

Addenda sheet
Clerical and control procedures
  manual
Data element dictionary
Distribution list
Errata sheet
Installation standards
Operator's manual
Organization manual

Playscript format
Policy manual
Procedure manual
Program manual
Stand-alone station
System manual
Text editing
Word processing

QUESTIONS

1. What is the difference in purpose and content between the organization manual and the policy manual?
2. Into what classifications may procedure manuals be divided?
3. What part of the content of the systems manual is appropriate for inclusion in the clerical and control procedures manual?
4. What are some of the characteristics of data that appear in the data element dictionary?
5. Name some areas of programming and practices that might be treated in the installation standards manual.

6. What are some of the reasons, or excuses, offered for poor documentation? How can they be overcome?
7. Name the "six Cs" of good procedure writing.
8. Name and describe the steps by which documentation is produced.
9. Use the Playscript format to describe how documentation might be kept on magnetic tape and updated by the use of punched cards.
10. Describe the functions of the programming secretary.
11. As systems and programming manager, you find that your documentation is already inadequate and getting further behind every day. Suggest possible steps you might take and select the best way to alleviate the problem.
12. What persons and equipment are included in a word processing system? How can they help to reduce the cost of producing documentation?
13. List three cycles involved in word processing and the steps into which the cycles are divided.

CASE STUDY
SUNCOAST COMMUNITY COLLEGE

As they continue with the detailed systems study of the alumni application, the Suncoast team members are careful to document each step fully. The assemble their working papers, notes of meetings, interview records, returns from questionnaires, record layouts, flowcharts, timetables, and charts for printed reports and display screens.

Sally Waters, Data Entry Operator, is designated as documentation librarian for the team. She is familiar with DOKUMENTR, a software package used in the computer center that permits the computer to aid in the documentation process. The line printers used by the IBM 4341 mainframe have only uppercase print. They are considered suitable for preparation of system and program manuals, but not for interim reports and correspondence. Marilyn Woods offers use of a memory typewriter in the Office of Institutional Advancement for preparation of those documents requiring letter quality.

At the end of each month Gerald Phipps, in consultation with other team members, drafts an interim report to be forwarded via Rick Jagsby and Mack Cordron to the Administrative Council. Sally Waters prepares the report on the memory typewriter, retaining the magnetic record for possible later use. Figure 5–6 illustrates one of the interim reports. The team members note that DOKUMENTR and the memory typewriter are not compatible, requiring duplication

---

DATA SYSTEMS INTERIM REPORT

To: Rick Jagsby, Director of Systems Development

From: Gerald Phipps, Project Manager

Project No.: ALUM-01   Date: 4/30/XX

Description of Project:

   This study designs and develops an online alumni record system that will produce desired labels and lists and maintain record of alumni gifts.

Progress to Date:

   1. Detailed study team of six persons has been selected.
   2. The state auditor will serve as part-time consultant on security and control.
   3. Phase I scope and objectives have been set.
   4. Interviews are scheduled with alumni directors from five nearby institutions and with local faculty and alumni.
   5. Overall flowchart, data gathering questionnaires, and alumni master record layout have been completed.
   6. DOKUMENTR has been chosen for preparation of system and program manuals.

Problem Areas Encountered:

   1. DOKUMENTR on IBM 4341 is not compatible with magnetic card typewriter for documentation.

Recommendations:

   1. Recommended later phase to install word processing system compatible with IBM 4341 mainframe.

Report Accepted and Distributed (✓)   Returned for Revision (   )

Rick Jagsby
Director of Systems Development

Figure 5-6. Interim report of detailed systems study. Periodic reports keep management informed on the progress of the study and prevent misunderstanding later.

of effort and knowledge of two separate systems. They resolve that later phases of the systems study will recommend a word processing system that can work as a stand-alone unit as well as a terminal to the IBM 4341 mainframe.

   Gerald Phipps constructs a data element dictionary for the newly designed donor file. He makes copies of the pages of the dictionary describing those elements in the student master file needed for the alumni application. This permits all elements to be described in a single document.

Team members agree that Phipps will be responsible for the system manual and the clerical procedures manual, while John Shirley, Senior Programmer, will produce the program manual and operator's manual. Documentation is an integral part of the design and development stages of the system.

QUESTIONS AND EXERCISES

1. Who is responsible for contributing to the documentation in the course of the systems study? When should documentation begin?
2. How would documentation be easier if the word processing system were fully compatible with the IBM 4341 mainframe?
3. Do you agree with the teams's choice of persons to complete the four manuals? Why or why not?
4. On the basis of the information on the system study to date, what items should be contained in the clerical procedures manual?

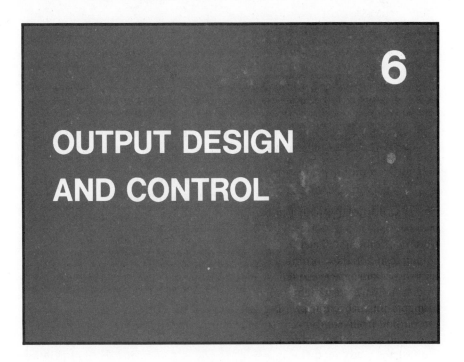

OUTPUT DESIGN
AND CONTROL

6

OBJECTIVES

At the end of this chapter, you should be able to:

1. Identify the principal devices and media for output of information.
2. State principles of design of display screens.
3. Distinguish between a business form and other printed documents.
4. Describe current trends in design and use of business forms.
5. Describe methods of constructing business forms.
6. Name the factors in designing and ordering forms that affect their cost.
7. Describe characteristics of a good records management system.
8. Describe conditions that affect the length of time and the form in which records must be maintained.
9. Describe design considerations of a management information system.

In Part II we have followed the steps followed by the systems department to define the objectives the data system must meet, to analyze existing systems, and to recommend one or more alternatives to top management. Following approval of the proposed project, the systems people should begin designing a complete system to meet the objectives defined earlier.

The four basic processing steps for computer systems are data entry, or input; processing; information storage; and output. However, for designing the system we often prefer to begin by specifying the output the system is to produce. First, we carefully determine what information the user needs and make sure it is presented in the clearest and most attractive form possible. Then we are ready to design the input necessary to provide that information, determine how it is to be stored until needed, and what processing steps will be undertaken.

The *design report* is a formal presentation to management. The presentation is often made to a steering committee comprised of systems and user personnel. The report is a detailed walk-through of the systems proposal, with a cost-benefit analysis and implementation schedule. Its purpose is to gain user acceptance and management approval before proceeding to the systems development phase. Its format and content are similar to those of the systems study report.

In this chapter we begin by reviewing the major types of output devices and media. Then we consider the design of display screens, presently the most common form of output. Next we disuss many considerations in design and control of printed forms. We continue with a number of advanced uses of the management information system and conclude with guidelines for records management and retention.

OUTPUT DEVICES AND MEDIA

Output of computers may be grouped into two broad types, called soft copy and hard copy. *Soft copy* includes information displayed upon a screen or given as an audible response. Soft copy is available for only a limited period and must be reconstructed to be reviewed later. *Hard copy* is in the form of printed paper reports, punched cards, or paper tape that can be kept and reviewed repeatedly.

Visual Displays

Because of the high cost and frequent shortages of paper in recent years and the growth of online systems, *visual display screens* provide the most common form of output. They are soft-copy devices since the image on the screen is no longer available for examination once it has been replaced by another image. Often it is possible to make a printed hard copy of the screen as a permanent record at the operator's option. Display screens are often called *cathode ray tubes* (CRTs).

The CRT may be considered *local* when it is connected directly to the computer through a cable for distances up to about 2400 feet, or *remote* when it uses telephone or telegraph lines from farther away. The CRT is usually attached to a keyboard that may be used for inquiry and response. Thus the CRT terminal may be used for both output and input.

Display screens are divided into two principal groups: (1) character displays and (2) graphics. *Character displays* are limited to the letters of the alphabet, the decimal digits, and certain special characters. Typically, 64 to 96 different symbols may be displayed. Some screens can show uppercase letters only, while others can display both upper- and lowercase letters. The display screens range from 8 to 10 lines of 40 characters per line to 24 or more lines of 100 or more characters each. A popular size is 24 lines of 80 characters each.

Many screens can display *graphics* in the form of lines, graphs, and drawings, as well as characters. The graphics are formed from small dots, each of which has its own separate location. It may be necessary to switch from character mode to graphics mode. Some screens allow combinations of graphics on the upper part of the screen and five or six lines of characters at the bottom of the screen for explanations or descriptions. Some screens permit graphics in as many as 15 different colors. High-resolution graphics increase the number of dots on the screen and make them smaller so that they can form even finer lines and denser drawings.

Printed Output

In spite of the tendency to reduce printed output in favor of visual display screens, today we have a wide choice among many print technologies, speeds, quality, designs, and devices. The *impact printer* has been and still is the principal output device for most computer systems. Printers normally use type bars, drums, dot matrix formation, Selectric ball, or daisy wheel. They may be *serial printers* printing one character at a time or *line printers* printing an entire line at a time. Speeds may range from fewer than 100 to more than 2000 lines per minute. From 64 to 96 characters are usually included in the set of characters that can be printed.

Nonimpact printers are usually one of four types: (1) thermal, (2) electrosensitive, (3) inkjet, or (4) laser. *Thermal printers* have heated printing heads, producing dots that form matrix characters on specially coated paper. Thermal printing devices are relatively inexpensive and quiet, but the paper is expensive, has a distinctive look, and may not be permanent. *Electrosensitive printers* shoot electrical discharges at aluminum-coated paper to form matrix characters on the surface. *Inkjet printers* create a matrix by spraying small jets of ink on the paper. Inkjet printing is silent, high in quality, and reasonably fast. High-speed *laser printers* can print more than 20,000 lines per minute using laser and photographic techniques similar to those used by copying machines. Laser printers are expensive and are justified only when the volume of printing is extremely high. All nonimpact printers have the disadvantage of being able to print only a single copy at a time.

Plotters provide another form of printed output. *Drum plotters* have the paper rolled around a large drum that can be rotated in either direction. In addition, a plotting pen is suspended from a rod placed horizontally across the paper. The combination of the horizontal movement of the pen and the vertical motion of the drum can cause a short line of perhaps 1/100 of an inch to be drawn in any of eight directions. The short lines can be combined to form characters, curves, straight lines, or circles.

Flatbed plotters have the paper spread over a large flat surface. Plots are made by moving a pen in any direction from mechanical arms suspended above the table.

Punched Output

Punched cards may be used as output from computer systems at rates of 100 to 300 cards per minute. In *serial punching* cards are punched from left to right, one column at a time. For standard 80-column cards, this requires 12 punch blades, one for each row, and up to 80 separate punching cycles per card. *Parallel punching* requires 80 punch blades which operate up to 12 times per card as the 12 rows pass the blades. In parallel punching the cards are fed past the punching blades from top to bottom.

Punched cards make effective *turnaround documents*. In this operation the computer punches or prints in optically readable characters on a card which is mailed to a customer or other addressee, who then returns the card with the payment, order, or whatever response is indicated. The card then may be read directly as input to the computer without keypunching or other manual entry of data.

Paper tape, once a common form of punched output, has largely been replaced by various forms of magnetic output that are faster and more reliable than paper tape.

Magnetic Output

Magnetic tapes, disks, drums, cards, and cartridges may also be used for output from computer systems. However, such output is not directly available for inspection by the user. Such output is usually for intermediate storage to be used as later input to the computer at the next stage of the data processing cycle. Magnetic output may also be used for distributing commercial software programs or transmitting files and report information from one computer system to another.

Computer Output Microfilm

Perhaps the greatest innovation in recording output data is *computer output microfilm* (COM). Microfilm is film of a size up to 105 mm with images which must be enlarged 8 to 40 times to be equivalent to normal paper documents. There are two major types of COM devices; *alpha-numeric*, which produce characters, numerals, and symbols; and *graphic*, which produce varied images and all types of drawings. In general, anything that can be shown on a CRT display tube can be placed on microfilm.

The basic components of a COM device are (1) the input, (2) the logic section, (3) the conversion section, (4) the deflection controls, (5) the display section, and (6) the film-handling section. Input may be from an online computer or an offline storage unit. Display is usually represented by the face of a CRT unit. Some units permit hard copy to be made from the enlarged microfilm image.

Many things must be considered in selecting COM hardware. If alphanumeric information is only archival in nature, film and equipment are relatively inexpensive. Special forms may be provided which overlay the computer-generated data and the image includes both. The most expensive equipment is required for high-speed retrieval systems. Microfilms may appear in such forms as rolls, cartridges, aperture cards, and microfiche. They may be positive or negative, and come in various sizes, such as 16, 35, 70, or 105 mm.

Microfilm offers the advantages of speed many times faster than that of an impact printer or plotter and highly compact storage of man-readable information. Its disadvantages include a cost from 4 to 10 times that of a high-speed printer and the fact that each copy made of the original image will tend to be of poorer quality, so that the third- or fourth-generation copy may be unreadable.

It is to be expected that continued technical improvements will be made in COM as in all other devices, so that it will become increasingly attractive and common as an output form.

Audio-Response Units

Some computers are able to transmit output in the form of the human voice through *audio-response units*. A limited vocabulary and voice style must be selected and prerecorded. The unit is able to convert such data as balances, amounts, or time of day to spoken words. Many microcomputers also can produce music or sound effects under program control.

Audio-response units can be found at many checkout counters nowadays reciting the amounts entered into the point-of-sale terminals.

DESIGN OF DISPLAY SCREENS

Display screens are often used for both input and output, so that the output designer must include instructions on the screen to guide the terminal operator in entering data and responding to messages.

The design of display screens has many factors that are similar to the design of printed output, but also many that are quite different. Displayed and printed output are similar in requiring that data be conveniently arranged, properly labeled, free from confusing or unexplained codes, uncrowded, and relevant. Headings, columnar arrangement, editing, and the sequence of presentation are designed in the same way for display screens as for paper forms.

However, many design requirements for screens are not encountered in designing the printed page. Screens usually have no more than 24 lines of 80 characters each, while printed pages have 50 to 55 lines of up to 133 characters each. Thus the screen can usually display only about one-fourth as much data at one time as the printed page will hold. Further, the entire screen must be retained in storage and then displayed as a unit, whereas printed lines are usually formatted and written out one at a time.

Alphanumeric Displays

The most common types of terminal screens use *alphanumeric displays*, sisting of alphabetic or numeric characters, plus some special characters,

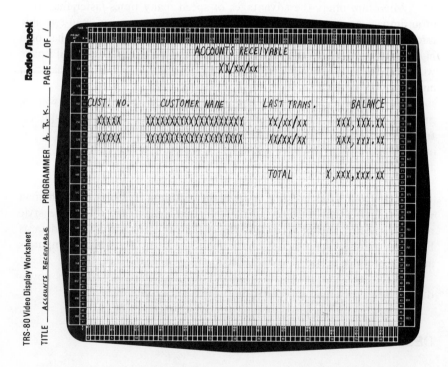

Figure 6-1. Video display worksheet. The worksheet permits exact spacing of headings, detail lines, and total lines to be specified by row and column on the screen.

such as periods, commas, asterisks, slashes, dollar signs, and so forth. Figure 6-1 shows a video display worksheet that may be used for designing the headings, columns, spacing, and other requirements of the desired output.

Since the entire screen must be set up in storage, it is not possible to use smaller type for headings, instructions, or captions as with custom printed forms.

The analyst needs a knowledge not only of the specific terminal that is used for the display but also for the data communications software that transmits data to and from the terminal. For each line to be displayed, it is necessary to set up a line of *attribute characters.* These characters show the starting positions of the various fields and how they are to be used. For example, constant fields may be *protected,* so that they cannot be modified by the terminal operator in keying data. Some fields may be limited to numeric data and others to alphabetic or alphanumeric data. Some fields may be displayed in high *intensity,* some medium intensity, and some blanked out.

The attribute characters also indicate the position of the *cursor.* Each screen has a cursor to indicate the position in which data is to be written out or keyed in. The cursor is usually a small dot, triangle, or underscore that moves along the screen as data is being keyed or written on the screen. Attribute characters indicate the initial position of the cursor as well as the positions to which it can be skipped. The cursor can be manually moved anywhere on the screen by using the keyboard, but data can be entered only in those fields designated as input fields by the attribute characters.

Each screen format used in a program must be stored internally in main storage of the computer or in a screens' file on magnetic disk. The designer should therefore try to use the minimum number of separate screens consistent with clarity and effectiveness to the user. Each screen designed to display information must be programmed to accept some response from the terminal operator. The responses might be a single key or short code to reduce the amount of keying required by the operator.

High-intensity lighting of certain fields on the screen can focus attention on the data that has been or should be entered. Flashing symbols are often used for displaying error messages resulting from incorrect data.

Figure 6-2 shows the constant information and attribute characters needed to produce a screen used in a college registration system. This particular screen allows a maximum of 80 columns and 24 rows.

Graphics Displays

Most microcomputers and many other terminals have powerful graphics features that permit the attractive display of information. For scientific use, the graphics may display function curves that often make beautiful artwork (see Figure 6-3). The ability to select up to 15 colors for any of the graphics dots enhances the clarity and beauty of the presentation.

For business uses, graphics may be used to present bar graphs, pie

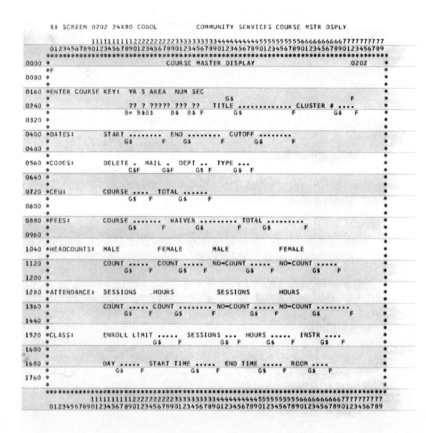

Figure 6-2. Constant information and attribute characters. The attribute characters indicate intensity of lighting, whether fields are alphabetic or numeric, whether data can be entered into a field, and other characteristics.

charts, and many other forms of pictorial representation for comparative statistics. Computer-aided design (CAD) employs graphics to simplify the complex drawings that go into the design of machine parts, electronic circuits, building plans, and aircraft.

Display Output Control

Display output is often available not only within the confines of the company offices but from anywhere within reach of a telephone. Special precautions are needed to safeguard the security of the data base. *Passwords* may be assigned to establish the identify of the person receiving the information and to limit access to certain files or data elements.

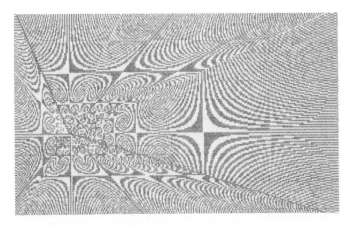

Figure 6-3. Graphics display screen. For displaying graphics, the screen
is divided into far more rows and columns than it is for
printing characters. Each position where a dot may occur
on the screen is called a pixel.

Each person authorized to use a terminal is assigned a password, and
sometimes an additional special password is required for especially sensitive
programs or confidential information. In addition, each program may have
its normal identification code and sometimes a secret password as well. The
terminal control system maintains tables that verify passwords and prevent
access by unauthorized persons to programs and files.

Passwords must be promptly changed in the case of a breach of security. As employees come and go, passwords must be changed and
reassigned regularly. Output design should ensure that passwords keyed
into a terminal for identification are not displayed upon the screen where
casual observers might see them.

FORMS DESIGN AND CONTROL

Business traditionally has devoted much attention to the problems of personnel selection and training. Similarly, it has spent much time and effort
analyzing capital expenditures for plant and equipment so as to get the
maximum value per dollar spent. But business forms have been one of the
most neglected aspects in our economy. Even though they are absolutely
essential to the operation of every business and procedure, they often have
been taken for granted.

Although a single form represents only a fraction of a cent in cost,
the forms industry in this country grosses about $1 billion per year. Even
more important, it has been estimated that for every dollar spent to buy a
business form, from $16 to $20 must be spent to process it. If the form is

poorly designed, difficult to understand, or confusing to process, it can cause a large amount of waste for an organization.

What is a business form? A form is defined as a document having constant printed information and space to add variable information. It is an essential link in an operational procedure and a medium for business communication. It may take a variety of shapes, sizes, weights, or construction, but it is customarily printed on some type of paper.

Obviously, not all pieces of paper are included in our definition of a business form. Printed materials such as advertising circulars, product labels, price lists, and customer instruction sheets normally are not considered business forms, inasmuch as they do not carry any spaces for entry of additional data. Inspection tags designed to be stamped and various ticket forms designed to be hand punched are likewise excluded from our definition of business forms.

Trends in Business Forms

For years, business has been concerned with the tremendous growth of the paperwork required to carry on its day-to-day functions. One of the heralded advantages of the computer has been its ability to spew forth reams of paper at high rates of speed in order to produce mountainous reports of great detail.

One trend resulting from so much output is the tendency to use plain stock paper rather than printed continuous forms. The computer is able to print column headings, page numbers, and simulated vertical and horizontal rulings. Thus a computer can produce not only readable but even attractive reports on plain paper. The second trend concerns input forms. Data is presented to a computer system not only through the medium of printed paper forms, but also through punched cards, documents and magnetic ink encoding, edge-punched cards, optical characters, and other specialized media. Here, the systems person often must be concerned not only with human ability, but also with a machine's ability to recognize and properly process the characters represented on the forms.

Concentrated efforts are being made to reduce the use of paper through direct computer input and through output via nonprinted means such as visual displays and microfilm. But the use of forms continues to be a major concern of systems work.

Let us look first at some of the technical points to be considered in forms design. Later in the chapter we will turn our attention toward the questions of responsibility and control of forms.

Design Considerations

Good forms must combine both practical and aesthetic qualities. They must suit the purpose for which they are intended. They must be easy to write, read, process, and dispose of. They must provide for capture of all necessary data, but must avoid duplication and extraneous material.

The best design practice calls for captions located above and to the left of the boxes for data entries. This arrangement permits the caption to be seen whether the data is to be entered by hand or by means of a typewriter. As much information as possible should be preprinted on the form in order to reduce the time required to prepare it. Where possible, blocks may be provided so that the respondent can check one or more of several choices.

Figure 6-4 shows a dual form with upper captions. The computer printing shows the present fields of a student record on magnetic disk. Handwritten additions or corrections are entered into the proper fields directly above the printed data. The changes are then keypunched, and the change cards are used to update the record on magnetic disk. The form can also be used for recording data to be punched initially to create a new record.

Both horizontal and vertical spacing should be considered in designing a form. Usually $1/4$ inch should be allowed between lines for a handwritten form and $1/3$ or $1/6$ inch for a machine-written forms. Most typewriters and computer printers use $1/6$-inch vertical spacing.

Computer printers may be adjusted to print eight lines per inch for such items as student academic records or property real estate descriptions, where it is important to get as much information as possible on a single form. Forms designed with improper vertical spacing require constant readjustment of the typewriter if the typewritten characters are not to fall right across one of the horizontal lines.

For horizontal spacing, sufficient room should be allowed on the form to enter the information asked for. Vertical rules may be of different thickness to make data stand out more clearly. For example, light vertical rulings or dotted lines might appear between the month, day, and year, with heavier vertical lines at the left and right side of the entire data field.

Colored inks and colored papers may add to the attractiveness and usefulness of a form, but they usually involve additional cost. Gray, green, brown, or blue ink afford better contrast then black between the printed data and that which is entered as the form is processed. Red ink is frequently used on credit memoranda, stop payment requests, rejection tickets, or other forms requiring special attention. Blue ink does not reproduce by certain photographic processes, and may be used as an outline for documents that are customarily photographed.

For multiple-part forms, different colored papers aid in the distribution of the forms to the proper departments and make it easy to spot any copy in the wrong group.

Wording printed on forms should be both precise and concise. Forms to be distributed outside the company should always include the company name and identification. On internal forms, the company name may be

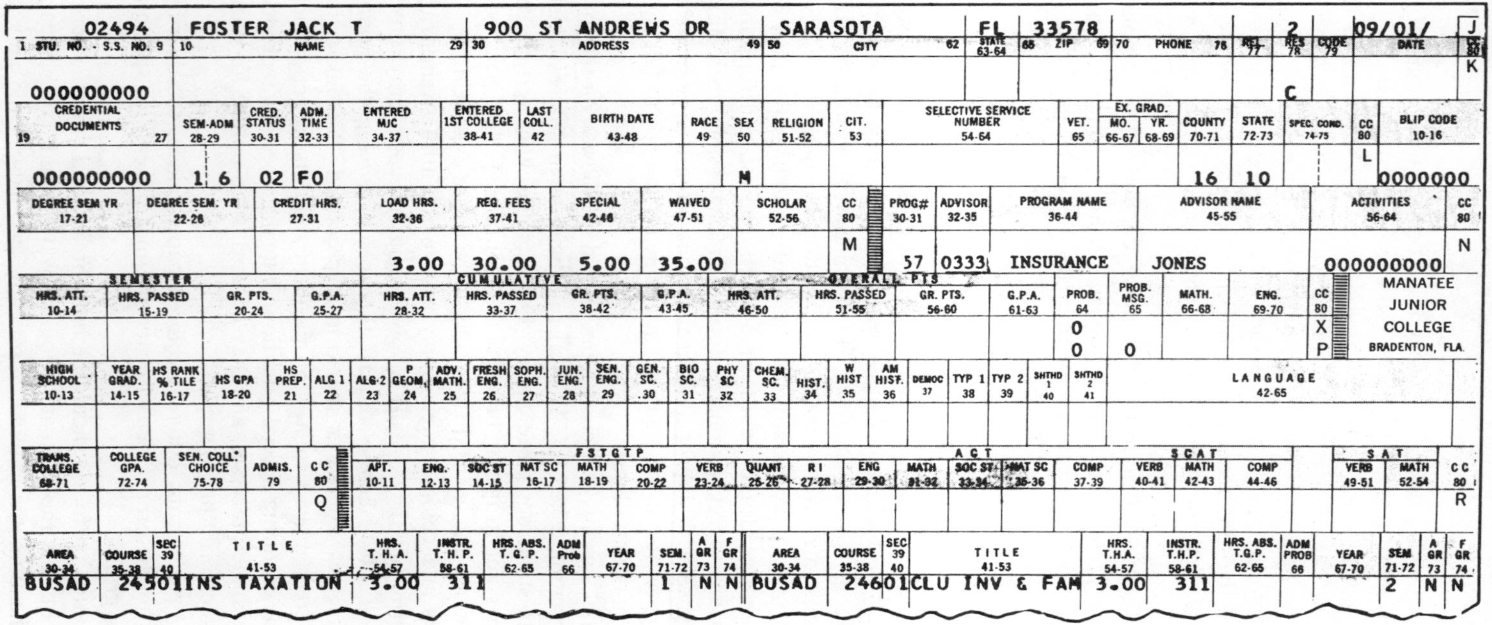

02494 | FOSTER JACK T | 900 ST ANDREWS DR | SARASOTA | FL | 33578 | 2 | 09/01/ | J
1 STU. NO. - S.S. NO. 9 | 10 NAME 29 | 30 ADDRESS 49 | 50 CITY 62 | STATE 63-64 | 65 ZIP 69 | 70 PHONE 76 | REL. 77 | RES 78 | CODE 79 | DATE | CC 80
000000000 | C | K

CREDENTIAL DOCUMENTS 19 27 | SEM-ADM 28-29 | CRED. STATUS 30-31 | ADM. TIME 32-33 | ENTERED MJC 34-37 | ENTERED 1ST COLLEGE 38-41 | LAST COLL. 42 | BIRTH DATE 43-48 | RACE 49 | SEX 50 | RELIGION 51-52 | CIT. 53 | SELECTIVE SERVICE NUMBER 54-64 | VET. 65 | EX. GRAD. MO. 66-67 YR. 68-69 | COUNTY 70-71 | STATE 72-73 | SPEC. COND. 74-75 | CC 80 | BLIP CODE 10-16
000000000 | 1 6 | 02 | FO | M | 16 | 10 | L | 0000000

DEGREE SEM YR 17-21 | DEGREE SEM. YR 22-26 | CREDIT HRS. 27-31 | LOAD HRS. 32-36 | REG. FEES 37-41 | SPECIAL 42-46 | WAIVED 47-51 | SCHOLAR 52-56 | CC 80 | PROG# 30-31 | ADVISOR 32-35 | PROGRAM NAME 36-44 | ADVISOR NAME 45-55 | ACTIVITIES 56-64 | CC 80
3.00 | 30.00 | 5.00 | 35.00 | M | 57 | 0333 | INSURANCE | JONES | 000000000 | N

SEMESTER: HRS. ATT. 10-14 | HRS. PASSED 15-19 | GR. PTS. 20-24 | G.P.A. 25-27
CUMULATIVE: HRS. ATT. 28-32 | HRS. PASSED 33-37 | GR. PTS. 38-42 | G.P.A. 43-45
OVERALL PTS: HRS. ATT. 46-50 | HRS. PASSED 51-55 | GR. PTS. 56-60 | G.P.A. 61-63
PROB. 64 | PROB. MSG. 65 | MATH. 66-68 | ENG. 69-70 | CC 80
0 0 | 0 | X P
MANATEE JUNIOR COLLEGE BRADENTON, FLA.

HIGH SCHOOL 10-13 | YEAR GRAD. 14-15 | HS RANK % TILE 16-17 | HS GPA 18-20 | HS PREP. 21 | ALG 1 22 | ALG-2 23 | P GEOM. 24 | ADV. MATH. 25 | FRESH ENG. 26 | SOPH. ENG. 27 | JUN. ENG. 28 | SEN. ENG. 29 | GEN. SC. 30 | BIO SC. 31 | PHY SC 32 | CHEM. SC. 33 | HIST. 34 | W HIST 35 | AM HIST. 36 | DEMOC 37 | TYP 1 38 | TYP 2 39 | SHTHD 1 40 | SHTHD 2 41 | LANGUAGE 42-65

TRANS. COLLEGE 68-71 | COLLEGE GPA. 72-74 | SEN. COLL. CHOICE 75-78 | ADMIS. 79 | CC 80
FSTGTP: APT. 10-11 | ENG. 12-13 | SOC ST 14-15 | NAT SC 16-17 | MATH 18-19 | COMP 20-22
VERB 23-24 | QUANT 25-26 | R I 27-28
ACT: ENG 29-30 | MATH 31-32 | SOC ST 33-34 | NAT SC 35-36 | COMP 37-39
SCAT: VERB 40-41 | MATH 42-43 | COMP 44-46
SAT: VERB 49-51 | MATH 52-54 | CC 80
Q | R

AREA 30-34 | COURSE 35-38 | SEC 39 40 | TITLE 41-53 | HRS. T. H. A. 54-57 | INSTR. T. H. P. 58-61 | HRS. ABS. T. G. P. 62-65 | ADM Prob 66 | YEAR 67-70 | SEM. 71-72 | A GR 73 | F GR 74 | AREA 30-34 | COURSE 35-38 | SEC 39 40 | TITLE 41-53 | HRS. T.H.A. 54-57 | INSTR. T.H.P. 58-61 | HRS. ABS. T.G.P. 62-65 | ADM PROB 66 | YEAR 67-70 | SEM 71-72 | A GR 73 | F GR 74
BUSAD | 24501 | INS TAXATION | 3.00 | 311 | 1 | N | N | BUSAD | 24601 | CLU INV & FAM | 3.00 | 311 | 2 | N | N

Figure 6-4. Dual form with upper captions. This type of form is used especially with batch processing applications. It shows the content of master files. When a field is to be changed, the correction is written directly above the printed data, and the form is sent to the data processing department for keypunching.

omitted or placed in subordinate position to the form title. Forms should be as self-explanatory as possible, and the use of confusing abbreviations should be avoided.

The size of the margins to be allowed on printed forms depends to a large extent on the method used for binding. If loose-leaf ring binders are used, ½-inch margins may be sufficient, whereas 1½-inch margins might be required for post binders. Forms may also be bound at the top or bottom in order to provide easier reference. Care should be taken to be sure that such important items as invoice number, date, names, or amounts are not hidden behind the binding. Snapout forms require a ½-inch gripper edge for removing the carbon paper from the multiple forms. Documents to be encoded in magnetic ink require that the bottom ⅝ inch of the form be reserved for the magnetic ink characters.

Business forms normally should be limited to a size of 8½ by 11 inches. This is a standard size for printing, processing, stocking, and filing. Smaller sizes may be appropriate where they can be conveniently handled, but they may require extra costs for trimming, special paper, and filing.

Forms printed by computers normally are larger than 8½ by 11 inches in order to gain the maximum number of printing positions at a single cycle. Printers usually range from 120 printing positions to 144. The standard printing size is 10 characters per inch, so that form sizes run from 12 to 14.4 inches actually printed. At least ½ inch is required on either side for the pin-feed holes, and additional space may be required for special punching or additional margin.

Forms design aids. Forms and card manufacturers customarily provide layout sheets to aid in proper design of forms and cards. The layout forms commonly are numbered horizontally across the page to correspond with the printing positions of printers which are attached to computers. The usual spacing is ten positions to the inch horizontally and six lines to the inch vertically. Frequently at the side is a facsimile of the carriage control tape, so that the proper channel and line number can be exactly matched to the spacing requirements of the form.

Even where no printing is used—that is, where all data is to be output from the computer—these form design sheets are invaluable for laying out headings, captions, and variable printing information on stock forms.

Even if one uses stock cards with no special printing requirements, multiple card layouts sheets may be employed to show the various columns to be used for fields in the cards. Other types of card design forms permit the calculation of the requirements for punching, interpreting, mark sensing, or optical card reading. Figures 6-5 through 6-8 show some of the form layout sheets that may be used.

The following pointers can help one achieve effective forms design:

1. Allow one printing position for each vertical rule on a form. The spacing

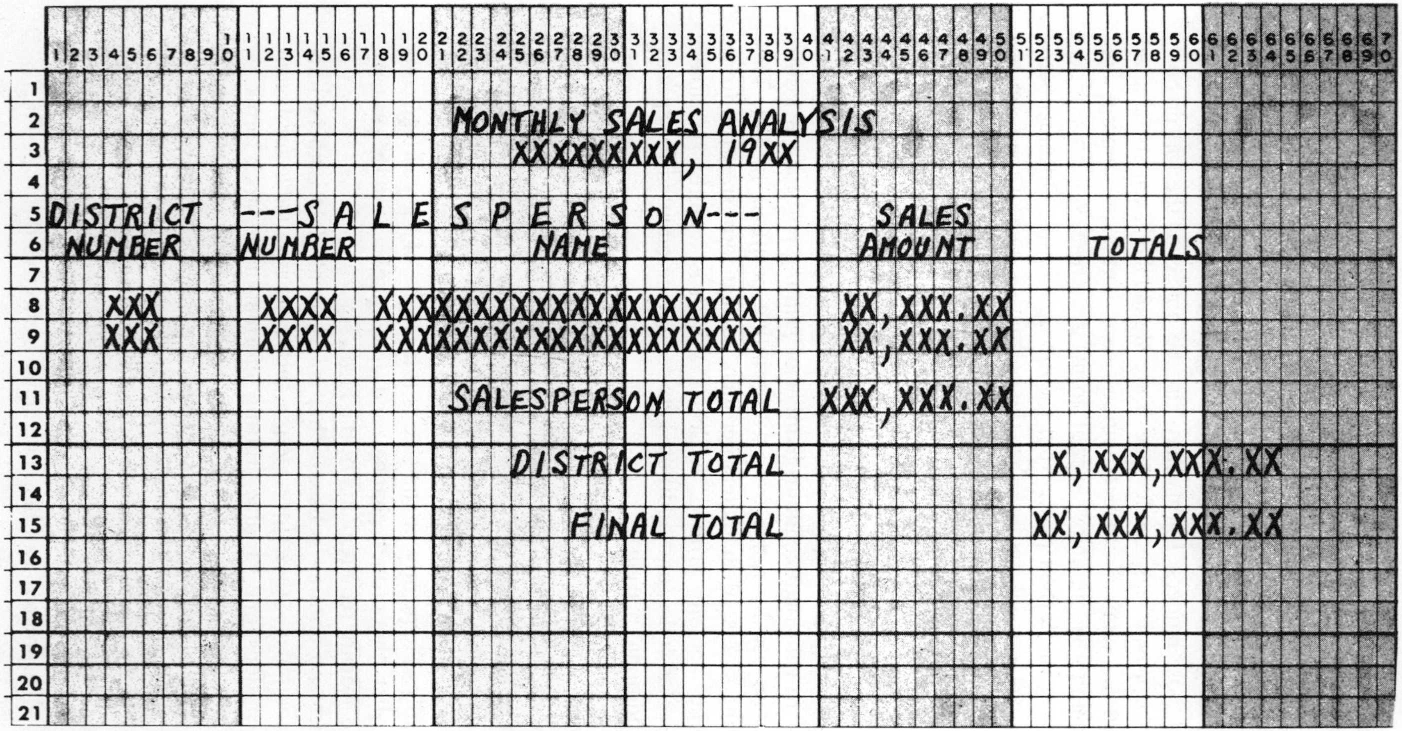

MONTHLY SALES ANALYSIS
XXXXXXXX, 19XX

DISTRICT	--SALESPERSON---		SALES	
NUMBER	NUMBER	NAME	AMOUNT	TOTALS
XXX	XXXX	XXXXXXXXXXXXXXXX	XX,XXX.XX	
XXX	XXXX	XXXXXXXXXXXXXXXX	XX,XXX.XX	
		SALESPERSON TOTAL	XXX,XXX.XX	
		DISTRICT TOTAL		X,XXX,XXX.XX
		FINAL TOTAL		XX,XXX,XXX.XX

Figure 6-5. Print chart for form layout. Printing positions across the page and lines down the page are numbered. The analyst can lay out heading, detail, and total lines exactly as they will appear on the printed page.

152

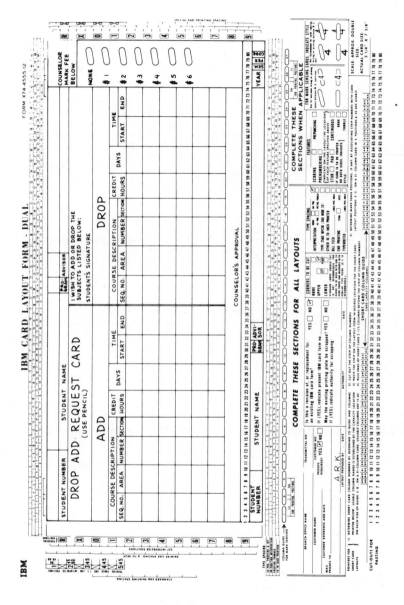

Figure 6-6 Dual card layout form for card design. Different scales appear on the form to provide for spacing by different machines that might punch or print on the cards.

153

FIELD LENGTH WORKSHEET					
Job No.: SCC 620	Record Name: Inventory Master				
		Length		Columns	
Field Description	Type	Trial	Final	From	To
Item number	N	5	5	1	5
Item description	A	20	22	6	27
Unit price	N	7	8	28	35
Quantity on hand	N	5	5	36	40
Reorder point	N	4	5	41	46
Quantity on order	N	5	5	46	50
Totals		46	50		

Figure 6-7. Field-length worksheet. This form enables the analyst to work out the best possible arrangement of data elements within a record.

at 10 lines per inch is too close to allow a line between adjacent characters.

2. Keep horizontal rulings to a minimum. Do not try to place them on the line immediately above or below a single line of printing.

3. In drawing a form layout sheet, put Xs in each position to be printed by the machine, so that the forms manufacturer can make precise measurements and allow proper tolerance (see Figure 6-9).

4. Arrange fields so that as much information as possible can be printed horizontally at one time. For example, printing the date, check number, and check amount on a single line rather than on three separate lines saves printing cycles on the output printer.

5. Print narrow forms side by side, two-up, three-up, or four-up, to take advantage of maximum printing positions per line. Forms printed this way not only are more readable but cost less than multiple-part sets.

6. Use shaded areas for captions and column headings to make the variable information printed on the forms stand out clearly.

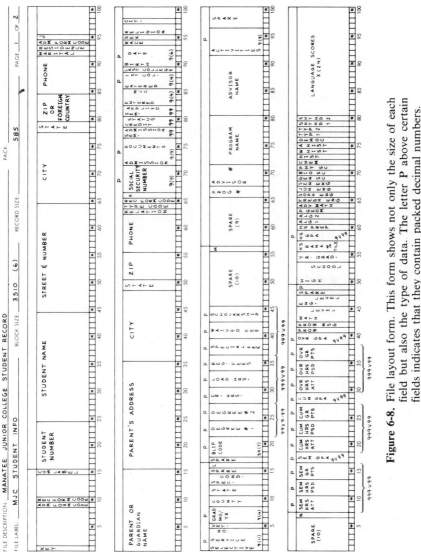

Figure 6-8. File layout form. This form shows not only the size of each field but also the type of data. The letter **P** above certain fields indicates that they contain packed decimal numbers.

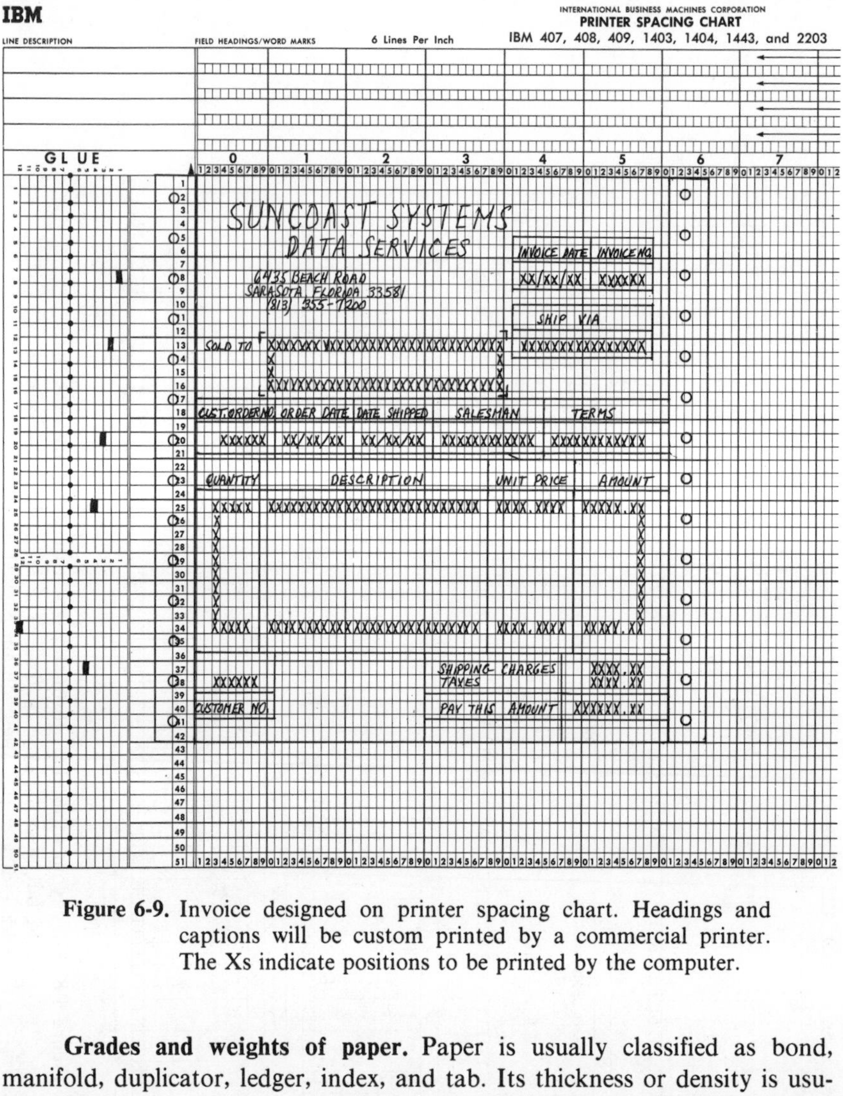

IBM

INTERNATIONAL BUSINESS MACHINES CORPORATION
PRINTER SPACING CHART

LINE DESCRIPTION   FIELD HEADINGS/WORD MARKS   6 Lines Per Inch   IBM 407, 408, 409, 1403, 1404, 1443, and 2203

Figure 6-9. Invoice designed on printer spacing chart. Headings and captions will be custom printed by a commercial printer. The Xs indicate positions to be printed by the computer.

Grades and weights of paper. Paper is usually classified as bond, manifold, duplicator, ledger, index, and tab. Its thickness or density is usually expressed in pounds. The number of pounds refers to the weight of 500 sheets of paper sized 17 by 22 inches.

Bond is divided into two types: rag and sulphite. The rag papers have the best appearance and durability. The quality varies according to the percentage of rag content, which is usually either 25, 50, or 100 percent. Sulphite bond papers, which are less expensive than rag, are used extensively for internal forms. Bond weights range from 10 to 24 pounds, with the higher weights usually being the rag content papers.

Manifold paper is also referred to as onionskin. The 9-pound weight is most common. Manifold is commonly used for the internal parts of multiple-part sets.

Duplicator papers, which range from 16 to 20 pounds, are intended for use with ditto or hectograph machines. They are specially prepared to transfer carbon from master copies using an alcohol spirit solution.

Ledger papers run from 28 to 36 pounds and are used for accounting records, visible record forms, checks, and so forth.

Index papers are very heavy, ranging from 72 pounds upward, they are used for printing cards of different types.

Tag stocks are very thick, ranging from 80 to 125 pounds. They come in various thicknesses. Tag is generally a lower grade of paper than those named above.

Types of construction. Forms may be assembled in many different ways, ranging from single unpadded sheets to complex assemblies of a great variety of sizes, colors, grades of paper, and methods of fastening.

Single sheets often can be produced in the company's own facilities, but more complex construction normally must come from a commercial printer. Because the cost of a printed form usually is only a fraction of the cost of processing it, the processing requirements of the type of construction one selects always must be taken into consideration. For example, a clerk can well afford to insert carbon paper manually if he or she uses only three or four copies of the form in a typical day, but if several hundred forms are used per day it is false economy to have the clerk spend time manually inserting carbons.

Commercial printers produce either stock forms or custom-designed forms. Stock forms, which make up much if not most of the continuous paper used in computer printers, are normally preprinted in large quantities and are of a generalized design which may be used by many different companies. They usually come in one to six parts in a wide variety of sizes, ranging from about 8½ by 3½ inches to 11 by 17 inches. The great majority of stock forms are printed with horizontal lines only, frequently three lines to the inch. Occasionally, special forms such as the 941A for reporting quarterly earnings of employees covered by social security are available as stock items. A popular version of stock forms calls for alternate green and white shaded areas rather than solid printed lines. Stock forms for computer use normally have pin-feed holes along both margins, with perforations along one or both sides.

Custom forms are more expensive than stock forms. They may be of almost any desired construction, combination of colors, number of parts, or types of paper. The printer's representative can give valuable aid and advice as to the selection of the best form for the money. Most large manufacturers have libraries of forms of various types that they have used for their customers all over the country. The representative is normally able to obtain a wide variety of samples of any given form, such as a payroll check or an invoice, from which the best features can be adapted to one's own use.

In addition to single sheets and continuous forms with single and multiple parts, printers can supply many other types of construction, such as fanfolds, snapouts, pasted pockets, and complex mailing sets.

Fanfold is the least expensive type of construction for extremely large quantities. In fanfold construction all copies of the form are printed on the same continuous roll of paper. They are then folded, and carbon paper may or may not be inserted. Railroad waybills are a typical example of fanfold forms.

Snapout forms provide a stub which joins the different copies of the form and the carbon paper. The form is designed so that it can be grasped at the opposite end from the stub and all the carbon paper removed with a single snapping motion. The stub may be at the top, bottom, or side of the form, depending on the type of machine in which the form is to be used. The side stub is not appropriate for a form to be used in a typewriter because it will be difficult to align properly. Having the stub at the bottom of a form to be used in the typewriter makes it easier to make erasures in the event of typographical errors.

Pasted pocket forms are designed to form a type of envelope into which charts, cards, or carriage control tapes can be placed to be sent along with the document after it has been printed.

Complex mailing sets designed for continuous feeding are now available in which forms are already inserted in envelopes. A single pass through the computer can produce eight or ten separate printed items, some of which may be detached and retained while the others are mailed directly to the outside user. By using carbonized spots or having segments cut out of the carbon paper, certain printed information will appear on additional copies and other data will be omitted. Earnings reports, student grades, insurance notices, and many other high-volume mailings can be prepared by having carbonized impressions inside an envelope which is addressed by the computer.

The method of making multiple copies may vary. Carbon paper is probably the most widely used, but it has the disadvantage of adding thickness to the set and requiring special disposal. NCR paper (no carbon required) is specially treated on the back of one part of the form and the front of the next part so that pressure causes the formation of an image by crushing microscopic ink capsules built into the paper. NCR paper costs about one-third more than carbon paper.

The backs of certain copies of the form may themselves be carbonized, so that they carry the impression to subsequent copies. This type of construction enables one to make a larger number of copies and is not as bulky as separate sheets of carbon would be. The disadvantage is that the form is permanently carbonized and will make a copy of anything written on it at any later time.

Forms intended for use on high-speed printing devices have to cope with many special problems not encountered with forms for typewritten or manual preparation. Paper undergoes tremendous strain when it is subjected to speeds of 2000 to 3000 lines per minute. Because the paper must start and stop very quickly, the fastening method must allow enough play so that different parts rotating slightly different distances around the printing platen will be properly aligned. It must not have so much play that the print line will dance up and down. Perforations must be deep enough to permit forms to be separated easily, but they must not allow the forms to come apart prematurely.

Pricing considerations. The analyst must be aware of all the factors that contribute to the cost of forms. Prices are made up of a combination of flat charges, which are constant regardless of quantity, and running charges, which vary according to the quantity of forms ordered. Flat charges include the preparation of the plate or plates and the setup of the printing press. (When a form is reordered, the flat charge normally will be less because the plate does not have to be prepared a second time.) Running charges include the paper, ink, glue, and the actual running time on the press.

The analyst should be aware of the standard sizes of forms. It is often less expensive to order a standard form slightly larger than one needs and to have it perforated in order to reduce it to usable size than it is to order a nonstandard smaller size.

Special art effects, such as lithography, screening, halftones, or offset may be used. Reverse block printing uses ink to fill in all around the lettering, but leaves the lettering positions unprinted, so that the original color of the paper shows through.

Special conditions, terms, agreements, or other instructions may be printed on the back of the form if they are too lengthy to be included on the face.

The type and weight of carbon paper has an important bearing on legibility. Nine-pound carbon paper is usually used in forms with up to four parts, and 7½-pound carbon paper for larger numbers of copies. A special type of blue carbon is used for handwritten forms.

Special charges are made for composition changes, where one part of the form has different printing from that which appears on other copies. Composition changes are particularly useful where one pass of the form through the computer can produce several different related documents all at one time.

Marginal words, which designate the person or department who is to receive each copy of the form, usually must be confined to a particular corner. Marginal words do not add much to the cost of the form and are a convenience to aid in proper distribution.

Most forms may be serially numbered in one or two places. Along with printed numbers, it is possible to get consecutive numbers printed in magnetic ink on certain types of checks and even punched in continuous form cards or card sets. Figure 6-10 shows typical banking forms using magnetic ink encoded characters.

One way to cut down on printing costs is to have forms constructed

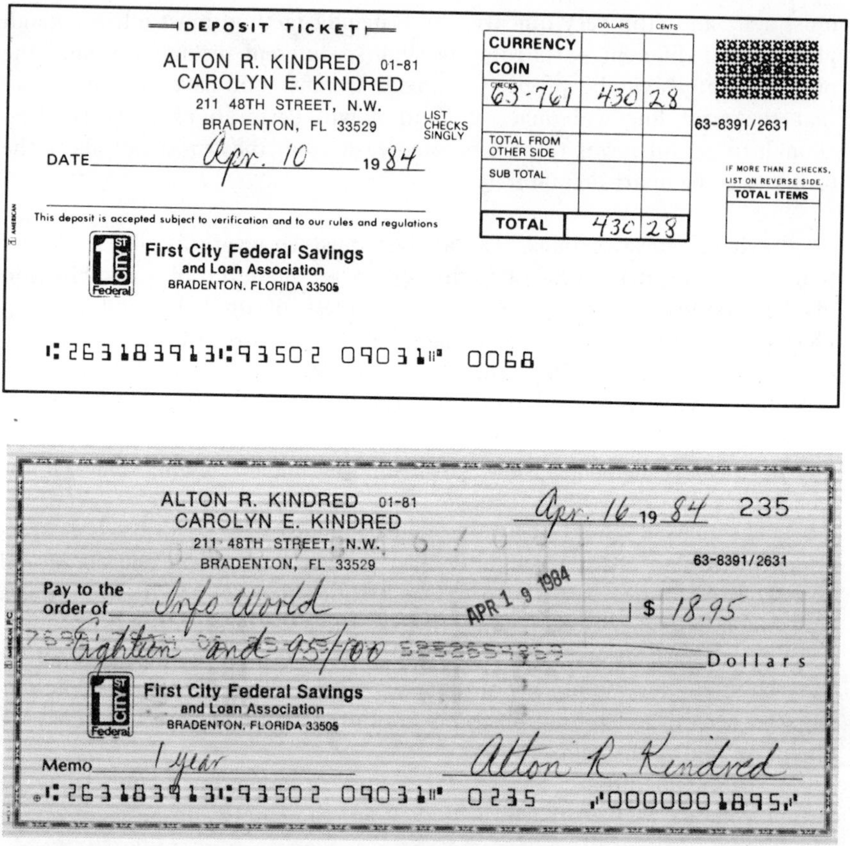

DEPOSIT TICKET

ALTON R. KINDRED 01-81
CAROLYN E. KINDRED
211 48TH STREET, N.W.
BRADENTON, FL 33529

DATE Apr. 10 19 84

LIST CHECKS SINGLY

	DOLLARS	CENTS
CURRENCY		
COIN		
CHECKS 63-761	430	28
TOTAL FROM OTHER SIDE		
SUB TOTAL		
TOTAL	430	28

63-8391/2631

IF MORE THAN 2 CHECKS, LIST ON REVERSE SIDE.

TOTAL ITEMS

This deposit is accepted subject to verification and to our rules and regulations

First City Federal Savings
and Loan Association
BRADENTON, FLORIDA 33505

⑆263183913⑆93502 09031⑈ 0068

ALTON R. KINDRED 01-81
CAROLYN E. KINDRED
211 48TH STREET, N.W.
BRADENTON, FL 33529

Apr. 16 19 84 235

63-8391/2631

Pay to the order of Info World $ 18.95

APR 1 9 1984

Eighteen and 95/100 Dollars

First City Federal Savings
and Loan Association
BRADENTON, FLORIDA 33505

Memo 1 year

Alton R. Kindred

⑆263183913⑆93502 09031⑈ 0235 ⑈0000001895⑈

Figure 6-10. Typical banking forms using magnetic ink encoded characters. The bottom ⅝ inch of the form is reserved for magnetic ink to indicate bank numbers, account numbers, and amounts.

two-up—that is, side by side. Printing two copies of a form side by side costs considerably less than constructing the two parts separately with carbon inserted in between.

Other ways for a company to reduce its expenses on forms include:

1. Using standard size paper
2. Reducing part-to-part composition changes
3. Using standard location for numbering
4. Reducing the form sizes by tighter spacing of composition
5. Taking advantage of quantity discount
6. Grouping forms of similar sizes and designs
7. Eliminating unnecessary cards
8. Eliminating nonessential use of colors
9. Avoiding folding

It is often possible to place a large quantity order and to arrange with the printer for delivery of part of the order at various times through the year. This procedure permits the printer to schedule production during slack periods and to pass the resulting savings on to the customer. It also means that in effect the printer is providing part of the warehousing service, which the customer would otherwise have to do.

Forms Control

There is a growing tendency to place the responsibility for the control of forms in special subdivision of the systems department. Because the systems department goes into all areas of the organization and is principally concerned with the interrelations that exist between departments, it seems natural that the responsibility for the business forms, which are the basis for communication between departments, should be vested with the systems department.

The first step in effective forms control is to gather a copy of every document being used in the organization. Usually, two samples are needed, one for a numerical and one for a functional file. The numerical file normally is arranged in straight sequential order, purely for the purpose of identifying each form. The numerical sequence provides the most convenient way to store most forms in the stockroom. Using this method, the stockroom has to reserve space for expansion in only one place, after the highest number previously assigned.

When forms are classified by function, a special coding system is required. One may be used as a prefix indicating the type of construction, such as flat sheet, book, snapout, fanfold, tab card set, or other designation. Three digits may be used to indicate the organizational departments in which the form is used. A final one or two digits can be used to indicate the type or purpose for which the document is used, such as requests, orders, movement of material, identifications, or reports and analyses.

Once all forms in the organization have been gathered and classified, it is important to tabulate exactly what data occurs in each form, where it is used, and what other forms use this same data. By carefully analyzing this output, it is possible to consolidate and to eliminate certain forms.

A common problem is the "bootleg" form. Often departments which feel the need for a new form simply design and run off copies and start using it without considering whether a similar or identical form is already in use. The forms control groups should be given the authority to approve all requests for purchase of printed forms, and even to approve in-house duplication or reproduction of forms beyond a certain quantity.

Report Output Control

If we have entered the correct data into a system and have processed it properly, the output should be correct. However, we still must continue to exercise control over the output reports and documents themselves.

The operator should *visually inspect* reports as and after they are printed, to be certain that paper is not wrinkled, ribbons are sufficiently dark, forms are properly aligned, and printing does not lap over ruled lines. The operator should ensure that the proper *number of copies* are printed and that they are *distributed* to the proper parties. Some reports that are *classified* as to security require special handling, receipting, and destruction when no longer needed for reference.

The *timeliness* of reports must be carefully controlled. If output time-tables are not followed, the value of information produced in reports declines rapidly. Reports must be produced in a *format* which can be clearly read and understood by the user.

There is a close relationship between the *processing span* and the time-liness of reports. The processing span is the time covered by the report. For example, annual reports that come out within two weeks of the end of the year are considered quite satisfactory, whereas daily reports that come out two weeks late are virtually useless. The shorter the span covered by the report, the more promptly it must be issued to be of value.

DESIGN OF THE MANAGEMENT INFORMATION SYSTEM

We will recall from Chapter 1 that the purpose of the management information system (MIS) is to provide useful timely information for decision making at all levels within an organization.

The lower management levels require detailed operational reports of daily processing for supervision and control. They use current exception reports and recent historical data to attain objectives and do short-term planning.

Middle management personnel require operating summaries and comparative data to spot short-term trends and define medium-range plans.

Top management needs external information on taxes, fashions, markets, investment opportunities, and actions of competitors, along with internal reports. They must set goals, make long-range plans, set strategy, and assure adequate return on investment. They will often want to use *simulation* techniques through use of mathematical models to explore the possible effects of various alternatives. Simulation helps provide answers to questions such as: What if we open a new branch? or What if we increase production levels?

Each successively higher management level trends to require more reliance on external information and less internal detail. Each higher level must look further into the future for planning and exercise a broader area of responsibility and control.

As we design the output of the MIS, we must bear in mind the specific requirements of each level of management. Breaking the large MIS into smaller subsystems helps to achieve control, distribute developmental work among the staff members, and get part of the system into operation while work continues on the rest of it.

Great emphasis must be placed on involving the management team in the MIS design. A good information system satisfies the needs of the people who set its requirements. The success of the system depends upon managers, and not just the programming or clerical staff, being happy with the results.

Economy, reliability, responsiveness, and modularity must be taken into account in the design of the system. These four requirements may best be achieved by beginning modestly and testing each phase of the MIS before proceeding to the next phase. A system design with a limited number of categories and classification is simpler than one having more elements and variables. But even such a limited management information system takes a long time to produce.

It is possible to design an MIS for either batch or online operation, or for both. Batch operation is suitable for producing detailed reports and certain exception reports. Online operation is preferable for making inquiries where an immediate response is needed. Online operation requires a method of gaining direct access to the desired record without examining the entire file, usually by referring to one or more indexes.

Online systems may be expanded to data communications networks serving not only all offices of a plant but also stations over a wide geographic area. The network may be centralized, so that the central computer is in a single site served by many terminals. Or the network may be distributed or dispersed so that part of the data base as well as part of the processing may be done at the outlaying stations.

Much of the output of an online MIS will be shown on display screens. The design of such screens requires the highest degree of clarity, convenience, conciseness, and flexibility. Easy interaction between the inquiries of management and the responses of the MIS is essential.

RECORDS MANAGEMENT AND RETENTION

The systems department might in some instances be made responsible for designing a program of records management and retention. Even where the functions of forms control and records management are combined, the systems department might well be consulted.

It has been estimated that almost three-quarters of any company's records are forms, while half of its reports are forms. Forms design therefore must consider storage requirements in terms of size, durability of paper, and position of binding, if any.

Records management is concerned with the production, distribution, storage, and retrieval of records. Even though an increasing number of a company's records are in magnetic form, the management of paperwork is still a major concern. Decisions are constantly needed as to how many copies of papers are needed, who gets them, who needs to keep them, and how long must they be retained.

For some types of records, single copies may be circulated as information among a number of persons, with each noting and passing the copy along to the next person on the list. This method is less effective if the record is needed for later reference than if each person has his or her own copy, but it is also less expensive.

An internal decision must be made as to how many copies of records might be produced and filed. As in most other management decisions, the question is whether the benefits derived from having multiple copies justify their cost.

However, it is often a question of federal or state law how long certain records must be retained. For tax purposes or required audits, some records must be retained for a number of years. Many public agencies and departments are required to retain some records permanently, while other records may be destroyed only after receiving specific approval of the division of archives. Some organizations must prepare a list of documents showing the retention schedule and the name of the person or office responsible for every record prepared or received. The intent is to ensure that all public records are available for review or audit as long as they may be relevant.

The systems department should be aware of requirements for records retention to safeguard against destruction of vital information before it has been properly authorized.

SUMMARY

Output from computers may be classified as soft copy or hard copy. Soft copy, such as visual displays or audible responses, is available for only a limited period. Hard copy in printed, punched, or magnetic form may be kept and reviewed repeatedly.

Display screens, called cathode ray tubes (CRTs), may be considered local or remote depending upon their distance from the central computer. Screens may display characters or graphics.

Printed output may be produced by impact or nonimpact printers. Impact printers may have solid characters or dot matrix and print either a character or a full line at a time. Nonimpact printers may be classified as thermal, electrosensitive, inkjet, or laser. Plotters also provide printed output using drums or flatbed devices.

Punched cards, now declining in popularity, make effective turnaround documents. Magnetic output on tapes or disks is used primarily for intermediate storage for later processing. Computer output microfilm can be produced faster than printed pages, stored in a highly compact space, and mailed inexpensively. Audio-response units permit a limited number of spoken words to be used as output.

Screens should be designed with the convenience to the user in mind. High intensity lighting, blinking characters, and graphics provide interest and emphasis for information presented. Attribute characters are used to show the purpose and limitations of each field. The same screen may be used for both input and output.

Printed forms should be practical, aesthetically pleasing, easy to use, and suited to the purpose for which they are used. They should be of standard sizes, which are convenient to process, handle, and file. Colored inks and paper may be used to add to the attractiveness of the form. The arrangement of information on the forms must provide for margins and binding.

The various grades of paper are bond, manifold, duplicator, ledger, index, and tag. These grades come in a variety of weights. The proper weight and grade should be selected for each job.

Types of construction range from single sheets, through padded or stub books, snapouts to fanfold. In designing a form one must also consider such features as punching, perforation, scoring, folding, die cutting, and fastening.

Control of forms may be improved by requiring approval of new forms before they are printed and by centralizing responsibility for design and approval of forms. Every attempt should be made to consolidate and reduce the number of forms, to maintain close control to ensure an adequate supply, to provide sufficient lead time in placing orders, and to order in the most economical quantities.

The management information system should be designed to make information available to all levels of the organization for decision making. The lowest level is concerned with internal information for direct operation and control. Middle management needs internal information with trends to define objectives for short-term plans. Top management needs summarized internal information along with external data to make long-term plans and strategy.

Records management is concerned with the production, distribution, storage, and retrieval of records. Federal and state laws often affect the length of time that records must be kept.

TERMS FOR REVIEW

Alphanumeric displays
Attribute characters
Audio-response unit
Business form
Cathode ray tube
Character display
Computer output microfilm
Custom form
Drum plotter
Electrosensitive printer
Flat charge

Flatbed plotter
Forms control
Graphics display
Hard copy
Impact printer
Inkjet printer
Laser printer
Line printer
Linear programming
Local
Marginal word

Mathematical model   Simulation
Nonimpact printer   Snapout form
Password   Soft copy
Processing span   Stock form
Remote   Thermal printer
Running charge   Turnaround document
Serial printer

QUESTIONS

1. What are the differences between hard copy and soft copy? Give some examples of each.
2. Distinguish between local and remote terminals.
3. What are some of the different types of impact printers?
4. Name four types of nonimpact printers and describe how each creates the printed characters on paper.
5. Distinguish between serial and parallel punching of cards.
6. What are some advantages and disadvantages to computer output microfilm for output as compared with paper documents?
7. What are attribute characters? How are they used in design of display screens?
8. How are passwords used in control of display output?
9. What is meant by a business form? What types of printed materials are not included in this definition?
10. Name the different grades of paper and give a typical use of each grade.
11. Distinguish between stock forms and custom-made forms.
12. What is meant by the term "construction" in the manufacture of forms? What is the difference between a snapout and a fanfold form?
13. What optional features in printing specifications are likely to incur extra costs?
14. What is the difference between flat charges and running charges in determining printing prices? What is the price per thousand for forms having a flat charge of $150 and running charges of $10 per thousand for an order of 10,000? For 100,000?
15. How would you go about implementing a forms control program in your company?
16. On a printer spacing chart, design and draw a payroll check and earnings stub. The check and stub together form a continuous tab card printed side by side. The bottom ⅝ inch of the check is encoded in magnetic ink with the bank identification number. The bank name is "Long Green Bank of Myakka City," number 63-999/631. The check

should include name of payee (20 spaces), date, check number (five digits), and amount. The stub includes Social Security number, hourly rate 9.999, hours worked 99.9, regular pay 999.99, overtime pay 99.99, gross 999.99, withholding tax 999.99, F.I.C.A. 999.99, four other deductions (numbers 1–4) each 99.99, and net pay 999.99. Only 120 printing positions may be used.

17. On a printer spacing chart, draw headings and column rulings for a payroll register to accommodate data printed on check and stub in Question 16. Put date at top of report instead of at side of each name. Write X in each position to be printed alphanumerically and 9 in each numeric position.

18. What is the role of the systems department in a records management and retention program for an organization?

CASE STUDY
SUNCOAST COMMUNITY COLLEGE

Gerald Phipps begins design of output for the alumni application with the master menu for selection of programs. Each program is given a four-character mnemonic name to be consistent with other online programs produced in recent years. Each operator using the system must enter a password to gain access to each program. The password will not be displayed on the screen when it is keyed.

Each program will also offer a menu for selection of available options and to prompt the entry of required information. These programs will be provided:

1. ALUM—Master menu for alumni application.
2. AGFT—Create, update, or delete donor record.
3. ALST—List of alumni sorted in various categories.
4. ALBL—Mailing labels sorted in various categories.
5. ADSP—Display alumni record.
6. AMST—Create alumni master file or add graduates following each commencement.

SCREEN DESIGN

Display screens used with the IBM 4341 network contain 24 lines of 80 characters each. The master menu screen provides space for entering a four-character program code, four-character terminal operator code, optional operator password of three to eight characters, and optional program security code of three to eight characters. Typing "HELP" as the program code causes the master menu of all programs to be displayed 20 entries at a time. Pressing the ENTER key shows the next 20 entries of the menu. Typing the proper four-character program name and terminal operator code will display certain programs and require entry of passwords for others.

The display screen for program ADSP is shown in Figure 6–11. Keying in the Social Security number causes the name and identifying data to be retrieved from the alumni master file and displayed. No donor data is shown on this screen. Program AGFT shows similar data and also allows entry, correction, and display of the donor record.

FORMS DESIGN

Phipps decides that where address labels are desired, the standard 1-inch labels will be used. This will permit five printed lines per label and leave a half-line margin at top and bottom. Most addresses are only three lines, but some are four. The additional line contains coded information useful in classifying the type of mailing sent out or the response received. The labels are 4 inches wide containing 40 characters per line.

Listings will be in a standard format, with only the sorting sequence to be changed. The standard listings will contain an identification line:

1.	Social Security number	11 spaces, edited in the form 999-99-999
2.	Name	20 spaces
3.	Address	20 spaces
4.	City	14 spaces
5.	State	2 spaces
6.	Zip	5 spaces
7.	Year graduated	4 spaces
8.	Degree	3 spaces
9.	Major	3 spaces
10.	Year graduated with second degree	4 spaces
11.	Second degree	3 spaces
12.	Second major	3 spaces

An optional second line of the standard listing will give a record of total contributions for each of the last five years. Each entry shows year in four spaces and total contributions with 12 spaces edited.

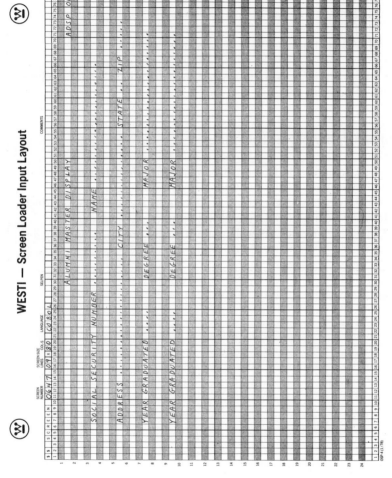

Figure 6-11. Display screen for alumni master record. The dots indicate the number of characters to be entered for each field.

169

Phipps calculates that, with spaces between fields, the listings will fit in 132 printing positions on standard 8½-by-14⅞-inch continuous forms.

Another printed report will show the detailed listing of contributions from the alumni member for the current year as the second line following the identification line. Two gifts can be printed side by side on the same line showing this information:

1. Date   6 spaces
2. Receipt number   5 spaces
3. Purpose code   7 digits
4. Amount of gift   12 spaces edited 9,999,999.99

As many lines as necessary are used to print all gifts received during the current year.

QUESTIONS AND EXERCISES

1. Name some of the factors to be considered in safeguarding data and privacy in design of output.
2. What are some advantages in producing listings on 8½-by-11-inch forms as compared with use of wider forms?
3. Draw a print chart showing listings to be produced by Program ALST.

7

INPUT DESIGN
AND CONTROL

OBJECTIVES

At the end of this chapter, you should be able to :

1. Identify the principal devices and media for input of information.
2. State general principles covering input design.
3. Describe processes used to verify input into data systems.
4. Calculate check digits using the Modulus 11 method.
5. Describe how totals are used in control of input.
6. Point out reasons for passwords for control of input from remote terminals.
7. Name reasons for use of codes in data processing.
8. Describe the most common types of codes.
9. Describe methods of assigning codes.
10. Show how standardization of codes eases transfer of data.

In any business organization data originates from *transactions* that take place. The exact nature of the transactions may vary from one organization to the next, but there are many common characteristics that apply to data from all sources. All data must be collected, recorded, classified, and often transcribed to get it into a form that computers can process.

INPUT DEVICES AND MEDIA

There are many different devices and media used for data entry, but they may be grouped into two major categories: (1) those used in online transactions, and (2) those used for batch data entry. Those used primarily for online data entry include keyboards with display screens, and optical scanners. Those used primarily for batch processing are magnetic ink character readers, punched card systems, and key-to-storage devices.

Keyboards with Display Screens

The most common types of online terminals have keyboards on which the operator enters data and display screens, or cathode ray tubes, that display both the keyed data and information returned to the operator from the computer. Keyed information is displayed on the screen to permit visual verification. Data returned from the computer may be displayed on the screen faster than it can be printed by the usual hard-copy terminal printer. As mentioned in Chapter 6, online terminals may accommodate alphanumeric data only, graphics only, or a combination of both. Terminals are usually called *dumb, smart,* or *intelligent* depending upon the number of functions they can carry out or the amount of programming that they are able to do.

In addition to a display screen, or sometimes instead of one, some keyboard terminals have a printer for producing hard copy. The printer may produce a single line at a time or may make an exact copy of what appears on the screen. Keyboard terminals may also be combined with *touchtone telephone devices* that permit a conventional telephone instrument, with a special adapter, to be used for transmitting data directly to a computer. Plastic cards, paper tape, punched cards, and the telephone dial can all be used for input. A touchtone system can use existing lines at very low cost, but is limited in speed and requires special data conversion equipment.

Point-of-sale terminals may be conventional keyboards with display units or special machines such as cash registers or bank teller machines. These devices permit data to be captured and transmitted directly to the computer at the point the transaction occurs. Special keyboards often are used to reduce the amount of keying the operator must do.

A special adapter, called an *acoustic coupler,* allows virtually any terminal to gain access to a central computer by dialing through ordinary telephone lines. After the number is dialed, the telephone receiver is placed in a cradle in the acoustic coupler to establish the connection.

Industrial *data collection* systems may be placed at various stations throughout a plant to transmit data to a central site. They are useful for cost control, industrial security, production control, labor distribution, and inventory control. They accept data from punched cards, plastic badges, and manual dials, and transmit it to magnetic tape, paper tape, or directly to the computer. These systems permit online capture of data as transactions occur.

Optical Scanners

Optical scanning equipment does not require keyboard entry, holes, or magnetic media of any kind; it reads marks or printed characters directly from printed or handwritten documents.

Most common of the optical scanners are those designed to read the *universal product code* (UPC), shown in Figure 7-1. This code now appears on almost every package, can, jar or bottle found in drug and grocery stores. The UPC consists of vertical marks of varying widths to stand for decimal digits. Below the marks the digits are recorded for the operator's use if necessary. The scanner is usually housed in a window in a recess on the checkout counter. As the clerk moves the container past the window, light beams sense the code and transmit data to the back of the store, where prices are obtained, inventory records are adjusted, and sales totals are accumulated.

Another type of optical scanner is the *reading wand.* The wand, about the size of a pencil, is attached to a cable that is connected to the terminal. The wand can be pointed close to the UPC or other coded information on a ticket or tag to sense the price, model, size, or other data recorded there.

Some optical scanners can sense only the presence or absence of a mark. Such scanners are often used for multiple-choice tests, surveys, meter readings, and other data entry purposes.

Figure 7-1. Universal product code. This code appears on boxes, cartons, and packages in retail stores and on other products such as magazines. It is sensed by optical scanners to control inventories and print customer receipts.

Optical character readers can be grouped in four classes, depending upon the type of input documents used:

1. Self-punch readers scan a 51-column punch card for printed data and punch data into the card itself. The card is then used as input to a computer. These readers are widely used for oil company credit card processing. The 51-column cards are standard 80-column cards that have been perforated to separate into a stub retained by the customer and a part to be returned with the payment.
2. Document readers are limited to handling small "turnaround documents," which are prepared by a computer printer, sent to the customer, and returned with the payment.
3. Page readers typically read up to a full page of data. Virtually all OCR manufacturers offer page readers.
4. Journal roll readers read cash register and accounting machine tapes optically.

The typical OCR machine consists of several operating segments: (1) document transport for paper handling; (2) scanning optics, or the visual segment; (3) recognition logic, or the software for identification; and (4) digital conversion for input to the computer.

Not all the technical problems associated with OCR have been solved. Handwritten data, certain type fonts, and machine reliability are still problem areas. The high initial cost of such equipment may be reduced with greater standardization of paper, fonts, and forms. OCR as a method of input is likely to continue to improve and to grow.

Magnetic Ink Character Recognition

Magnetic ink encoders are used principally by the banking industry, but are also suitable for credit cards, tickets, and retail merchandising. The magnetic ink characters are usually imprinted along the bottom edge of the form. Encoded documents can be read by sorter-readers both online into the computer system at high rates of speed and offline for physical sorting of the documents.

Magnetic ink has proven to be highly reliable for use on documents that must be handled manually under all types of conditions. A specially designed type style called *E13-B font* (Figure 7-2) may be read by either machines or human beings. However, its limited character set of only 14 characters and the need for preprinting and pre-encoding data are disadvantages.

Punched Cards

Punched cards for many years were the chief form of computer input. The 80-column Hollerith card was named after Herman Hollerith, who first developed a means of recording data in punched cards for the 1890 census.

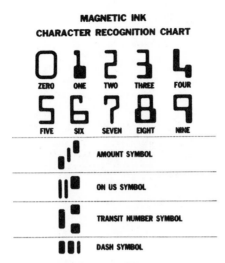

Figure 7-2. E13-B font. This type style was designed by the banking industry to be readable by both human beings and machines.

The punched card measures 7⅜ inches long by 3¼ high, containing 80 columns, each having 12 rows for punching rectangular holes. Each column contains one or more punches, which form the code to represent a letter, number, or special character.

The 96-column card measures 3.25 inches by 2.63 inches and uses small circular holes instead of the rectangular holes that appear in the 80-column card. These cards were introduced for the IBM System/3 computer and are used by small business systems. Both 80-column and 96-column cards (Figure 7-3) are made of fairly rigid, high-quality paper stock that is easy to handle and has long life.

The *keypunch,* or card punch machine, is used to transcribe data from documents such as lists, payroll sheets, inventory lists, orders, or student schedules into holes in cards. The cards are typically collected into batches and then read into the computer by *card readers.* Some types of card readers also double as card punches for output from the computer. Readers for 96-column cards are called multifunction card processing machines (MFCPs). They not only read cards as input, but also perform functions such as sorting, collating, reproducing, and interpreting the cards.

Key-to-Storage Systems

Key-to-storage systems were once considered a simple replacement for punched card data entry; now they have many added features that make them valuable in distributed processing systems. Key-to-storage systems include key-to-tape, key-to-disk, key-to-diskette, and intelligent terminals.

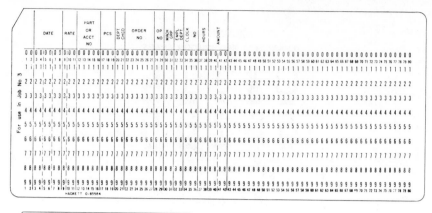

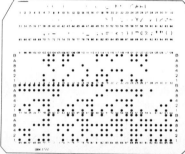

Top: 80-column transcript card.

Bottom: 96-column card for IBM System/3.

Figure 7-3. Punched cards having 80 and 96 columns. The 80-column cards typically have only one, two, or three punches per column to represent numbers, letters, or special characters. The 96-column cards may have as many as six.

They can substantially reduce data entry costs and increase throughput.

Key-to-storage machines can be used for data entry, verifying, editing, and searching. The tape or disk media can be reused. They are lighter to handle and transport and more compact to store than cards. Keying may also be faster than punching cards because of the ease of making corrections.

Other Input Devices

Cash registers and adding machines can produce machine-readable output in the form of printed paper tape, punched paper tape, continuous forms, or magnetic-ink-coded documents. They have the advantage of producing computer input as a by-product of recording the transaction at its point of origin, but they are less effective for input at other points.

Other types of readers permit the automatic transcription of retail sales item information from prepunched tags for sales analysis and inventory control. These readers typically produce punched cards, magnetic tape, or direct computer input. Point-of-sale data recording is possible, but tags must be prepunched with data to be recorded when the sale is made, and they are difficult to alter if prices change.

Magnetic tapes, disks, and diskettes may be used for input to computers. Purchased software often is delivered in magnetic form so that it can immediately be loaded and executed. A very common practice is to use output at one stage of the data processing cycle as input at a later stage. In this sense, virtually all types of master files may be used as input media. Using magnetic media in this way eliminates the need for additional data entry by keying or optical scanning.

INPUT DESIGN PRINCIPLES

Data should be arranged for input so that the data entry operator records the data elements in the same order in which they appear on the source document. Careful planning will ensure that all data elements later required will be captured at the source and that only those elements needed will be recorded. Often in the past much data has been collected that has seldom, if ever, been used.

For online transaction entry from a keyboard, data is often organized into *lists*. A list is simply a series of data elements, separated by commas or, in some systems, by blanks. Each element is stored separately in the form of a *variable* for later processing in the program. Elements in lists may be one of three types: (1) alphanumeric data, or character strings; (2) integers, also called fixed-point numbers; and (3) real numbers, also called floating-point numbers, written with a decimal point. For example, in response to the message:

ENTER CUSTOMER NAME, ACCOUNT, AND BALANCE

the operator might enter the list

"ANTHONY B. ROLLY", 45678, 1234.75

Character strings containing spaces or commas must often be enclosed in quotation marks.

For batch processing, such as punched cards, input data is usually in the form of *records*. Each record consists of several *fields*, each containing one data element (Figure 7-4). The collection of records organized for a particular purpose make up an input *file*.

Records are said to be *fixed-length* when a given field, such as a name, is always the same length in each record. *Variable-length* records may have fields such as a name with a length of, say, 12 bytes in one

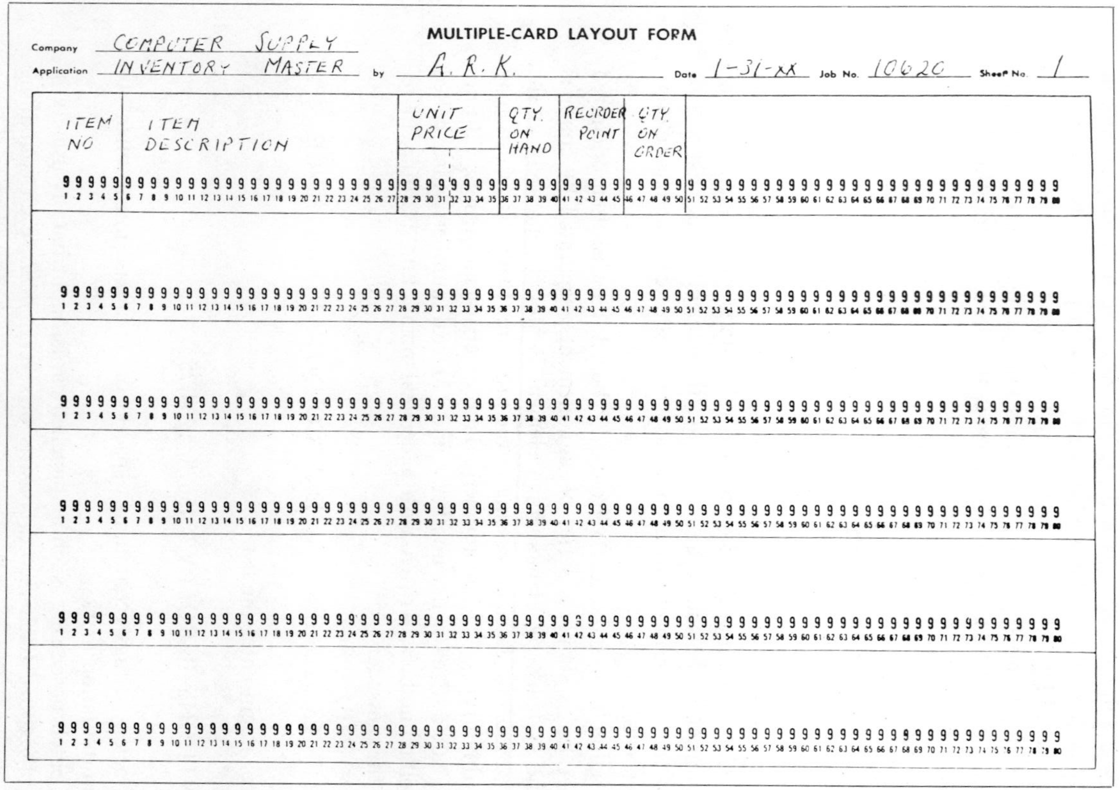

Figure 7-4. Record divided into fields. Solid lines indicate divisions between fields. Dashed lines indicate locations of assumed decimal points.

178

record and 20 bytes in another record. Such variable-length records require a special character, or *delimiter,* to designate the end of the field and another delimiter for the end of the record. Delimiters are usually such characters as slashes (/) or dollar signs ($) that are not found in the regular data elements themselves.

Design of Input Screens

A crucial point in design of display screens for input is to be certain that the operator knows exactly what to enter. To this end, a *menu* may be provided giving a choice of the desired programs or functions the operator wishes to execute. The menu is designed so that the operator needs to enter only a single number or letter to make the selection. Then another menu may be offered to refine the choice further. Figure 7-5 shows a menu designed on a video display worksheet.

A message called a *prompt* is usually sent to the terminal by the program to guide the operator in entering the data in the proper length and form. The data entry operator responds to the prompt by keying in the desired data item. Then another prompt is sent to obtain the next data item.

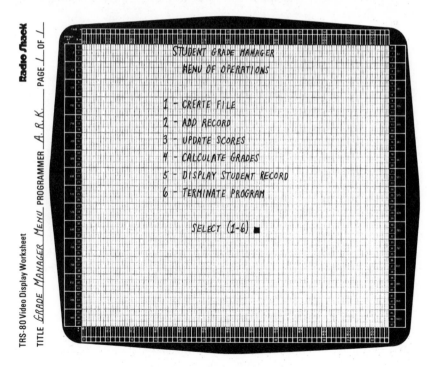

Figure 7-5. Menu on video display worksheet. The worksheet shows the specific number of rows and columns on the screen of a specific computer to aid in designing useful and attractive reports.

An entire screen might be formatted, using *attribute characters* as described in Chapter 6. These attributes define the length of each field, whether the data in the field is alphabetic or numeric, whether the data displayed can be changed, and another design features. The *cursor* moves from one field to another on the screen under program control to guide the operator in entering the data, just as one would fill in a blank form on a typewriter.

Intelligent terminals, or microcomputers used as terminals, may be programmed in BASIC or another high-level language for data entry. Special commands may be used to position the cursor for display of output messages or for the receipt of input data. Some cursor commands found on popular microcomputers include:

VTAB—position the cursor to a specific vertical line.
HTAB—position the cursor to a specific column of a line.
PRINT@—print at a specific relative position on the screen.
HOME or CLS—clear the screen and set the cursor at the upper left.

General design principles that apply to most display screens used for input include:

1. Clearly identify the specific data element that should be entered.
2. Display dots to indicate the number of characters to be keyed (Figure 7-6).
3. Indicate whether data should be alphabetic or numeric.
4. Leave plenty of space for maximum readability.
5. Verify each field as it is received and request reentry if data does not meet required form, length, or range of values.
6. Limit each screen to related fields of a single record, such as name, address, age, major, and other information about a student.

Design for Optical Scanning

Input may be sensed optically in many different forms. In this section, we will consider the location of the universal product code (UPC), the positioning of marks to be read optically, and the selection of type fonts for optical character reading.

Universal product code. The UPC is usually placed on the bottom of the container holding the product or near the bottom of the front or side panel. This placement enables the clerk at the checkout counter to draw the container past the sensing station without additional handling or turning. The sensing device on the scanner that reads the UPC is remarkably flexible. It can read the code straight, reversed, upside down, or from an angle. An audible beeper indicates whether the code was properly read.

```
                              MJC REGISTRATION                              0:35

                                                                           TYPE  R

ENTER:  SSN .........  YEAR/TERM ...

NAME:  ............................  ADDRESS:  ............................

CITY:  ..............  STATE:  ..  ZIP:  .....  PHONE:  ...  ...  ....

PROGRAM:  ....  ADVISOR:  ....  VETERAN:  .  VA BENEFITS:  .  GRADUATION:  .  OVERLOAD  .

    SEQ     AREA  NMBR  SEC     TITLE        HOURS  DAYS  START  END  ROOM  INST

   .....  .....  .....  ....  ..................  .....  .......  ....  ....  ....  ....

   .....  .....  .....  ....  ..................  .....  .......  ....  ....  ....  ....

   .....  .....  .....  ....  ..................  .....  .......  ....  ....  ....  ....

   .....  .....  .....  ....  ..................  .....  .......  ....  ....  ....  ....

   .....  .....  .....  ....  ..................  .....  .......  ....  ....  ....  ....

   .....  .....  .....  ....  ..................  .....  .......  ....  ....  ....  ....

   .....  .....  .....  ....  ..................  .....  .......  ....  ....  ....  ....

   .....  .....  .....  ....  ..................  .....  .......  ....  ....  ....  ....

   .....  .....  .....  ....  ..................  .....  .......  ....  ....  ....  ....

   .....  .....  .....  ....  ..................  .....  .......  ....  ....  ....  ....

   .....  .....  .....  ....  ..................  .....  .......  ....  ....  ....  ....

   .....  .....  .....  ....  ..................  .....  .......  ....  ....  ....  ....

   .....  .....  .....  ....  ..................  .....  .......  ....  ....  ....  ....

   .....  .....  .....  ....  ..................  .....  .......  ....  ....  ....  ....

   .....  .....  .....  ....  ..................  .....  .......  ....  ....  ....  ....

FEES:  REG ...... + SPEC ...... + SPF ...... - SCHL/WAIV ...... = TOTAL ......

HOURS:  CREDIT ......  LOAD ......                    PAY FEES BY:  .........
```

Figure 7-6. Visual display screen with dots showing number of characters in fields. This screen differs from many others in that it
can show up to 15 different detail lines representing courses
taken by a student.

Typically, the UPC contains 10 digits. Five indicate the manufacturer
and the other five designate the specific product of that manufacturer.

Optical mark sensing. Optical mark readers operate by reflecting a
beam of light off the paper containing the marks and measuring the
amount of light reflected. The mark absorbs some of the light so that the
reflection is not as intense as that in the unmarked areas of the paper. No.
2 pencils should be used for marking. Various inks reflect too much light so
that the mark is not correctly sensed. Other pencils do not deposit enough
graphite on the paper to be measured accurately.

Optical mark sensing requires precise positioning of the marks on the
form to be read. On the standard form used for test scoring (Figure 7–7)

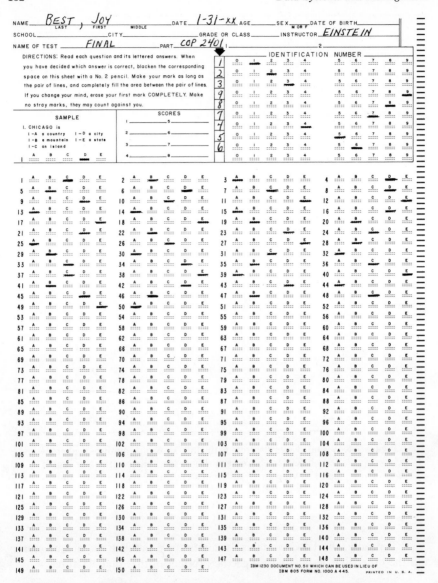

Figure 7-7. Standard form used for test scoring. Student responses are read by optical mark readers directly into computers, punched into cards, or recorded on magnetic tape.

there are four questions per line, with each question having five possible answers. Each of the 20 possible marks must be in a precise position. Any stray mark on the sheet will be misread. Timing marks along the right side of the sheet cause the light beams that sense the marks to be turned on as the answer sheet passes through the sensing mechanism.

Ink used for printing instructions, question numbers, and frames for the answers must be in a color of ink that the sensing device does not recognize. Colors usually chosen for background printing are light blue, green, red, or brown.

The input designer must know what machine is to sense the marks. Some machines sense vertical marks, some horizontal, and some circular. The number of marks per line and the spacing of lines varies according to the type of machine.

Optical character readers. A wide selection of type styles, or *fonts,* is available for printing characters to be read optically (Figure 7–8). The characters may be printed on pages, small cut forms, or continuous rolls of paper. The characters may be printed as output from cash registers, adding machines, typewriters, or computer printers. They are often used on turn-

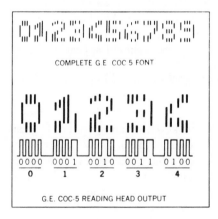

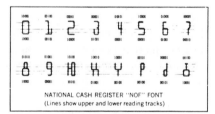

Figure 7-8. Optical character fonts. (Reprinted with permission of Datamation Magazine, Copyright by Technical Publishing Co., a Division of Dun-Donnelly Publishing Corporation, a Dun & Bradstreet Company, 1969, all rights reserved.)

around documents, on which bills printed by the computer and sent to a customer are returned by the customer with the payment to be read optically for input during the next processing cycle.

Some optical readers can read handwritten characters that are large, plain, block style, without connecting lines in clearly defined blocks on the input form.

Magnetic Ink Character Recognition

The banking industry is the major user of *magnetic ink character recognition* (MICR). Checks, deposit tickets, and other documents used for input are imprinted along the bottom $5/8$ inch of the form. A special style of type, called E-13B font, was designed for this purpose. It consists of 14 different characters, illustrated in Figure 7–2.

Figure 7–9 shows a layout form for designing checks using magnetic ink. Notice that the width of the document must be between 6 and $8^3/4$ inches and the height between $2^3/4$ and $3^2/3$ inches. No magnetic ink other than the prescribed MICR characters and symbols should appear in the $5/8$-inch band on the bottom edge of the form.

Identifying information about the bank and the customer number are printed on the checks before delivery to the customer. After the customer writes the check, the first bank receiving the check imprints the amount field using a magnetic ink encoding machine keyed by an operator. Thereafter, no manual keying or punching is necessary. Checks may be sorted by clearinghouse number and bank number on which the checks were drawn and amounts calculated by sensing the numbers by MICR sorter-readers. The bank on which the checks were drawn sorts on customer number to post the customer account and return the checks to the customer.

Card Design

Not many years ago the whole field of punched card design was considered a specialty in itself. Now, however, with the growth of different methods of inputting data into a computer, card design has become more a branch of form design. Cards are becoming more and more an integral part of other forms. Tab card sets, in which the first or the last copy of the set is a 51-column card while the other copies are paper, are used in such commonplace applications as credit card billing.

It is also possible to get continuous form cards in single or multiple parts, or printed side by side. Figure 7–10 shows a planning sheet for data on continuous cards to be printed side by side. Continuous form cards sets can come prenumbered and prepunched with a check number or other type of sequence number.

There are several types of cards in common use. The *transcript* card is one which is punched completely from another document and is used pure-

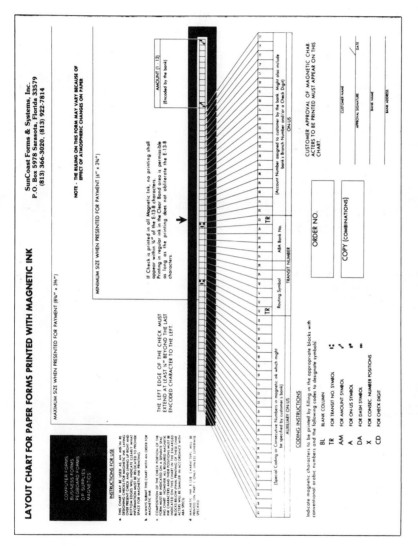

Figure 7-9. Layout chart for paper forms printed with magnetic ink. Maximum and minimum allowable sizes of the checks are indicated. (Courtesy of Suncoast Forms and Systems, Inc.)

185

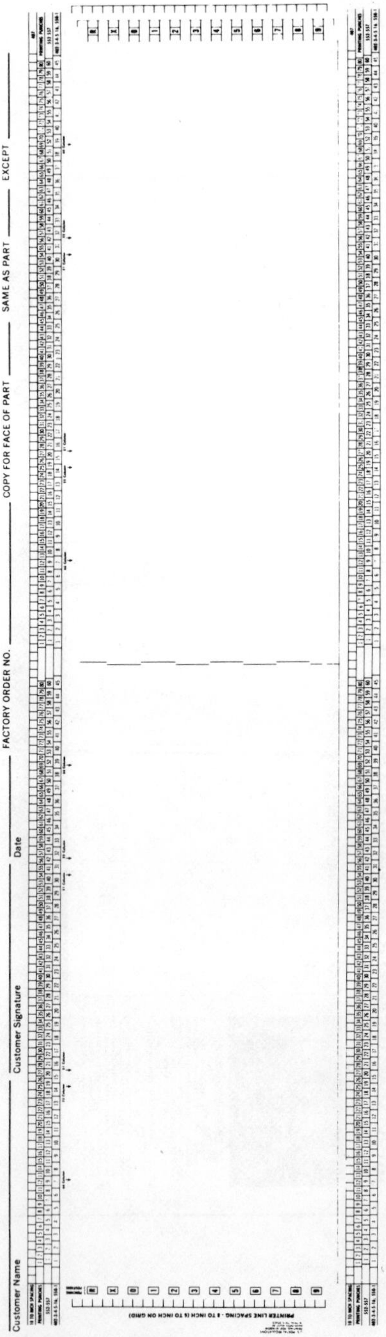

Figure 7-10. Continuous card tab layout form. Printing cards side by side (two-up) eliminates need for carbon paper. The multiple scales at top and bottom of the card provide spacing for many different types of machines.

ly for the purpose of entering information into a computer system. Of course, it may be further processed by sorting, collating, or reproducing.

The *dual* card is a source document which is printed or handwritten where a transaction occurs. Later, the data is keypunched into the same card for machine processing. It is very difficult for a keypunch operator to read a card which is being punched, because of the jerky motion of the card through the keypunch machine.

Mark sensing cards may be either dual or transcript type. They include small printed ovals or circles (called bubbles) which the respondent fills in with a pencil. Punching is done automatically by machines capable of reading the marks electrically or optically. This eliminates the need for separate key action by the operator.

The IBM *Port-a-Punch* card has deep scoring in each possible punching position of the card. With a special needle, the scored portion may be punched out manually. The Port-a-Punch card is sometimes used in such applications as elections, test scoring, or inventory control.

One popular use of punched cards is as *turnaround documents*. In this operation the computer punches or prints in optically readable characters on a card which is mailed to a customer or other addressee, who then returns the card with his or her payment, order, or whatever response is indicated. The card then may be read directly as input to the computer without keypunching or manual entry of data.

Among the optional features which affect the price of cards are striping at the top or at other points throughout the card, color of card stock, printing on both sides, and special punching or scoring. Figure 7–11 shows examples of different card types and design. Certain types of cards have marks, bar codes, or printed characters that may be read by optical readers. The spacing and location of the areas to be read are the critical considerations in designing this type of card. Indeed, the arrangement of data on a card is an important factor in all card design. Its sequence depends upon four things:

1. The location of identical data in other cards with which the new one will be processed
2. The sequence of data on the source document from which the card will be punched
3. The machines or programs to be used during processing
4. Manual operations in which the card will be used

As far as possible, information to be printed or interpreted on a card should be between the punching positions so that it will not be obliterated when the card is punched.

It is sometimes desirable to have punched information printed on the card from the keypunch itself or from a separate interpreter. In such cases, the top line above the 12 row of the card should be set up for keypunch spacing, 80 positions to the card, while the lower interpreting lines might be set up with 60 interpreter positions per card.

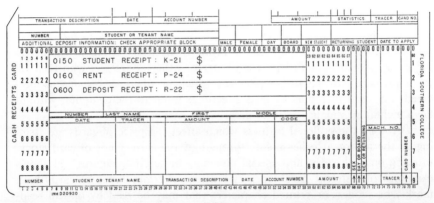

MARK SENSE

DUAL

OPTICAL MARKS

Figure 7-11. Specially designed punched cards. Each is designed to capture data from marks or handwriting placed on the card itself.

INPUT VERIFICATION AND CONTROL

Any data processing system is only as good as the original data on which it works. One aim of systems planning is to reduce the number of times when data must be recorded or copied between its origin and its final entry into a computer system.

The traditional way of producing input to a computer has been to record a transaction on some paper document, collect the source documents into batches, transmit them to the data processing department for keypunching, key verify the punched cards against the original documents, and read the cards into the computer. This is still a very common practice, and it may be the best obtainable for certain types of applications.

Magnetic tape encoding machines permit the same device to be used for both data recording and verifying. Another advantage of magnetic tape records is that they can be corrected in place, whereas punched cards have to be repunched and the erroneous card thrown away.

Optical character reading bypasses both the keypunching and key verifying steps. The original printed or handwritten documents are read directly into the computer under program control. Optical character readers, however, are very expensive and are not yet able to read all types of input documents.

Remote or local terminals may be attached directly to a computer or to an input device such as tape or disk. Data at the point of origin may be verified visually on the terminal printer or screen of the cathode ray tube. In some instances, data can be listed and proofread in order to give sufficient accuracy.

Limiting the number of persons who can originate data permits a higher degree of training, skill, and accuracy. However, a limited number of points of origin might produce bottlenecks that reduce production rates.

Where possible, it is good practice to have the person who made an error be responsible for correcting it. This calls the error to the person's attention and helps to prevent a repetition.

Control of Clerical Procedures

Certain practices are recommended to ensure that clerical operations associated with data processing are carried out accurately, promptly, and in a standard manner. One fundamental principle is to divide duties in such a way that one person's work serves as a check on the accuracy of another. For example, a cashier should receive money and record the amount received. A second person should post the receipt to the proper accounts and balance to the cashier's totals. A third person might be responsible for preparing the daily deposits, which must balance to previous totals.

The control of source documents can be aided by using prenumbered forms, color coding copies, validating documents with control numbers, or other similar techniques. A knowledgeable supervisor can detect many errors simply by scanning through documents prepared by a clerk. Good training and thorough understanding of procedures are important attributes of good control.

Check Digits

Various formulas may be used for calculating the check digit. One of the most common is called the Modulus 11. To demonstrate this formula let us assume a basic account number of six digits in addition to the check digit. A typical number might be 376-925-X, where X is the check digit. Since there will be seven digits in all, we assign weights to each digit, starting with 7 for the leftmost digit, 6 for the second digit, and so on. The calculation proceeds as follows:

1. Multiply each digit by its weight:

$$
\begin{array}{cccccc}
3 & 7 & 6 & 9 & 2 & 5 \\
\times\,7 & \times\,6 & \times\,5 & \times\,4 & \times\,3 & \times\,2 \\
\hline
21 & 42 & 30 & 36 & 6 & 10
\end{array}
$$

2. Add the products together:

$$21 + 42 + 30 + 36 + 6 + 10 = 145$$

3. Divide the sum by 11 and save the remainder.

$$\frac{145}{11} = 13 \qquad \text{remainder } 2$$

4. Subtract the remainder from 11. The difference is the check digit. $11 - 2 = 9$ (check digit). The complete account number is then 376-925-9.

In later processing for verification we multiply each digit by its weight, including the check digit with a weight of 1, add the products and divide by 11. If the remainder is 0, the entire number and check digit are correct.

A number of variations for calculating check digits is possible. One is to divide the entire number by a prime number such as 7 and use the remainder as the check digit. This would limit the check digits to the range of 0 through 6. Another is to multiply the first digit by 7, the next by 3, and the next by 1, and then repeat the cycle. The products are then added together and divided by 11 as shown above. The method selected should be convenient to use and should detect the most common types of errors, such as:

1. *Transpositions.* Where two adjacent digits are transposed, such as record-

ing 367 instead of 376, the check digit formula should generate a different check digit and thus reveal the error.

2. *Slide.* A slide results when the entire number is displaced by one position. This would result if an identification number started in column 4 of a card instead of column 5.

3. *Incorrect keying.* Common keypunch errors involve striking a 0 instead of a 3 or a 6 instead of a 3, since both numbers are punched with the ring finger of the right hand. Similarly, a 2 might be struck instead of a 5, or a 7 instead of a 4 on the keypunch.

4. *Incorrect shifting.* Incorrect use of the shift key on a keypunch would result in punching a letter U instead of a number 1 or a letter L instead of a number 6.

Control Totals

A very common means of verifying the accuracy of amounts in source data is to run an adding machine total from the original documents. This adding machine tape may then be compared with totals generated in entering the amount into the computer. If these *proof totals* agree, we normally can be assured that the proper figures have been entered. Occasionally, of course, there may be an offsetting error so that the proof total comes out correct even though the individual amounts are wrong, but such coincidences will be rare.

It is also possible to use *hash totals* as a method of verifying data. The term "hash total" is applied to the sum of account numbers, codes, or other types of numbers which normally are not accumulated. The sum of the student numbers of all persons in a class normally has no meaning, but it can be used as a means of verifying the accuracy of these numbers in the same way the proof totals are used for dollar amounts or quantities.

It is also common practice to count the number of records processed, the number of documents in a batch, or the number of cards punched. A *record count* does not ensure that the data is correct, but if any records are missing then certainly the batch or the file will not be correct.

In a real-time system using data transmission, *message counts* also may be kept as an aid toward verifying accuracy. If the number of messages received at the central processing station does not agree with the number of messages sent from one of the terminals, then we will know that data has been lost in the transmission.

Passwords

Data input from terminals requires special precautions. Often this data goes directly to create or update master files without the usual proving and balancing functions. Along with other forms of input verification mentioned in this chapter, *passwords* are often used to establish the identity of the data entry operator and to limit access to update programs.

Each person authorized to use a terminal is assigned a password, and sometimes a special password in addition for special security for especially sensitive programs. In addition, each program has its normal acquisition password and sometimes a secret password as well. Each program using the terminal must be able to determine that the correct password has been entered before the data will be accepted.

Provision must be made for passwords to be changed readily in case of a breach of security. It is no easy matter to maintain the secrecy that such passwords must have and still notify authorized users when a change is necessary.

CODING AND CLASSIFICATION OF DATA

Whatever type of data system we have, we must be able to identify each data item clearly, to classify it in connection with other similar data items, and to sort, retrieve, or otherwise process it by means of machines. In data processing, then, we make widespread use of codes, and a good portion of the system analyst's work is to develop, maintain, and analyze codes of various types.

A *code* may be defined as a brief title, composed of either letters or numbers, used to identify an item of data and to express its relationship to other items of the same or similar nature.

In developing codes, we must raise several questions:

1. Who originates the data and who else uses it?
2. What is the data used for, and in how much detail is it maintained?
3. How frequently is the data used, and what are the priorities of its users?
4. Is the data relatively permanent, or is it temporary and constantly changing?

Using the answers to these questions, we attempt to develop codes which will be expandable, precise, concise, convenient, meaningful, and operable.

Reasons for Coding

A good code should serve most or all of the following objectives:

1. *Uniqueness.* A large file of university students or of bank depositors may contain dozens of persons with the same name. A unique student number or customer number positively identifies the person in question.
2. *Brevity.* The codes M and F are shorter than the descriptions *male* and

female. Other codes may show an even more dramatic reduction in length.

3. *Speed.* Most machines are able to process coded data much more rapidly than they can handle the original descriptive information.

4. *Sequencing.* Codes may be assigned in such a way that data may be placed in any desired sequence. Codes may thus be assigned according to geographic area, frequency of use, cost, or any other desired sequence that bears no relationship to alphabetic order.

5. *Uniformity.* Codes make it possible to identify similar items, even though the terminology used to describe them may differ. Colleges and universities are attempting to work out uniform course numbering systems to facilitate transfer of credits from one institution to another. The federal job classification codes uniformly identify various occupations. Code numbers used on federal income tax and social security forms, such as W2, 940-A, and 1040, are familiar to almost all business people and many private citizens.

Coding Types

Codes may be numeric, alphabetic, or alphanumeric. Numeric codes may be further converted into binary, packed decimal, or octal codes to reduce storage space in computers or in magnetic files.

Numeric codes spring largely from unit record ancestry. Many of the original punch card machines were not able to handle alphabetic information, and those that could handle alphabetic data required additional operations. For example, sorting alphabetic data on a card sorter required two passes per column as compared with a single pass for numeric data. Numeric codes are still widely used, primarily for their convenience for showing the classification or hierarchy of related data items. The five-digit zip code is an example of a purely numeric code familiar to all United States' citizens.

Binary codes are especially useful in conserving space in large files of data. Most present-day computers use an 8-bit code to represent one decimal number, letter, or special character in storage. Considering the eight bits as a binary number, it is possible to represent 256 distinct codes as separate combinations of 0s and 1s. In 16 bits, or two storage locations, 65,536 different codes may be indicated. Any numeric code can readily be converted to binary form by computer instructions. Where used, such codes can offer savings of 40 to 65 percent over the storage required to use the codes in straight decimal form.

Purely *alphabetic* codes offer symbols which are readily recognized as abbreviations or mnemonic codes for the terms for which they stand. For example, the two-character abbreviations of the state names are used almost uniformly in connection with the zip code by large business organizations. Days of the week appear on many college class schedules as MTWRF. Assembler language programmers readily recognize that MVC, LR, and A are mnemonic computer operation codes meaning "move characters," "load register," and "add," respectively.

Alphanumeric codes take one of two forms. Either certain characters of the code are always alphabetic or always numeric, or both numbers and letters may appear in any position. Many state license numbers have adopted alphanumeric codes to derive a larger number of unique codes using fewer positions. For example, by using four numerals we can get only 10,000 distinct codes, 0 through 9999. By using the 10 numbers and 26 letters in each of the four positions we have a total of 36^4, or 1,679,616, unique codes, in the same amount of space.

Methods of Assigning Codes

The *serial* method of coding is the simplest to use and apply. It is simply the assignment of consecutive numbers, beginning with 1, to a list of items as they occur. This method, almost universally used for numbering checks, invoices, and other documents, may also be applied to numbering students or employees.

Serial coding makes no provision for classifying groups of like items, nor does it permit alphabetizing except where the items were in alphabetic order when the numbers were originally assigned. The advantage of the serial code is its ability to code an unlimited number of items using the fewest possible digits. A serial code that uniquely identifies one item may be combined with other types of codes which classify and place in sequence.

Block coding is a minor modification of serial coding in which a series of consecutive code numbers is divided into blocks, each block of numbers being reserved to identify a group of items having some common characteristic. For example, in coding hand tools, codes 1 through 15 might be applied to different types of pliers, 16 through 30 to hammers, 31 to 45 to wrenches, 46 to 60 to saws, and so forth.

Group classification codes are those which designate major classification with the high order digits and intermediate and minor classifications by the successive lower order groups of code digits. The length of the code or the number of groups depends upon the refinement of classification desired. Many accounting systems are based upon a code structure where a high order digit of 1 represents assets, 2 liabilities, 3 capital accounts, 4 through 6 income accounts, and 7 through 9 expenditure accounts (Figure 7-12). One powerful feature of modern computers is the ability to construct codes from virtually any field within a set of records, assigning one field as the major group for one sorting or processing operation and another group as the major group for another processing step.

Significant digit codes are those in which all or some of the code digits describe weight, dimension, distance, capacity, or other characteristics of

```
1000    ASSETS

1100       Current Assets
1101          Cash in Office
1102          First City Bank
1105          Notes Receivable
1110          Accounts Receivable
1150          Merchandise Inventory

1200       Deferred Assets
1205          Prepaid Rent
1210          Prepaid Insurance

1500       Fixed Assets
1510          Land
1520          Buildings
1530          Plant Equipment
1540          Office Equipment

2000    LIABILITIES

2100       Current Liabilities
  .
  .

2500       Long-term Liabilities
  .
  .

3000    EQUITY ACCOUNTS
  .
  .
```

Figure 7-12. Group classification code. The leftmost digit indicates the major classification. Digits to the right indicate successively lower classifications.

the items themselves. For example, the code TSRWE78-14 might describe an automobile tire, steel-belted radial, white sidewall, size E78-14.

Final-digit coding is a technique which uses the last digit of a code to indicate some simple separation of items in a classification. Large private telephone switchboards commonly are assigned numbers ending in zero; additional direct lines coming through the switchboard then end in the digits 1 through 9.

Extracted codes are used widely by magazine publishers and direct mail houses to convert names and addresses into codes which can be sorted to facilitate mail distribution. For example, the zip code might make up the first five digits of the extracted code, four low-order digits of the street number the next four, the first three characters of the street name as the initials as the final two characters of the code. When sorted in this sequence, the address labels are grouped in a way that greatly expedites the delivery of the mail.

Standardization of Codes

Wherever possible, it is convenient to use codes developed by someone else. Doing so facilitates interchange of data between organizations and saves a tremendous amount of systems time. Certain computer user groups, trade associations, federal and state governments, and educational institutions have banded together to develop uniform codes.

The state of Florida has developed a uniform course numbering system for all public colleges and universities in the state. The first three codes are alphabetic to reflect the discipline or area of specialization, while the last four digits are numeric to give the specific content of the course within the discipline. The first of the four numeric digits gives the level at which the subject is taught. For example, AMH 1010 would indicate American History taught at the freshman level.

The National Commission for Higher Education Management Systems (NCHEMS) has done extensive work in developing a program classification structure for higher education. It is a method of dividing all college activities into primary programs, such as 1.0 Instruction, 2.0 Research, and 6.0 Institutional Support. Then each primary program may be further subdivided into subprograms, categories, and sectors. Instructional programs are classified down to the level of the individual course section. Figure 7-13 shows a segment of this code.

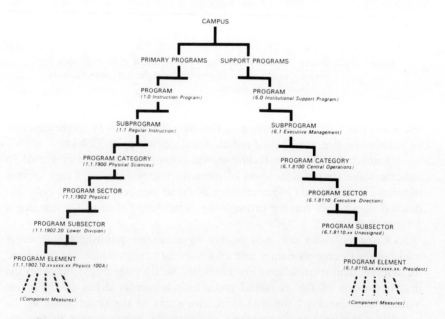

Figure 7-13. Program classification structure nomenclature. This group classification code is widely used by colleges and universities to group together various revenues and expenditures.

The federal and state governments provide standard codes to be used by their agencies and subdivisions in maintaining records and making reports.

Dates may be coded in various forms. While the most common form is month, day, and year (12/25/80), showing the year first (80/12/25) permits more convenient sorting and comparing. The Julian date, showing year and day of the year (80/360) is being commonly used for its ease in computing elapsed days.

The 24-hour clock, also called military time or European time, elimates the need for A.M. or P.M. designations. It also simplifies the calculation of elapsed time.

Proper names are almost universally arranged last name first, then first name, then middle name or initial, and finally the suffix such as Jr. or III. Apostrophes, hyphens, and blanks are customarily omitted in surnames. This arrangement permits names to be sorted in strict alphabetic sequence. A relatively simple computer routine can rearrange the names so that the last name appears last for addressing or check writing if desired.

Before sorting long fields of alphabetic data became practical by computer, numeric codes were often assigned to permit proper names to be arranged into alphabetic sequence without sorting on the names themselves. Some remnants of this practice may still be found. It is especially helpful with names of customer or vendor organizations where the most important keyword in the name for alphabetic purposes is not the first word of the name.

SUMMARY

Input devices and media may be used online or in batch data entry. Online devices include keyboards with display screens and optical scanners. Batch devices include magnetic ink character readers, punched card systems, and key-to-storage devices.

Keyboard terminals are classified as dumb, smart, or intelligent depending upon the number of functions they can do. Point-of-sale terminals permit data to be captured at the source and transmitted directly to the computer. The acoustic coupler permits a terminal to gain access to a central computer from any telephone.

Optical scanners can read marks or characters. The universal product code is widely used in stores to identify a product and its manufacturer. The reading wand, resembling a pencil, may be used to sense optical characters. Optical characters may be printed on pages, small cut forms, or continous rolls of paper.

Magnetic ink characters are widely used in banking. The E13-B font identifies the bank, the customer, sometimes the check number, and the amount of the check. The magnetic ink characters appear on the bottom $\frac{5}{8}$ inch of the check or deposit ticket.

Punched cards may contain 80 columns or 96 columns. Cards may be designed in sets of multiple parts or manufactured side by side. Transcript cards, dual cards, mark-sensing cards, and Port-a-Punch cards are some of the varieties available. Key-to-storage systems record data on magnetic tape, disk, or diskette. They are faster to use than cards and more compact to store. Printed tapes and punched paper tape may provide other forms of input.

Input to terminals is often in the form of lists, with items separated by commas or other delimiters. Batch input is usually in the form of records, with each record having fields containing the various data elements. Records may be fixed-length or variable-length.

Good screen design often employs a menu, from which the operator chooses programs or options by entering a single letter or digit. The program should prompt the operator to make the proper entry at each stage of input.

Input data should be thoroughly verified at the time of entry. Generally, those who enter data should be responsible for correcting it. Check digits are calculated on the digits of an identification number to verify their correctness. Proof totals, hash totals, and record counts are methods to verify the accuracy of batches of input data. Passwords identify users of terminals and protect access to programs and files.

Coding and classification of data are necessary to permit data to be processed effectively through modern machines. Numeric, alphabetic, and alphanumeric codes all have their uses in data systems. Standardization in the use of codes makes the transfer of data easier between different organizations and agencies.

TERMS FOR REVIEW

Acoustic coupler	Group classification code
Alphanumeric code	Hash total
Block code	Hollerith card
Check digit	Intelligent terminal
Code	List
Control total	MICR
Cursor	Optical character recognition
Delimiter	Optical mark sensing
Dumb terminal	Optical scanner
E13-B font	Point-of-sale terminal
Extracted code	Prompt
Field	Reading wand
File	Record
Final-digit code	Serial code
Fixed-length record	Significant digit code

Smart terminal	Transposition
Touchtone telephone	Universal product code
Transcript card	Variable-length record

QUESTIONS

1. What are the two major categories of data entry devices and media? Name some of the devices in each category.
2. What determines whether a terminal is dumb, smart, or intelligent?
3. What is the purpose of the acoustic coupler? How does it work?
4. What applications use the universal product code? How is it read or sensed?
5. What are the advantages of optical scanning versus keying as a means of data entry? What are the disadvantages?
6. Compare the relative merits of key-to-storage systems with those of punched cards.
7. What are some considerations in design of input screens?
8. Compare and contrast the relative characteristics and advantages of optical mark sensing and optical character recognition.
9. What industry makes wide use of magnetic ink character recognition? Where on input documents are the MICR characters placed?
10. Calculate check digits using the Modulus 11 method described in the text for account numbers 147-239, 111-111, and 753-249.
11. Name some of the types of control totals and show how they are used in input control.
12. What are some of the reasons for using codes rather than full descriptions of data elements?
13. Calculate how many unique automobile license numbers can be assigned using only alphabetic characters in the first three positions and only decimal digits in the last three.

CASE STUDY
SUNCOAST COMMUNITY COLLEGE

Data entry to the alumni master file comes from four sources:

1. The original master record will be extracted by batch processing from the student master file. A file creation program will be written to read the student master file and create an alumni record for each graduate. Gerald Phipps, in consultation with Neal McGill,

Dean of Admissions and Records, estimates that there are between 11,500 and 12,000 graduates. Oddly enough, the exact number has not been determined because of the fact that some students receive two degrees. A nonduplicated count has not been made.

2. A second source will be a batch addition to the alumni master file following each graduation period. Students are graduated in December, May, June, and July, although graduation exercises are held only in May. The additions will also include students already in the file who may be receiving a second degree.

3. A record will be added to the master file each time a nongraduate makes a first contribution to Suncoast. As the record is created in the donor file, the master file is checked to see if it contains a record for the donor. If it does not, the alumni master record is built from data elements extracted from the student master file and inserted into the alumni master.

4. Changes to the alumni master file are to be made online from a terminal in the Office of Institutional Advancement. Since most data in this file is historical, changes are expected only to name or address.

SCREEN DESIGN

Input to the donor file will be exclusively by online terminal from the Office of Institutional Advancement. Phipps designs a screen to facilitate creation and updating of the donor record each year (Figure 7-14). Social Security number is the key to the donor record. When this number is entered, identifying information from the master record is displayed. The data entry operator then enters the appropriate data for one or more donations. Each subsequent access of the record will show any previous contributions and will position the cursor in the proper position to add later gifts.

The basis for data entry is a handwritten receipt prepared by the cashier in the Business Office. The cashier is responsible for original recording of all cash receipts. One copy of the receipt form goes to the terminal operator in the Business Office and two copies to the Office of Institutional Advancement. One of these latter two copies is used to update the donor record. The other is sent to the donor with a letter of thanks.

CODING OF DATA

Receipt numbers are standard five-digit sequential codes assigned the Office of Institutional Advancement.

The code for the purpose of the gift is a group classification

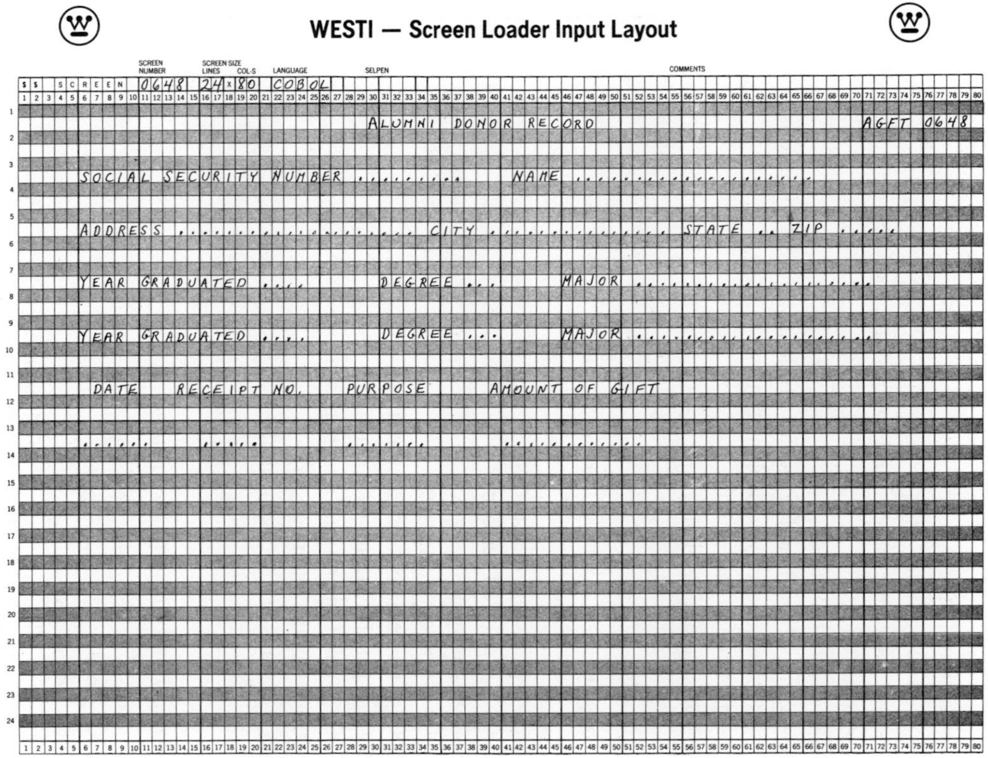

WESTI — Screen Loader Input Layout

Figure 7-14. Display screen for updating donor record. The upper four lines print data from the alumni donor record. Data about new gifts is entered on the bottom line from the terminal keyboard.

201

code in two parts. The first digit gives the fund number (general fund, restricted, endowment, and so forth) and the next four indicate the project or department for which the gift is intended, such as varsity basketball or student scholarships. The last three digits give the object classification, such as buildings, equipment, or personal services.

Code for fund:

    1—general fund
    2—restricted fund
    3—auxiliary enterprises fund (bookstore, food service)
    4—loan fund
    5—scholarship fund
    6—agency fund (funds held for students and organizations)
    7—unexpended physical plant fund
    8—debt retirement fund
    9—investment in plant fund

Major categories for the project or department:

    1000—academic instruction
    2000—organized research
    3000—community service
    4000—academic support
    5000—student services (counseling, activities)
    6000—general administration
    7000—plant operations and maintenance
    8000—student financial aid
    9000—transfers between funds

Major categories for object classification code:

    100—assets
    200—liabilities
    300—capital accounts and fund balances
    400—revenues
    500—personnel expenditures
    600—general current expenditures
    700—capital outlay
    800—unassigned
    900—unassigned

QUESTIONS AND EXERCISES

1. List the four sources of data entry to the alumni master file.
2. Draw a systems flowchart for the procedure for preparation and recording of contributions.
3. Is proper separation of duties observed in handling cash receipts?
4. Prepare a segment of the object classification code for personnel expenditures. Allow for division into such categories as full-time faculty, part-time faculty, administrative salaries, clerical and support personnel, contractual payments, and contributions to retirement fund. Include as many expenditures directly related to personnel as you think appropriate.

8

SEQUENTIAL FILE DESIGN AND PROCESSING

OBJECTIVES

At the end of this chapter, you should be able to:

1. Define each basic term used in this chapter relating to files.
2. Describe file characteristics such as volatility and activity.
3. Differentiate between file maintenance and file processing.
4. Give characteristics of each of the major file storage devices.
5. Name and describe the principal methods of file organization.
6. Describe file labels and tell their purpose.
7. Calculate the capacity of disk tracks and files for records of different sizes and blocking factors.
8. Give the principal features of an input/output control system.
9. Describe the principal techniques for updating sequential files.
10. Describe techniques for searching sequential tables and files.
11. Name and describe methods for sorting sequential files.

Human beings cannot remember everything they need to know and use in going about their daily work. A computer also has a limited capacity in its central storage, or memory. There must therefore be some organized way of calling in information as needed, processing it, and storing the results back where it can again be retrieved later as needed.

THE NATURE OF FILES

When we collect data and organize it for a particular purpose, we term it a *file*. The file may be thought of as an extension of memory, whether for an individual or a computer. It may be *temporary* or *permanent*, depending upon its retention time. It may be a *static* history file, recording a single event that has occurred, or a *dynamic* status file, showing changing balances, averages, or other conditions.

Files may use different devices as well as different media. Each separate input/output device attached to a computer is classified as a file. Paper, cards, film, magnetic tapes, and disks are commonly used as media for files.

Data is organized in a regular hierarchy ranging from its smallest elements to its largest, most complete structure. The terms used to describe the different levels of the hierarchy are fairly well standardized.

File Terminology

In computer systems, the smallest unit of data is the *bit*, or binary digit. A bit can have a value of either 0 or 1. It is represented mechanically or electronically in a number of ways. Bits are combined in sets of 6 or 8 to form *bytes* representing digits, letters, or special characters, or in larger sets of 16, 24, 32, or 64 to represent large binary numbers, called *words*.

The *character*, or *byte*, is the smallest unit of data that can be manipulated in many high-level programming languages. In manual systems the character is the smallest unit into which data is subdivided.

Bytes or characters are combined into *fields*, or *data elements*. Examples are names, Social Security numbers, descriptions, or other meaningful combinations. The general, or generic, term associated with a field is called a *data element*, such as a name or address, while the specific value stored in the data element is a *data item*, such as John Smith or 10 Downing Street.

Data elements are combined into *records*. A record is defined as a collection of data elements related to a common identifier, or key. The key may be a person, place, or any other piece of information which the data element describes. We should distinguish between the *logical* record, which consists of all those data elements that have a logical relationship to each other, and the *physical* record, which is made of all data which is actually read or written in a single machine operation. Several logical records usually are grouped together to form a physical record, or *block,* to permit more efficient use of magnetic tape or disk devices.

A collection of records organized for some particular purpose is called a *file.* The term *file* may refer to a physical unit, such as a cabinet or drawer, or to the collection of data within the physical unit. The term *data set* is often used as a synonym for file.

A reel of magnetic tape or a magnetic disk pack which may contain files is referred to as a *volume.* For small to medium-sized files it is customary to use a single volume, or reel, for each file. Larger files require more than one reel to contain them, and are called multivolume files. In a few cases, more than one file might be placed on a single tape volume, which would then be called a multifile volume. Magnetic disk packs nearly always will have more than one file on a single volume, although they too may require more than one pack, or volume, for very large files.

The identifier which uniquely identifies a record is called the *key.* For convenience in handling, keys are frequently numeric in form, even though they stand for alphabetic information. For example, a Social Security number is a more appropriate key for a payroll file than a name because more than one person may have the same name. Similarly, numeric codes frequently are used for inventory items, bank customers, magazine subscribers, or any of the other logical entities which are likely to have records in a file.

File Purpose

The chief purpose for which files are designed and organized is to make the information contained therein available when and as needed. The number and types of data elements selected to make up the record depend upon the purpose for which the file is intended. A simple mailing address file needs to contain only name, street, address, city, state, and zip code. A more generalized mailing file might include such elements as codes for occupation, level of education, political or religious affiliation, income, number of members in family, type of automobile, or other descriptive information. Such a file could then be used for selective mailing to reach a particular class or type of addressee.

Data in files is a valuable resource that can be subjected to the same type of treatment as other resources. It can be catalogued, inventoried, generated, stored, handled, retrieved, copied, validated, corrected, and destroyed just like other materials. To be useful, data must be accurate, timely, in the right form, at the right place, and with clear meaning. As defined in Chapter 1, *data* consists of raw facts; it becomes *information* when it is combined into meaningful form. The two terms will be used more or less interchangeably in this chapter relating to files.

For our purposes, information can be classified into at least three types:

1. Operational information needed in the day-to-day conduct of the business.
2. Management information to provide the basis for both current and long-range decision making.
3. Information required for governmental reports, tax records, and other statutory purposes.

File Characteristics

In addition to the purpose for which the file is to be used, there are other characteristics to be considered in planning both the manner in which the file is to be organized and the manner in which it is to be processed. Among these are volatility and activity.

Volatility refers to the addition and deletion of records from a file. A *static* file is one that has a low percentage of additions and deletions, such as the membership of the Baseball Hall of Fame, where two or three members are added each year and no one is deleted. A *volatile* file is one that has a high rate of additions and deletions, such as the residents of a hotel or the passengers on an airplane. A highly volatile file requires either that a large amount of unused space be allowed for records to be added, or else that the file be constantly rearranged to keep the active records in the proper sequence.

Activity refers to the number of records actually processed or updated during a single run through the entire file. Activity is considered from three standpoints: (1) percentage, (2) distribution, and (3) amount.

The percentage of the records in a file having activity has an important bearing on how they should be accessed. All the students in a college receive a grade at the close of the semester. A high percentage of the bank patrons having checking accounts write checks frequently throughout the month. Where most of the records in a file have activity in one processing run, the records normally are accessed one after another and posted or bypassed as appropriate. If the percentage of activity is very low, it is a waste of time and effort to access every record in the file and some means should be devised to select only those records that require updating.

The distribution of activity refers to the fact that some records in the file may have a high percentage of activity while others may have little activity. In an inventory, some items may be received and issued many times daily while other items move slowly or at only certain times of the year. The most active items in the file should be placed where they can be accessed most readily.

The amount of activity refers to the frequency with which the file is used. In some cases 100 percent of the records of a file may have activity only once a year. Even a large file so seldom used can be kept in punched cards or even in some manual form. Other files may have a high percentage of use daily or even more often. Such files should be on tape or disk so as to take advantage of rapid processing time.

Record Length

Records in a file may be organized several different ways with respect to length. The most common method and the easiest to use is a single record of *fixed length.* Where records of up to several thousand characters can be conveniently stored and processed, this method is very satisfactory. Fixed-length records can be blocked so that each block is also of fixed length, except the last block, which may be shorter.

Variable-length records permit each record to have a different number of bytes. Usually the first four bytes of the record are reserved to designate its length. The term *repeating structure* refers to a system in which a segment of the record is of fixed length, followed by a variable number of additional fixed-length segments. For example, in an accounts receivable application, the fixed portion of the record might contain customer number, name, address, and other descriptive information, while a variable number of segments is used to describe each invoice number, date, and amount due.

FILE STORAGE DEVICES AND MEDIA

As defined earlier in this chapter, a file may consist of a physical unit or of the data contents of the unit. We may also think of the file as being made up of the *media* on which the data is recorded, such as paper documents, punched cards, magnetic tape, or magnetic disks. Here we will review some of the principal features of the media and devices which hold files in magnetic form.

Magnetic tape devices typically hold two tape reels, one for the tape to be read or written on and the other for takeup. The tape, typically ½ inch wide and from 800 to 2400 feet long, passes by one or two read-write heads between the reels at speeds ranging from 37.5 to 200 inches per second. There are either seven or nine channels running the length of the tape to correspond with the number of bits per character on the computer system. One of the channels is used for a parity bit. Bits recorded in the remaining channels are interpreted as numbers, letters, or characters. The recording density of the bits ranges from 200 to 6250 bits per inch. The speed of data transfer between the tape unit and internal storage depends upon both the tape speed and the recording density.

Records may be of any length that may be practically contained in internal storage of the computer. Logical records normally are blocked to make the physical record as long as practicable. Between each block there is an interblock gap, usually about ½ to ¾ inch in length. A tapemark is a special physical record of only one character written at various places in the file to indicate the start of the file, the end of identifying labels, the end of the file, or the end of the volume. (On IBM System/370 computers a tapemark is represented by one byte containing a 0 bit followed by seven 1 bits, or hexadecimal number 7F.)

Magnetic tapes can accommodate massive files and are feasible wherever records have a high percentage of activity. They can be processed only sequentially.

Other forms of magnetic storage can be grouped under the general heading, *direct-access storage devices* (DASD). Of these the most common are magnetic disks and drums. *Disks* may be fixed in place or arranged in interchangeable packs. Because of their great flexibility, packs have become more common than fixed disks. Disks resemble phonograph records which are mounted rigidly upon a central core or shaft, with about ½ inch of space between each disk. Disks are most commonly arranged in stacks of 6 or 11 to the pack; because the top and bottom faces of the pack are not used for recording magnetic data, the packs provide 10 or 20 recording surfaces. Data is recorded in concentric tracks, usually with 100 or 200 tracks to each disk surface. The tracks located directly above one another on the various disk surfaces jointly constitute a *cylinder,* so that there are as many cylinders per pack as there are tracks per surface. Figure 8-1 shows a disk pack.

Magnetic read-write heads for disk units are arranged in an assembly in such a way that, without moving the assembly, the heads can read or write every track on a given cylinder. To move to the next adjacent cylinder, however, either the assembly must move, or *seek,* to that cylinder or there must be another circle. Sectors typically consist of 100 or 200 characters, and from one to all the sectors on a cylinder may be read or written at one time.

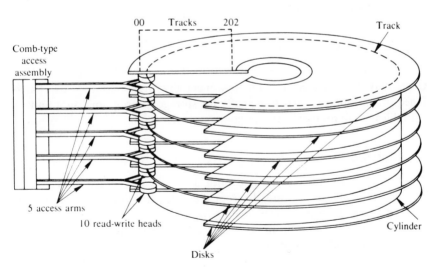

Figure 8-1. Disk organization of IBM 2311 access mechanism. All the tracks directly above one another constitute a cylinder. The entire cylinder can be read without moving the read-write heads. (Courtesy of International Business Machines Corporation.)

Magnetic *drums* provide faster access than disks because they usually have separate read heads for each track. Tracks run around the outside of the drum surface. Drums are not interchangeable, so they usually are used for frequently referenced data, such as tables, programs, or subroutines.

All DASD units require that gaps be left between the blocks of data recorded on the tracks. The length of the gap must be taken into account when computing the number of records that may be placed on a track.

METHODS OF FILE ORGANIZATION

There are at least five principal methods of organizing a file: (1) sequential; (2) partitioned; (3) indexed; (4) indexed sequential; and (5) direct, or random.

Sequential Files

In a sequential file, records are organized purely on the basis of their successive physical location in the file. In most cases the records are arranged in a sequence based on their keys, but records may be in a file in chronological order or in no particular order at all. It usually is not possible to find an individual record without examining all the records that precede it physically in the file, or to delete or add records without rewriting the entire file. Sequential organization is most effective for files having a high percentage of activity.

Partitioned Files

A partitioned file is one that is divided into several members, each of which may have many individual sequentially organized records. Partitioned organization is used principally for storage of programs, subroutines, and tables in connection with operating systems.

Indexed Files

Indexed files must be created on a direct access storage device, since it must be possible to go directly from the index to the appropriate record in the file without reading all preceding records.

Records need not be in sequence when the file is created. As each record is built and added consecutively to the file, an index is made which contains the key to each record and its disk address. After all records are written, the index is sorted in sequence by key.

Records may later be added to the main body of the file in any order. However, the index need to be sorted again after new entries are made to reflect the added records.

Indexed files are discussed more fully in Chapter 9.

Indexed Sequential Files

Indexed sequential (IS) organization, which can be used only with direct-access storage devices, combines the advantages of both sequential and random processing. The essential features of IS files are:

1. A prime data area of records which must be in sequence according to their keys.
2. One or more indexes which permit individual records to be located without reading the entire file.
3. One or more separate overflow areas where records are placed when additions are made to the file.

Indexed sequential files are discussed more fully in Chapter 9.

Direct (Random) Files

The direct (random) method of organization is based upon some predictable relationship between the key to the record and its location within the file. In its simplest form—which is rarely possible in practice—the key would be the address of the disk location where the record is placed. With this system, the location of the record is known as soon as the key is known, so that the record can be read directly.

In actual practice, the key is usually subjected to some type of calculation which produces the address where the record should be placed. A common practice is to divide the key by the number of tracks in the file, take the remainder, and add it to the location of the first track in the file to produce the track where the record should be written or read.

Direct files are discussed more fully in Chapter 9.

CONTROL IN FILE PROCESSING

In processing files, we must be certain that we are reading the correct file, that we do not overwrite existing files, and that we can recover and restart if processing is interrupted because of power failure or machine malfunction.

In this section we will consider two features that contribute to control in file processing: (1) file labels and (2) checkpoint records.

File Labels

In processing files, we must be able not only to identify each record within the file and each field within the record, but also the file itself. Decks of cards or rolls of paper tape customarily are placed in boxes or trays and labeled with paper stickers or marked with ink or crayon as to the contents of the file. Most computer systems nowadays use cards and paper tape primarily for input only, with both transaction and master files on magnetic tape or disk.

Labels on magnetic files are both exterior and interior. An *exterior* label of gummed material is placed on the outside of the volume—that is, the disk pack or reel of tape which is the physical unit handled by the operator—to tell the operator the name of the file, the date of creation, whether or not it is to be retained, its expiration date, and other details.

The *interior* label is recorded magnetically on the tape or disk just as data is. Interior labels may be read or written by the programmer as the program is executed, or they may be processed by the operating system as a part of the input/output control system (IOCS).

It is possible on either tape or disk to have a single file on one volume, several files on one volume (multifile volumes), or large files requiring several volumes (multivolume files). Each volume normally has its own label, which uniquely identifies it quite apart from any file which it may happen to contain. The volume label normally is recorded when the volume is first placed into use and not changed throughout its life. Figure 8-2 shows the standard volume label used by the IBM Disk Operating System.

On magnetic tape it is customary to use a *header* label preceding the data records of a file and a *trailer* label following the last data record for the file in addition to the volume label, which is normally the first thing written on the tape. The contents of the header and trailer labels for a file are the same, except that the block count of data records appears in the trailer label only and the character HDR are used to identify the header lable and either EOF (end of file) or EOV (end of volume) to identify the trailer label. The content of the standard tape file label may be seen in Figure 8-3. Users may design and process their own labels in any way they wish, either in place of or in addition to the standard labels processed by the IBM Disk Operating System.

On magnetic disk files, as well as on drums and magnetic cards, the file labels are not physically located with the data area of the files. They are in a separate area called the *disk directory* or *volume table of contents.* Because each record on a disk file can be individually addressed, the label contains the highest and lowest addresses, or *extents,* used by the file. It is therefore possible to check that a new file being created will not overlap an existing file that is still active. Other data included in the standard file labels for direct access storage devices are the type of file organization, creation and expiration dates, key and record lengths, number of extents for the file, upper and lower limits of each extent, and other identifying data.

Figure 8-4 shows the standard file label for direct-access storage devices used by the IBM Disk Operating System. Labels with other formats are used for the master or cylinder index for indexed sequential files, for files having more than three extents, and for the disk directory (volume table of contents) itself.

Other manufacturers having other operating systems use labels of dif-

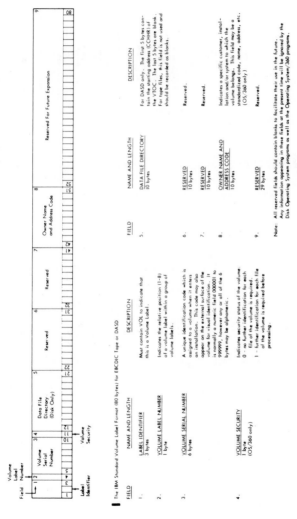

The IBM Standard Volume Label Format (80 bytes) for EBCDIC Tape or DASD

FIELD	NAME AND LENGTH	DESCRIPTION
1.	LABEL IDENTIFIER 3 bytes	Must contain VOL to indicate that this is a Volume Label.
2.	VOLUME LABEL NUMBER 1 byte	Indicates the relative position (1-8) of a volume label within a group of volume labels.
3.	VOLUME SERIAL NUMBER 6 bytes	A unique identification code which is assigned to a volume when it enters an installation. This code may also appear on the external surface of the volume for visual identification. It is normally a numeric field 000001 to 999999, however any or all of the 6 bytes may be alphameric.
4.	VOLUME SECURITY 1 byte (OS/360 only)	Indicates security status of the volume. 0 - no further identification for each file of the volume is required. 1 - further identification for each file of the volume is required before processing.

FIELD	NAME AND LENGTH	DESCRIPTION
5.	DATA FILE DIRECTORY 10 bytes	For DASD only. The first 5 bytes contain the starting address (CCHHR) of the VTOC. The last 5 bytes are blank. For tape files, this field is not used and should be recorded as blanks.
6.	RESERVED 10 bytes	Reserved.
7.	RESERVED 10 bytes	Reserved.
8.	OWNER NAME AND ADDRESS CODE 10 bytes	Indicates a specific customer, installation and/or system to which the volume belongs. This field may be a standardized code, name, address, etc. (OS/360 only.)
9.	RESERVED 29 bytes	Reserved.

Note: All reserved fields should contain blanks to facilitate their use in the future. Any information appearing in these fields at the present time will be ignored by the Disk Operating System programs as well as the Operating System/360 programs.

Figure 8-2. Standard volume label, tape or DASD. Volume labels are normally recorded on the tape or disk only once and never changed. (Courtesy of International Business Machines Corporation.)

The IBM standard tape file label format and contents are as follows:

FIELD	NAME AND LENGTH	DESCRIPTION
1.	LABEL IDENTIFIER 3 bytes, EBCDIC	identifies the type of label HDR = Header -- beginning of a data file EOF = End of File -- end of a set of data EOV = End of Volume -- end of the physical reel
2.	FILE LABEL NUMBER 1 byte, EBCDIC	always a 1
3.	FILE IDENTIFIER 17 bytes, EBCDIC	uniquely identifies the entire file, may contain only printable characters.
4.	FILE SERIAL NUMBER 6 bytes, EBCDIC	uniquely identifies a file/volume relationship. This field is identical to the Volume Serial Number in the volume label of the first or only volume of a multi-volume file or a multi-file set. This field will normally be numeric (000001 to 999999) but may contain any six alphameric characters.
5.	VOLUME SEQUENCE NUMBER 4 bytes	indicates the order of a volume in a given file or multi-file set. This number must be numeric (0000 - 9999). Multiple volumes of an output file will be numbered in consecutive sequence.
6.	FILE SEQUENCE NUMBER 4 bytes	assigns numeric sequence to a file within a multi-file set.
7.	GENERATION NUMBER 4 bytes	numerically identifies the various editions of the file.
8.	VERSION NUMBER OF GENERATION 2 bytes	indicates the version of a generation of a file.

FIELD	NAME AND LENGTH	DESCRIPTION
9.	CREATION DATE 6 bytes	indicates the year and the day of the year that the file was created: Position — Code — Meaning 1 — blank — none 2-3 — 00-99 — Year 4-6 — 001-366 — Day of Year (e.g., January 31, 1965 would be entered as 65031).
10.	EXPIRATION DATE 6 bytes	indicates the year and the day of the year when the file may become a scratch tape. The format of this field is identical to Field 9. On a multi-file reel processed sequentially, all files are considered to expire on the same day.
11.	FILE SECURITY 1 byte	indicates security status of this file. 0 = no security protection 1 = security protection. Additional identification of the file is required before it can be processed.
12.	BLOCK COUNT 6 bytes	indicates the number of data blocks written on the file from the last header label to the first trailer label, exclusive of tape marks. Count does not include checkpoint records. This field is used in trailer labels.
13.	SYSTEM CODE 13 bytes	uniquely identifies the programming system.
14.	RESERVED 7 bytes	Reserved. Should be recorded as blanks.

Label fields layout:

Label Identifier / File Label Number	File Identifier	File Serial Number	Volume Sequence Number	File Sequence Number	Generation Number	Version Number of Generation	Creation Date	Expiration Date	File Security	Block Count	System Code	Reserved
1, 3, 5	6	3 / 21 22 / 27 28	31 32	35 36	39 40 41	42	47 48	53 54	55	19 09	13 73 74	80

Figure 8-3. Standard tape file label. The header (HDR) label precedes data records in each file, and the end-of file (EOF) label follows them. (Courtesy of International Business Machines Corporation.)

214

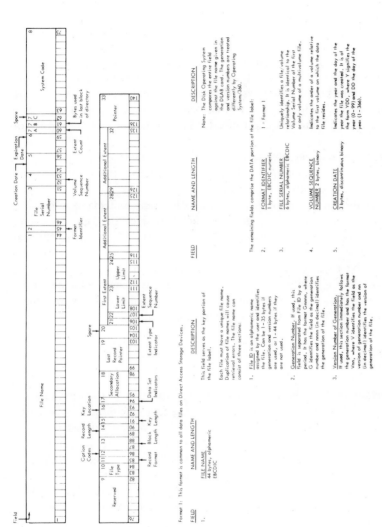

Figure 8-4. Standard DASD file labels, format 1. DASD labels are physically apart from disk files and appear in the disk directory, or volume table of contents (VTOC). (Courtesy of International Business Machines Corporation.)

215

ferent formats and content. Many of them require only a file name or identifier. The operating system takes over all details of determining the number
of extents required and the exact addresses assigned to each file.

Checkpoint Records

With computer programs requiring extremely long processing time or
several hours of printing, provision is often made to take checkpoints at
various intervals throughout the run. A checkpoint consists of writing out
the contents of all or a part of storage, together with the content of certain
files, at a certain point in processing. The checkpoint records normally are
written on magnetic tape or a sequential disk file. In some instances, checkpoint records may be interspersed directly in output files written on tape or
disk.

The purpose of the checkpoint record is to enable the program to be
restarted in the event of power failure or other interruption without having
to rerun the entire job from the beginning.

Where files are updated in place, as with online systems, it is possible
that certain records have been modified on disk since the last checkpoint
was taken. It is necessary to make the records in the file return to the status they had at the time of the last checkpoint. One way to do this is to
maintain a log of all transactions that occur. A special routine must be
used to back out all transactions that occur after the checkpoint up to the
point of interrupt. Then the program can be started with files and main
storage in agreement as of the time of last checkpoint.

CALCULATING FILE CAPACITY

An important part of the file design and organization is to determine the
optimum size of each record and the blocking factor to produce the maximum utilization of disk space. For example, if a disk is organized with sectors containing 512 characters, and our records have a length of 256
characters, we can block two records and use all of the available disk area.
But if we plan our records to be 260 characters, we can get only one record
per sector and waste 252 positions, almost half of the available amount.
Where the sector is the basic addressable unit, some systems do not allow
the block length to exceed sector length.

It is also necessary to know with some accuracy the number of
records in the entire file. If the extent allocated to the file is too small, it
will soon fill up and require reorganization. If the extent is too large, valuable disk space is wasted. Even where the operating system automatically
allocates space for a file as needed, the retrieval may be complicated and
slowed because the file is spread out among a number of disconnected extents.

Where the track is the principal addressable unit on disk, gaps are left between blocks of data on the track. Gaps also may appear between the different parts of the block. For example, IBM's Disk Operating System requires that each block have an address marker, a count area, and a data area. In addition it may have a separate key area (see Figure 8-5). The gap between each of these areas varies somewhat with the specific device used as well as with the length of the key or the block. Special formulas are available that enable the system designer to compute the number of records of various sizes, with or without separate keys, that may be fitted into a track on each of the devices.

From Figure 8-6, we may calculate the number of records per track, per cylinder, and per drive for the IBM 3348 disk. For example, assume that 150-byte unblocked records are to be recorded without separate key fields. By following down the left-hand column, we can find that 26 logical records per track will fit. In fact, we could still get 26 records even if the length were increased to 161 bytes. From the same row, we find we can get 312 records per cylinder, 108,576 records per Model 35, and 217,152 records per Model 70.

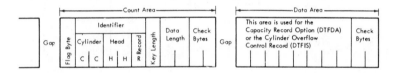

Schematic Representation of Record Zero

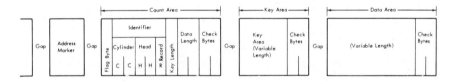

Schematic Representation of a DASD Record with a Key Area

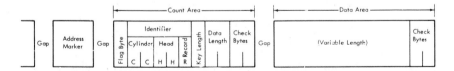

Schematic Representation of a DASD Record without a Key area

Figure 8-5. IBM disk track organization with and without separate key area. Sequential files normally do not have a separate key field; indexed sequential and direct files normally do have a separate key. (Courtesy of International Business Machines Corporation.)

NUMBER OF BYTES						NUMBER OF RECORDS			
Without Keys			With Keys						
Max. per record	Per 3348		Max. per record	Per 3348		Per track	Per cylinder	Per 3348	
	Mod. 35	Mod. 70/70F		Mod. 35	Mod. 70/70F			Mod. 35	Mod. 70/70F
8368	34,944,768	69,889,536	8293	34,631,568	69,263,136	1	12	4176	8352
4100	34,243,200	68,486,400	4025	33,616,800	67,233,600	2	24	8352	16704
2678	33,549,984	67,099,968	2603	32,610,384	65,220,768	3	36	12528	25056
1966	32,840,064	65,680,128	1891	31,587,264	63,174,528	4	48	16704	33408
1540	32,155,200	64,310,400	1465	30,589,200	61,178,400	5	60	20880	41760
1255	31,445,280	62,890,560	1180	29,566,080	59,132,160	6	72	25056	50112
1052	30,752,064	61,504,128	977	28,559,664	57,119,328	7	84	29232	58464
899	30,033,792	60,067,584	824	27,528,192	55,056,384	8	96	33408	66816
781	29,353,104	58,706,208	706	26,534,304	53,068,608	9	108	37584	75168
686	28,647,360	57,294,720	611	25,515,360	51,030,720	10	120	41760	83520
608	27,929,088	55,858,176	533	24,483,888	48,967,776	11	132	45936	91872
544	27,260,928	54,521,856	469	23,502,528	47,005,056	12	144	50112	100224
489	26,546,832	53,093,664	414	22,475,232	44,950,464	13	156	54288	108576
442	25,841,088	51,682,176	367	21,456,288	42,912,576	14	168	58464	116928
402	25,181,280	50,362,560	327	20,483,280	40,966,560	15	180	62640	125280
366	24,454,656	48,909,312	291	19,443,456	38,886,912	16	192	66816	133632
335	23,782,320	47,564,640	260	18,457,920	36,915,840	17	204	70992	141984
307	23,076,576	46,153,152	232	17,438,976	34,877,952	18	216	75168	150336
282	22,375,008	44,750,016	207	16,424,208	32,848,416	19	228	79344	158688
259	21,631,680	43,263,360	184	15,367,680	30,735,360	20	240	83520	167040
239	20,959,344	41,918,688	164	14,382,144	28,764,288	21	252	87696	175392
220	20,211,840	40,423,680	145	13,321,440	26,642,880	22	264	91872	183744
204	19,593,792	39,187,584	129	12,390,192	24,780,384	23	276	96048	192096
188	18,842,112	37,684,224	113	11,325,312	22,650,624	24	288	100224	200448
174	18,165,600	36,331,200	99	10,335,600	20,671,200	25	300	104400	208800
161	17,480,736	34,961,472	86	9,337,536	18,675,072	26	312	108576	217152
149	16,800,048	33,600,096	74	8,343,648	16,687,296	27	324	112752	225504
137	16,019,136	32,038,272	62	7,249,536	14,499,072	28	336	116928	233856
127	15,380,208	30,760,416	52	6,297,408	12,594,816	29	348	121104	242208
117	14,657,760	29,315,520	42	5,261,760	10,523,520	30	360	125280	250560
108	13,981,248	27,962,496	33	4,272,048	8,544,096	31	372	129456	258912
99	13,229,568	26,459,136	24	3,207,168	6,414,336	32	384	133632	267264
91	12,540,528	25,081,056	16	2,204,928	4,409,856	33	396	137808	275616
84	11,926,656	23,853,312	9	1,277,856	2,555,712	34	408	141984	283968
76	11,108,160	22,216,320				35	420	146160	292320
70	10,523,520	21,047,040				36	432	150336	300672
63	9,734,256	19,468,512				37	444	154512	309024
57	9,045,216	18,090,432				38	456	158688	317376
51	8,306,064	16,612,128				39	468	162864	325728
46	7,683,840	15,367,680				40	480	167040	334080
41	7,019,856	14,039,712				41	492	171216	342432
36	6,314,112	12,628,224				42	504	175392	350784
31	5,566,608	11,133,216				43	516	179568	359136
26	4,777,344	9,554,688				44	528	183744	367488
22	4,134,240	8,268,480				45	540	187920	375840
18	3,457,728	6,915,456				46	552	192096	384192
14	2,747,808	5,495,616				47	564	196272	392544
10	2,004,480	4,008,960				48	576	200448	400896
7	1,432,368	2,864,736				49	588	204624	409248
3	626,400	1,252,800				50	600	208800	417600

Figure 8-6. Track capacity table. To get five physical records per track, records without keys may be as long as 1540 bytes. With keys, they cannot exceed 1465 bytes. The gap between the key and data fields takes up space that could otherwise be used for data. (Courtesy of International Business Machines Corporation.)

If we place the 150-byte logical records in blocks of 10, the physical record length becomes 1500. Now from the fifth row of the table we find we can get five physical records per track, or 50 logical records, compared with 26 per track for unblocked records. Blocking the records has almost doubled the number of bytes that can be stored on each track, because there are fewer gaps between physical records.

If our 150-byte unblocked record includes a separate key field of, say, 8 bytes (data length = 142, key length = 8), we can get only 21 records per track because of additional disk space taken by the gap between the key area and the data area for each record.

Sometimes the file designer has little control over the size of a logical record, which is dictated by file content and the amount of related data that must be kept together. But he or she can alter the number of logical records that are combined to make one physical record, or block, in order to get the most efficient space utilization on the track.

Special calculations are required for indexed sequential files. The prime data area contains the track index on the first track of the cylinder, the prime data area on some tracks, and the cylinder overflow area on still other tracks. The records in each of the three areas are of a different size. The calculations of space requirements in thus more complex for this type of file. Formulas are available to compute the number of records for each type of track.

CLASSIFICATION OF FILES

Files may be classified according to use. An *input* file is an existing one from which records are read into the computer for processing. Input files may very well come from one medium, such as punched card or magnetic tape, when the output from processing goes to some other device, such as a print line, another tape unit, or a terminal device. Input files are sometimes called *source* files.

Output files, sometimes called *destination* files, are those which are written out onto some device after some input and processing have taken place. One very common way of processing sequential files is to read one input file, called a *master* file; to read one or more separate input files, designated as *transaction* files; to apply the transactions to the master file; and then to create a separate output file, which becomes a *new master* file for later processing.

This method is sometimes called *father-son* processing where the old master file is the father and the new master file is the son. Most devices accommodating sequential files use the father-son method of updating.

Each time a new master file is created it is considered a new generation. Consequently, the generation preceding the present "father" file is called the "grandfather" file. It is customary to retain the latest three generations of each master file in order to be able to recreate the current one in the event it is destroyed or lost for any reason. Even if both the newest "son" file and the preceding "father" file are destroyed, it is possible to recreate them if the "grandfather" file and all transaction files that occurred since it was created are still available.

A very few sequential files, principally those on magnetic disk, permit updating directly on the old master file. The same file is both the input and the output file; hence it is called an *I/O* file, or *source-destination* file. A punched card may also be a source-destination file if updated information is punched back into an unused field of the original input card. Normally it is not possible to change the size of a record in a source-destination file because the bytes of data which are added to the original length would overlap into the next adjacent record.

A *piggyback* file is a special type of destination file which permits records to be added onto the end of an existing file. First the end-of-file marker of the original file is located, then records are added on the end, and finally a new end-of-file symbol is recorded. Not all operating systems or languages accommodate piggyback files.

Work files are those which may be processed as an extension of main storage. The usual procedure is to write out data on a device such as a magnetic tape or disk, and later to read this information back for further processing. Intermediate results or temporary data developed at one stage of processing can thus be available for later processing. Work files may be retained from one job to the next, or they may be deleted at the end of the job if no longer needed.

Checkpoint records may form a special type of file. In some operating systems they are called *rescue dumps* or *breakout records.* Checkpoints are a special form of data storage which preserve the contents of internal registers, the program being executed, certain data files and tables, or other information that permits a program to be restarted at a given point if it is interrupted for any reason. Checkpoints normally are taken during very long processing runs involving the printing of hundreds of records or several hours of processing time. In the event of some unanticipated interruption because of power failure, equipment trouble, damage to printed forms, or other cause, processing may be restarted at the checkpoint rather than from the beginning of the entire job.

MAINTENANCE AND PROCESSING OF SEQUENTIAL FILES

File *maintenance* is the term that describes creating a file, adding or deleting entire records, or deactivating a file. *Processing* or *updating* refers to inserting, modifying, adding to, or deleting fields of data within the record. In short, file maintenance changes the number of records in a file, while processing changes the content of the records.

The best managerial practice normally dictates that maintenance and updating operations be separated. It can readily be seen that a checking account record, for example, should be created and placed in the active file before checks are drawn upon it.

Usually, it is impractical to try to put everything that relates to a particular record in the file. There are practical limits to the amount of data that can be stored and even more restrictions on the ease with which it can be retrieved later for any useful purpose. Files therefore usually are classified as either master or transaction files.

Master files contain relatively permanent identifying or descriptive information about the record. They also contain cumulative totals and data about current status. They normally do not attempt to retain all the individual transactions or postings that produced the present totals or balances.

Transaction files contain information about specific events that have some effect upon master files. Transactions include such events as the receipt of cash, the sale of a commodity, the issuance of a paycheck, or the making of a hotel reservation. Transaction files normally are created in the order of occurrence, but they may be sorted into some other sequence for processing.

There are two principal methods of processing files: (1) sequential and (2) random, or direct. The *sequential* method—sometimes called *consecutive* —requires that transactions be batched for a certain period of time, sorted into the same sequence as the key of the master file, and then processed against the master file. Punched card or magnetic tape files can be processed only sequentially. Disk files also may use sequential processing effectively. This method, in which every record in the master file must be read, is efficient for files having a high percentage of activity. If there is no transaction, the old master record is written out unchanged in a new master file. If there are any transactions, they are added to the old master and the new updated master is written out. Because transactions must be in the same sequence as the master file, usually only one master file can be updated at one time. Transactions must be resorted on another key in order to be applied against another master file.

Sequential files require less sophisticated hardware and software than do other types.

Random, or *direct*, processing takes transactions in the order in which they occur and applies them against every master file that is affected by the transactions. Random processing requires a capability of locating and reading any record in the file about as readily as any other. After updating, the record is rewritten into the same location on the disk. No other records are affected in the file until another transaction occurs.

Sequential files are most commonly arranged in ascending order according to one field in each record of the file designated as the key. Records may be sorted before the file is created, or the file may be created in any order and later sorted into the proper sequence by key. Sequential files may be created on different media and devices. With many types of equipment only sequential files may be processed. The chief characteristic of sequential files is that each record must be processed starting at the beginning and continuing serially through the entire file. Punched cards, paper tape, magnetic tape, paper documents read optically, and magnetic ink documents are examples of files that can be processed only in sequential fashion. Likewise, printed output is considered to be a sequential file where each line is a separate record within the file.

DATA MANAGEMENT SYSTEM

Nearly every modern computer system includes data management routines, sometimes called input/output control systems (IOCS), as a part of its operating software. There are two levels of IOCS: *physical* and *logical*. Physical IOCS is used by all programs run within the system. It provides for executing commands from the central processing unit to the I/O channel to start and stop I/O operations, to test for the completion of the transfer of data, to handle interruptions, and to test for error conditions.

Logical IOCS consists of macroinstructions and routines which serve as a link between the user's programs and physical IOCS. Macroinstructions are single statements used by the programmer that call forth a whole group of statements that either define characteristics of a file or specify what processing steps shall take place. Some of the functions of logical IOCS are:

1. To request execution of appropriate channel programs by physical IOCS
2. To handle end-of-file and end-of-volume conditions
3. To block and deblock records
4. To switch between input/output areas when more than one area is specified as a file buffer

File Definitions and Specifications

In most computer languages, the programmer supplies some or all of the following information about each file in the form of parameters to certain macroinstructions:

1. File name used in the program
2. I/O device type
3. File organization structure
4. Access method
5. Record format and size
6. Number and location of I/O areas
7. Location and size of key fields
8. Type and content of labels
9. Error options
10. Other optional information

In RPG and NEAT/3, this information is entered by the programmer on file specification sheets from which cards are punched in a rigid format and incorporated in the user's program. COBOL requires certain entries in the ENVIRONMENT DIVISION of each program to specify file device type, structure, access method, and key information. Other entries in the

DATA DIVISION define the block and record length, type of file labels, and names of fields within records.

Assembler language provides for including some or all of this information as parameters in DTF (define the file) macroinstructions. Some of the devices that may be used for sequential processing include:

DTFCN—console typewriter
DTFCD—card read punch
DTFPR—line printer
DTFMT—magnetic tape
DTFPT—paper tape
DTFOR—optical reader
DTFMR—magnetic ink character reader
DTFSD—sequential direct-access storage device (disk, drum, or magnetic card)

BASIC and FORTRAN usually provide standard file definitions automatically for such devices as the display screen, card reader, or printer, and no definition statements are required by the programmer.

In using magnetic tape or direct-access storage devices, it is customary to block several *logical* records together to make one physical record. Because the block is the amount of data which is always physically transferred between main storage of the computer and the input/output device, fewer such transfers are required, thus expediting the speed of program execution. Blocking reduces the number of interrecord gaps on magnetic tape or direct-access devices, thus allowing utilization of a higher percentage of the magnetic storage.

In defining internal storage, it is necessary to have one or more *I/O areas* large enough to transfer a block of data physically between the device and storage. Defining more than one I/O area permits internal processing to proceed with one of the blocks while a second block is being read into or written from storage. It is further possible to define a *work area* for processing an individual logical record from the block of data in the I/O buffer area.

Thus the I/O area is normally the size of one physical block and the work area is the size of one logical record. For certain types of output files, the I/O area must include additional bytes for special disk control purposes, the key field when written separately from the rest of the data, or the length indicator for variable-length records.

Sequential Processing Instructions

In this section we will describe some of the most common processing macros and the operations which they perform on files of different types and characteristics.

Open. Before any file can be processed it must first be opened. In some languages files are automatically opened if the programmer does not issue the specific instruction. OPEN tests that the specified device is turned on, ready, and not busy with another job. For magnetic tapes, it positions the tape at the load point marker. If an input tape is labeled, the OPEN reads the header label and compares it with label cards in the job control stream. For output labeled tape, OPEN first checks to be sure that there is not a previous unexpired label on the tape reel, then writes the new label as supplied through job control, writes a tapemark, and positions for the first data block to be written.

For direct-access storage devices, all of which must be labeled, OPEN examines the disk directory, or volume table of contents, compares both label and extent with information supplied through job control, and positions the read-write head at the beginning of the data area. For output files, OPEN verifies there is no overlap of unexpired files, enters the label and extent information in the disk directory, and positions the read-write head at the beginning of the data area on disk.

Close. CLOSE is issued to deactivate a sequential storage device. Normally, once a device is closed, it cannot be read or written until it has been reopened. CLOSE usually deactivates an output file by writing the last block from the output area, an end-of-file record, and output trailer labels if any. For magnetic tape files, CLOSE provides whatever rewind option has been specified in the file definition. As a general rule, when a file has been closed and then reopened, the device is repositioned to the first record in the file. Some systems permit a file to be reopened for a different purpose from the original. For example, an output file may be closed and then reopened and processed as an input file in the same program.

Get. The GET macro, or READ statement in many languages, is the main way by which a programmer gets access to a record in a file. The first GET issued transfers a physical block from the device to the I/O storage area specified. If the records are to be processed directly in the I/O area, the address of the first record in storage is placed in a special register so that the data within the record can be properly addressed. If a work area is specified, the first logical record in the block is transferred to the work area.

Figure 8-7 shows the effect of GET on blocked records without a work area. Figure 8-8 shows processing with GET using a work area.

The next GET in processing blocked records does not read additional data from the device. Rather, it places in the I/O register the address of the second record within the block so that it can be processed or, if a work area is being used, it moves the second record into the work area for processing. Only when sufficient GETs have been issued to process all the records in the first I/O area will the next block be transferred from the I/O device into storage.

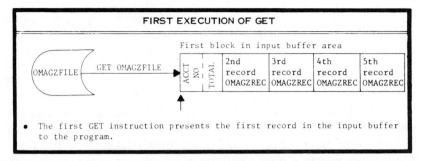

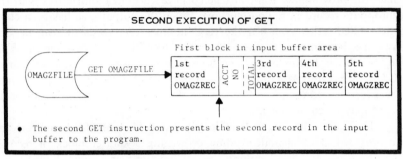

Figure 8-7. Processing blocked records without a work area. Each successive GET moves a pointer to the next record in the block in the input buffer area. (Courtesy of NCR Corporation, Dayton, Ohio.)

We thus can see that by using logical IOCS, the programmer is able to concentrate purely on the content of a single logical record without regard to modifying addresses in registers, counting the number of records per block, or actually determining when to transfer an additional block to storage. When a GET macro encounters the end-of-file character, an auto-

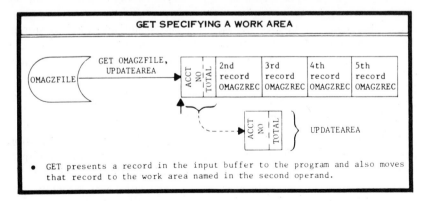

Figure 8-8. Processing blocked records with a work area. Each successive GET moves the next record in the block to the work area for processing. (Courtesy of NCR Corporation, Dayton, Ohio.)

matic branch is taken to the address which the user has designated as the name of the end-of-file routine. If a GET reaches the end-of-volume on either magnetic tape or disk before encountering end-of-file, it initiates automatic volume switching to the new volume so that processing may continue.

Put. The PUT macroinstruction, or WRITE statement in some languages, places a logical record into an output file in either of two operations: *move* or *locate*. In the move operation, PUT takes the logical record which the programmer has constructed in a work area and moves it to the appropriate record in the output area. When the output area has been completely filled—that is, when the total number of records making up one block has been moved to the I/O area—then PUT transfers the block to the I/O device. In the locate operations, which is used without a work area, PUT does not move the logical record into the output area, but places into a register the address of the segment of the I/O area where the next logical record may be constructed.

There are other sequential file processing functions for which macros are provided. They include reading or writing a shorter block of records than the usual one and handling control functions on various I/O devices, such as rewinding, spacing, or backspacing tape; skipping or spacing the printer to a new page or line; and selecting stackers for cards or documents.

UPDATING SEQUENTIAL FILES

As indicated earlier in this chapter, the usual way of updating sequential files in the father-son technique, whereby a new version of the old master file is created after applying transactions, additions, and deletions to the old file.

Source-destination files on punched cards and direct-access storage devices may be updated by rewriting the updated master record directly over the old master record. Usually, the rewrite technique does not allow the size of the record to be changed or records to be added to the file.

Father-Son Technique

Normally, only one master file is updated at one time, but multiple transaction files may be applied against the master during the same processing run. Transactions should be sorted into the same sequence as the master file before starting the update run. The father-son technique presumes that no two master records will have the same key, but that multiple transactions may have the same key.

Processing proceeds as follows:

1. A record is read from a transaction file.
2. A record is read from the master file.
3. The keys of the master and transaction records are then compared. If the keys are equal, the transaction is added to or subtracted from the master record and a new transaction is read.
4. If the key of the master record is lower than the key to the transaction file, the master record is written to the new master, or *son* file, and the next master record is read.
5. If the transaction key is lower than the master key, it indicates either that there is a new record to be added to the master file or that an error occurred. As mentioned earlier, additions to the file normally are kept separate from update activities.
6. This processing continues until all the transactions have been applied against all of the master records. As a normal situation, not all of the master records will have transactions during a single processing run. Those having no activity are written unchanged on the new master file. There may also be multiple transactions on a single master record.

When reaching the end of either the master or transaction file, place all 9s in the key field for that file. This will simplify the logic of programming. It is not necessary to have separate logic to handle the remaining records when either file reads its end-of-file signal. All unprocessed records on the master file will continue to be written out because they will have a key lower than the 9s on the transaction file. Similarly, remaining transactions will compare lower than the 9s on the master file and will be processed as usual. Processing may terminate when master and transaction keys are equal and either contains 9s. Figure 8-9 shows the logic for father-son processing of a sequential file.

Rewrite Technique

A record from punched card files or from direct-access storage devices (DASD) can be read, processed, and transferred back to the same storage location or card from which it was read. An unblocked physical DASD record or card is transferred to main storage by a GET instruction. After the record is processed, the next PUT instruction causes the updated physical record to be written back in the same disk location or punched in the same card from which it was read. If records are blocked, the next PUT instruction does not actually result in a rewrite to the physical device, but simply sets up an indication for the next GET instruction, which accomplishes the transfer.

A GET instruction must always precede a PUT instruction, and only one PUT can be issued for each record. If a particular record does not require updating, the PUT instruction may be omitted.

If no PUT instruction is issued for an entire block of records, this in-

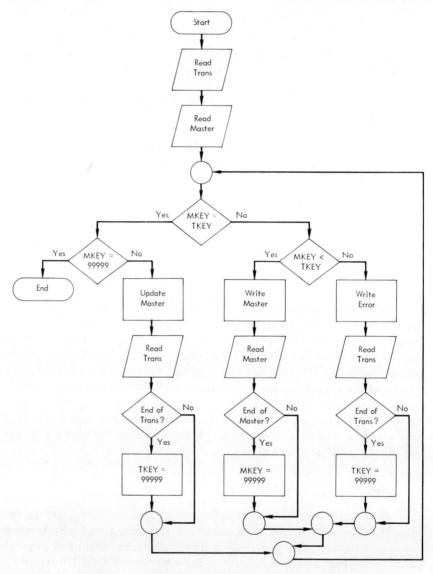

Figure 8-9. Logic for father-son processing. The father file represents the old master file. The son file is the new version of the master file. Records are updated whenever the key to the transaction file matches the key to the master file.

dicates that the original block has not been changed in any way, and no rewriting takes place for that particular block.

The proper entries must be supplied in the file description to use the rewrite technique for updating.

SEARCHING TECHNIQUES

Four methods of searching a table for a particular key may be applied to the problem of retrieving a particular record from a file. The programming for a search in core is simpler than the search of a file, but the principles remain the same. The four methods of search are (1) sequential, (2) spaced sequential, (3) probability, and (4) binary.

The *sequential* search is the most commonly used method. If the table is not in sequence, each item in the table must be examined until the desired item is found or the end of the table is reached. With this method the maximum number of compares is the number of items in the table, and the average number to find any given item in the table is half that number. If the table is in ascending sequence, the problem may be shortened slightly. As soon as a key in the table is found that is higher than the argument (the key being searched for), we know that the item is not present and the search can be discontinued.

The *spaced sequential* method moves a little more quickly toward items that may be located higher in the table. Instead of comparing every item in the table, every tenth key is compared with the search argument. When a key is found higher than the search argument, we back up nine items and then move forward one item at a time until we find the desired item or determine that it is not present.

The *probability* search requires special arrangement of the table so that items are placed in the table in order of their expected frequency of occurrence. If determining the relative frequency of the different table items has been done correctly, the table item most often used will be placed first in the table and will be located on the first compare. The second most frequently used reference item will placed second and will be located with only two compares.

The *binary* search requires that the table be in ascending sequence. The maximum number of compares is 2 raised to whatever power gives one the number of items in the table. A table of 16 items requires only four compares, since $2^4 = 16$. A table of 256 items requires only eight compares, since $2^8 = 256$.

Using this method one begins the search with the center item of the table. If the search argument is higher than the key of that item, the lower half of the table can be discarded and the search continues with the center item in the upper half. Each successive compare discards half of the remaining table until the desired item is found or is determined to be not in the table.

Figure 8-10 shows a generalized BASIC routine using a binary search technique. Note that there are two ways to terminate the search: (1) to find a key in the table which agrees with the search argument, and (2) to narrow the search down to the point where the highest location still to be searched in the table is lower than the lowest location to be searched.

```
200 LET L = 1                           'SET LOW RANGE
210 LET H = N                           'SET HIGH RANGE    ,
220 LET M = INT ((L + H) / 2)           'CALCULATE MIDPOINT
230 IF X(M) = K OR H < L THEN 280       'DOWHILE X(M) <> K AND H >= L
240   IF X(M) < K THEN LET L = M + 1    '   IF KEY LOW, RAISE LOW RANGE
250   IF X(M) > K THEN LET H = M - 1    '   IF KEY HIGH, LOWER HIGH RANGE
260   LET M = INT ((L+H) / 2)           '   CALCULATE NEW MIDPOINT
270 GOTO 230                            'END OF DOWHILE LOOP
280 IF H < L THEN 310                   'IF X(M) = K
290   PRINT K, Y(M), Z(M)               '   THEN PRINT TABLE DATA
300 GOTO 320                            'ELSE
310   PRINT K; "NOT IN TABLE"           '   PRINT ERROR MESSAGE
320 RETURN                              'RETURN TO MAIN PROGRAM
```

Figure 8-10. Binary search technique in BASIC. The binary search is the fastest searching method. A table of 1000 elements can be searched using only 10 comparisons.

The power of the binary search is dramatically revealed when we see that for a table of 1000 items straight sequential searching would require a maximum of 1000 compares and an average of 500. Binary searching would require only 10 compares.

SORTING AND MERGING TECHNIQUES

Many types of files can be processed only sequentially. When reports are to be prepared in some sequence other than the one in which the file was originally organized, it becomes necessary to sort the file on some other element of data rather than its original key. Even where it is possible to access records directly, without regard to their original sequence, it still is frequently helpful to sort the records for particular report purposes.

Let us first examine some basic terms used in sorting. Most files originally are organized in sequence by a particular *key*, or *identifier*. For example, social security number would be a logical key for personnel or payroll records. However, for specific reports it might be desirable to sort the personnel or payroll records into order by department, pay classification, rate, or some other sequence. The field that contains the desired classification then becomes the key on which the records are sorted. The key is normally a numeric code, although it may be alphabetic description. Numeric data can be organized in binary, signed decimal, unsigned decimal, or character format. It is important to know the exact form in which the key is expressed so that the proper compare instruction can be given in sorting the file.

The *sequence* of sorting normally is ascending order but it may be descending. The sequence depends in part on the coding structure designed for the particular computer. For example, the IBM System/370 computer considers numbers to have a higher collating sequence than letters, whereas the NCR Century series considers letters to be higher in collating sequence than numbers.

A *string* is a series of keys in the desired sequence. The string is broken whenever a key is out of the desired sequence and a new string begins. For example, the keys 1, 6, 9, and 4 constitute two strings, the second string beginning with 4 which is lower in sequence than the preceding 9.

The collection of items of keys or records to be sorted makes up an *array*, or *table*. Each entry in the array or table is referred to as an *element*, or *item*. A *subscript* is used to designate which item in the table is referred to.

A *pass* consists of a series of inspections whereby all items in the table are compared, or all items not previously placed in sequence are compared to determine what changes of sequence still need to be made.

An *interchange*, or *swap*, refers to the changing of position between two items in a table. Because most sorting techniques will take place in core storage of a computer, and because moving into a storage location destroys the previous contents of the location, it is necessary to use a *save area* large enough to hold one record whenever records are interchanged.

Sorting Methods

It is possible to use any one or a combination of many different methods of sorting data. Two methods described here are relatively easy to understand and to code in application programs.

Bubble sort. The bubble sort, or *exchange method,* works in this fashion to place records in ascending order by key. The first key is compared with the second and the records are interchanged if the first key is higher than the second. Then the second key is compared with the third and each successive adjacent pair of keys is compared, interchanging records where necessary. When the next-to-last key is compared with the last key the first pass is complete. This procedure tends to push the highest key to the last position in the table on the first pass, the next to the highest key to the next to last position on the second pass, and so forth.

For each successive pass, we may make one less compare than we made for the preceding pass. The last pass requires comparing only the first and second items in the table and interchanging them if necessary.

It is necessary to keep track during each pass whether or not an interchange was made. Because two adjacent items in the table are always being compared, if a complete pass can be made with no interchange required, no further sorting is necessary and the file is in sequence.

Suppose that we begin with keys in an original sequence of 54, 69, 23, 41, and 37. Pass 1 proceeds as follows:

Compare No.	*Positions*	*Values*	*Interchange*
1	1 and 2	54 and 69	No
2	2 and 3	69 and 23	Yes
3	3 and 4	69 and 41	Yes
4	4 and 5	69 and 37	Yes

The first pass will always require one less comparison than the number of items in the table. At the end of the first pass, the records have a sequence of 54, 23, 41, 37, 69. Three interchanges were made, and therefore we must make another pass.

For pass 2, we return to the first item in the table, but because the last item already contains the highest key, it will not be necessary to compare it again, and we will stop with the fourth item in the table. Thus:

Compare No.	*Positions*	*Values*	*Interchange*
1	1 and 2	54 and 23	Yes
2	2 and 3	54 and 41	Yes
3	3 and 4	54 and 37	Yes

The sequence at the end of the second pass is 23, 41, 37, 54, 69, and three interchanges were made. Notice that the two highest keys are now in the two highest positions, but that the remaining positions are not necessarily in sequence.

Pass 3 continues as follows:

Compare No.	*Positions*	*Values*	*Interchange*
1	1 and 2	23 and 41	No
2	2 and 3	41 and 37	Yes

The sequence at the end of the third pass is 23, 37, 41, 54, 69, and one interchange was made. We then continue with pass 4, comparing the first two items, and complete the sort.

Compare No.	*Positions*	*Values*	*Interchange*
1	1 and 2	23 and 37	No

The sequence at the end of the last pass is 23, 37, 41, 54, 69.

In this example, ten comparisons were required and four passes. This was necessary because the original data was almost completely reversed in its sequence. If the original data had been in ascending sequence, only one pass would have been necessary to verify the fact that no interchanges were required, and no further sorting would be necessary. The exchange method takes maximum advantage of the degree in which the keys are already in sequence. It is a relatively easy method to code (see Figure 8-11), it requires only enough space for one key or record to be saved during the interchange, and it is a satisfactory method for internal sorting in core storage.

Under no circumstances would the bubble sort ever require more than $N - 1$ comparisons for N items in a file, and it might require only the one verification pass to prove that the records were already in sequence.

The bubble sort can move a high key from a low position all the way to the end of the table in a single pass. But a low key can move only to the next-lower position in each pass. Therefore, the slowest sorting occurs when the lowest key is in the highest position of the table.

Shell sort. The Shell sort, named after its inventor, Donald Shell, speeds up the procedure. Instead of comparing adjacent items in the table, each pass, an interval, or *gap* separates the items to be compared. On the first pass, the gap is equal to the half the number of items in the table, unrounded. For 100 items in the table, the first item would be compared with the 51st, the second with the 52nd, and so on, until the 50th is compared with the 100th. When an interchange is made, the high keys will

```
100 REM BUBBLE SORT SUBROUTINE
110 REM VARIABLES USED:
120 REM    N = NUMBER OF ELEMENTS IN ARRAY
130 REM    X(N) = ARRAY TO BE SORTED
140 REM    I = SUBSCRIPT FOR COMPARING
150 REM    T = TEMPORARY SPOT FOR EXCHANGING ELEMENTS
160 REM    E = SWITCH FOR EXCHANGE MADE
170 REM    M = ENDING SUBSCRIPT FOR EACH PASS
200 LET M = N - 1                      'SET SUBSCRIPT TO NEXT TO LAST ITEM
205 REM                                'REPEAT
210    LET E = 0                       '  SET EXCHANGE SWITCH OFF
220    FOR I = 1 TO M                   '  DOWHILE I <= M
230       IF X(I) <> X(I+1) THEN 280    '    IF PAIR OUT OF SEQUENCE
240          LET T = X(I)               '      INTERCHANGE THE PAIR
250          LET X(I) = X(I+1)
260          LET X(I+1) = T
270          LET E = 1                  '      SET EXCHANGE SWITCH ON
280    NEXT I                           '    ENDIF
290    LET M = M - 1                    '  DECREMENT ENDING SUBSCRIPT
300 IF E <> 0 AND M>0 THEN 210          'UNTIL NO INTERCHANGE OR LAST PASS
310 RETURN                              'RETURN TO MAIN PROGRAM
```

Figure 8-11. Bubble sort in BASIC. Adjacent elements in an array are
compared and interchanged if necessary to place into the
proper order. In each pass, the highest keys tend to move
("bubble") toward the highest positions in the array.

move toward the top and the low keys toward the bottom of the table more rapidly.

The second pass and third, if necessary, are repeated using the same interval until no interchanges are made. Then the gap is divided by 2, unrounded, and the process is repeated. The last several passes will have an interval of 1, so that adjacent items in the table will be compared for the final fine sort. When the interval becomes 0 (half of 1, unrounded), the sort is complete. Figure 8-12 shows the Shell sort in BASIC.

To illustrate the Shell sort, take a string of ten keys in the original sequence of 54, 69, 23, 41, 37, 19, 81, 96, 48, and 15. The interval is 10 divided by 2, or 5. The sorting proceeds as follows:

Pass No.	Compare No.	Positions	Values	Interchange
1	1	1 and 6	54 and 19	Yes
	2	2 and 7	69 and 81	No
	3	3 and 8	23 and 96	No
	4	4 and 9	41 and 48	No
	5	5 and 10	37 and 15	Yes

Values at end: 19, 69, 23, 41, 15, 54, 81, 96, 48, 37

2	1	1 and 6	19 and 54	No
	2	2 and 7	69 and 81	No
	3	3 and 8	23 and 96	No
	4	4 and 9	41 and 48	No
	5	5 and 10	15 and 37	No

Values at end: 19, 69, 23, 41, 15, 54, 81, 96, 48, 37

3	1	1 and 3	19 and 23	No
	2	2 and 4	69 and 41	Yes
	3	3 and 5	23 and 15	Yes
	4	4 and 6	69 and 54	Yes
	5	5 and 7	23 and 81	No
	6	6 and 8	69 and 96	No
	7	7 and 9	81 and 48	Yes
	8	8 and 10	96 and 37	Yes

Values at end: 19, 41, 15, 54, 23, 69, 48, 37, 81, 96

Note that when no interchanges were required during pass 2, the gap for pass 3 was divided by 2 (5/2 = 2 unrounded). Results for the remaining passes would be:

Pass 4, gap 2, compares 8, interchanges 2, values at end 15, 51, 19, 54, 23, 37, 48, 69, 81, 96

Pass 5, gap 2, compares 8, interchanges 1, values at end 15, 41, 19, 37, 23, 54, 48, 69, 81, 96

Pass 6, gap 2, compares 8, interchanges 1, values at end 14, 37, 19, 51, 23, 54, 48, 69, 81, 96

Pass 7, gap 2, compares 8, interchanges 0, values at end 15, 37, 19, 51, 23, 54, 48, 69, 81, 96

Pass 8, gap 1, compares 9, interchanges 3, values at end 15, 19, 37, 23, 41, 48, 54, 69, 81, 96

Pass 9, gap 1, compares 9, interchanges 1, values at end 15, 19, 23, 37, 41, 48, 54, 69, 81, 96

Pass 10, gap 1, compares 9, interchanges 0, values at end 15, 19, 23, 37, 41, 48, 54, 69, 81, 96

Total passes 10, total compares 77, total interchanges 15

Comparison of sorting methods. It will be noted that for a small number of items to be sorted that the bubble sort may require fewer passes and comparisons than the Shell sort. However, as the number of items to be sorted increases, the Shell sort shows dramatic improvement. As an experiment by the author, tables of random numbers of different sizes were generated and sorted by both methods. The results were:

Table Size	Method	Passes	Compares	Interchanges
5	Bubble	4	10	7
5	Shell	5	17	3
10	Bubble	5	35	16
10	Shell	7	52	12
20	Bubble	15	180	81
20	Shell	13	212	45
50	Bubble	46	1219	631
50	Shell	22	959	184
80	Bubble	69	3105	1728
80	Shell	25	1779	315
100	Bubble	90	4905	2465
100	Shell	28	2533	405

Note that even with small tables, where the Shell sort takes more passes and compares than the bubble sort, it usually requires fewer interchanges. As the number of items in the table increases, the Shell sort takes fewer passes, compares, and interchanges than the bubble sort. Actual time savings depend upon the speed of the equipment being used and whether the table is in main storage or secondary storage.

```
100 REM SHELL SORT
110 REM VARIABLES USED:
120 REM      X(N) = ARRAY TO BE SORTED
130 REM      N    = NUMBER OF ELEMENTS IN ARRAY
140 REM      I    = SUBSCRIPT FOR COMPARING
150 REM      G    = INTERVAL BETWEEN ITEMS COMPARED
160 REM      T    = TEMPORARY SPOT FOR EXCHANGING
170 REM      E    = SWITCH FOR EXCHANGE MADE
200 LET G = INT(N / 2)
210 IF G = 0 THEN 330
220    LET E = 0
230    FOR I = 1 TO N - G
240       IF X(I) <=X(I+G) THEN 290
250          LET T = X(I)
260          LET X(I) = X(I+1)
270          LET X(I+1) = T
280          LET E = 1
290    NEXT I
300    IF E = 1 THEN 220
310    LET G = INT(G / 2)
320 GOTO 210
330 RETURN
```

Figure 8-12. Shell sort in BASIC. The Shell sort is faster than the bubble sort. Items to be compared are separated by a gap. When interchanges are made, the elements move farther upward or downward toward their final positions. Fewer interchanges are required to complete the sort.

Sort Packages

One of the main utilities normally provided with any operating system is the sort-merge package. Such a package normally is generalized to the extent that it will accommodate a variety of record and block sizes, key types and lengths, and input/output devices; will sort ascending or descending sequence; will construct multiple field keys; and will meet all of the normal requirements of the user. Information is supplied to the sort routine in the form of parameter cards.

Most sort packages use a form of *tag sort*. The tag consists of the key of the record in the leftmost digits and the disk address of the record as the rightmost part of the tag. One pass of the file is required to build the tag. The tags are then sorted by one of the methods in common use, such as the bubble or Shell sort, and the records may then be retrieved in the new sequence by reading them directly from the address specified on the tag.

Figure 8-13 shows a group of seven job control statements for use with the IBM DOS Sort-Merge routine, immediately following the //EXEC DSORT statements. In Figure 8-13 the RECORD parameter indicates that the records are fixed-length and that both input and output records will be 160 characters.

The SORT parameter shows that the key is to be constructed with

```
// JOB ARKLSORT
// ASSGN SYS002,X'193'         INPUT
// ASSGN SYS001,X'192'         OUTPUT
// ASSGN SYS014,X'193'         WORK
// DLBL FILEW,'SORT WORK FILE',0,DA
// EXTENT SYS014,999999,1,0,40,60
// DLBL FILEA,'UNSORTED LAW ENF. ADDRESSES',0,SD
// EXTENT SYS002,999999,1,0,10,30
// DLBL FILEO,'SORTED LAW ENF. ADDRESSES',99/365,SD
// EXTENT SYS001,000000,1,0,1210,30
// EXEC DSORT
 RECORD TYPE=F,LENGTH=(160,,160)
 SORT FIELDS=(66,2,A,1,24,A,81,35,A),FORMAT=BI,FILES=1,SIZE=350
 INPFIL VOLUME=1,BLKSIZE=(3200,X),INPUT=D
 OUTFIL BLKSIZE=3200,OUTPUT=D
 OPTION LABEL=(S,S)
 END
/*
/&
```

Figure 8-13. Control statements for sort-merge package. RECORD,
SORT, INPFIL, OUTFIL, and OPTION statements give
precise specifications of the file to be sorted.

the leftmost two characters coming from columns 66 and 67 of the record,
the middle 24 characters from columns 1–24, and the last 35 characters
from columns 81–115, all to be sorted in ascending order. The format of
the key is binary, and the size of the file is approximately 350 records.

The INPFIL parameter indicates that there is a single input volume
on disk, with a block size of 3200 bytes. The output file, as specified by the
OUTFIL parameter, is also on disk with a block size of 3200 bytes. The
only OPTION is that both input and output files will contain standard labels.

Most commercial software houses provide sort packages, each
claiming superior speed, versatility, or ease of handling. Some sort packages
may be called as subroutines by user programs, while others are executed
as regular programs in the course of the normal job stream. Sorting con-
sumes a large portion of processing time, and the selection of effective sorting methods and packages can materially affect production efficiency in an
installation.

SUMMARY

Files are the highest level in a hierarchy of data items that progress successively from the bit to the byte or character and then through the word or
field to the record and finally to the file. Files are collections of records organized for some special purpose. The purpose dictates the data elements to
be included and suggests methods of organization, processing, and retrieval.

Interest in computer files is centered primarily in magnetic tape or di-
rect access storage devices, which include disk, drum, and magnetic cards.
Files on any device may be processed sequentially, but only those of
DASDs may be processed randomly.

Volatility refers to the number of additions and deletions of records in a file. Activity refers to the number or distribution of records that have transactions to be posted during any given pass of the file. Master files consist of relatively unchanging descriptive information and current summary status figures. Transaction files contain data about events that affect some of the data in master files.

The principal methods of file organization are sequential, partitioned, indexed, indexed sequential, and direct or random. The latter four can be employed only on DASDs.

Files may be identified by both exterior labels on the outside of the tape or disk volume and interior labels written electronically along with the data. Labels may be processed by the program itself or, in some systems, by the operating system. They are used to check that the proper file is being accessed, that existing files are not overwritten, that the records and keys are of the right size, and other pertinent facts.

To make the most efficient use of available disk space, the system designer must be aware of the capacity of each sector or track and must use the proper blocking factor for each file. Track capacity formulas assist in the calculation of the number of records of different sizes that may be placed upon each device, allowing for the space required for the gap between records.

Files may be classified as input, output, input/output, and piggyback. The first three types are often referred to as source, destination, and source-destination files.

The input/output control system (IOCS) consists of a series of prewritten routines that handle most of the details of input/output programming. Physical IOCS handles the actual channel commands for the transfer of data between the device and the central processing unit. Logical IOCS uses a group of macroinstructions to permit the programmer to concentrate entirely upon the logical content of each individual record.

The characteristics of each file must be spelled out in the form of parameters that define the file for the particular device used. Sequential processing macroinstructions, such as OPEN, CLOSE, GET, PUT, and others, are used whenever the programmer is concerned logically with reading or writing a record.

Sequential files may be updated using either the father-son technique or the rewrite technique. The father-son technique results in a new master file being written out after any updating, additions, or deletions have been made to the original file. The rewrite technique provides that the master record is written in its original location after updating has taken place.

Four methods are described for searching a table: sequential, spaced sequential, probability, and binary. Although an entire file rarely can be held in core storage, a portion of it may be read into central storage, searched as a table, and additional parts read in until the desired record is either found or determined not to be present.

The selection of a sorting method is determined by the sequence desired, the key location and length, the number and size of records, the size of core storage, and type of auxiliary storage, and the degree of original ordering.

Two sorting methods are discussed: bubble and Shell. They are widely used for tables or arrays already in core.

Tag sorting requires direct-access storage devices. One pass is made where the address of each record can be extracted and combined with the key to the record into a tag in a separate file. After the tags are sorted, each full record can be retrieved from the address which is associated with each key.

Sort packages are provided with most operating systems to handle files of many types and sizes on different devices. Information is supplied to the sort package by means of parameter cards.

TERMS FOR REVIEW

Activity	Parameter
Binary search	Pass
Bubble sort	Physical record
Cylinder	Piggyback file
Destination file	Probability search
Direct-access storage device	Sequential search
Extent	Shell sort
Interior label	Source file
I/O area	Source-destination file
IOCS	Spaced sequential search
Key	String
Logical record	Tag sort
Macro	Transaction file
Master file	Volatility

QUESTIONS

1. What is the difference between operational information and management information? Give some examples of each.
2. Distinguish between volatility and activity with respect to files.

3. What is the difference between a volume label and a file label?
4. Distinguish between file maintenance and file updating. Why should the two forms of processing not be combined into a single run?
5. Distinguish between logical and physical IOCS.
6. What is meant by a "file definition"? Describe how files are defined in RPG, COBOL, and assembler language.
7. Why is work area used? What are the advantages of using one? Can you name any disadvantages?
8. Draw a program flowchart to show the logic involved in updating a sequential file using the father-son technique. How does the use of a dummy record with a high key at the end of the master file and another at the end of the transaction file simplify the logic?
9. Which kinds of file devices allow updating to be made by rewriting in the original location? Which kinds do not?
10. For a table of 1000 items, does the spaced sequential search or the binary search use the fewer compares to cover the entire table? How many items must be in the table before the number of compares is the same for the two methods?
11. Using Figure 8-6, calculate how many physical records can be placed on each track of the IBM 3348 disk for the following record lengths:

Record Length	Separate Key Length
1600	None
1200	15
600	15
100	10

12. How does the position of magnetic tape labels with respect to data records differ from that of the labels on disk?
13. You have the keys 44, 16, 78, 91, and 37 to be sorted by the bubble sort. Show the order of the keys at the end of each pass and the number of interchanges required during each pass.
14. Sort the keys 44, 16, 78, 91, and 37 using the Shell sort. Show the order of the keys at the end of each pass and the number of interchanges required during each pass.
15. What problems do you see in trying to perform a tag sort on magnetic tape files?
16. If you have access to a computer with an operating system, make up the parameter cards for its sort routine to do the following job:

Input: Tape with standard labels, record size 40, blocked 10
Output: Disk with standard labels, record size 40, blocked 20
Key: Positions 5–9, then 30–34, then 42–44 (all in ascending order)

CASE STUDY
SUNCOAST COMMUNITY COLLEGE

Gerald Phipps and John Shirley work together on designing the files for the alumni application system. They decide the alumni master file should be organized as indexed sequential so that the records of alumni making contributions during any given years can be retrieved directly as needed. They temporarily defer further work on this file.

They consider various alternatives for design of the alumni donor file. One possibility is to attach additional fields to the master records to show contributions received. Indexed sequential files under DOS/VSE do not support variable-length records. Therefore, it would be necessary to allow enough space for the largest number of contributions any alumni member would be likely to make over an entire lifetime. Such a large record would be highly wasteful of disk space if many alumni should make no contributions at all.

Another option would be to create a file annually showing identification and only those contributions made during the current year. This would require recreating the entire file each year although only a small percentage of the alumni would make one or more contributions.

Therefore, they decide to create a separate donor file each year for only those who actually make contributions. The key to the file will be Social Security number, so that a link can be made to the indexed sequential file containing the alumni identification information. The donor file will be a sequential file with variable-length records containing from one to a maximum of 50 gifts per year. This method of file organization, they believe, will provide an efficient method of using disk space and also permit efficient processing of current records.

They propose to retain in the current files the most recent five years of donor records. Older records can be retained in inactive files as permanent records that can be recopied into the active files if desired to make comparisons of giving for the current year with ten or more years ago.

Record layout for the donor file is in this form: Root segment:

Record length field	4 bytes
Social Security number (key)	9 bytes
Number of gifts this year	2 bytes

Variable segment (1 to 50 segments):

Date	6 bytes
Receipt number	5 bytes
Purpose	8 bytes
Amount (two decimal places)	9 bytes

The minimum-sized record will therefore be 43 bytes (15 bytes for the root and 28 bytes for the first segment). The maximum-sized record will be 1415 bytes (15 for the root and 1400 for the 50 gift segments of 28 bytes each). The most common size is expected to be 99 bytes (15 bytes for the root and three gift segments of 28 bytes each). They refer to the track capacity table in Figure 8-6 and calculate that the input/output area for this file should be 1423 bytes. This will accomodate the 4-byte block length field and one maximum-sized block of 1415 bytes, 14 of the most common-sized records of 99 bytes, or 33 of the minimum-sized records of 43 bytes.

The alumni application requires extensive sorting of gifts by year of graduation, by major field of donor, and in other ways. The SORT feature in COBOL accepts input from indexed sequential files or from variable-length sequential files. All programming is expected to be done in ANS COBOL74, which supports the SORT feature fully.

QUESTIONS AND EXERCISES

1. Why did the team decide to use variable-length records for the donor file?
2. How are the alumni master file and the donor file to be related or tied together?
3. Suppose that two bytes were added to the variable segment of the donor record. Calculate the size the I/O area must be to hold the maximum-sized record. Then calculate how many records per block there can be of the most common size and the minimum size?

9

DATA BASE
DESIGN AND
PROCESSING

OBJECTIVES

At the end of this chapter, you should be able to:

1. Explain the difference between traditional file organization and the data base concept.
2. Describe the elements of the data base.
3. Relate the stages in the evolution of the data base.
4. State the objectives of data base organization.
5. Compare and contrast the three views of the data base.
6. Define data base management systems and describe the elements that comprise them.
7. Describe the ways in which data is structured logically within the data base.
8. Distinguish between indexed files, indexed sequential files, and direct (random) files.
9. Describe steps taken in processing each of the three types of files.
10. Give advantages and disadvantages of the use of a data base as compared with traditional files.

The traditional way of designing and using files has been to begin with the output required to produce a certain report. Then, working backward, processing steps necessary to produce that output were worked out. Next, input data elements needed for processing were defined. Finally, one or more files were created to supply the input data.

This procedure meant that the same data element might be present in many different files, a condition called *redundancy*. Every program using the same file had to describe it in complete detail. If one data element had to be added to a file to meet the needs of one program, then every program that referred to that file had to be modified to reflect the change in the file. Programmers came to spend more of their time on program modification and maintenance than on writing new applications.

THE DATA BASE CONCEPT

To overcome these objections, the data base approach came to be used in the late 1960s. The intent of a data base is to provide a large, integrated store of data that any user can tap as needed. It may be stored in a centralized location or dispersed among the various users and connected by data communications networks.

Data is created or used whenever *events* occur. An event is any incident that arrives, comes, occurs, happens, or takes place. *Event analysis* is performed by constructing a table listing events across the top of a page and the data elements involved in each event down the left side. Thus we can readily see in how many events each data element appears (see Figure 9-1).

A data base may be defined as a collection of interrelated data stored so as to serve multiple applications with minimum redundancy. The description of the data is intended to be entirely independent of the instructions that process it in application programs. The data base system permits new records to be added or existing records to be modified or deleted without changing all the application programs that refer to that data. This ability is called *data independence*.

The data base organization is necessarily highly complex. It must be able to serve batch processing, online systems, and real-time interacting users. Related data in various areas of the file must be able to be created, retrieved, updated, or deleted. Data elements need to be interrelated by means of chains, lists, pointers, and rings to permit retrieving the desired data without having to examine all records in the file.

ELEMENTS OF THE DATA BASE

The data base is composed of five elements: (1) the data collection, (2) direct-access storage devices, (3) the data element dictionary, (4) the data base administrator, and (5) the data base management systems.

Data Elements	Time Card	Payroll Register	Pay Check	Earnings Stub	Employee Payroll Master	Overtime Report	Deduction Register	Labor Distribution
Date	x	x	x	x	x	x	x	x
Hours worked	x	x		x	x	x		
Pay rate		x		x	x			
Regular pay		x		x	x			
Overtime pay		x		x	x	x		
Gross pay		x		x	x			x
Social Security tax		x		x	x		x	
Federal income tax		x		x	x		x	
Group insurance		x		x	x		x	
Contributions		x		x	x		x	
Other deductions		x		x	x		x	
Net pay		x	x	x	x			
Check number		x	x	x	x			
Department number	x	x			x	x		x
Employee number	x	x	x	x	x	x	x	x
Employee name	x	x	x		x	x	x	x
Employee address			x		x			

Figure 9-1. Event analysis table. This table shows each of the reports or documents in which each data element appears.

The Data Collection

Terms employed in data base design differ somewhat from those used in traditional file processing. In Chapter 6 we defined a record as a collection of data about some person, thing, or event. In data base terms, the subject about which the information is stored is called an *entity*. The term *entity set* is therefore used to refer to the file or collection holding information about entities.

Just as records are divided into fields, entities have *attributes,* or *properties,* such as name, dollar value, or size, that we may wish to record. Much of the work of the data base is to associate the attributes we wish with the proper entity, or with similar attributes in other entities.

Each entity normally has a *key,* or *identifier,* that is unique for that entity alone. The name or description of the entity is often not necessarily unique and therefore does not serve as a positive identifier. Attributes for each identifier are usually stored in coded form as separate fields along with the key and descriptive data to make up the record for the entity. Thus we can visualize data as stored in a form where each record consists of a single line in which each field, or attribute, makes up a column. A series of records might thus appear as separate lines on a page. Data stored in this form is often referred to as a *flat file.*

The different values that relate to one entity are sometimes called a *tuple* (pronounced "tupple"). A tuple with two values, such as name and age, is called a pair. For more than two values it is called an *N-tuple*, where *N* refers to the number of values. Some data management systems refer to a *record*, some to a *tuple*, and some to a *segment* to describe the identifier of an entity with its related attributes. Figure 9-2 shows examples of entities, attributes, and tuples.

Direct Access Storage Devices

Data base processing requires that we be able to get rapidly from one entity to another without reading all other entities between them. Standard sequential files do not permit such processing. Therefore, direct access storage devices, which include magnetic disk, drum, and magnetic cards, are needed. For simplicity, because all three types of devices may address records directly, we will use the general term *disk* to refer to any direct access device.

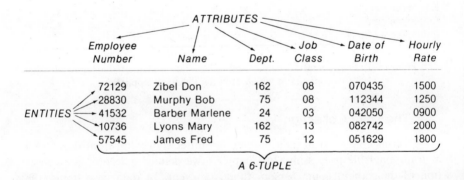

A 6-TUPLE

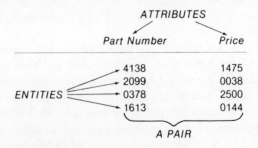

A PAIR

Figure 9-2 Entities, attributes, and tuples. The entity resembles a record, while its attributes resemble fields. The tuple indicates the number of attributes contained within the entity.

Some disk files are organized with the *sector* as the principal address-able unit. Each track on the disk is divided into segments, or sectors. Figure 9-3 shows a track divided into sectors.

Other types of disks are organized with the track as the main address-able unit, and each track may hold one or more physical records, or *blocks.* A *cylinder* consists of those tracks directly above one another on the various surfaces of the disk pack. The read-write assembly can read a full cylinder without repositioning. Figure 8-1 shows the disk organization of the IBM 2311 access mechanism.

Data Element Dictionary

The data element dictionary defines each piece of data that appears in the data base. The definition includes such details as:

1. Length of size of the data
2. Type (whether alphabetic, alphanumeric, or numeric)
3. Minimum and maximum values the data can take

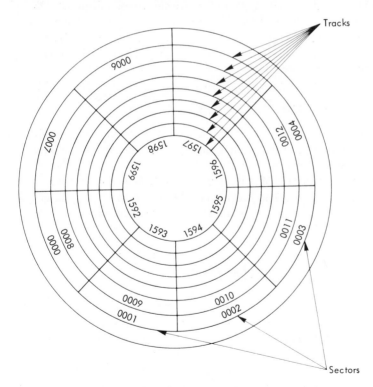

Figure 9-3. Disk track divided into sectors. Sectors are numbered con-secutively around each track working inward from the out-ermost track.

4. Source of the data
5. Codes for all files in which the data element appears
6. Editing pattern, if appropriate

The dictionary may be kept manually, with each element appearing on a separate page. Or it may be maintained by a data definition language through software, that may be either a part of or separate from the data base management software.

Data Base Administrator

The data base administrator (DBA) plays both a technical and administrative role in the organization and use of the data base. The functions of the DBA may be carried out by a single individual or by a group of persons in large organizations.

The *technical* aspects of the DBA's job deal with the design of the data base and its interfaces with the operating system and applications. The *administrative* areas deal with setting policy for data access and control and for resolving conflicts among data users within the organization. The duties require a combination of diplomacy and authority. Even though the data base administrator may be a member of the data processing department when the data base is first being formed, eventually he or she should report directly to top management.

Data Base Management Systems

Data base management systems include the specialized software necessary to create and process the data base. In some instances, the data definition language is also a part of the data base. The intent of the data base management system (DBMS) is to make the data base independent of the applications programs that use it. The DBMS provides the interface between the application programs and the operating system.

The DBMS is described more fully later in this chapter.

EVOLUTION OF THE DATA BASE

The data base as we conceive it today has come through four stages. In the first stage, prior to the third generation of computers in the middle 1960s, files were typically organized in a serial manner. The logical and physical structure of the files were the same. Most processing was serial in nature, and batch processing was the typical mode. Application programmers usually created the files they needed for each specific application, with little regard to the needs of the next application.

By the late 1960s the second stage involved the use of file access methods to permit both serial and random access to records. Some distinction was noted between the logical and physical organization. Many details of reading and writing records to files were handled by input/output control systems, but the application programmer was still heavily involved in many aspects of data management and processing methods.

In the early 1970s the third stage brought early data base systems. The same physical data could be viewed in different logical ways by different applications. Through complex organization, redundancy was sharply reduced. Data could be retrieved at the field or group level rather than requiring complete records to be retrieved in every instance. Data management systems bridged the gap between the logical file descriptions of the application programmer and the physical arrangement of the data base.

In the fourth stage of the present day, elaborate software provides both logical and physical data independence. The creation and maintenance of the data base is the responsibility of the data base administrator who may use a data description language for the overall logical organization of the files. Application programmers may describe only the data and relationships that they require in specific programs. Data base management systems may provide a form of command language to retrieve data from the data base and present it to the application programmers in the form they require. Some software provides a data interrogation language directly to the user to provide quick and convenient access to data not requiring application programs.

OBJECTIVES OF DATA BASE ORGANIZATION

A number of bodies have devoted attention to problems of data base definition, organization, and processing. The Conference on Data Systems Languages (CODASYL), the IBM users' groups SHARE and GUIDE, the Association for Computing Machinery (ACM), and the American National Standards Institute (ANSI) X3 SPARC/DBMS Study Group have all issued important reports.

The final objective of data base systems is to find easier, cheaper, faster, and more flexible ways to make data available to application programs. By concentrating in one place all the data required by an organization, it should be possible to make it more accurate, private, and safe from intentional or unintentional damage.

The data base provides a huge pool that serves as a resource to each application programmer or other user to draw from as needed. The programmer or user need not know all the details of where the data is physically located or in what form it is stored. It should be possible to add or delete data items without affecting programs already written. The data base should be capable of expansion or rearrangement in such a way as to be transparent to the user.

The primary objectives of data base organization may be summarized in the following statements:

1. The data base is the foundation for easier, cheaper, faster, and more flexible application program development.
2. The data may be used in many different ways according to the needs of different users.
3. Changes may be made in the data base without the need for redoing or modifying application programs.
4. Users may see clearly what data is available to them and be able to use it easily in a variety of ways.
5. Unanticipated requests for data can be handled readily through some form of high-level interrogation language.
6. Change and growth in the data base may be made easily without affecting processing methods.
7. The cost of maintaining and changing the data base can be kept low.
8. Data proliferation and redundancy can be avoided.
9. Adequate controls will ensure that data is safeguarded from damage or unauthorized use.
10. Privacy of individuals about whom data is maintained will be safeguarded.

THREE VIEWS OF THE DATA BASE

A single data element is not very useful in itself. Only as it is associated with other data elements do we build usable information. The relationships that may exist between data elements may often be shown by *mapping*. These relationships are the crux of data base organization.

There are three distinct types of organization for the data base. Two of these types are logical and one is physical. They are often called (1) global logical data organization (schema), (2) external organization (subschema), and (3) physical storage organization.

The Schema

The overall logical description of the data base is called a *schema*. This term was originated by the CODASYL Data Base Task Group and has become widely used. The schema might also be termed a model of the overall data. The schema forms a chart giving the names of entries and attributes and the relationships between them. It is a framework into which might be fitted the specific values assigned to the data elements at any given time. The values at any given time are called an *instance of the schema*.

Schemas are often drawn in the form of a block diagram. Solid lines between blocks represent relationships that may or may not be apparent from the data elements themselves. Dashed lines show cross-references to other records that might supply additional related information. Figure 9-4 illustrates a schema.

The data base administrator is greatly concerned with the schema as representing the total requirements of all programs and users of the data base. He or she must be aware of the forms of organization that best serve the needs of all users and be sure that all data elements that are likely to be needed will be available and accessible. The administrator is concerned with the logical arrangement of the entire data base and not just the needs of a single program.

The Subschema

The term *subschema* refers to the more limited view of the data held by the application programmer. Many different subschemas may be derived from one schema. They need not follow the same logical structure as the schema from which they come. It is the function of the data base software to be able to present the data to the application programmer in the form in which he or she wishes to use it. Other terms that are sometimes used for the subschema include *logical view* or *submodel*.

The subschema represents the view of data described within the application program, such as the COBOL DATA DIVISION. It will not necessarily be at all similar to the manner in which the data is actually stored in the data base. Figure 9-5 shows a subschema.

The Physical View

Systems programmers and systems designers have the third view of the data base—that of the physical layout on the storage devices. They must be concerned with such details as what method will be used to locate the data, what fields are to be used as pointers to other records, what techniques might be used to reduce storage space, and what security measures will be employed. The physical view is sometimes called the *internal schema*.

Later in the chapter we will deal in detail with the physical organization and processing of data on direct access storage devices.

ELEMENTS OF DATA BASE MANAGEMENT SYSTEMS

The software that enables a data base to be defined, created, used by a variety of users, and modified as needed is called a data base management system (DBMS). It must work as an interface between the application programming language, such as COBOL or PL/I, the operating system, and possibly a data communications control system.

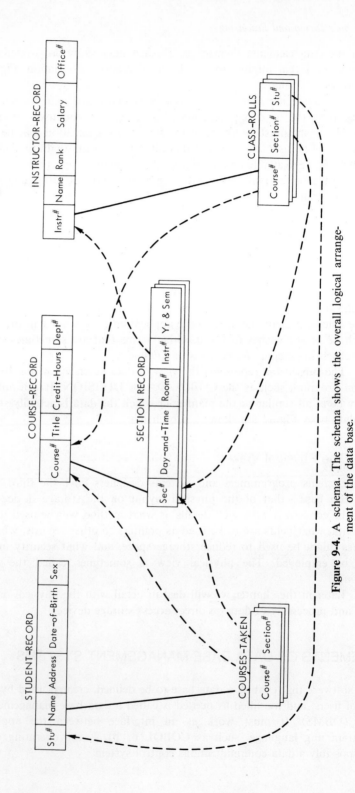

Figure 9-4. A schema. The schema shows the overall logical arrangement of the data base.

Subschema for student schedule:

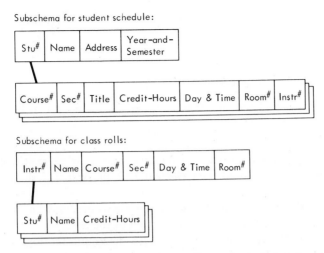

Subschema for class rolls:

Figure 9-5. A subschema. The subschema shows the logical arrangement of data needed for a specific program or application.

DBMS Languages

At least five languages may be involved in data base management to some degree.

1. The application must be written in a conventional programming language. This language must often have some extensions of special features to permit processing of the data base by linking to a DBMS.
2. The data manipulation language may either be imbedded in the applicattion language by means of special verbs (FIND, GET, MODIFY, INSERT, etc.) or be accessible by means of CALL statements as a subprogram. The data manipulation language is the means by which the application programmer directs the DBMS to provide the data or carry out other functions on the data base.
3. The subschema description language offers a means for the programmer to declare the data elements and records that he or she wishes to use in the program. This language might be a part of the DATA DIVISION in COBOL, a separate feature of the DBMS, or an independent data description language.
4. The schema description language enables the data administrator to describe the entire global logical data organization. It may be desirable to have this language independent of the DBMS so that the data descriptions will not have to be rewritten if the DBMS software or hardware is changed.
5. The physical data description language might be termed the device-media control language. Although the time might come when the physical description of the data might be mapped automatically from the schema

description language, the state of the art has not reached that point as this is written.

DBMS Functions

Functions of the data base management system might be described in terms of these events:

1. The application program requests a record to be read and gives the name of the desired data element and the value of the key where it might be found.
2. The DBMS must refer to the subschema as described in the application program to get the proper description of the data.
3. The DBMS refers to the schema to determine the logical data types that are needed.
4. The DBMS refers to the physical data description to determine which physical records are to be read.
5. The DBMS issues a command to the operating system to read the required record.
6. The operating system performs the physical operation of transferring the record between the storage device and the system input/output areas.
7. By comparing the subschema and schema, the DBMS builds the logical records needed, making any necessary conversions in the form or arrangement of the data elements.
8. The DBMS transfers the data from the system input/output areas to the work areas of the application program.
9. The DBMS provides the application program with status or error information regarding the result of the call for data.
10. The application program then performs the desired operations on the data in its work area.

The specific technique or formula for addressing and searching for a record in the data base may appear in any one of three places:

1. A routine in or called by the application program
2. A part of the data base management system
3. A feature of the operating system access method

Placing the routine in the application program tends to reduce the degree of data independence. Relying exclusively on the operating system may reduce flexibility. The data base management system offers the best opportunity to combine flexibility, new forms of data organization, and new techniques.

Back-End Processors

As DBMS development becomes more efficient and increases capability, it also increases system overhead. The DBMS requires more storage and linkage complexity, both in main storage and on auxiliary devices.

Data is described logically in terms of its key, content, or value, while the physical description refers to its location in storage. To convert from one reference scheme to the other takes overhead both in processing time and storage. *Back-end processors* are being used to reduce overhead in the same way that front-end processors have been handling data communications for some years. The back-end processor would use hardware to perform many of the functions presently being done by DBMS software.

Many back-end processors use an associative memory approach, which allows data to be addressed and searched by content or value rather than by physical address. This approach requires five basic hardware elements.

1. The data register contains the key or value being sought.
2. The mask register limits the part of the value currently being searched for.
3. The word select register flags the words to be included in the present search that have perhaps been selected in a previous search using a different mask.
4. The search results register flags records that satisfy all search criteria.
5. The multiple match resolver points to the first record that satisfies all criteria.

Figure 9-6 shows an example of the associative memory approach.

LOGICAL DATA STRUCTURES

The logical organization of the data base requires a number of ways to link related entities and attributes together. Some of the methods include pointers, lists, rings, and inverted files. One or a combination of these methods may then be used to organize the data into a specific structure. Three structures described in this chapter are flat files, trees, and plex structures.

Pointers

A field that contains the address of another record is called a *pointer.* An index is usually merely the key of a record and a pointer to the address where it is located on disk. Pointers may also be called *links, chaining records, sequence links,* or other names denoting a way of tying together.

Lists and Rings

Often records that are not in physical sequence have pointers that enable them to be processed in a desired sequence. There must be a pointer (usually at the start of the file) to direct us to the first desired record. That

KAREN	BECK	SECY	SALES	DATA REGISTER

0------0	1------1	0------0	0------0	MASK REGISTER

	BECK			WORD SELECT REGISTER	SEARCH RESULTS REGISTER	MULTIPLE MATCH RESOLVER
	BECK			1	1	1
				1	0	0
				1	0	0
	BECK			0	0	0
				0	0	0
	BECK			1	1	0
				1	0	0
	BECK			0	0	0
	BECK			1	1	0

Figure 9-6. Associative memory approach. A series of registers permit back-end processors to search the data base by use of hardware instead of software.

record in turn has a pointer giving the address of the second desired record, and so on. The last record has some special symbol indicating that it is the end of the sequence. Where the pointers go in one direction only, the organization is called a *simple,* or *one-way, list.*

It is also possible to have forward and backward pointers, so that each record has one pointer giving the address of the following record in sequence and one pointer specifying the preceding record. This structure is called a *ring.* Figure 9-7 shows examples of lists and rings.

In complex files where we wish to be able to show many relationships, it may be necessary to have a separate pointer for almost every field in the record. The task of modifying pointers each time a record is added or attributes within a record are changed can be formidable.

Inverted Files

An *inverted file* is one in which the key to the file is an attribute and the data fields are pointers to each of the records that contain that attribute. Inverted files are normally variable-length records, since the number of records containing the same attribute would vary widely. For example, an inverted file for the attribute *female* would certainly have more pointers than a record for the attribute *Ph.D.* An inverted file is illustrated in Figure 9-8.

One-Way List				Ring			
Record Number	Name	Forward Pointer		Record Number	Name	Forward Pointer	Backward Pointer
0	Pointer to first record	3		0	Pointer to first record	3	7
1	Onley	5		1	Onley	5	8
2	Saunders	10		2	Saunders	10	5
3	Beck	9		3	Beck	9	*
4	Washington	7		4	Washington	7	10
5	Riggsbee	2		5	Riggsbee	2	1
6	McCord	8		6	McCord	8	9
7	Webb	*		7	Webb	*	4
8	McMillen	1		8	McMillen	1	6
9	Hebert	6		9	Hebert	6	3
10	Silver	4		10	Silver	4	2

* Denotes end of list.

Figure 9-7. List and ring structure. The list contains a pointer in each record to the next record in sequence within the file. The ring contains pointers to the next record going either forward or backward.

In traditional files we visualize a table in which one row represents one person or thing and the columns represent its characteristics, or attributes. In an inverted file, the attribute becomes the row and the pointers to the individuals become the columns.

Stacks

Stacks are data structures named after the stacks of plates often found in spring-controlled wells in cafeteria lines. Just as only the top plate is available to the diner, so only the top element in the stack is normally available to the programmer (Figure 9-9).

A stack is usually stored in the form a single-dimensional array. A pointer is maintained that points to the last element currently in the array, which is the top of the stack. The *push* operation adds an item to the stack. It increases the stack pointer by one and stores the item in the designated element in the array.

The *pop* operation removes an item from the array. It stores the last item pointed to in some other location if it is to be retained and subtracts one from the stack pointer to indicate the new top of the stack.

Records in conventional file:

Record No.	Name	Sex	Major	Dorm	Class
1	Abbey	F	Eng	A	Fr
2	Connor	M	Biol	C	Jr
3	Garrison	M	DP	D	Sr
4	Loughlin	F	Math	A	Soph
5	Mackay	F	DP	B	Fr
6	Ross	M	Eng	C	Sr

Records in inverted file:

Attributes		Pointers to Record Numbers		
Sex:	F	1	4	5
	M	2	3	6
Major:	Eng	1	6	
	Biol	2		
	DP	3	5	
	Math	4		
Dorm:	A	1	4	
	B	5		
	C	2	6	
	D	3		
Class:	Fr	1	5	
	Soph	4		
	Jr	2		
	Sr	3	6	

Figure 9-8. Conventional and inverted files. An inverted file is a special type of index giving some characteristic or attribute and containing pointers to all records having that attribute.

Stacks are often used to store a series of addresses as the data base is being searched for specific records. They are also widely used to hold the return addresses to the main program after subroutines are executed.

Flat Files

Earlier in this chapter we mentioned the *flat file,* in which each record contains the same set of fields so that the file can be represented in two-dimensional form. The record may be viewed as a line in which the fields are the columns. A *relational data base* is constructed principally from flat files, using a technique called *normalization.* Normalization is a step-by-step process for simplifying complex relationships between data with associations in the form of two-dimensional tables. Such tables have these properties:

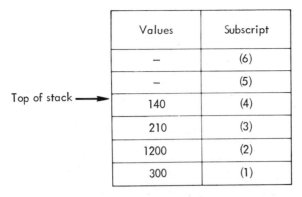

	Values	Subscript
	—	(6)
	—	(5)
Top of stack ⟶	140	(4)
	210	(3)
	1200	(2)
	300	(1)

Figure 9-9. A stack. New values are added (pushed) only to the item above the current top of the stack. Values can be removed (popped) only from the top of the stack. The top of the stack is indicated by the subscript of the highest item currently in the stack.

1. No items in a table entry are repeating groups.
2. All items in each column are of the same kind.
3. Each column is given its own name.
4. All rows (table entries) are unique; there are no duplications.
5. Both rows and columns may be viewed in any sequence.

To change complex structures to flat files, the use of a secondary key is often indicated. For example, if student number is a key in a record containing several occurrences of course number, the structure may be normalized by creating a flat file that has student number as the primary key and course number as the secondary key.

Trees

A second logical form of data base organization is the use of the *tree structures*. The tree is usually represented upside down, with the root at the top and the leaves at the bottom. The tree is made up of a hierarchy of elements called *nodes*. There can be only one root node, but every other node is related to one (and only one) *parent* node at a higher level. The lower nodes are called *children*. Nodes at the ends of branches (with no children) are called *leaves*. Figure 9-10 shows a tree representing data described in a COBOL DATA DIVISION.

Trees may be used to show both logical and physical relationships. Data tends to fall into a hierarchy of categories. One department may have many employees, each of whom has certain job skills, physical characteristics, or "children." The CODASYL Data Base Task Group defines a two-level tree of records as a *set*. Hierarchies with more than two levels are regarded as being made up of multiple sets.

```
01 PAYROLL-RECORD.

    02 EMPLOYEE-DATA.
        04 SOC-SEC-NO              PIC 9(9).
        04 EMP-NAME                PIC X(20).
        04 EMP-ADDRESS.
            08  CITY               PIC X(14).
            08  STATE              PIC XX.
            08  ZIP                PIC 9(5).

    02 CURRENT-PAY.
        04 RATE                    PIC 9(3)V99.
        04 EXEMPTIONS              PIC 99.
        04 HOURS-WORKED            PIC 9(3)V9.

    02 CURRENT-DEDUCTIONS.
        04 FICA                    PIC 9(3)V99.
        04 WITHHOLDING-TAX         PIC 9(3)V99.
        04 OTHER.
            08 OTHER-DEDUCTIONS
               OCCURS 5 TIMES      PIC 9(3)V99.
```

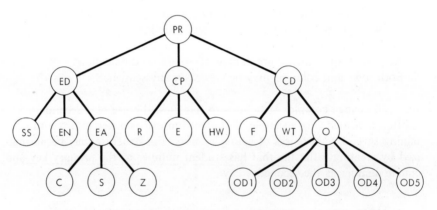

Figure 9-10. A tree representing data described in a **COBOL DATA DIVISION**. The tree is upside down, with the root at the top and the various branches coming downward. The structure of a tree may also be shown by level number and by indentation as in this illustration.

Plex Structures

A third form of data base organization is the use of a *network,* also called a *plex structure.* The plex structure is more complex than the tree, because any item may be linked to any other item. A child can have more than one parent, or there may be no indication of the parent-child relationship. A family tree showing only the father of each generation would be a tree structure, whereas one showing both parents would be a plex structure.

Figure 9-11 shows a plex structure of a schema in which each supplier for a company might carry more than one kind of product, and each of the products might be obtained from any of several suppliers.

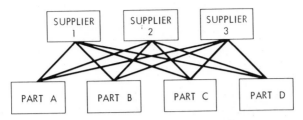

Figure 9-11. A plex structure where each supplier can offer any required part. This structure is contrasted with a tree, in which each branch can come only from one node.

FILE ORGANIZATION FOR THE DATA BASE

In Chapter 8 we described the physical characteristics of direct-access storage devices and mentioned the three principal types of file organization that are usually supported by file management software for operating systems. In this section we will describe further the organization and processing of these three types of files. They are (1) indexed files, (2) indexed sequential files, and (3) direct (random) files.

Indexed Files

Records of an *indexed file* may be written on the disk in any sequence. An *index* is maintained in a separate part of the file, showing the key to each record and a pointer to its location on the disk. The index is kept in sequence by key. We can retrieve the records in sequence by referring to the index and following the pointer directly to the location of the record on the disk (see Figure 9-12).

Indexed Sequential Files

As mentioned in Chapter 8, indexed sequential files have a prime data area, one or more indexes, and one or more overflow areas. To create such a file, records are placed in the *prime data area* in sequence according to key, with as many records as possible in a block and as many blocks as possible on a track to gain the maximum disk utilization. The first track of each cylinder contains a *track index,* giving the highest key that occurs on each track within that cylinder. Normally the last one or two tracks of the cylinder are reserved for an *overflow area,* which does not contain records when the file is first created.

In a separate location of the disk is placed a *cylinder index,* which gives the highest key appearing on each cylinder within the file. There may be a third index, the *master index,* but this is not required. It contains the highest key on each track of the cylinder index.

The number of tracks per cylinder and the number of cylinders per

Index:

Key	Record Number
00137	8
07435	4
19190	2
23576	10
49043	7
52531	1
67748	9
69415	6
71382	3
94467	5

Data Records in Order of Creation:

Record Number	Key	Name
1	52531	Celebrity Films
2	19190	Nashville Music
3	71382	Worldly Tours
4	07435	Green Thumb
5	94467	Instant Data
6	69415	Grimm Futures
7	49043	Ultra Fashions
8	00137	Caloric Foods
9	67748	Dyme Stores
10	23576	Hunt & Peck, Typists

Figure 9-12. Indexed file organization. Records are added to the end of the file, regardless of the key. The index contains each key with a pointer to the proper record number in the file. The index is kept sorted in key sequence.

disk may vary from one device to another. Magnetic cards have additional portions of the address referring to the cell, subcell, and strip, but the basic principle that each record has a specific address which can be found without searching the entire file still holds fast.

Since some operating systems may differ in specific details, the characteristics of the IBM System/370 DOS described below are fairly typical of the way indexes may be used.

Indexed sequential files may be processed in random or sequential order. Records may be blocked or unblocked, and may be processed directly in the I/O area or in a work area. All physical data records must contain key areas, and all key areas must be the same length. Data records must be fixed length only. For files requiring more than one volume, all volumes must be online at one time for loading, adding, or retrieving randomly or sequentially.

Direct (Random) Files

We will remember from Chapter 8 that there is some definite relationship between the key of a record and its address on disk in files with direct organization. Thus an index need not be used and the records in adjacent positions on disk are not necessarily in sequence according to their keys.

There are two principal forms of organization. One requires that each record have a separate key field written on the disk next to the data record. In this instance, the track is the basic address computed, and the operating system will search the track for the particular key in question. The second method is to use the record number (ID) on the track as well as the track number as part of the address. In this instance, no separate key field is required and the address computation goes directly to the desired record location of the track for writing a new record or accessing an existing record.

Either fixed or variable-length records may be used in a direct file, but records may not be blocked unless the programmer is responsible for all details of blocking and unblocking.

PROCESSING INDEXED FILES

Indexed files, we will recall, need not have the records in sequence but do require that an index be kept in sequence by key. Each entry in the index contains, besides the key, a pointer to the location of that record within the file.

Creating the File

As each record is written in the prime data area of the file, an entry is made in the index giving the key of the record and its location of disk. The index may be kept entirely in main storage if the file is relatively small. Otherwise, each entry is written into the index portion of the file as it is prepared. The pointer may refer to the relative record number of the record within the file or to the physical location, such as sector number or cylinder and track number.

Once the file is created, the index must be sorted in sequence by key so that the index can be efficiently searched to retrieve the records for processing.

Adding Records

New records are merely added to the end of the existing file (see piggyback files in Chapter 8). As each new record is written, an entry is added to the index. At the conclusion of the additions, the index is again sorted to the key sequence.

Deleting Records

Any of several methods may be used to delete records from an indexed file. Perhaps the simplest is to write a code, such as the hexadecimal number FF, in the index entry for the record. Processing programs would make a test to bypass that record in the future.

Another possibility is to change the key in the index entry to zeros or all hexadecimal FFs so that sorting will place all deleted entries at the start or end of the index.

Ordinarily, the actual records remain on disk until the file is recopied, at which time they are not transferred to the new file. If an index entry is deleted, there is no practical way to retrieve the actual record from the file.

Updating Records

To find a specific record for updating, the index is searched using any of the methods described in Chapter 8 to find the key that is equal to the desired transaction key. Using the index pointer, the desired record is read into main storage and updated. Then it is rewritten to the same location on disk.

PROCESSING INDEXED SEQUENTIAL FILES

Most current operating systems have operating system software for processing indexed sequential files. Macros are used in assembler language and statements on **COBOL ENVIRONMENT, DATA, AND PROCEDURE DIVISIONS** to make the complex processing of these files more convenient for the programmer. Many data base management systems would have these features incorporated into their software.

Creating and Extending the File

The records must be in sequence according to key, and there must be no duplicate records when the file is created. Appropriate entries in the file definition statements indicate that an indexed sequential file is to be created. The OPEN statement for such a file verifies the label and extent information supplied by the job control cards, checks that the desired space is available on the disk by verifying the disk directory, and writes the label information in the disk directory.

Index areas are next initialized by writing a dummy record for each entry in the cylinder and the track index that might be used if the file is fully loaded.

Each logical record is then presented to the load routine for creating the file. Records may come from more than one input file and may be merged as they are presented to the load routine. Blocked records are first assembled in an output area and transferred to the disk only when the block is filled.

When all records have been loaded, the last block of records is written, followed by an end-of-file record. Entries in the index are completed, and the file is closed, or deactivated.

Extending the file refers to the addition of records to a file when all the keys are higher than the previous record in the file. The same program that initially loads an indexed sequential file can extend it. The only change necessary is in one field of a job control card to designate that the file is already in existence and is not to be created from the beginning.

Figure 9-13 shows an indexed sequential file after creation before any records have been added to the overflow area.

Adding Records to Overflow Area

Adding records to an existing indexed sequential file is the most complex and time consuming of all the functions. For this reason, when a file is highly volatile—that is, when many additions are made at frequent intervals—it is often better to avoid using the overflow area by reconstructing the file. This involves merging the records from the original file with those to be added, thus creating a brand-new file.

When an instruction is given to write the added record, the software must search the indexes to locate the proper block where the record is to be inserted. Then the last record on the track is shifted to the overflow area, and all other records on the track following the position where the record is to be inserted are moved forward one position. Then the new record is inserted in the proper location. This operation may rearrange each block on the track completely by one record position. The last track in the file may have usable space after the last record and may not shift a record to the overflow area.

Two changes then must be made in the track index to reflect the added record. The normal entry is changed to show the key to the last record presently on the prime data area track, and the overflow entry is changed to give the cylinder, track, and record number of the first record belonging to this track in the overflow area.

Figure 9-14 shows an indexed sequential file after several additions to a prime track.

Even though records in the prime data area may be blocked, those in the overflow area are not blocked but have a 10-byte pointer attached to the record. The pointer designates the next record in sequence in the overflow area which came from this particular track. The pointer in the last

Cylinder Index:

Key	Cyl.	Track
125	41	00
348	42	00
561	43	00
779	44	00
995	45	00

Track Index, Cylinder 41:

Normal Entry				Overflow Entry			
Key	Cyl.	Track	Rec.	Key	Cyl.	Track	Rec.
018	41	01	00	018	41	01	00
037	41	02	00	037	41	02	00
058	41	03	00	058	41	03	00
096	41	04	00	096	41	04	00
125	41	05	00	125	41	05	00

Prime Data Area, Cylinder 41:

Cyl.	Track	Record 0	Record 1	Record 2	Record 3	Record 4	Record 5
41	01	xxx	003	007	011	015	018
41	02	xxx	022	025	029	034	037
41	03	xxx	040	043	048	055	058
41	04	xxx	065	071	077	089	096
41	05	xxx	102	109	114	119	125

Overflow Area, Cylinder 41:

Cyl.	Track	Record 0
41	06	xxx
41	07	xxx

Figure 9-13. Indexed sequential file before additions. No records are in the overflow area. Normal and overflow entries in the track index are identical.

record in sequence from each track contains a hexadecimal FF to designate the end of the chain. The pointer on each record in the overflow area is called a *sequence link*.

The principal advantage to having an overflow area for each cylinder is that it eliminates the movement of the read-write heads whenever an overflow record needs to be written or accessed. However, the presence of the overflow area reduces the amount of prime data area available for the original records. To avoid this drawback it is possible to specify an *independent overflow area* on a different cylinder to be used either in addition to or instead of the cylinder overflow tracks.

Cylinder Index:

Key	Cyl.	Track
125	41	00
348	42	00
561	43	00
779	44	00
995	45	00

Track Index, Cylinder 41:

Normal Entry				Overflow Entry			
Key	Cyl.	Track	Rec.	Key	Cyl.	Track	Rec.
012	41	01	00	018	41	06	03
037	41	02	00	037	41	02	00
055	41	03	00	058	41	06	02
096	41	04	00	096	41	04	00
125	41	05	00	125	41	05	00

Prime Data Area, Cylinder 41:

Cyl.	Track	Record 0	Record 1	Record 2	Record 3	Record 4	Record 5
41	01	xxx	003	007	008	011	012
41	02	xxx	022	025	029	034	037
41	03	xxx	040	043	048	051	055
41	04	xxx	065	071	077	089	096
41	05	xxx	102	109	114	119	125

Overflow Area, Cylinder 41:

Cyl.	Track	Record 0	Record 1	Record 2	Record 3
41	06	xxx	018 C41,T01,RX'FF'	058 C41,T03,RX'FF'	015 C41,T06,R01
41	07	xxx			

Summary of Changes:

Record added	Placed on track	Record shifted to overflow area	Record number in overflow area	Last record now on prime track
12	01	18	1	15
51	03	58	2	55
08	01	15	3	12

Figure 9-14. Indexed sequential file after addition or records 12, 51, and 08. Records are shifted to the overflow area to make room for records in the proper sequence on the prime data tracks. Overflow records have pointers to the next record in sequence from their respective tracks. Normal and overflow entries are updated to show the new location of records.

Sequential Processing

Sequential retrieval from an indexed sequential file may begin with the first record of the file or with some other specified record. The desired key is placed in a special field referred to as the *key argument*. Retrieval may begin either with that exact key (if it is present), or with the first key having the same high order digits as the key argument. For example, a key argument of 12345000 should be specified to begin retrieval with the first key in the file beginning with 12345 and then continue in sequence throughout the rest of the file.

Sequential retrieval requires not only that records from the prime data area be read into storage, but that the overflow entries in the track index and chaining records in the overflow area be followed to present each record in its proper sequence.

If records are to be updated sequentially, processing steps are the same as those described in Chapter 7. If no record in a given block has been updated, the block need not be rewritten to the file. Only those blocks that have had any record changed need be rewritten.

It is not possible to combine the functions of sequential retrieval with those of addition of records to indexed sequential files.

Direct Processing

Different file definition statements and processing instructions are required to retrieve records directly from indexed sequential files. The programmer first places the key of the desired record into the key argument field. The direct retrieval routine searched the indexes to locate the track containing the desired record and then searches the track for that record and transfers it to main storage if it is found.

The programmer may then extract data from the record or update the record and rewrite the updated record back to the file. The key argument field must not be altered between reading and rewriting.

Direct processing is the most common way of handling indexed sequential files.

A special 1-byte field is used by IBM's Disk Operating System to record the status or condition following each operation on an indexed sequential file. This field indicates such conditions as duplicate record, record out of sequence, or prime data area full while loading the file. During other processing, it might indicate no record found, end-of-file during sequential retrieval, duplicate record during addition, or overflow area full. Some of these conditions are normal and expected, while others may cause an abnormal termination of the program.

Copying and Reorganizing the File

Because it takes longer to access records from an overflow area than from a prime data area, it is important to reorganize the file as soon as the overflow records become numerous. A set of statistics, maintained by the operating system, allows the programmer to know the status of the file. This set includes the prime record count, the overflow record count, identification of available independent overflow tracks, identification of cylinder overflow areas full, and the number of references made to records that are the second or higher links in an overflow chain.

Some systems of indexed sequential files permit the deletion of a record by tagging a certain signal, normally hexadecimal FF, in the first byte of the record. The IBM System/370 DOS does not permit this particular procedure. To delete a record, some flag may be placed in the record to indicate it is to be omitted when the file is reorganized. Reorganization is accomplished by creating a new version of the file using the existing version as input. The original file would be described for sequential retrieval, any records to be added to the file as a separate input file for sequential processing, and the reorganized file as an output file to be loaded.

Advantages and Disadvantages

Some of the advantages of the indexed sequential file are:

1. The programmer is relieved of a tremendous amount of housekeeping detail in maintaining indexes, overflow areas, and chaining fields.
2. The system provides very fast access for records for both sequential and direct processing.
3. With relatively static files the overflow area may be eliminated or kept very small, giving a very high percentage of disk utilization.

Some of the disadvantages of indexed sequential organization are:

1. For a highly volatile file, adding records can require an excessive amount of time as overflow areas become filled.
2. Compared to direct processing, searching the indexes takes a longer time to retrieve records.
3. Variable-length records cannot be accommodated.

PROCESSING DIRECT (RANDOM) FILES

Direct files do not require an index. Instead, some computation is made on the key to transform it into a disk address. This section describes methods to initialize tracks for the file, create the file, calculate addresses, add records, and process both sequentially and directly.

Initializing the Tracks

The principle of direct access files is that any given record may be written or read from the file without regard to what precedes or follows it. Accordingly, before a file can be loaded we should remove all previous data from former files which may have used these same locations. There are available standard disk initialization routines which blank out all data on the track and reset the *track capacity record* on each track to indicate that it is clear. The track capacity record normally is the first record (record zero) on each track. It contains the record number of the last record currently on the track and the number of bytes still available where additional records may be written.

Creating the File

The file loading or creating process works as follows:

1. A record is read from an input file. It need not necessarily be in any particular sequence.
2. Some computation is made on the key to the record to determine a disk address. The address may be expressed as a decimal or binary number giving the relative track number to the beginning of the file, or as the actual cylinder, track, and record number. This address is placed in a special field called the track reference field in some languages or the AC-TUAL KEY in COBOL.
3. Depending upon the option chosen, the operating system then writes the record following the last record previously written on the calculated track, or at the exact record location specified in the track reference field. The operating system checks the track capacity record to see if there is enough room on the track for the record. If so, after writing, the operating system updates the track capacity record to show the last record number written and the number of bytes remaining on the track.

A 2-byte field is used to record an error and status code following each operation. Some conditions encountered might include no room found on the specified track or track address outside the file extent.

Normally, if no room is found on one track in creating the file, the record may be written on the next available track or in a separate overflow area.

Addressing Techniques

Under ideal circumstances, which rarely exist, each record would be exactly one track in length and each key would be the physical address of the track. Because this is seldom the case, some calculation or randomizing formula normally must be used on the key to convert it to a specific track address. Any technique that reduces a longer name or identification number into a shorter code or address is called *hashing*. One of the most common hashing formulas is to *divide the key by a prime number* close to the number of available tracks on the disk. The *remainder* is used as the relative address of the track within the file. The relative address added to the beginning track of the file gives the actual address.

Example 1. Suppose that 100 tracks are required for a file. Ninety-seven is a prime number close to 100. Divide the key by 97 and the remainder of 00 to 96 is the relative track address. Key 12345 divided by 97 equals 127, with a remainder of 26. The record's home address is relative track 26.

Example 2. Assume that 100 tracks are required for the file with five records per track randomized to record address. There is therefore room for 500 records in the file. A prime number close to 500 is 499. We divide the key of 12345 by 499 and then divide the remainder (369) by the number of records per track (5). The quotient (73) is the relative track address; the remainder (4) plus 1 ($= 5$) is the record number on that track.

This method of calculation can be used with nonnumeric keys because the normal alphanumeric codes represent usable binary numbers.

A second method of computing the key is *folding*. Here the key is split into two or more parts which are added together. The sum, or part of it, is used as a relative address. For example, take the key 123456. Splitting the key in half gives $123 + 456 = 579$. Splitting the key in thirds gives $12 + 34 + 56 = 102$. Taking alternate digits gives $135 + 246 = 381$.

Another hashing method is *transforming the key to a different radix* or base. For example, the key 123456 might be converted to radix 11 to produce a four digit address. $(1 \times 11^5) + (2 \times 11^4) + (3 \times 11^3) + (4 \times 11^2) + (5 \times 11^1) + (6 \times 11^0) = 161051 + 29282 + 3993 + 484 + 55 + 6 = 194871$. Use 4871 as the relative address.

Another possibility is to *square the key* or *take its cube* and use certain of the middle digits of the result.

Any method which distributes the relative addresses evenly throughout the file and reduces the number of duplicate calculations, called *synonyms*, will be acceptable.

Adding Records

Unlike indexed sequential files, where the addition of records is a completely different procedure from loading the initial file, direct-access files use virtually the same procedure to add as to load. An input record is read, its key is manipulated so as to produce the track address, and a seek is made to the desired track. Then the track capacity is read to determine the next available location on the track and the record is written at that point. The only problem occurs if there is no room on the home track to hold the record. If the specified track is full, the user must supply another track address on which the overflow record can be written.

There are two basic approaches to the handling of overflow records: *chaining* and *progressive overflow*. One record, normally the first after the track capacity record, is used as a chaining record to provide a link between the home track and an overflow track. The first record that cannot be written on its home track is written on the next available track. The chaining record on the home track then must be changed to give the address of the track on which the record was written. Later, it will not be necessary to search each subsequent track to retrieve that record, for one can go directly to the track specified by the chaining record. A blank chaining record indicates that no overflow from this particular home track has yet occurred.

Under the progressive overflow method, there is no chain from the home track to the overflow track. The overflow track is simply the next consecutive track. A typical procedure is to allow overflow to occur to successive tracks within a single cylinder. If the record will not fit on its home track, each following track may be tried until the end of the cylinder is encountered.

The chaining method of handling overflows is somewhat more complicated to program because IOCS does not handle chaining records, but it may result in shorter search for overflow records. Progressive overflow is simpler to program and will supply as fast timing on retrieval if most of the overflow records can be written on the first track following the home track.

If certain records in a direct access file have more activity than others, they should be loaded first so that they have the greatest probability of being placed on their home track.

Sequential Processing

Records may be retrieved sequentially according to their position on the track by supplying each trach and successive record number to the track reference field before issuing the read instruction. This method may be used for mass changes affecting all or the majority of the records within the file or for recopying the file. Remember that the records on the track are not necessarily in sequence by key.

If the records are to be processed in sequence by key, a separate finder file must be used to find them. Each key in turn is placed in the key argument field, the track address is calculated, the read instruction is issued, and the status byte is tested to see if the record is found.

Direct Processing

The most common way of using direct files is of course in the direct or random fashion. An input record, which can be in any sequence, is read and a calculation is performed on its key to determine the track where the search shold be made for a key equal to that of the input record. If an equal key is found, the record is transferred from disk into central storage where it may be updated.

Two reference fields are required—the key argument and the track reference field. Both must be initialized properly by the programmer before the record can be retrieved.

If the record is not found on its home track, an option may be indicated to permit the search to be continued throughout the remaining tracks of the cylinder. When located, the record is rewritten after updating. Care should be taken not to change the contents of either the key field or the track reference field between reading and rewriting.

If the file is organized by record number on the disk rather than by key, the programmer must supply both the track address and the record address in the track reference field before issuing the read instruction.

Remember that no record found does not necessarily indicate an error. For example, if a file contains the license numbers of stolen automobiles, one would not expect a record to be found in checking out the license plates of a car involved in a minor traffic violation.

Advantages and Disadvantages

Some of the advantages of using direct files are:

1. Access is extremely rapid. No indexes need be searched, and the first seek is made directly on the track where the record is expected to be found.
2. Great flexibility is offered to the programmer, who may use chaining records if desired, address by record ID or by key, or use fixed- or variable-length records.

Some of the disadvantages of direct processing are:

1. Records cannot be accessed in sequential order by key without the use of a separate finder file.
2. A certain portion of the disk will remain unused because of the necessity of maintaining space for adding records to the file.
3. The higher the percentage of disk utilization, the greater the likelihood of having overflow records written on some track other than their home track, with correspondingly slower access time.

SUMMARY

The intent of data base organization is to provide a large, integrated store of data that any user can tap as needed. Data should be defined and stored independent of the limitation of any specific program. Related data in various areas of the files must be able to be created, retrieved, updated, or deleted.

Elements of the data base are the data collection itself, direct access storage devices, the data element dictionary, data base administrator, and data base management systems. The data base has evolved in four distinct phases to reach the current level.

There are three views of the data base, two logical and one physical. The logical views are the schema, or global organization, as seen by the data administrator, and the subschema, or more limited external view held by the application programmer. The physical view of the systems programmer is concerned with the actual appearance of the data on the I/O devices.

Data base management systems may involve at least five different languages to describe and process the data base. They perform a variety of functions to interface the needs of the application program, the operating system, and possibly the data communications software. A back-end processor may perform some of these functions on hardware rather than the usual software.

The data base requires a system of pointers, lists and rings, and inverted files to show the relation of the various elements. Flat files, trees, and plex structures help to describe the relationships.

Physical file organization may be in the form of indexed files, indexed sequential files, and direct (random) files. Operating system routines are available to assist in creating and processing files of these three types.

TERMS FOR REVIEW

Attribute

Chaining record

Data base administrator

Data base management system

Data description language

Data element dictionary

Data independence

Entity

File reorganization

Flat file

Hashing

Hierarchical file

Inverted file

Key argument

Mapping

Plex structure

Pointer

Prime data area

Progressive overflow

Redundancy

Ring structure

Schema

Sequential access

Stack

Subschema

Synonym

Track capacity record

Track reference field

Tree structure

Tuple

Updating

QUESTIONS

1. What is the difference between the traditional file organization and the data base concept?
2. Name and describe the five elements of the data base.
3. Through what four stages did the data base evolve? Do you foresee further changes?
4. What are the objectives of data base organization? To what extent do you believe they have been achieved to date?
5. What are the three views of the data base? What person or group of persons is concerned with each of the views?
6. What do we mean by data base management systems? What elements comprise them?
7. What is a back-end processor, and what is its purpose?
8. Distinguish between lists and rings as means of associating data elements. Give an example of each.
9. Define and give an example of an inverted file. What is its purpose?
10. What are the main characteristics of flat files? What do we mean by normalization in constructing them?
11. Define a tree structure and name its parts. Why is it useful in data definitions?
12. In what way do tree structures differ from plex structures? Which can be more complex to define?
13. Distinguish between the organization of indexed files and indexed sequential files. Which has the more distinct features or components?
14. What steps are required by the operating system to add a record to an indexed sequential file?
15. What is the function of the track capacity record on a direct file? Where does it appear within the file?
16. Using the division-remainder method and 97 as the prime number divisor, calculate the relative track on which a record with key of 54321 should be placed.
17. Describe the differences between the chaining method and the progressive overflow method for handling overflow records on direct files.

CASE STUDY
SUNCOAST COMMUNITY COLLEGE

From the earliest stages of systems design, Gerald Phipps and John Shirley have determined that the alumni master file should be organized as an indexed sequential file. Indexed sequential files may be processed sequentially or directly. The sequential processing will be convenient for making listings, building special report files, and reorganizing the file when the overflow areas become full. The direct processing will permit full identifying information to be obtained about each donor by using the Social Security number in the donor file as a pointer to the corresponding master record.

The alumni master record contains these fields:

1. Delete code (blank for active, X'FF' for deleted)	1 byte
2. Social Security number	9 bytes
3. Name	20 bytes
4. Address	20 bytes
5. City	14 bytes
6. State	2 bytes
7. Zip code	5 bytes
8. Date first admitted to Suncoast	6 bytes
9. Latest date attended	6 bytes
10. Date graduated with first degree	6 bytes
11. First degree earned	3 bytes
12. First major field	3 bytes
13. Date graduated with second degree	6 bytes
14. Second degree earned	3 bytes
15. Second major field	3 bytes
16. Honors and activities (10 2-byte fields)	20 bytes
Total	127 bytes

All these fields are currently present in the student master file, although in different relative positions. Program AMST will create the alumni master file initially only for graduates of Suncoast Community College. At the end of each graduation period, in May, June, July, and December, Program AMST will add new graduates to the file through a batch application.

Program AGFT will add records to the alumni master file of nongraduates who make contributions to the college. This will be an online application. As each contribution is recorded, Program AGFT will check the alumni master file to see if the record of the donor is present. If not, it will be extracted from the student master file and inserted into the alumni master file. Phipps and Shirley believe that this procedure will keep active records readily available without building a huge file of former students who neither graduate nor make contributions to the college.

A number of online applications already available to all terminals will be useful to the alumni application. They include:

1. *SALP—student alpha listing.* This permits the first three or more characters of a student name to be entered. All students whose names begin with those characters are displayed on the screen, with corresponding Social Security numbers.
2. *SRDM—student record display.* This displays any or all of five portions of the record of a student whose Social Security number is keyed in.
3. *SNUM—student numeric listing.* This gives the name of a student whose Social Security number is keyed into the terminal.

QUESTIONS AND EXERCISES

1. Using track capacity table in Figure 8-6, calculate the best blocking factor for the 127-byte records in the prime data area of the alumni master file if the maximum block length is 2000 bytes? Remember that the 9-byte Social Security key must be added to the block length before determining the maximum number of blocks per track.
2. How many overflow records may be placed on each track, allowing for the 9-byte separate key field and the 10-byte sequence link field that is attached to each record? Remember that records in the overflow area of an indexed sequential file are unblocked.
3. As records of new graduates are added to the alumni master file after each graduation period, should they be placed in the overflow area, or should the file be reorganized to merge in the new records into a new file? Give reasons for your answer.

10

HARDWARE
EVALUATION
AND SELECTION

OBJECTIVES

At the end of this chapter, you should be able to:

1. Name the major categories of computer hardware.
2. Give typical examples of each of the major categories of hardware.
3. Describe applications for which various types of hardware are suited.
4. Name at least four alternatives to purchase as a means of acquiring hardware.
5. Name the four steps in procurement of equipment.
6. Describe methods of determining workload requirements of the new system.
7. Describe a systematic approach to determining system specifications.
8. Employ a rating and weighting scale to compare relative merits of different hardware proposals.
9. List typical errors in evaluating hardware.
10. Cite the principal features that should be incorporated into a computer contract.

In Part III of the text we considered all the aspects of systems design. Systems design results in a *design report,* which describes the system *to be built.* Its purpose is to gain approval of users and top management before investing further resources in the project. If the report is approved, systems personnel proceed with the detailed development phase.

Now in Part IV we describe the development stage. This stage involves selecting and ordering hardware, selecting or writing programs, testing the programs thoroughly, and completing the data communications that are a part of most modern computer systems.

Selection of computer systems is often a frustrating and bewildering task at best. The technology is complex and rapidly changing. There are many possible ways in which any system design can be developed. Competition is strong between well-informed and highly motivated vendors. Enormous sums of money may be involved. In fact, some systems departments do not rely on analysts and designers to select hardware, but call on technical support specialists when new or different hardware must be ordered.

Choices of computer systems range from tiny hand-held computers costing less than $100 to huge mainframe networks costing millions of dollars. In recent years, hundreds of thousands of microcomputers have been purchased for business or personal use each year. Each of these computer systems was selected for many reasons, some good and some bad. One of the great tragedies of the relatively short computer era has been our unwillingness or inability to profit from the experience and mistakes of others.

In this chapter we shall review the major classes of computer hardware and then point out some techniques that have been successful in evaluating and selecting computer equipment, as well as some pitfalls that can be avoided.

TYPES OF HARDWARE

All the types of hardware have been discussed in previous chapters. One cannot design output, input, processing, and storage without giving attention to the media and equipment that are to be employed. However, it is not only possible, but probable, that we might have gone deeply into the design of display screens, printed forms, data base, and access methods without considering which actual model or manufacturer of equipment will be selected.

One of the first steps in systems development is to determine the hardware on which the entire computer system is to be based. Often, current equipment is adequate for new or expanded systems. At other times, additional hardware is specified to expand, upgrade, or replace existing equipment. Because a long lead time is often required for equipment to be delivered, timely selection and ordering of hardware are essential.

Not only are there many ways to acquire equipment and hardware services, but also many types of equipment to perform the various data processing operations. Systems developers should refer to current trade journals for comparisons of the characteristics of various classes of hardware. Subscription services such as **DATA PRO REPORTS** or Auerbach provide detailed information comparing all types of computer hardware and software. Tables showing data entry equipment, for example, might compare the primary functions, typical application areas, data media, operating speed range, data volume, cost range, principal manufacturers, and major advantages and disadvantages.

Input Equipment

The systems design phase produces specifications on which selection of input equipment will be based. But there still remain many questions to be considered before equipment is placed on order. For example, even though we may have decided upon keyboard with display screen as our principal method of data entry, we have to answer such questions as these:

1. How many input stations are needed, and where are they to be located?
2. Are dumb, smart, or intelligent terminals needed?
3. Will transactions be sent immediately to the host computer or batched for later transmission?
4. Will screens need color and graphics capabilities?
5. Does each station need disks or diskettes for storage?
6. What size, color, and shape should the screen be?
7. Should keyboard and screen be a single unit or separate ones?
8. How many terminals and what kinds can be supported by a single control unit?

Similar questions must be answered for each other form of data entry equipment to be used by the system. Punched cards may have 80 columns or 96 columns. Card readers may need to sense optical marks as well as punched holes. Card punch machines may punch holes immediately as keys are pressed or only after the entire 80 or 96 columns have been recorded into a storage unit.

If optical scanners are to be used, we must make the final choice between mark readers and character readers. We must consider the character types, or fonts; the media to be read; the type of recognition equipment; and the relative merits of competitive vendors. Ordinary typewriters equipped with special optical fonts provide an effective, economical form of OCR input.

Other data entry forms we might need to evaluate include the key-to-storage systems, such as key-to-tape or key-to-disk. Magnetic ink encoding is another data entry alternative.

Central Processors

The user has many options in selecting the central processing unit, or CPU. Computers may be designed to serve a *special,* limited purpose, or they may be the *general-purpose* type used in most business applications. *Analog* computers measure physical quantities, forces, velocities, or movements and represent their values along a continuous scale. *Digital* computers count specific, discrete values and represent them by a number system, usually binary.

The central processing unit contains the control, arithmetic-logic, and main storage units. The control unit directs operations, selects and interprets instructions, and acts as a central nervous system. The arithmetic-logic unit performs arithmetic functions, tests conditions, and moves, shifts, or compares data in various forms. The main storage unit may be composed of *magnetic cores, semiconductors,* or *silicon chips* capable of being readily magnetized and demagnetized to represent binary digits.

Internal data organization may be of fixed word length or variable word length. With *fixed-word-length* organization, 16, 24, 32, 36, or 64 bits constitute one binary word to be stored and processed as a single unit. Fixed-word machines are described as "word-addressable" because an address or location in storage refers to an entire word. Fixed-word organization is most efficient for scientific processing. Often a number of registers, each capable of holding one word, are provided to speed and facilitate processing. Both *fixed-point* (integer) and *floating-point* data usually may be handled.

Computers using *variable word length* are called "character-addressable." Each address in storage refers to a single character of 6 or 8 bits rather than to an entire word. Fields of data vary in length according to their content.

Virtually all computers use some form of binary representation internally, because the digits 0 and 1 can readily be represented by an "either-or" condition. Magnetization may be clockwise or counterclockwise along magnetic cores; a switch may be open or closed; a hole in a card is either present or absent. However, many different codes may be used to represent numbers, letters, and special characters within main storage.

Because visually interpreting the value of a string of 0s and 1s is difficult, binary digits are often grouped and represented in another number system. For example, by taking any number of binary digits and dividing them right to left into groups of three, we may convert each group to one octal digit. Similarly, we may express each group of four binary digits from right to left as one hexadecimal digit. Octal or hexadecimal notation thus serves as a convenient shorthand for indicating the contents of any storage location which uses a 6-bit or 8-bit code. Figure 10-1 shows some examples.

Main storage units in recent years have utilized new technological developments, such as *semiconductors, charge-coupled devices,* and, to a limit-

Decimal	Binary	Binary in 3s	Octal	Binary in 4s	Hexadecimal
0	0	000	0	0000	0
1	1	001	1	0001	1
2	10	010	2	0010	2
3	11	011	3	0011	3
4	100	100	4	0100	4
5	101	101	5	0101	5
6	110	110	6	0110	6
7	111	111	7	0111	7
8	1000	001/000	10	1000	8
9	1001	001/001	11	1001	9
10	1010	001/010	12	1010	A
11	1011	001/011	13	1011	B
12	1100	001/100	14	1100	C
13	1101	001/101	15	1101	D
14	1110	001/110	16	1110	E
15	1111	001/111	17	1111	F
16	10000	010/000	20	0001/0000	10

Figure 10-1. Comparison of decimal, binary, octal, and hexadecimal numbers from 0 through 16. Binary digits in groups of three convert directly to one octal digit. In groups of four they convert directly to one hexadecimal digit.

ed extent, *magnetic bubbles.* These devices have reduced both the size and the cost of storage as compared with the magnetic core. In addition to being simpler in structure than core, they use less power, give off less radiant heat, and some of them hold stored information even in case of power failure.

Increasingly, CPUs of large mainframes, minicomputers, and microcomputers are employing *read-only memory (ROM)* to increase their flexibility. ROM is faster than main storage and is often used for frequently used routines. ROM is often placed on a single silicon chip that can easily be inserted in the CPU. Instructions, called *microcode* or *microprogramming,* are placed in ROM by the manufacturer or systems programmer. The application programmer can read and use the microcode but cannot alter or add to it in any way.

By microprogramming, it is possible to make one computer execute instructions designed for another computer. The microcode may be modified or replaced at times to give variety to the instructions the computer can execute. Manufacturers may elect to carry out many internal functions either by hardware or by microprogramming. In many microcomputers language translators such as BASIC or even operating systems may be placed in microcode to allow the random access main storage (RAM) to be used entirely by application programs. Figure 10-2 shows the main storage layout of a typical microcomputer.

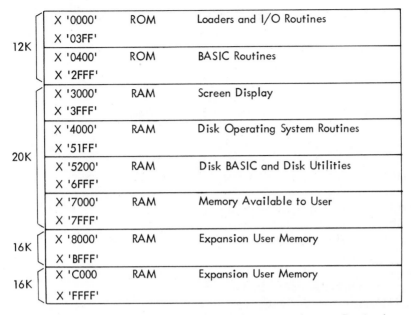

Figure 10-2. Typical microcomputer main storage layout. Read-only memory (ROM) contains routines that can be used but not changed by the programmer. Random access memory (RAM) not required by the operating system is available to the programmer.

Mass Storage

The most commonly used media for storing mass files are magnetic tapes, disks, drums, and magnetic cards. *Tapes* come in two forms, *cassettes* and *reels.* Cassettes are used primarily with mini- and microcomputers for storing both programs and files. Reels are used on larger systems. Tapes are the least expensive of the mass storage media, but they have the disadvantage of not permitting direct access of information. On larger systems, they are used to process files that are not highly active, or to hold backup copies of disk files.

Drums are relatively expensive compared to disks and magnetic cards. They are used primarily for tables, programs, and libraries rather than user data files.

Disks are the most common form of mass storage. They may be either *fixed* in place or in demountable *packs.* The packs are interchangeable so that the same drives may be used for different files at different times. *Diskettes,* also called *flexible* disks or *floppy* disks, come in single units. Some diskettes may now be read on both sides when mounted in place. They are used primarily with small computers, but on some larger computers they may be used in conjunction with read-only storage to record microcode.

As in all other hardware evaluation, storage devices must be compared in terms of their characteristics, and the best combination of features at lowest relative cost should be selected. Some of the characteristics that are commonly compared are:

Storage capacity in millions of bits, bytes, or words
Average time to position head over proper track ("seek time")
Average rotational time
Addressable positions per disk or drum
Number of tracks per cylinder
Number of cylinders per pack or unit
Cylinder capacity
Transfer rate for reading or writing
Number of channels for access
Recording density in bits per inch
Recording code
Data format
Maximum number of units per system
Total storage capacity of entire system
Number of reading heads
Maximum number of tracks one head must read

Output Equipment

Most data systems now being designed will center around the keyboard with display screen for both input and for output. Many of the questions to be answered during the development phase were raised earlier in the chapter. Advertisements, articles, circulars, catalogs, and separate price lists are sources of information needed to choose the proper devices for display of output.

For printed output, choices must be made between impact and nonimpact printers, between fully formed characters and matrix printers, and between character printers and line printers. Prices may range from $200 or $300 for a small nonimpact matrix character printer to more than $100,000 for laser printers capable of producing 20,000 or more lines per minute.

Magnetic output in the form of magnetic tape, disks, drums, or diskettes is usually to create or update mass storage rather than for the ultimate user of the information. Occasionally, magnetic tape or diskettes may be used for distributing software or for transmitting report information such as quarterly reports of Social Security earnings.

Punched cards or forms printed with optical characters may be produced for turnaround documents. Bills or other forms requiring response are punched or printed at one stage of the data processing cycle and sent out to the customer. When returned with the payment or other answer, the punched or printed data can be read into the computer without rekeying.

Computer output microfilm provides a compact, permanent, fast form of output. The high initial cost of the COM equipment can be offset by large savings in storage cost or in mailing to users. The equivalent of a 200-page book can be reproduced in a single microfiche card measuring about 4 by 8 inches and mailed for the cost of a first-class letter. The contents of a four-drawer filing cabinet take less space than a shoebox when reduced on microfilm.

Minicomputers

Small, general purpose computers began to be used for laboratory applications around 1962. By 1968 new advances in transistors and use of integrated circuits produced a whole flood of new products and manufacturers.

These machines came to be called *minicomputers.* The prefix "mini" grew from the fact that originally these devices were limited in size, price, performance, and software support from the manufacturers. Through the 1970s hardware advances continued, so that many of these limitations disappeared. The main distinction between general-purpose mainframes and minicomputers became one of scale rather than major difference in design or capability.

Most minicomputer central processing units have an instruction set of 64 to 100 instructions, although some have over 200. Word length is typically sixteen bits. Most instructions are contained in a single word. Arithmetic operations are typically done in fixed-point binary, but optional floating-point arithmetic may be available for scientific use.

The use of magnetic core for main storage has declined, while increased use of semiconductor solid-state memory has brought lower cost and greater internal speed. Read-only memory is often provided to give greater speed and flexibility to program execution.

While originally limited in their use of input/output devices, most minicomputers now have controllers for a wide range of the standard I/O equipment. A whole new industry has grown up to meet the growing need for minicomputer peripherals, and many independent manufacturers have emerged to meet the growing demand.

Software development has reached the point where many vendors supply operating systems capable of supporting time-sharing and real-time operations.

Minicomputers have been used in five general categories of applications. The categories, with examples of each, are:

1. *Computation:* accounting, inventory, production scheduling
2. *Word processing:* text editing, typesetting, photo composition
3. *Communications:* message switching, front-end processor, remote batch terminal

4. *Data acquisition:* data reduction or conversion, medical test analysis
5. *Process control:* numerical tool control, traffic management

In performing any of these applications, minicomputers may be used in three different ways:

1. As stand-alone computer systems programmed to do a variety of jobs on a small scale
2. As dedicated computers doing a single job day after day
3. As modules or terminals to a large computer system performing some functions on their own or calling on the larger system to transmit or receive data from a central data base

The greatest advantage of the minicomputer is that the user can buy the exact amount of computing power needed for a job. Within the limits of size, the mini can perform any of the functions that a larger computer can. It becomes feasible to locate minicomputers directly at each user's site rather than in a single central location.

The greatest disadvantage of minicomputers has been the limited amount of good software and, sometimes, of maintenance service. Both of these disadvantages have been reduced in recent years.

Microcomputers

Even smaller and lower in cost are the *microcomputers.* Their distinguishing characteristic is the *microprocessor,* often placed upon a minute silicon chip, that performs the basic functions of the central processing unit. Some chips no larger than a fingernail can hold hundreds of thousands of electronic circuits. When the input, output, and storage subsystems are also placed in a small set of chips, the system is called a microcomputer.

Hundreds of thousands of microcomputers are now marketed each year through retail radio stores and newly formed computer stores. They have reached a whole new group of small business users who could not afford the cost of large mainframes in past years. They also attract users for personal reasons, ranging from game playing to keeping household accounts and managing personal investments. Just as minicomputers increased their capability over time, so the microcomputers have added peripherals, software, and storage capacity. An inexpensive microcomputer may control numerous devices, including keyboard, display screens, printers, plotters, cassettes, diskettes, hard disk, light pens, joysticks, audio output, security locks, and heating and cooling systems.

Microcomputers can serve as front-end processors for computer networks, back-end processors for data base management systems, process controllers in manufacturing applications, and stand-alone devices. Their low cost, small size, power, and durability make them viable choices for many business and personal applications.

STEPS IN PROCUREMENT

Selecting computer equipment is a lengthy process beset by uncertainties. If a company is choosing its first computer, it often lacks precise definitions of its needs in terms of timing, volume, and capacity. If it is already using a computer, the problem of choosing among alternative hardware approaches is more difficult than comparing apples and oranges.

Not only are there many suppliers to be considered, but many models and various approaches offered by the same supplier. Often political or economic forces are at work quite beyond the control of the systems department. Nevertheless, there are selection practices that can and should be employed to fortify the final decision with as many facts, performance measures, and comparative figures as possible.

The steps involved in selecting and procuring computer equipment may be divided into four groups: (1) design, (2) solicitation, (3) evaluation, and (4) negotiation (Figure 10-3).

Design

By this time in our process of systems analysis and design, we should have many firm conclusions about the type of hardware that is required. The file design and processing procedures dictate to a large degree the kind of hardware that is suitable. However, we must continue our design activities in more specific ways by (1) formulating objectives and (2) determining system specifications (Figure 10-4).

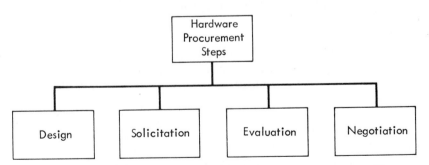

Figure 10-3. Hardware procurement steps. The design step specifies hardware needs. Solicitation invites bids. Evaluation selects the best bid. Negotiation arranges final acquisition details.

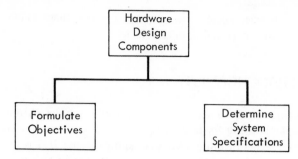

Figure 10-4. Hardware design components. The design phase involves formulating objectives the hardware must meet and then setting exact specifications for the equipment.

Formulating objectives. The objectives should take fully into account not only the present needs but also short-range developments of the next two to three years and long-range projections from three to ten years ahead. Some of these objectives undoubtedly have already been set forth in the system study.

One major objective of any installation is to provide capacity for an expanding work load. Another is to increase throughput—that is, the quantity of work accomplished on a steady, normal basis. A third is to reduce turnaround time, the time elapsed between the input of data into a system and the return of useful information from it.

Most, if not all, of the following items usually appear on a list of objectives or goals of an installation:

1. Provide new applications.
2. Improve capability for production and/or computation.
3. Increase throughput and reduce turnaround time.
4. Reduce costs of equipment, programming, and operations.
5. Make a smooth transition for the previous system.
6. Ensure compatibility with present and future systems.
7. Provide for flexibility.
8. Furnish specified information as requested.
9. Use support of vendors and consultants.
10. Establish the desired mode of operations, whether open or closed shop, online or batch.

Determining system specifications. For each of the objectives that have been set forth, detailed specifications must be prescribed. Workload description includes both current and past volumes and quantities as a basis for future projections. Descriptions of current equipment and activities presently performed are needed to clarify planned activities.

The requirements of the specifications are both *mandatory* and *option-*

al. Mandatory requirements must be provided if the system is to operate at all, while optional requirements will enhance it to the extent that they can be made available. There is probably a tendency to include too many items on the mandatory list at first. Each requirement must be carefully reviewed to be certain whether it is entirely essential or merely a desirable addition.

Availability must also be considered in determining system specifications. This term refers to that fraction of the day or week that the computer system can do useful work. It is always less than one because of the need for equipment maintenance or the numbers of operating shifts scheduled. In another sense, availability refers to devices or features that may be acquired within the constraints of cost or current state-of-the-art technology. There is no point in specifying a system that no one can deliver at the price you expect to pay.

Throughput refers to the total number of jobs processed per unit of time. Sometimes specifications are written in terms of the number of instructions the computer can execute per second. While this may be an important concern where numerous calculations are required, in most situations input/output speed or functions of the operating system are more crucial to throughput.

Specifications must also consider *elapsed time* that each job spends within the computer system. Manual steps in handling jobs outside the computer, such as finding and mounting tape reels or disk packs, contribute more to total program time than hundreds of thousands of executed instructions internally.

A final consideration in specifications is the *resources* used in processing each job. The total work load consists of CPU time, amount of core storage required, input/output channels, quantity and type of disk storage, number of lines printed, and many other factors.

Careful statement of specifications permits vendors to submit realistic proposals and helps to avoid misunderstanding and possible litigation at a later time.

Solicitation

When specifications have been established and made known, the next step is to receive proposals from manufacturers or used equipment dealers. Until very recently one had only two choices in acquiring equipment: either rent it or buy it from the original manufacturer. The matter is far more complex now. Not only are there numerous choices among types of hardware, but the number of options for sources of hardware and services has multiplied. Figure 10-5 shows the components of the hardware solicitation phase.

Alternatives to purchase. Even without considering different types of equipment, some of the choices available for acquiring hardware include:

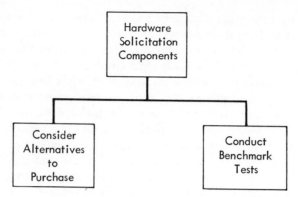

Figure 10-5. Hardware solicitation components. Leasing and lease-purchase arrangements are alternatives to purchase of equipment. Benchmark tests involve running the same program on different equipment and comparing the results.

1. Buy equipment from the manufacturer.
2. Rent from the manufacturer.
3. Buy used equipment.
4. Lease from a leasing company.
5. Purchase service from a time-sharing company, using terminals in the user's office or plant.
6. Engage a facilities management firm. Such a firm provides all computer services, including systems analysis and design, programming, operations, hardware, and supplies. The firm will use your own equipment or supply its own to work either in your facilities or in its own.

In recent years an upsurge in the number of leasing companies and used computer dealers has taken place. There are two distinct types of leases: (1) the financial lease, or the full-payout lease; and (2) the operating lease, or non-full-payout. The first type is similar in many ways to a loan for purchase of the equipment. This plan has been used for many capital assets, such as aircraft, freight cars, automobiles, and machinery, in addition to computer equipment. Under the second plan, the lessee is committed only to a series of rental payments over the term of the lease.

The advantages for the lessee (user) under a third-party lease are:

1. Rental payments are normally 10 to 30 percent less than those charged by the original manufacturer.
2. The minimum monthly maintenance contract from the vendor is usually paid by the lessor.
3. Additional system time may be used at no additional direct rental charge.
4. Flexible schedules of rental charges are often available.

Some disadvantages of third-party leasing are:

1. Leasing companies frequently require a longer lease than do the vendors.
2. Vendor support may apply only in the original location where equipment is installed, and may be canceled if equipment is moved.

In evaluating proposals from computer leasing companies, the following questions should be posed and satisfactory answers received:

1. Is the lease flexible?
2. What equipment does the lease cover?
3. Can equipment be added?
4. What happens if the system fails to operate satisfactorily?
5. How are federal taxes affected?
6. Is a termination penalty included?
7. How are personal property taxes treated?
8. What insurance provisions are included?
9. How will the lease be financed—independently or through a bank?
10. Does the lease contract contain unusual clauses?

Benchmark tests. Once all possible sources of hardware have been considered, they may be invited to submit *benchmark tests* as one means of comparing performance. Benchmark techniques seek to represent the total data processing workload by sample programs. These programs are then run on each proposed machine using the operating systems and compilers proposed by the different vendors to provide the desired data.

Advantages of this system are that the actual operating system, compiler, and machine components are tested. Total throughput can be verified. Actual programs from the current installation may be used where feasible, or new programs for the proposed system may be tested.

Some disadvantages to using benchmarks include:

1. Uncertainty that the benchmark programs and test data are good samples of the prescribed work load.
2. Cost of providing and running the benchmark programs.
3. Difficulty in getting a vendor configuration for testing that is precisely the same as that proposed for the new system. For example, it may be difficult, if not impossible, to run a benchmark with an online system having 50 terminals.
4. Possible need for different versions of programs for each vendor.

Whether or not benchmarks can be used, proposals usually are solicited by an invitation to bid. Even here conflicts can arise. If no preselection of vendors is made, bids might well be received from unreliable firms concerned primarily with cutting prices. If invitations are extended only to bidders who are considered valid candidates, then some charges of favoritism or discrimination might be made. At any rate, bids should be prepared on a uniform format showing cost tables, equipment speeds and performance specifications, software included with equipment, maintenance and support, and other characteristics. It is often fruitful to hold discussions with all vendors between the time of issuing the invitations to bid and the time for receiving bids to amplify and clarify what is needed.

Evaluation

A clearly defined procedure for evaluation of bids for hardware should be spelled out. Criteria to be used for comparison are then established. A rating system provides an objective method of comparing competitive features. Trade-offs between cost, convenience, and time are often necessary. Errors in evaluating hardware made by other users in the past need to be identified and avoided. Components of the hardware evaluation phase are shown in Figure 10-6.

Designating procedures for evaluation. An effective system of evaluation of equipment bids and proposals incorporates the following six steps:

1. List major technical attributes of hardware that you consider important, and identify important subheadings under each attribute.
2. Give each attribute a weight showing its relative importance in your plans.
3. Assign a rating to each vendor for each attribute to show how well the vendor is able to supply that attribute.
4. Multiply each vendor's rating for each attribute by its weight, and get a total of the products.
5. Rate each vendor by cost attributes.

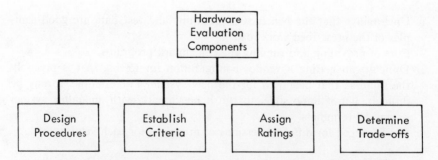

Figure 10-6. Hardware evaluation components. Procedures for evaluation are first designed. Then criteria for comparison are made. Equipment from different vendors is rated. Selection is made on most benefits for least cost.

6. Add together the weighted products of both technical and cost attributes to show a composite comparison of each vendor's total proposal.

Establishing criteria for comparison. It should be obvious from a review of the hardware objectives and specifications that some features are more important than others. By carefully reviewing the system requirements, you should list those attributes that are critical to the operation of the new system and give them a relatively high weight. Desirable features of less importance are given lower weights.

The process of selecting criteria to be evaluated can be highly subjective. The combined opinions and judgments of several evaluators should be obtained. It is important to include each attribute that is to be rated. The weights can reflect differences between installations. For example, a batch installation might attach no weight at all to terminal devices, whereas an online nationwide communications network would have to weigh the attribute of terminals very heavily.

One advantage of this evaluation procedure is that it provides a good balance between objective measures and subjective judgment. Listing every attribute and rating each manufacturer in a comparable way makes the evaluation as objective as possible, while the use of weights still permits individual judgment to be brought into play.

Stating objective ratings. Once the list of attributes, maximum ratings, and weights has been completed, you are ready to begin comparing the vendors. Make a separate column for each vendor, and divide it into two parts. In the first part place the rating that you assign to that vendor's capability to supply that attribute. In the second show the product of that rating multiplied by the weight assigned to that attribute.

Finally, for each vendor add the sums of the products and show them at the bottom of the list of attributes. Figure 10-7 shows a possible table for a simple comparison.

Determining trade-offs. The technical portion of the proposals should be evaluated independently of the cost proposals. Some trade-offs undoubtedly will be required, with some speed or capacity having to be sacrificed in the interest of economy. But it is possible to ease the tradeoff process by assigning relative weights to performance and to cost. The best overall system is that which gives the best performance per dollar of expenditure.

Some ways to compare costs between vendors are:

1. Measuring the cost of executing similar individual instructions
2. Determining the cost of executing each segment or portion of a program
3. Determining the cost of executing a typical mix of instructions
4. Costing out the run of a single benchmark program or a group of best programs

Attribute	Weight	Vendor A		Vendor B	
		Rating	Product	Rating	Product
A. Hardware:					
1. Compatibility with present equipment	4	7	28	9	36
2. Main storage capacity	3	9	27	9	27
3. Reliability	2	9	18	10	20
4. Expandability	3	9	27	8	24
5. Communications handling	3	8	24	9	27
6. Virtual storage capacity	3	7	21	8	24
7. Internal cycle time	2	9	18	8	16
Total			163		174
B. Financing:					
1. Cost	5	9	45	7	35
2. Flexible financing plans	5	9	45	8	40
Total			90		75
C. Maintenance:					
1. Local maintenance personnel	3	5	15	8	24
2. Travel distance	3	5	15	8	24
3. Backup technical personnel	2	6	12	9	18
4. Guaranteed response time	2	6	12	8	16
Total			54		82
D. Software support:					
1. Compatibility with present software	4	7	28	9	36
2. Local support personnel	2	6	12	8	16
3. Availability of training	2	8	16	8	16
4. Additional technical support	2	7	14	7	14
Total			70		82
Overall totals			377		413

Rating Scale: 1 = least favorable;   10 = most favorable

Figure 10-7. Hardware attribute weight and rating form. Weight determines relative importance of each attribute. Rating shows relative standing of each vendor for that attribute. The products of weight times rating are added to give overall standing to each vendor.

Typical errors in evaluating hardware. Even the most careful approach to hardware evaluation and selection is fraught with dangers. The following list points out some of the more common errors with the hope that they might be avoided:

I. Errors in evaluating suppliers:

1. Considering seriously only one manufacturer or vendor
2. Accepting only what a manufacturer or vendor offers, not what it *has* available to offer
3. Failing to define your own needs clearly in sufficient detail
4. Grossly underestimating total costs, especially those of system development, programming, and conversion
5. Failing to pool your needs with other potential users to share costs
6. Failing to check equipment performance with other users of that type
7. Accepting half-truths or statements about performance elsewhere rather than being sure equipment meets your own needs
8. Failing to recognize self-interest, generalizations, and lack of understanding of your problem on the part of vendor representatives

II. Errors in the evaluation of the hardware itself:

1. Failing to run actual tests on your data
2. Failing to recognize the vital role of the operating system and the performance of the supporting software or hardware
3. Failing to calculate the marginal utility of adding certain hardware
4. Failing to compare hardware costs against other alternatives, such as additional shifts, clerical operations, or contracted services
5. Selecting equipment before fully defining system needs
6. Sticking with traditional concepts such as detailed printed reports rather than exploring ways of displaying only the specific information desired
7. Failing to anticipate the effect of *Parkinson's Law*—that the real or imagined needs of users expand quickly to fill up available computer time
8. Failing to consider independent peripheral suppliers

Negotiation

Once competing proposals have been analyzed and fairly evaluated, the next step in the procurement process is negotiation. In this section, guidelines for the selection of the successful vendor are presented, and then a checklist of points to be considered in drawing a computer contract is set forth. Figure 10-8 shows components of the hardware negotiation phase.

Guidelines. In the solicitation phase, guidelines may have been established for minimum and maximum ranges of cost and performance. Using these guidelines, one might choose any of the following:

1. The best performer having effective cost less than the maximum
2. The lowest-cost equipment whose performance exceeds the minimum standard

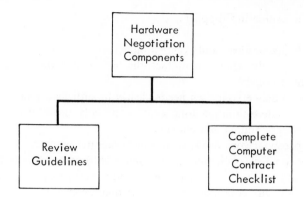

Figure 10-8. Hardware negotiation components. Negotiation involves review of acquisition guidelines and of a detailed checklist of details to be included in the final contract.

3. The equipment that satisfies cost and performance standards and has the highest performance-cost ratio

During the negotiation phase any questions not completely clarified in the bid proposals must be resolved. Before any contract is signed, it should be thoroughly reviewed by all interested parties.

Computer contract checklist. This section gives a list of items in contracts for computer equipment and services which systems personnel, data processing managers, and management should consider when installing or expanding a system. Contracts should also be discussed with the organization's legal counsel.

1. *System design:* details about applications the system is supposed to handle; critical features such as accuracy standards, job scheduling, normal and peak volumes, and personnel availability
2. *Responsibilities:* user; consultant; manufacturer; leasing company (if any); communications company; supplier of forms, software, furniture, etc.; contractor for site preparation; and movers
3. *Basic system specifications:* performance specifications of each piece of hardware; specifications for accessories, such as ribbons, cards, and forms; software specifications such as utility routines, assemblers and compilers, application packages, documentation requirements, ownerships rights, limitations on use
4. *Site preparation:* advance notice to permit construction of necessary facilities; operating and environmental requirements for air conditioning, power and light, floor-load limits, fire protection, and wiring; space requirements for equipment, service areas, storage, offices, and power rooms

5. *Personnel training:* who gets the training, length of course, when and where given, who gives the course, who pays for it

6. *Delivery and acceptance:* delivery dates for software and hardware; special arrangements for installation; testing time before and after installation; system checkout; time of first rental or purchase payment

7. *Finances:* rental arrangements; purchase of equipment and software; taxes; discounts; site preparation; shipping and installation costs; penalties

8. *General operations:* permissible temperature and humidity; permissible power-range limits; personnel matters, such as unionization, training, injuries

9. *Maintenance:* reliability of equipment, such as downtime, repair time, backup; kind and frequency of routine maintenance; modification or upgrading of equipment

10. *Modification and termination of contract:* improvements by suppliers; modification by user; conversion of systems; conditions of termination

11. *Miscellaneous contract terms:* length of agreement; warranties; right to assignment to another party; governing law; other documents included in contract; arbitration

HARDWARE MAINTENANCE

Systems developers often fail to take account of the overriding importance of hardware maintenance service. With large-scale mainframes, maintenance is usually provided by the manufacturer under a monthly service contract for each piece of equipment or special feature. Charges usually vary with the distance maintenance personnel must travel. Developers must consider the location of the nearest maintenance personnel to determine both cost of service and time required to correct problems. For distances beyond 100 miles, charges of $40 or $50 per hour for travel time alone might be required.

Where equipment is purchased, maintenance service is rarely if ever included in the purchase price. But costs of rentals or leases usually do include maintenance. All costs of hardware acquisition and maintenance must be considered in deciding which alternative to choose.

For large mainframes, it is impractical to take hardware to a maintenance center for service. Thus all service is performed at the installation site. Several choices are usually available that vary the hours during which maintenance service will be performed or the way it will be billed:

1. Contracts may specify that service will be performed upon call during normal working hours, perhaps eight or nine hours per day. Extended service at higher cost can be contracted for up to 24 hours per day. Service calls after the contract hours are subject to additional charge.

2. Provision is usually made that requests for service will be answered within a reasonable time, such as two hours or four hours from time of call.

3. The monthly payments for full maintenance contracts usually cover all labor and materials except equipment damaged through negligence of the user. Repair or replacement of damaged equipment is billable at extra cost.

4. Factory warranty maintenance agreements may be offered at less cost than full maintenance contracts. These provide for a lower monthly cost, but require additional hourly charges whenever service is performed.

5. With increased use of inexpensive silicon chips for intricate electronic components, the tendency is to replace defective parts rather than attempt to repair them at the site. Defective chips may be returned to the manufacturer's maintenance headquarters for repair or salvage.

Contracts for microcomputer maintenance differ widely from those for large mainframes. Service may be offered by the original manufacturer, by the local franchised dealer, or by independent maintenance companies. Many microcomputer users elect not to carry maintenance agreements at all, but to take their chances on getting service when needed and paying for only for service as rendered. Many maintenance companies give low priority to work performed without a continuing contract and charge a higher hourly rate. They also charge for all parts repaired or replaced.

A second type of service for microcomputers carries a monthly charge that covers parts and work done at the maintenance center. This requires that the user deliver the equipment to the maintenance center and pick it up when ready.

A third type of service agreement provides for full maintenance performed at the user's site. This type of service is most expensive of the three, but eliminates delay in getting equipment back in order and the bother of disassembling and transporting equipment to the maintenance center.

SUMMARY

In this chapter we have reviewed some of the principal types of hardware, with particular emphasis on different methods of input and output. Online terminal devices are rapidly replacing keypunches as the principal data entry devices. Optical character recognition (OCR) offers great promise for ultimately reducing or eliminating the need to key and verify source data. Computer output microfilm (COM) provides fast output, compact storage, and convenient reproducing of data in human-readable form.

The four steps in procurement of hardware are design, solicitation, evaluation, and negotiation. Design involves the formulating of objectives and determination of system specifications.

Before soliciting bids, one must consider the many alternatives to purchase, such as renting or leasing, acquiring used equipment, use of a time-sharing service, or engagement of a facilities management firm. Benchmark tests permit direct comparison of rival bids on sample programs and test data.

Evaluation involves assigning a rating to each type of equipment and vendor. The rating is multiplied by a weighting factor showing the relative importance of that item, giving a product. The sum of the products gives the relative technical merits of each manufacturer. These merits must be compared against the cost of the equipment.

Negotiation requires guidelines to determine the basis for awarding the contract. A list of items to be spelled out in the contract is furnished.

The availability and cost of hardware maintenance must be considered when choosing equipment. Contracts may call for full service on-site or for service when equipment is delivered to the maintenance center. Users may elect to carry no regular maintenance agreement and pay only for services as they are performed.

TERMS FOR REVIEW

Analog computer
Benchmark test
Cathode ray tube
Computer output microfilm
Digital computer
Diskette
Font
Hardware maintenance
Impact printer
Magnetic bubbles
Magnetic core
Magnetic ink encoders
Microcomputer
Microprogramming

Minicomputer
Negotiation
Nonimpact printer
Optical character recognition
RAM
ROM
Semiconductor
Silicon chip
Solicitation
Third-party lease
Throughput
Touchtone telephone
Trade-off

QUESTIONS

1. Give some of the relative advantages and disadvantages between keypunching cards and using magnetic tape encoders as a means of originating source data for computers.

2. What features contribute to the growing popularity of online terminals for data entry?
3. What reasons have tended to slow the adoption of optical character readers as input devices?
4. Under what circumstances are line printers better to use than microfilm for computer output? When or where might microfilm be better?
5. Give advantages and disadvantages of minicomputers as compared with large-scale mainframe computers.
6. What are some of the applications for which microcomputers are being used?
7. What are the four steps in procurement of computer hardware?
8. Describe the most common objectives of any data processing system.
9. What are included in the system specifications?
10. Name and evaluate the various alternatives to purchase of computer hardware.
11. What is meant by the term "technical attribute?" Give several examples.
12. Distinguish between the terms "rating" and "weighting" in connection with hardware evaluation.
13. What errors are often made in evaluating suppliers? In evaluating hardware itself?
14. What areas need special attention in negotiating computer contracts?
15. Prepare a rating scale similar to Figure 10-7 to evaluate hardware needed for some application with which you are familiar. Then assign weights to the attributes, multiply each attribute by its weight, and add the products.
16. Describe alternative methods of obtaining hardware maintenance and compare the costs, convenience, and promptness of the different methods.

CASE STUDY
SUNCOAST COMMUNITY COLLEGE

The team studying the alumni application system considers several possible hardware configurations. One alternative is to have a completely separate microcomputer system for the Office of Institutional Advancement. The second alternative is to have a terminal tied to the existing network. The first approach has several advantages:

1. The main thrust of the office is to promote Suncoast Foundation, a separate nonprofit corporation organized to solicit donations for the benefit of Suncoast Community College. Ownership of a sepa-

rate system is cleaner than having to share facilities between two separate organizations.

2. Eventually, the alumni application will be combined with other Suncoast Foundation mailings, records, and activities. A single computer system serving both alumni and other donors might be convenient.

3. The microcomputer system can combine record keeping of the donor files with word processing functions in preparing and mailing financial campaign materials.

There are several disadvantages to a separate microcomputer system:

1. The capacity to store and process files on disk is much more limited than that of the IBM 4341.

2. The present IBM 4341 system is not equipped to receive input from any microcomputer.

3. If the microcomputer cannot be online to the larger mainframe, all alumni master records will have to be created manually from printouts from the present student master file.

As a second alternative, the team considers utilizing the existing IBM 4341 network and disk files and adding only a terminal in the Office of Institutional Advancement. They determine the cost of an additional terminal to be about $1650 for purchase or $65 per month for lease. The lease price includes maintenance, but the purchase price does not. Necessary cabling can be run between buildings by the college maintenance staff. The added terminal can utilize the present operating system and take advantage of all present network software. They conclude that, initially at least, it is more practical to utilize the present IBM 4341 network and data base, with data entry by regular terminal.

The team determines that the only hardware to be acquired is the additional terminal in the Office of Institutional Advancement. The 1100-line-per-minute printer in the Computer Center can prepare all reports, labels, and listings. Present disk storage space is adequate for the alumni master file and the donor files for the next several years.

Terminals presently in use are manufactured by three different vendors. Although they have minor differences on the keyboards and control keys, essentially they are interchangeable. Screens have 24 lines of 80 characters each. Common attribute characters among all makes of terminals permit special display features such as field protection, flashing characters, and high-intensity lighting for emphasis. The decision for selecting the brand of terminal therefore concerns only price and availability. All three brands have maintenance available in the immediate vicinity with guaranteed response to service calls within two hours.

Gerald Phipps prepares specifications for the terminal and sends them through Rick Jagsby to Mack Cordron. Cordron issues requisition for lease of one terminal. The Purchasing Department issues request for bid to the three different suppliers. At the appointed time the bids are opened. All three suppliers are found to meet specifications and so the lowest price is approved. Purchase order is issued with delivery date set for September 15.

QUESTIONS AND EXERCISES

1. List the reasons the alumni systems study team decided against use of a separate microcomputer system and chose to add a terminal to the existing system.
2. Give reasons why the lowest price for equipment is not necessarily the best buy.
3. Should the study team have recommended obtaining bids from vendors other than the three who already are supplying terminals to the college installation? Why or why not?

11

SOFTWARE EVALUATION, SELECTION, AND DEVELOPMENT

OBJECTIVES

At the end of this chapter, you should be able to:

1. Describe the stages of the evolution of software services.
2. Name the parts of a computer operating system.
3. Name and describe the hardware features required by operating systems.
4. Define multiprogramming and state the hardware and software considerations to make it possible.
5. Describe each of the libraries of the IBM Disk Operating System and the types of statements and programs stored there.
6. Describe the steps taken and the purpose of system generation.
7. Compare and contrast the three principal sources of software described in the chapter.
8. Name the principal programming languages and the major features of each language.
9. Describe areas of programming specialization and career paths that may be followed by programmers.
10. Name the major applications for which software may be acquired.
11. Describe tax considerations and legal problems involving patents and copyrights that have created confusion about software.

Software is broadly defined as the detailed instructions, or programs, which are fed into a computer to tell it what to do. The function of software is to match the general capabilities of the computer to the particular needs of the user at low-level cost.

In designing a computer, engineers often have to choose between using hardware to accomplish some particular function or operation or doing the same job through the use of software. No matter what its design, internal processing speed, storage capacity, or the number of instructions it can execute, no computer system can be truly effective without good software.

STRUCTURED PROGRAM DEVELOPMENT

Detailed *programming* nearly always will be done during the development phase. The original systems design normally has indicated the type of work to be done, and even the record layouts and data flow, but not the actual detailed programs. The development phase requires estimates of the time required to write, compile, and test all programs needed by the system. Estimating program requirements is a difficult matter. Not only do programmers work at different rates, but they use different approaches to a problem. One programmer might require 50 percent more instructions to perform a given routine than another. Asking each programmer to make his or her own estimate of the time it will take to write a given program is one solution to this problem. The programmer should make three estimates: the most optimistic, the most likely, and the most pessimistic. All the estimates can be averaged together, or those from the programmers most likely to be assigned to the project can be used to come up with a realistic estimate.

Structured programming is a rigorous form of modular programming. It has three major objectives:

1. Greatly reduced testing time
2. Improved programmer productivity
3. Greater clarity and comprehension of programs

Now used by many computer manufacturers, user organizations, and universities, it is considered the best way of teaching beginners how to write programs.

Structured programming embodies three major concepts. *Top-down design* (Figure 11-1) begins with identifying major functions and then breaking those functions into successively smaller functions. *Top-down coding* (Figure 11-2) refers to the idea of writing the code so that higher levels of design are coded before the lower levels are even designed. *Top-down testing* involves testing the higher levels of logic within a program, with the lower levels represented as dummy modules or "stubs." This whole approach is in direct contrast to the classical approach of testing first individual modules, then programs, and finally systems.

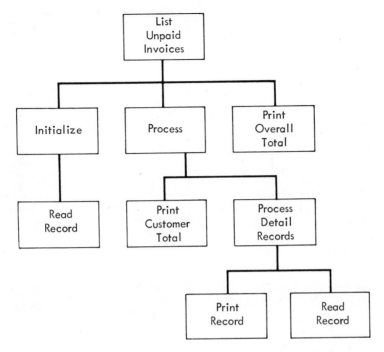

Figure 11-1. Top-down design. This hierarchy chart shows the main program module with each subordinate module. Major functions appear toward the top of the chart. Some lower-level modules are utilized by more than one other module.

The theory behind structured programming comes from the works of E. W. Dijkstra, C. Bohm, and G. Jacopini. It is based on the notion that any proper program can be constructed from three basic building blocks known as (1) process boxes, (2) IF-THEN-ELSE mechanisms, and (3) DO-WHILE mechanisms. These diagrams are shown in Figure 11-3.

Not all languages are equally convenient in employing these structures. Pascal, COBOL, and PL/I have features that permit them to be readily used, but programmers in FORTRAN, RPG, or assembly language must simulate these features.

Along with structured programming have come many other extensions and refinements, such as the use of programming teams, programming librarians, and special charts such as shown in Figures 4-7 through 4-11. The structured walk-through is a method of discussing with other members of the team the proposed approach a programmer plans to take before coding is started. The collective review of the approach is useful in detecting flaws in logic or design before program writing is commenced.

Some other features of structured programming that have gained wide acceptance include:

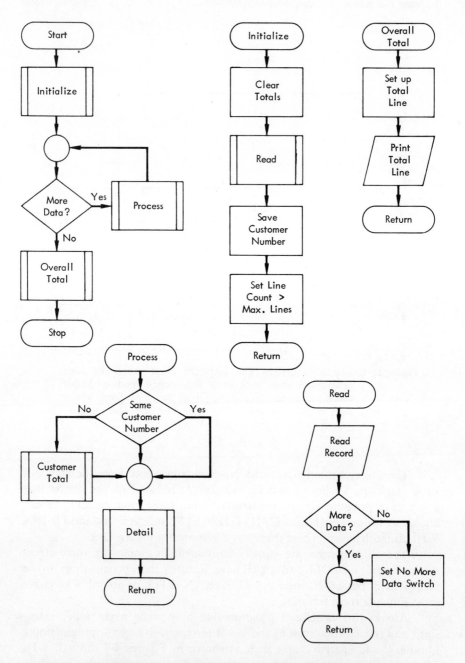

Figure 11-2. Top-down coding. Each module from the hierarchy is represented by a program flowchart. Each module has a single entry and single exit point, and ideally is contained on a single page of coding.

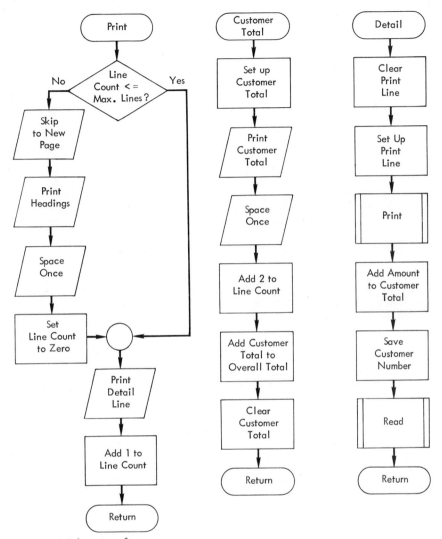

Figure 11-2 (*continued*)

1. Avoidance of GO TO statements to make it easier to follow program flow
2. Limiting each module to a single page of coding
3. Use of standard method for formulating names of files, records, and working-storage items
4. Indentation and spacing of entries in programs to show hierarchical relationships
5. Giving paragraph names numeric prefixes to facilitate finding their location within long programs

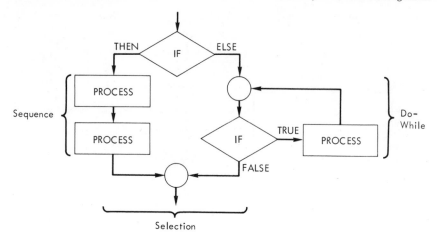

Figure 11-3. Structured programming basic building blocks. The three
basic blocks can be combined in any way necessary to
represent the most complex program logic.

6. Placing file and record descriptions, as well as processing routines, in the
   source statement library from which they can be copied into each source
   program that uses them
7. Standard methods of opening, closing, and processing files, and providing end-of-file routines
8. Providing only one entry point and one exit from every module

There are many advantages to using a structured programming approach. In its most complete form, structured programming involves the
use of a team consisting of a lead programmer, additional programmers and
coders as required, and a program librarian or secretary. The program is
developed from top down, first with the overall logic and then with each
function spelled out in more detail.

EVOLUTION OF SOFTWARE SERVICES

The term *programming* roughly refers to the producing of software, and the
term *program* traditionally has been applied to the software itself.

The development of software has progressed through five distinct
phases:

1. The early development, when the limited software available was developed jointly by the user and the computer supplier
2. The development of user groups to interchange ideas and problems as
   well as to define software packages and aids
3. The change of attitude toward programming brought about by conversion to third-generation computers

4. The beginning of a separate software industry apart from the computer manufacturer
5. The growth and proliferation of software services

Early Development

When the first computers became available commercially in the 1950s, nearly all programming had to be done in machine language. There were very few outside services, and the production of programs was divided almost evenly between users and manufacturers. Management generally was in favor of the development of computers and accepted the high start-up costs. In general, only large users could afford the early computers and the expenses associated with getting them on the air.

User Groups

The second period in software development ran from the late 1950s to the middle 1960s, roughly the time of second generation computers. During this time user groups such as SHARE, GUIDE, and COMMON came into being. The need for high-level languages was established, and the first compilers began to appear. Programmers became more expert in the applications with which they were working, principally payroll, inventory, and other accounting applications. The first generalized software began to appear. User groups provided voluntary exchange of programs, and a new cost consciousness came into being. Another clear need which emerged during this stage was the need for some alternative to batch processing.

Changing Attitudes

With the conversion to third-generation systems, the critical role of software became even more apparent. A third-generation system generally was dependent upon an operating system, often one of such bewildering complexity that much of the software provided by the manufacturer was necessary simply to make the computer work at all. Users still felt the need to become more self-sufficient in the development of their own applications programs. Severe personnel shortages were encountered, frustration grew, the cost of programming in many cases exceeded the cost of equipment, and users generally had to take a long hard look at their capability to produce software.

Beginning of an Independent Software Industry

In the last few years of the 1960s, outside services began to form, offering everything from education and training to proprietary packages and contract programming assistance. The so-called "unbundling" step taken by IBM in 1969 and followed by some other manufacturers provided for separate pricing of hardware and software services. Many capable programmers launched software houses of their own, of which a good number met with great success. Users found that in many cases they could purchase software that was both cheaper and more reliable than that which they could produce themselves.

New legal complications sprang up. Software became the subject of patent and taxation litigations. It also became an antitrust issue.

Software Service Growth

The reliance that a user once placed upon the vendor is now undergoing rapid change. It is still customary for vendors to supply the operating system, assemblers, compilers, and utility routines. Some applications packages are available from vendors, but under the unbundling policy most of these require an additional fee. Consequently, EDP managers and systems personnel now have to consider whether programming services are to be obtained from the computer manufacturer, from outside services, or from an in-house programming staff. Even more fundamentally, they must consider what role each of these should play or what combination of resources will produce the best result.

The appearance of mini- and microcomputers on the computing scene has brought greatly enlarged opportunities for software houses. Most of these low-cost systems are sold with little or no software provided by the manufacturer. Many of the purchasers are small businesses who have no experienced programming staff. A huge market has developed for application programs for small users. Some useful programs have been distributed through radio stores and retail computer stores on magnetic cassettes or floppy disks for prices as low as $5 to $10.

On the other end of the scale, users of large computer systems have found it preferable in many instances to purchase or lease tested software for data communications, data base management, and other applications rather than spend the time, money, and frustration on in-house development.

OPERATING SYSTEMS

Most modern computers operate under the control of an operating system, which consists of a collection of programs that enable the computer to take over many of the chores formerly performed by the operator. The operating system normally is provided by the manufacturer and should be evaluated as carefully as the hardware. In the long run, it may be more important in total throughput than computer cycle time or the number of instructions executed per second.

Purposes of an Operating System

The operating system is designed to:

1. Increase the throughput, or the volume of work that can be handled over a given period of time.
2. Assist the operator in running production programs and programmers in writing, compiling, debugging, and testing programs.
3. Help to reduce and detect errors.
4. Provide standardized service programs and libraries where these service programs and user-written problem programs may be stored for ready access.
5. Permit higher utilization of computer facilities through multiprogramming, time-sharing, and smoother job flow.

The complexity of the operating system will vary with the amount of core storage available, the number and types of peripheral devices, and the internal capability of the computer. Most computer operations can be performed either by hardware or by programming. Cost and speed determine which of the two approaches is used for any given operation.

Hardware Requirements

An operating system as we know it today would not have been possible with some of the earlier computers. Certain hardware features which were not available earlier are needed to permit the operating system to function. Some of the special hardware requirements are:

1. *Magnetic disk files* for the storage of the operating system and its associated programs and work areas. Tape files may be used for operating systems, but are far less efficient because they cannot be processed randomly.
2. *Interrupt facilities.* There must be some type of hardware interrupt features to signal some conditions so that the operating system can take control, correct the problem if possible, or else proceed to the next job.
3. *Input/output channels.* I/O channels, also called *data channels* or *buses,* serve as small special purpose computers to carry out input or output operations independently of internal operations.
4. *Large main storage.* Because a portion of the operating system using many thousands of bytes normally resides in main storage, the storage requirements for modern computers are much higher than those of earlier machines.
5. *Communications ability.* By being able to connect to commercial communication lines, modern computers are able to service many users over a widespread geographical area through the use of online terminals.

Multiprogramming

On every computer, the time required for input/output operations is much longer than that required for internal processing. The central processing unit therefore spends a large percentage of its available time waiting for data to be read from or written to the I/O devices. One way to reduce idle time is to use a combination of hardware and software features in such a way as to permit more than one program to reside in main storage and for each program to be executed in turn on a priority basis. *Multiprogramming,* then, is the interleaved execution of several jobs, or the ability to run multiple programs concurrently.

The job with the highest priority is started first. As soon as a program in that job issues a command to an I/O channel, control is passed to the program with the next highest priority. That program, in turn, continues until it either issues its own I/O command or is interrupted by the completion of the I/O operation of the higher-priority program. Then control is returned to the first program. On larger computers this successive interruption and transfer of control can service as many as a dozen different jobs.

The following considerations should be kept in mind about multiprogramming:

1. Main storage must be large enough to hold the desired number of jobs. Storage may be divided into fixed partitions, each of a preestablished size, or it may be allocated dynamically during execution to accommodate the different sizes of the programs being executed at any time.
2. The hardware must provide an interrupt signal as each I/O operation is completed.
3. The software must determine the priority of jobs and keep track of the instruction being executed in each program when an interrupt occurred, so that control can be returned to that point at a later time.
4. Storage protection must be included to prevent one program from writing or storing data into a section of storage being used by another program.
5. Programs must be relocatable, so that they can be executed in whatever part of storage is available.

Parts of an Operating System

Even operating systems designed by different manufacturers or by independent software houses share a number of common features. It is beyond the scope of this book to attempt to examine all operating systems in detail. Instead, we will concentrate on the Disk Operating System (DOS) used by the smaller models of the IBM System/370 computer family as an example of a typical operating system.

Operating systems consist of *control programs* and *processing programs.* Control programs provide functions such as handling of input/output operations, error detection and recovery, program loading, and communication between the operator and the program. In other words, control programs control the operating system. There are three principal control programs:

1. The supervisor, also called in other machines by such names as executive, monitor, controller, or nucleus
2. Job control
3. Initial program loader (IPL)

Processing programs are those which are loaded, executed, and supervised by the control programs. Processing programs accomplish the work that is to be done in a data processing installation. There are three principal types of processing programs:

1. Language translators. DOS provides five such translators: assembler, COBOL, FORTRAN, PL/I, and RPG.
2. Service programs supplied by the manufacturer. These include linkage editor, librarian, sort-merge, utilities, autotest, and emulator.
3. User-written problem programs.

The first two types of processing programs, language translators and service programs, normally are contained in the operating system supplied by the manufacturer. The third type, user-written problem programs, includes all those written by the user to solve the problems peculiar to each installation. The great bulk of the processing programs are in this third group.

Programs of the operating system are stored in various forms in three *libraries:*

1. Source statement library
2. Relocate library
3. Core image library

Let us now consider control programs, processing programs, and libraries in somewhat more detail.

Control programs. During normal operation, the *supervisor* remains in a portion of core storage. Its purpose is to control loading and execution of all other programs and to handle all requests for input/output operations. The supervisor is loaded into core storage from the systems residence disk pack at the start of each day, or at other times following an interruption in processing, by the *initial program loader* (IPL), which then transfers control to the supervisor. At the time, the date and time of day may be supplied and devices may be added or deleted from the table of available equipment. The supervisor displays messages to the operator as programs are executed and receives responses from the operator to select certain options or inquire into the status of certain parts of the operating system.

The *job control* program reads and interprets information contained on job control statements, sometimes called the job stream. The statements contain information giving the names of programs to be executed, label information for tape and disk files, and assignments of specific hardware devices to program files. Figure 11-4 shows a series of typical job control statements. A job may consist of one or more job steps. Each job step consists of a program to be executed, indicated by a / / EXEC statement.

Processing programs. The IBM Disk Operating System provides five different languages that may be translated into relocatable object programs, or modules. They are assembler language and the four high-level languages, COBOL, FORTRAN, PL/I, and RPG.

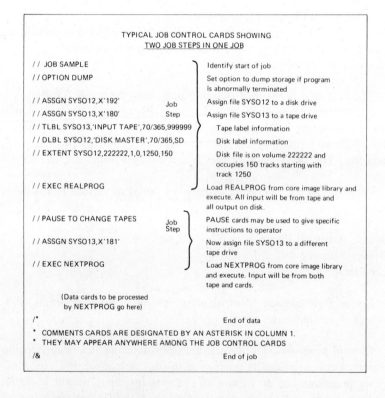

Figure 11-4. Typical job control statements showing two steps in one job. Each program executed constitutes one job step. Every job must have one or more job steps. Job control statements indicate the sequence in which the job steps will be carried out.

The *linkage editor* takes the relocatable object programs produced by the language translators and converts them to executable form. To do so, it must link together modules written by the programmer with other modules (principally input/output subroutines) supplied by the operating system. The linkage editor also assigns specific addresses according to the portion of core storage in which the program is to be loaded and executed.

The *librarian* is a group of routines that maintains and services the libraries of the operating system. Some of the librarian features are:

1. Cataloging (or adding) programs to the libraries
2. Deleting programs from libraries
3. Renaming, condensing, and reallocating entries in libraries
4. Displaying (or printing) and punching elements from the libraries
5. Displaying directories for all libraries

The *sort-merge program* provides for sorting of records to be done on magnetic tape or disk files. Specification cards provide the location and size of key on which sorting is to be done, the sequence desired, the number of input files, size of records, number of records, and other data.

Utility programs are provided to copy data files from one storage medium to another. Card to tape, tape to disk, disk to disk, and disk to printer are only a few of the combinations available.

The *basic telecommunications acces method* (BTAM) controls the transmission and reception of messages over telecommunications lines. BTAM provides asynchronous transmission to permit the various terminals to be polled by the central processing unit on a regular basis. Any terminals having a message to send may transmit it. Data communications are treated more fully in Chapter 12.

In addition to these processing programs supplied with the operating system, most application programs will be written or acquired by the programming staff of the installation.

Libraries. Each entry in the *source statement library* is called a book. Books may consist of macro definitions or assembler or COBOL source statements. Macro definitions are the series of statements which are to be executed each time the macroinstruction is used. The source statement library is divided into two sublibraries, one for assembler and one for COBOL. Each book in a sublibrary consists of any number of source statements which can be incorporated into any user's program by using a COPY statement.

Figure 11-5 shows the series of statements necessary to place a book in the source statement library. Each book in the source statement library is compressed—that is, each blank field is replaced by one or more bytes giving the count of blanks of that field and the count of nonblank characters in the preceding field. When source statements are brought from the li-

CATALOG MACRO DEFINITION INTO ASSEMBLER
SUBLIBRARY AND BOOK OF COBOL SOURCE
STATEMENTS INTO COBOL SUBLIBRARY

```
//  JOB CATALBK                              Identify start of job

//  EXEC MAINT                               Load MAINT from core image library and
                                             execute. MAINT is a librarian program
                                             for all libraries.

CATALS A.ADDX                                Catalog into assembler sublibrary under
                                             name ADDX

BKEND A.ADDX
    MACRO
& NAME ADDX    &X,&Y,&Z                       Book to be catalogued; note that BKEND
       L       0,&X                           statements precede and follow the
       A       0,&Y                           macro definition statements
       A       0,&Z
       ST      0,&X
       MEND
BKEND A.ADDX

CATALS C.ISFILE                              Now catalog into COBOL sublibrary under
                                             name ISFILE

BKEND C.ISFILE
     FD ISFILE, RECORDING MODE IS F,         The second book may be catalogued
        LABEL RECORDS ARE STANDARD,          into a different sublibrary by the
        DATA RECORD IS DISK-RECORD,          same program
        BLOCK CONTAINS 12 RECORDS,
        RECORD CONTAINS 60 CHARACTERS.
BKEND C.ISFILE
/*                                           End of data
/&                                           End of job
```

Figure 11-5. Job control statements to catalog a macro definition into the assembler sublibrary and a book of COBOL source statements into the COBOL sublibrary. Contents of each book are enclosed in bookend (**BKEND**) statements giving the name of the book.

brary, the blanks are restored so that source statements look the same as they did in the original input.

Each entry in the *relocatable library* is called a module. Modules are the output from the language translators. Modules may consist of complete programs which have been translated, subroutines or subprograms for specific purposes, or input/output control system (IOCS) modules.

These relocatable modules, which already have been compiled and are in machine language form, may be combined together into a single executable program by the linkage editor. Figure 11-6 shows the control statements necessary to catalog a relocatable module into the relocatable library.

Entries in the *core image library* are called phases. They are the output of the linkage editor and are ready to be loaded into core storage and executed. Programs are loaded from the core image library into core storage by job control under the command of a // EXEC statement. Programs

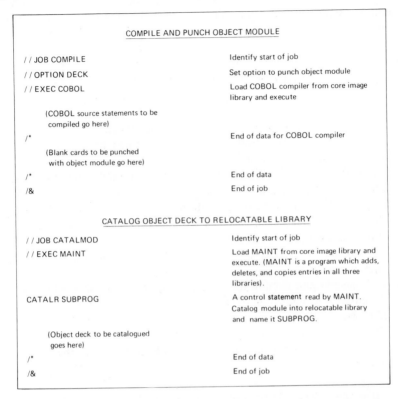

COMPILE AND PUNCH OBJECT MODULE

/ / JOB COMPILE	Identify start of job
/ / OPTION DECK	Set option to punch object module
/ / EXEC COBOL	Load COBOL compiler from core image library and execute
(COBOL source statements to be compiled go here)	
/*	End of data for COBOL compiler
(Blank cards to be punched with object module go here)	
/*	End of data
/&	End of job

CATALOG OBJECT DECK TO RELOCATABLE LIBRARY

/ / JOB CATALMOD	Identify start of job
/ / EXEC MAINT	Load MAINT from core image library and execute. (MAINT is a program which adds, deletes, and copies entries in all three libraries).
CATALR SUBPROG	A control statement read by MAINT. Catalog module into relocatable library and name it SUBPROG.
(Object deck to be catalogued goes here)	
/*	End of data
/&	End of job

Figure 11-6. Job control statements to punch and catalog a relocatable object module. Another option is to record the object "deck" on a disk work area and catalog it into the library from there.

also may be loaded from the core image library by the LOAD and FETCH macros executed in an assembler program.

Language translators, service programs, and all of the most commonly used user programs are cataloged into the core image library.

System Generation

Operating systems are being revised continuously. Errors are discovered and corrected, new utility routines are developed, compilers are expanded, and other improvements are made. Once or twice a year, the manufacturer or software firm that developed the operating system will release a new version. The new version normally is designed on a very generalized basis so that it can accommodate all the devices and features available to the computer system.

Few installations will wish to use all of the features supplied with the standard system. Instead, they will tailor the operating system to their own specific requirements. This procedure is called system generation.

In generating the system, the user must plan to assemble a supervisor to handle his or her exact configuration. There are eleven steps in the process of system generation, which normally requires several hours:

1. Initialize the disk pack that will contain the system.
2. Copy the IBM-supplied tape or disk onto the new pack.
3. Retrieve sample problems.
4. From the sample problem output, delete unwanted programs from all libraries of the system.
5. Allocate the proper size to each library.
6. Place standard labels for the linkage editor file and work files into the standard label area of the supervisor.
7. Assemble a new tailor-made supervisor, producing an output object deck of cards.
8. Linkage edit and catalog the supervisor into the core image library.
9. Assemble the relocatable IOCS modules that fit the user's particular hardware configuration.
10. Catalog the IOCS modules into the relocatable library.
11. Delete the supervisor and unwanted IOCS macros from the relocatable library.

It is often desirable to copy the contents of the library into a backup pack several times during the system generation process so that the system generation can be restarted in the event of error or machine failure.

SOURCES OF SOFTWARE

Data processing managers and systems personnel may draw upon three principal sources to meet their software requirements: (1) the computer manufacturer; (2) independent software firms, and (3) in-house programmers. Often, a combination of sources will provide the most economical and efficient balance.

Computer Manufacturers

Computer manufacturers generally offer some or all of the following five services:

1. System software
2. Applications software
3. Customized software

4. Educational services
5. Certain processing services

The first of these, systems software, formerly was offered without separate charge along with the equipment itself. Most of the remaining four services are subject to an extra cost, which may be a flat charge, monthly lease, or a charge subject to a negotiated contract. In some instances, software furnished without cost prior to the unbundling announcement of 1969 continues to be offered without additional charge by the manufacturer. However, new applications packages, educational courses, or systems work are charged for separately.

Independent Software Houses

The great growth of the separate software industry in recent years is evident in at least eleven major categories of services offered by nonmanufacturers. Most of these eleven categories can be further divided into separate, nonduplicated subgroups. These categories of services include the entire spectrum of people-based support activities within the information processing field.

1. *The service bureau.* There are three principal subdivisions of the service bureau: batch processing, online services, and dedicated service bureau, which may be either batch or real-time.
2. *Contract programming.* Basically, there are three types of service offered; peakload processing, conversion from one language or machine or another, and specialized skills or knowledge of an application or industry.
3. *Consultation services.* These include audits, management advice, systems planning, evaluation, and other activities that are normally associated with consulting firms.
4. *Personnel services.* Activities under this category involve recruiting, testing and measuring, and staff evaluation.
5. *Package suppliers.* Packages generally appear in four different groups: systems packages, conversion aids, applications packages, and documentation software. Giving a brand name to a package of one of these types is becoming a popular practice.
6. *Proprietary software.* Companies that offer this service usually work on site to provide tailor-made systems or programming aids for the user.
7. *Facilities or installation management.* This type of service implies the complete management and staffing of an organization's data processing activities by the service company. Services are provided either on the user's own site or on a remote processing basis.
8. *Dedicated applications.* In this growing area of software activity, the firm concentrates on a single unique service. Frequently the service will

be based upon a large, specialized data base. Examples include attorney's reference service for legal precedents, credit bureau investigation, investment portfolio analysis, and even dating service.

9. *Time sharing.* Regional and national networks already exist to offer problem-solving service, usually in FORTRAN or BASIC. Services also exist to permit problems to be phoned in by voice to a central station, where the problem is solved and the answer returned by telephone.

10. *Turnkey services.* This type of market usually provides single use, low-cost systems frequently based on minicomputers.

11. *Educational services.* Many software firms, as well as computer manufacturers, are finding the educational market to be very lucrative. In terms of professional instructors, number of students served, and dollar value, many of these organizations are rivaling the nation's largest universities. There is a great variety of offerings, from custom designed courses on site to standardized, continuing programs in the vendor's own schools. There are two-day management seminars and programmer training courses lasting many months. Publishing of textbooks, programmed instructional materials, and audiovisual materials is mushrooming.

We see from these examples that the software industry is growing rapidly and that the number of options available to the systems planner is almost unlimited.

In-House Programming

The majority of applications programs probably will be produced by the user's own personnel. In evaluating software, the systems analyst must be acquainted with the relative strengths and weaknesses of the traditional programming languages. The systems analyst should also be familiar with the concepts of structured programming as a tool for improving the quality of programming and documentation.

Comparison of Languages

It is probably an oversimplification to say that FORTRAN should be used for scientific jobs and COBOL for business-related jobs. But we should realize that these languages were specifically designed for these principal uses and that enormous libraries of programs in FORTRAN and COBOL have been accumulated over many years.

FORTRAN probably is the oldest of the computer languages in common use and seems to have more individual practitioners than any other language. It is convenient for the mathematician, engineer, or scientist with a specific problem to solve, but severely limited in working with massive files, and input/output operations are slow. FORTRAN is implemented on a large number of different computers, placing at the disposal of the programmer a wide variety of mathematical functions and fully debugged subroutines. It is certainly advantageous to the programmer in giving a quick and convenient approach to problem solving. Its disadvantage is the large amount of core required and the relatively slow execution time for high volume activities.

ALGOL is another scientific mathematic language. Considered by many mathematicians to be superior to FORTRAN, it has had wide acceptance in Europe but has been less popular in this country. Few ALGOL compilers are available on business-type computers.

The BASIC language was developed at Dartmouth College in connection with the General Electric Company, primarily for the use by students for learning computation under a time-sharing system. Although BASIC is an extremely easy language to learn to use, it nevertheless has advanced features which make it as powerful as most other mathematical languages. BASIC has been implemented on a number of nationwide time-sharing services. Although not intended originally for commercial use in processing large numbers of business records, BASIC has been adopted on many mini- and microcomputer systems as the principal language. Improved formatting instructions and file handling capability have been introduced, and some versions permit interactive processing of online data. From a limited beginning for problem solving and instructional use, BASIC now serves many users of small stand-alone systems or stations on distributed data processing networks.

COBOL is the most widely used business-oriented language. An outgrowth of a conference of major manufacturers, university people, and industry representatives under the leadership of the federal government, it has limited mathematical ability but can do the computations necessary in typical business problems. It is specifically designed and well suited for handling masses of data on a variety of files. Equally adept at servicing cards, tapes, disks, and high-speed printers, it is able to process fixed- and variable-length records and to make widespread use of common English terms and ordinary decimal number notation. It is implemented on virtually all of the major medium- and large-scale computer systems.

COBOL compiles extremely efficient programs at a high rate of speed. Its advantages include the use of familiar terms, a large amount of self-documentation, ease of conversion from one computer type to another, ability to handle many types of files, and efficiency of machine code which approaches that of the best assembly language programs. In the absence of compelling reasons to the contrary, most business data systems use COBOL as their fundamental language.

Pascal is the most recent programming language to gain widespread general acceptance. It was officially described by Niklaus Wirth in Zurich in 1971. Compilers have been developed for many computers, including several microcomputers.

Pascal was the first language designed specifically to support the concepts of structured programming. The structures of both data and algorithms permit top-down development. Well-written programs are easy to read and to understand. Pascal is popular as a first programming language in computer science courses.

Pascal programs follow a precise form. The heading starts with a PROGRAM statement giving the name of the program and the types of files to be employed. Then follow definitions and declaratives of constants and variables. Then come the statements separated by semicolons that express the logical design of the program. Statement groups such as IF-THEN-ELSE, REPEAT-UNTIL, WHILE-DO, and FOR-DO permit the use of selection and repetition in structured programming.

PL/I was developed by IBM in order to bring together the diverse features of mathematic and business programming. It has some characteristics derived from FORTRAN and others from COBOL, but it also has extensions and improvements contained in neither of the first two languages. PL/I is an extremely powerful language, but at present appears to be somewhat more difficult to learn than either FORTRAN or COBOL. Earlier versions seemed to require a great deal more core storage for instructions than do programs written in other languages. So far, major manufacturers other than IBM have not implemented PL/I compilers.

Report program generators (RPG) provide a quick and simple way of extracting information from files of many types. RPG also is likely to require a large amount of core and to have a fairly slow execution time in comparison with other languages. It is the principal programming language for some of the smaller computers, but with larger models it is used principally for extraction of one-time information or for other programs not intended to be used for regular production.

APL is an extremely powerful programming language based on special mathematical notation developed by Kenneth Iverson, an IBM employee. Available on a few dedicated time-sharing services throughout the country, it provides amazing computational ability with a relatively small number of keystrokes. Designed specifically as a terminal language, APL has not been implemented as a fundamental language for batch-type processing.

Assembly languages in the hands of a skilled programmer usually provide the most efficient use of core storage and execution time. They generally require more programming time and effort and a higher level of skill than some of the high-level languages. Without question, the greatest disadvantage of assembly languages is the fact that they normally can be used only on the computer for which they are designed. Whenever a change is made to a different computer, all assembly language programs must be rewritten. Occasionally, a manufacturer or software supplier has provided an emulator or simulator to permit assembly language programs written for one machine to be executed on another, but emulation or simulation usually increases execution time.

Even where other languages are used, certain routines, principally those concerned with telecommunications, may need to be written in assembly language. Practically all modern computers can link together program segments written in different languages. This feature permits a high-level language to be used for the bulk of the programming effort which is most time consuming, while assembly language routines can be written for those operations that cannot be done in the high-level language.

TRENDS IN PROGRAMMING

Within the past few years, programming has reached the point where many persons call it a profession. Like other new and rapidly emerging fields, it lacks maturity, standardization, and clear criteria for training and for evaluating performance. Without question, however, programming has now reached the point where it has become the principal factor in the use of the computer and no longer plays merely a supporting role.

Here we shall examine some of the current and developing trends in the field of programming. It matters little whether the programmer is employed by a user or a software house; in either case one generally will have the same career paths, opportunities for specialization, demands placed upon one, and rewards.

Although there is still some place for the programmer who is concerned primarily with coding routines and doing repetitive tasks under close supervision, the real demand today is for programmers and analysts of far greater expertise and imagination. The need for specialization grows greater as our operating systems and applications become more complex. No one can become expert in everything, and by limiting his or her field of concentration a programmer can become known as an expert in a chosen field.

Career Paths

In general, programmers can follow three basic lines of progression in advancing through an organization. Figure 11-7 shows the possible way which programmers might move from an entry position toward the top level in one of the three areas.

The administrative-technical avenue, as the name suggests, requires not only programming and systems ability but also the ability to manage and administer a department. Managerial talent is not always associated with the interest in detail and the analytical ability that are needed in programming. This area generally leads to the highest potential salary of the three groups.

The systems avenue appeals to programmers who have not only tech-

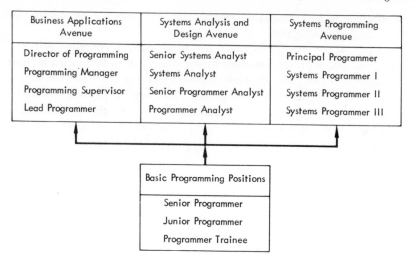

Figure 11-7. Career paths in programming. Programmers are more
likely to enjoy their work and remain loyal to their companies if they have a variety of opportunities for professional growth and advancement.

nical know-how but also an interest in the broader relations between people, methods, and materials. A skillful systems analyst may be of far
greater value to his or her organization in analyzing, designing, and
implementing new systems than in attempting to work as a manager or administrator.

The technical programming avenue allows talented programmers who
are interested neither in administration nor in systems work to advance to a
high salary and proficiency level within their own field of interest. It is
sometimes contended, though, that there is an inherent limit to the output
rate of a pure programmer which will not justify a top-level salary.

The Peter Principle, formulated by Laurence A. Peter, is an astute
formulation of the fact that a person tends to rise to his or her level of in-
competence. With the three career paths available for programmers mentioned above, it should be possible for capable programmers to avoid this
trap and advance to their highest level of both competence and interest.
The person who enjoys solving difficult algorithms or designing new
approaches to problems might make a miserable administrator. The organization is best served by recognizing and rewarding superior ability in each
of the three career paths.

Areas of Specialization

The form of specialization a programmer chooses might depend upon
the nature of the organization for which he or she works, or it might reflect
the programmer's educational background, personality, or recent experience. Some of the more common areas of programming specialization are:

1. Business data processing
2. Mathematic or scientific programming
3. Systems programming
4. Computer games

Business data processing is probably the largest of the four groups. This type of programming often does not require a high level of mathematical ability but may involve very complex logic, be subject to constant change, tie together systems which are basically dissimilar, and require close time scheduling. For this reason it appeals to programmers who have backgrounds in business administration, accounting, or liberal arts, with only a relatively short period of specialized programming training. Because the beginning programmer may be employed with little or no experience or specific training, the true value of the superior business programmer often is not fully appreciated.

Most mathematic or scientific programmers have bachelors or advanced degrees in mathematics, physics, or engineering. Programming in this area tends to be almost exclusively in FORTRAN and concerned with large amounts of mathematical manipulation and calculation. In many cases there is no need for detailed knowledge of complex data structuring. Subareas of specialization in scientific programming tend to be carved out more in terms of the specific disciplines than in terms of the differences in the nature of the programming itself. Although the educational level and mathematical knowledge of this group of programmers generally are higher than of those involved in business data processing, there is no indication that the programming itself is as difficult.

Systems programmers are employed mostly by hardware manufacturers and software firms. They include the compiler writers, operating system people, utility routine programmers, and applications packages developers. Such persons are likely to be heavily machine-oriented, but their backgrounds and preparations tend to be quite diverse. This area of specialization should be attractive to the expert programmer who is not interested in systems analysis and design or in a managerial position.

The advent of the microcomputer for personal use has opened a high market for computer games. Many software writers have found it highly challenging and financially rewarding to concentrate on producing such games.

It seems obvious that anyone who is going to work directly with a computer must specialize in some fashion. The question is the degree of specialization one seeks. It is true that the narrower the field on which one concentrates, the easier it is to become an expert in the history, theory, and practice involved in that field. One may specialize either because one is genuinely interested in a field or because one feels that specialization offers a simpler way to reach a position of recognition and authority.

The generalist, by definition and nature, probably will have less depth in any particular area, but should be more adept at relating and balancing a variety of experiences. It seems apparent that systems analysis and design involve a greater degree of generalization than systems or applications programming. The big problem in any programming organization is to provide the proper balance between technical depth and proficiency with broad understanding and appreciation of interrelated problems.

Applications Development without Programmers

A growing trend is for users to be able to design and implement applications without the need for programmers. Eventually, this trend may sharply reduce or even eliminate the need for application programmers.

It works in this way. The operating system or software package includes general-purpose programs that permit the user to specify the data elements to be used, the format to be presented, the sequence, control fields, accumulated totals, and other specifications of the desired information. Such report generators take the user's specifications and produce the information exactly as desired. The need for a special application program is eliminated.

Microcomputers are being employed by many users who are not accomplished programmers. Three software packages that are widely available at modest cost have been found to meet almost all the data processing needs of many users: (1) a word processing program, (2) a file management system, and (3) an electronic spreadsheet program.

After a short orientation session, most users can begin using the word processing program to produce memoranda, correspondence, form letters, reports, manuals, and files. Such documents can be retained, modified, or updated as needed, and reprinted automatically at high rates of speed.

The file management system permits creation, searching, sorting, updating, and merging of files of customer accounts, mailing lists, and other useful records.

The electronic spreadsheet permits the user to do extensive data analyses, tabulations, projections, and simulations. The results are displayed upon a screen or printed out as hard copy.

Recent developments such as microcomputers, portable computers, and dial-up networks put users into direct contact with many data bases. Generalized software enables them to extract the data they need and present it in the form they wish. They need not depend upon application programmers to supply their information.

SOFTWARE APPLICATIONS

As the software industry has grown, the number of applications has likewise expanded enormously. Now it is possible to purchase or lease software of every description, from complete operating systems to turnkey applications for entire industries, such as automobile dealers, banking, or education. The great majority of programs for sale are written in BASIC or COBOL, but many systems programming products are written in assembler language. The number of companies offering software has mushroomed. It is not the purpose of this book to promote any company or software product. Dozens of advertising pages appear in computer-related newspapers and trade magazines. Many programs have sold thousands of copies at prices above $50,000. In addition to the software that is offered to the general public, many organizations offer to share software they have developed for specific applications with other users on a cost-reimbursement basis. For example, many colleges and universities offer student record systems, registration packages, and other educational programs to their sister institutions at only the cost of copying on tape or disk.

Two applications bear special mention: (1) data communications and (2) data base management systems.

Data Communications

Recent hardware developments have simplified the task of programming for online systems. But most computer networks still require complex routines to maintain a file of screen formats to be transmitted over communications lines and to carry out the actual sending and receiving commands. Online systems also must make it possible for each terminal in the network to have access to a number of separate programs and to have the same program available to a number of terminals at the same time.

Often data must be compressed or compacted by eliminating blanks or other repeated characters before sending it over transmission lines. Then at the other end of the line, the compressed data must be expanded so that it can be correctly read.

Specialized communications software performs many of these functions. In almost all such software, the choice must be made between the amount of internal storage required to house the software and the speed with which responses can be sent to inquiries from the terminals. Communications software introduces still one more level of programming, all of which must interface smoothly if the system is to run to specifications. The application program, communications software, and operating system must all convey their requests back and forth to one another so that each can perform its own functions.

Data Base Management Systems

The software that enables a data base to be defined, created, used by a variety of users, and modified as needed is called a data base management system (DBMS). It must work as an interface between the application programming language, such as COBOL or PL/I, the operating system, and possibly the data communications control system. At least five languages may be involved in data base management to some degree. These languages are detailed in Chapter 9.

The specific technique or formula for addressing and searching for a record in the data base may appear in any one of three places:

1. A routine in or called by the application program
2. A part of the data base management system
3. A feature of the operating system access method

The power and availability of data base management software can be expected to continue to increase as more users accept the admitted complexity of data base organization in order to reap its benefits.

SOFTWARE PROBLEMS

One of the major thorns in the side of management with regard to software evaluation is the fact that software includes principally labor. Labor is the most expensive and unpredictable quantity in software development. It is difficult at best to predict the length of time expected for programming, and this is especially true in a new, untested application. The quantity of a programmer's output can be measured fairly well but its quality is difficult to measure.

Software can account for as much as two-thirds of the annual cost of a given computer installation. A chronic shortage of qualified personnel has led to considerable job hopping. Someone has said that software is the only business where all of its assets walk out of the door at 5:00 P.M., and there may be some question as to whether they will come back the next morning. As soon as programmers become reasonably competent, they seem to become disposed to seek greener fields with another company or to set up their own programming business.

Software has built-in limitations. Complete standardization is, if not impossible, at least years away. Even the so-called common languages, such as FORTRAN, COBOL, or BASIC, actually have so many variations that the same program run on different machines does not always produce the same results. But beyond the language itself, standardization of applications is even more difficult. Individual users feel that their own problems and needs are unique. Even when they purchase or acquire a software package instead of developing it themselves, they are likely to spend considerable time and effort in making modifications. To be sure, it is more economical and efficient to make some changes in an existing program than to develop one from scratch, but many such changes are the result of whim and do not make real improvements in the quality of the program.

Software development has traditionally lagged behind new hardware development. New computers have been marketed without supporting software or with operating systems full of bugs. Where in the early years of computers, 80 percent of costs were in hardware and only 20 percent in software, now the percentages are just reversed. The cost of hardware has steadily declined, while the cost of software and its production time have increased dramatically. Some authorities state that if program development takes as long as two years, the program will almost certainly be obsolete before it can be used.

Many newly established software houses have been founded by talented programmers with limited managerial experience and even more limited capital. Software houses have the same problems in attracting and retaining capable people as do established users. The quality of software, amount of support, and the stability of the company should be carefully investigated before contracting for software services. Users should be aware that if they make changes in purchased or leased software, they may subject themselves to withdrawal of vendor support and have to pay for assistance provided by the vendor in debugging or testing for software errors.

Anyone considering the selection and purchase of software packages would do well to consider the 25 points shown in Figure 11-8 before making a final decision.

Tax Considerations

Some states consider that purchased software is subject to state sales tax. Others consider it to be in the nature of nontaxable services. Software written by the programmers within the installation itself is usually not taxed. Software has been assessed intangible taxes in some states. Courts have not ruled consistently in all cases involving taxation of software.

The federal Internal Revenue Service has issued guidelines concerning federal income tax treatment of software costs. The most important features of the guidelines are summarized as follows:

1. All computer users must separate the costs of developing software from all other data processing costs. Users may elect to treat such costs either as current expense or as intangible assets to be amortized over a maximum of a five-year period. They cannot change method of accounting without permission of the Internal Revenue Service.
2. Software packages which are purchased must be treated as an intangible asset.
3. Costs of software packages leased or licensed must be treated as current expense.
4. The guidelines do not specifically answer the tax treatment of:
   a. Costs of outside software services such as systems engineers and contract programmers.
   b. Fees paid to outside services for consulting, facility management, or other software development.

Questions by Systems Analysts	Questions by Programmers
1. Is the package adaptable to our needs? 2. What changes must we make to use it? 3. What costs are involved? 4. Is it well designed and efficient? 5. Will it require additional equipment? 6. How good is the system documentation? 7. Can our present staff implement the package? 8. How good is the vendor support? 9. What are opinions of other users? 10. How stable is the vendor? 11. How does the package fit our overall systems plan? 12. What in-house technical support will it require? 13. Is programming language hardware independent? 14. Does the package meet valid user criteria?	1. What is the quality of programming? 2. Are appropriate file processing techniques used? 3. Is package compatible with present (or planned) software? 4. Are peripheral devices used effectively? 5. How good is the program documentation? 6. Are programs easy to maintain? 7. Do programs use computer mainframe efficiently? 8. Does the package have to be modified for our use? 9. Are programs well structured? 10. Does the package utilize effective data collection techniques? 11. Are effective controls and backup provided?

Figure 11-8. Twenty-five questions to ask about software packages. Both the systems analysts and programmers should review the software to see how well it meets their specific needs.

The effect of income tax regulations may strongly influence the decision as to whether to develop software in-house, to purchase or lease a package, or to contract for customized programming.

Patents and Copyrights

There still are cloudy areas on the question of patents or copyrights for computer programs. The interchange of programs among users, practiced so freely during the past generations, is likely to become rare as programmers and companies move to protect their proprietary interests in the software they develop.

The U.S. Patent Office has generally held that software could not be patented, since it involved mental rather than mechanical processes. However, a few patents have been issued.

Several hundred computer programs have been copyrighted. Copyright protection primarily gives authors the right to prevent others from copyrighting their work. The *idea* of a program may not be copyrighted, but only the form in which it is presented.

The best form of protection of software is still being debated. Some persons believe that a new type of classification, such as registration of programs under a special law, is needed.

SUMMARY

Structured program development embodies top-down design, top-down coding, and top-down testing. Its objectives are to reduce testing time, improve programmer productivity, and improve clarity and comprehension of programs. All program logic is assumed to be based on three basic structures: (1) sequence, (2) IF-THEN-ELSE, and (3) DO-WHILE.

We have looked at many of the factors involved in evaluating software. We have looked at the sources of obtaining software, whether from in-house, from manufacturers, or from independent software suppliers. We have seen that the development has come through five distinct phases. At least eleven major areas of specilization are identifiable in present-day software activity. Each of these major areas is further subdivided so as to provide a wide proliferation of choices in types of software and services available to the user.

Operating systems provide software of great sophistication and complexity. They have contributed greatly to the development of the computer services by providing a batched job facility where jobs may be stacked one after another. Remote batch processing allows job control statements, programs, and data to be entered from a remote terminal.

Operating systems provide bookkeeping services and file management facilities. They permit large central computer systems to be time-shared by a number of users scattered over a wide geographic area and provide large data bases which may be accessed and updated from many locations.

Operating systems greatly extend the power and scope of computer systems and use machines to perform many jobs that formerly required operators and programmers. Inasmuch as the operating system is an integral and indispensable part of the modern computer, it is perhaps the most important single software product to be selected.

Some of the problems involved in selecting software may be traced to the lack of a sufficient number of well-trained personnel, the very rapid growth of the field, the number of untested new firms, the instability caused by job hopping, and the failure on the part of managers to understand the complex nature of programming.

We have examined the principal characteristics and some of the advantages and disadvantages of selecting FORTRAN, ALGOL, BASIC, COBOL, PL/I, RPG, or assembler language.

Programming as a career continues to become both more demanding and more rewarding to one who seeks to establish it as a profession. Programmers may advance along the administrative-technical avenue, the systems avenue, or the technical programming avenue on their way toward the top level of their chosen career. They may choose to specialize in business data processing, in the mathematic or scientific computing, or in software development. Or they may prefer to become generalists in systems analysis and design.

Commercial software may now be purchased or leased for a wide variety of applications. Two of the most important areas serviced principally by commercial software are data communications handlers and data base management systems.

Software development faces many problems. Included in them are the questions of treatment for tax purposes and of protection by means of patents or copyrights.

TERMS FOR REVIEW

APL	Phase
Book	Processing program
Control program	Sequence structure
Data base management system	Structured walk-through
Facilities management	Supervisor
IF-THEN-ELSE structure	System generation
IPL	Top-down coding
Job control	Top-down design
Library	Top-down testing
Module	User group
Multiprogramming	Utility program

QUESTIONS

1. What are the objectives of structured programming? How does the structured walk-through help to meet these objectives?
2. Draw the flowchart symbols that represent the three principal building blocks in structured programming.

3. Name some of the features of structured program development.
4. What is the relationship between the five distinct cycles in the development of software and the three generations of computers?
5. What have been some of the effects of the unbundling policy (that is, the separate pricing of hardware and software) on the user? On the manufacturer? On the independent software supplier?
6. What hardware features, present on third-generation but not on second-generation computers, are needed to allow operating systems to function?
7. Name the three libraries found with the IBM System/370 Disk Operating System and describe the types of entries found in each.
8. What is done in system generation of the operating system? What is its purpose?
9. What is the difference between control programs and processing programs? Give some examples of each.
10. Give as many examples as you can of the eleven software services provided by nonmanufacturers.
11. What career paths are available to programmers in working their way up to the top in their profession?
12. What is meant by the Peter Principle and what does it have to do with the promotion of programmers?
13. What are the circumstances under which you might select an assembly language rather than COBOL as the basic language to be used in your programming?
14. Summarize the major characteristics of each of the programming languages described in this chapter.
15. What is the purpose of software for data communications? What are some of the functions it must perform?
16. List and describe the five possible languages that may be incorporated into data base management systems.
17. What are some of the problems regarding software development that are not present in developing other kinds of products? How may they be overcome?
18. What are some of the taxes to which software has been subjected in various states? What guidelines for income tax treatment have been issued by the Internal Revenue Service?

CASE STUDY
SUNCOAST COMMUNITY COLLEGE

The team making the detailed systems study of Suncoast alumni application turns its attention to the selection or development of software. Regular team members Gerald Phipps, Senior Systems Analyst, and John Shirley, Senior Programmer, confer with Rick Jagsby, Director of Systems Development, Saundra Dean, Director of Programming, and Mack Cordron, Dean of Data Systems. After a survey of available software, they conclude that application programs will have to be written in-house. They decide to use COBOL, the language in which virtually all in-house programs have been written.

Referring to the objectives of the alumni application developed earlier, they determine these programs will be needed:

1. AMST—a batch program to pull alumni master file from student master file. This program will have two modules. The first will create the original file by pulling the record of every student who has graduated as indicated by the presence of an entry in one or both fields showing data of graduation. The second module will search the student master file after each graduation date and create alumni records for each student who graduated on that date. The alumni master records will be organized as an indexed sequential file, with Social Security number as the key.

2. AGFT—an online program with one module to enter donor records into the donor file and another module to view the donor record. The donor file will be a sequential file with Social Security number as the key. Records will be variable-length, with space for 50 gifts per year. A new file will be created each year. As Social Security number of each donor record is entered, the alumni master file will be checked to see that a corresponding record exists. If it does not, a record will be pulled from the student master file and added to the alumni master file. The first donation received from an alumni member or former nongraduate will result in a new record being created in the donor file. Subsequent donations that year will add new segments to the donor record.

3. ALBL—a label printing program to print labels of students by year of graduation, by city, by major, or by other specified category. The program has one module to produce a work file for sorting and another module to print out the sorted records. The standard COBOL SORT feature will perform the sorting.

4. ALST—a program to list alumni or nongraduate donors in a

number of sequences. Options to the program will permit detailed contributions for the current year or annual contributions for the past five years to be included.

5. ADSP—an online screen display showing alumni master for any student whose Social Security number is entered. The screen will be consist of 24 lines of 80 characters each. The display program will have an option that will allow correction of name, address, or other data under carefully controlled conditions.

John Shirley is assigned to do the actual programming and completes the program design, coding, and testing on schedule. A date of October 15 is set for implementation. This will permit master records to be created for the most recent May, June, and July graduates. The busy fall semester registration and reporting period will be concluded, and the rush of registration for the spring semester will not yet have begun.

QUESTIONS AND EXERCISES

1. Which of the programs for the alumni application do you think should be written first? Why?
2. What advantages are there to have Program AMST written with two modules as described rather than writing two separate programs, one to create the original alumni master file and the other to add records of recent graduates?
3. Draw a high-level program flowchart for Program AGFT to enter the records into the donor file or to view the donor records.

12

DATA COMMUNICATIONS SYSTEMS

OBJECTIVES

At the end of this chapter, you should be able to:

1. Name six essential parts of a data communications system.
2. Distinguish between the purpose and function of modems and transmission control units.
3. Compare the different types of communications lines as to connections, grades of service, and speed.
4. Describe different types of terminals that may be used in data communications.
5. Distinguish among the features and characteristics of star networks, ring networks, and distributed data bases.
6. Name seven critical factors that must be considered in planning data communications systems.
7. Name ways to contribute to the accuracy and control of data communications systems.
8. State the principal features of online reservations systems.
9. Describe online financial applications and electronic funds transfer systems.
10. Describe the use of data communications in education and law enforcement.
11. Describe legal aspects and problems involving data communications systems.
12. Cite problems in auditing data communications systems and ways to cope with them.

The ability to send information over communication lines is not new. Messages were sent by telegraph and telephone well back in the nineteenth century. Rapid communication between distant points played a vital part in the development of our nation. As early as 1940, communications equipment was used by the U.S. Army Air Corps at Wright Field in an inventory control application. Punched cards were converted to paper tape for input to a teletypewriter network, and the paper tape output at the receiving station was transferred back into cards. Later developments permitted direct card to card transmission over telephone lines. By the late 1950s special-purpose, fixed program machines were used for both industrial processes and time-dependent business problems such as airline reservations systems.

With the arrival of the third generation of computers, data communications experienced a tremendous growth and became a standard feature of most modern computers. The ability to tie a central computer to remote stations in order to provide online, real-time systems has become a way of life. All indications are that data communications will become an even more significant part of the data processing industry as time goes on.

Various terms describe data communications. There are no standardized definitions for these terms, and some are used interchangeably. In this text, we shall make the following distinctions. *Telecommunications* refers to communication by electromagnetic systems, or the transmission of signals over long distances. Standard telephone and telegraph transmission entirely unrelated to a computer falls under this definition. *Teleprocessing* consists of a data processing system with communication ability; the term refers specifically to data transmission between a computer and remote devices. *Time sharing* relates to the servicing of many terminals concurrently from a central system, allocating each a portion of the total system time. Each user in a time-sharing system has the impression that he or she alone is using the computer. *Data communications* has been defined as that part of an overall system which permits one or more users to access a remotely located computer.

ELEMENTS OF A DATA COMMUNICATIONS SYSTEM

It takes much more than establishing the proper electrical connections to digital computers to develop a data communications system. It involves working together many different technologies of communications and computation coming from different backgrounds and requiring service from different vendors. No such system can be complete without the following six elements:

1. Central processing unit
2. Direct-access storage devices
3. Communication control devices, primarily to translate the coding of the

characters from the form used within the central processor to that used over transmission lines

4. Communication lines
5. The terminal devices at the remote stations, which may be any of a variety of types of hardware
6. The programming systems which control incoming messages and make the facilities of the computer system available to the user

In planning a data communications system, one must take into account all six of these major elements. It is impossible for the total system to function effectively if any one element is neglected. Figure 12-1 presents a data flow diagram showing the relationship of these six elements.

Central Processing Unit

Perhaps even more than with batch processing, a central processor for a data communications system must be expandable. The first applications are usually limited, but as experience is gained and more applications can be tied together, the need for a larger and faster processor should be anticipated.

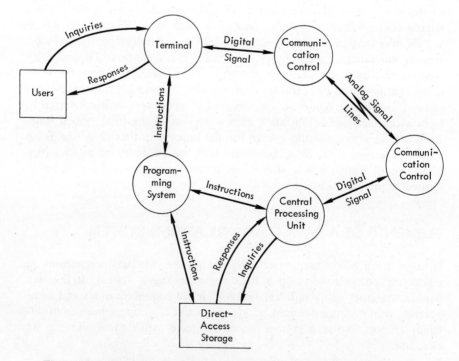

Figure 12-1. Elements of a data communications systems. Such systems are much more elaborate than batch data processing systems because of special hardware and software to control the transmission of data over communications lines.

Few systems today can afford to dedicate the central processor solely to data communications. The processor needs the ability to do multiprogramming, carrying on the terminal activity in the foreground while conventional data processing is done in the background. The rate at which data can be transmitted over communications lines is very slow compared with the internal speed of a processor. It is important to be able to interleave other work during the time intervals between transmission of messages. The ability to handle interrupts is of course essential.

Direct-Access Storage Devices

No central processor possibly can contain enough core economically to maintain all of the control programs, data files, and other information to be referenced by the remote users. Large direct-access storage devices (DASD), normally disk units, supplement core storage. The nature of the data in storage will vary depending upon the particular use for which the system is designed. In some instances, it will be primarily programs which the user may call for execution. In other cases it may be a large data base containing information to be retrieved at the control of the user. The data base may be constructed, modified, and updated by the user, or the user may be restricted solely to receiving a display of the data contained in the system.

DASD storage capacity must be large enough to maintain all of the data to be used by the system and accessible enough to meet the requirements of retrieval.

Communication Control Devices

As mentioned in Chapter 8, input/output operations are normally handled by means of a channel so that the central processing unit can be doing other useful work as data moves along the channel. Still additional hardware devices are required for transmission of data over communication lines.

Transmission control units and modems are two devices that must be added to arrange data for transmission over lines.

Transmission control units. Transmission control units are peripheral devices that allow the computer to communicate with the elements of a network. They vary greatly in size and function, but they almost always perform at least these functions:

1. Convert data from the serial, or byte-by-byte, form in which it is usually stored in the computer to the parallel bit-by-bit form in which it is transferred over the line.
2. Provide an interface between the computer and the modem.
3. Provide basic error recognition capability.

Modems. Digital data from the transmission control unit must be converted to a form—usually analog—that is suitable for transmission over the line. This process is called *modulation.* Similarly, at the other end of the line the signal must be converted back to digital form, or *demodulated.* The device that performs these functions is the modulator-demodulator, *modem* for short. Thus there must be a modem at each end of a communication line.

The modem transfers not only the data but also signals regarding the status, timing, and control of the data transfer.

A wide range of speeds can be in use at the same time among different terminals. The modems must accommodate the differences in speed of operation and in communication codes. Regardless of how many lines are required for a system, they all must be handled simultaneously. The modem therefore must provide for multiplexing, or carrying several channels over one telecommunications facility; the terminals may be interleaved.

Communication Lines

Many options are available to the analyst in the selection of the type of communication line facilities to suit the specific requirements of his system. Lines may be classified as *local* and *remote.* Local lines are those which may be somewhat apart from the central processor but which do not pass through the switching stations of the communications companies. Examples of local lines are those between buildings at the same site. Local lines usually are limited to about 2400 feet in length. Remote lines, using common carriers, may be any distance which can economically be justified, up to thousands of miles.

Three basic types of data connections, or channels, may be made between two points:

1. A *simplex* connection permits transmission in one direction only. A doorbell uses a simplex channel. Simplex connections are not commonly used in data communications because a response is required to acknowledge or reject each transmission.
2. A *half-duplex* connection permits transmission in either direction, but in only one direction at a time.
3. A *full-duplex* connection permits simultaneous transmission in both directions, as with the common telephone. Full duplex may cost around 10 to 25 percent more than half duplex.

The mode of transmission may be either (1) serial by character, serial by bit; or (2) serial by character, parallel by bit. Transmission that is *serial by bit* implies only a single transmission channel. The bits follow one another along the channel until the proper number of bits—five, six, seven, eight, or nine—have been received and converted by the modem into the proper character.

Transmission that is *parallel by bit* requires a separate path for each bit, so that all the bits for one character may be sent simultaneously. There may be six or eight separate wires, so that each wire carries a separate bit constituting the character; this is termed *space-division multiplexing*. Or a single channel may be divided into subchannels, each of which carries one bit; this is referred to as *frequency-division multiplexing*. Parallel transmission is not likely to be feasible on long-distance, low-speed lines, but it is commonly used for short distances where wires are laid down by the user. Lower terminal cost is possible with parallel transmission.

Transmission also may be classified as asynchronous or synchronous. *Asynchronous* transmission, also called "start-stop" transmission, is used on keyboard devices without a buffer, with varying interval between keying operations. Only one character is sent at a time, preceded by a START signal (a 0 bit) and followed by a STOP signal (a 1 bit). Because the keying is slow relative to transmission time, the channel may use *time-division multiplexing*, which means that the channel serves one terminal during one interval of time and another during the next interval. Machines using start-stop transmission usually are less expensive than those that are synchronous.

In *synchronous* transmission, characters are sent along the line in a continuous stream, or block. The receiving terminal must be in phase (synchronized) with the transmitting terminal. There is no pause between characters, and no START or STOP bits. This method, while more expensive, gives faster overall transmission, more efficient line utilization, and fewer errors.

There are three major types of communication facilities available:

1. The dial-up operation, or switched network, using regular long-distance telephone lines.
2. Leased line facilites whereby the lines are leased on a monthly basis from a communications common carrier.
3. Privately owned lines set up and maintained by the user.

A dial-up operation may be suitable for a limited number of stations where the rate of transmission of data is relatively slow. Charges are the same as those for any other long-distance service.

The wide-area telephone service (WATS) also provides dial-up facilities, but charges are assessed in terms of one of six geographical zones. Zone 6, for example, permits calls to be made anywhere in the United States, zone 5 is slightly smaller, and so forth.

Leased line charges are made up of the charge for the line itself, plus the channel termination charge (based on the connection between the leased line and the local switching office) plus local loop (the charge from the switching office to the terminal).

Certain grades of service are available within the three types of facilities mentioned previously:

1. Subvoice grade permits transmission of data only and not the human voice. This is used only for telegraph transmissions.
2. Voice grade permits transmission of both data and the human voice. This is far and away the most commonly used grade.
3. Broad band offers a broader band than the typical voice-grade circuit; it is capable of being subdivided into either subvoice or voice-grade channels.

With regard to speed, the communication lines are divided into the following four categories:

1. Low speed: 15 to 20 characters per second
2. Intermediate: up to 150 characters per second
3. Medium: up to 600 characters per second
4. High speed: up to 28,800 characters per second

Low-speed devices will operate over subvoice channels or over the higher-speed communication channels. The intermediate and medium-speed devices normally operate over voice-grade lines. High-speed devices normally require broad-band channels.

Speed of transmission is sometimes measured in bits per second. The term *baud* is applied to a rate of one bit per second of the binary signal or one 3-bit value per second in a train of signals each of which can assume one of eight different states. The term *hertz* is a measure of cycles per second.

On one system it is possible to mix together *point-to-point* lines and *multipoint* lines. A point-to-point network has one terminal device per line connected to the system; a multipoint network has more than one device per line. Where multipoint lines are involved, communications line control provides for either a *contention* or a *polling* system. Under a contention system, individual operators at their terminals attempt to get control of the line when they need it. Under a polling system, the central processor addresses each terminal in turn and invites it to send any messages which it may have ready.

Figures 12-2 through 12-6 show some of the variations possible in a communications network.

Terminal Devices

The element of the data communications system which is of most interest to users is the terminal, for this is the part they literally can get their hands on. A great variety of terminals may be chosen. It is vitally important that terminals be selected in the context of the total requirements of the system.

Terminals may be classified by *application* into one of three categories:

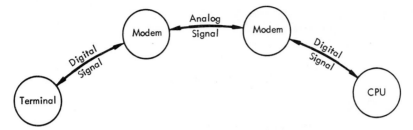

Figure 12-2. The point-to-point line has a separate line for each terminal. A modem at each end of the line converts the digital
signal from the terminal or the central processor into an
analog signal to be sent over the line.

1. Transaction terminals, which send a single transaction and receive a one-
   time acknowledgment or response from the computer. The user is said
   to be in a *conversational mode* with the computer.
2. Batch terminals, which transmit a group or batch of transactions at
   scheduled intervals rather than one at a time.
3. Retrieval terminals, which provide the ability to inquire into the status
   of certain files and to receive appropriate response.

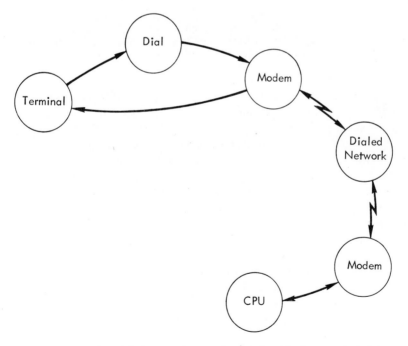

Figure 12-3. The dialed network uses the regular telephone system to
establish the line connection to the modem.

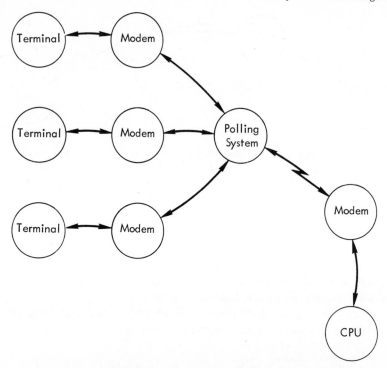

Figure 12-4. The polling system monitors each terminal on a definite
cycle and accepts messages from any terminal that is
ready to send at that time in the cycle.

Terminals may also be classified as being *general purpose* or *special purpose*. Special-purpose terminals are oriented toward particular industries rather than applications.

The lowest-priced terminal is a *teletype* unit with a typewriter keyboard which can be used to key messages to the computer and receive automatic typed responses on paper. Used in lieu of or in addition to the typewriter is the *cathode ray tube* (CRT). The CRT, sometimes called a display station, typically can display up to 24 lines of up to 80 characters per line of response on what looks like a small television screen. In some models it can display graphical illustrations as well as alpha-numeric information. The inquiry is displayed as it is keyed in to permit the operator to verify it visually, and the response will remain displayed on the screen until it is erased, either by the teminal operator or by the computer under program control. A *cursor* is a smaller indicator which may point to any character in any line for purposes of making corrections or focusing special attention.

Some models of the CRT permit the terminal operator to respond to messages simply by touching the screen with a probe which can be

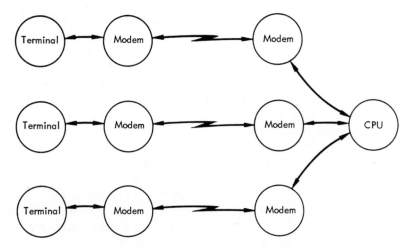

Figure 12-5. Dedicated lines. Each terminal has its own line to the central processor that is constantly available without the need for dial-up facilities.

electronically sensed or by using a light pen. Other forms of terminals permit slides or filmstrips to be displayed on the cathode ray tube and to be synchronized with recorded sound messages. This type of equipment is particularly useful in computer-assisted learning programs for students of all ages.

A *point-of-sale* terminal is installed directly at the point in a service

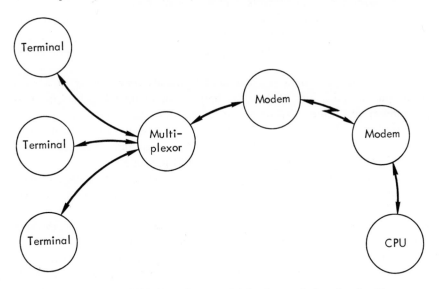

Figure 12-6. The multiplexor is a special hardware device that is able to merge messages from a number of terminals to transmit over the line in a single stream.

department or store where a sale is recorded. Some terminals have their own storage unit or recording media for capturing data about the sale, while others are online to a computer in the store or elsewhere.

Many of these terminals use an optical *reading wand* that can sense prices and product information from the box or can as the cashier moves *the reading wand* back and forth over the label on the can. The *universal product code* is a series of vertical lines of varying widths printed on each package or container. The first five digits of the code identify the manufacturer and the last five the product.

Data collection systems are widely used for such functions as control of plant production, attendance reporting, labor distribution, inventory update and maintenance, or recording receipt and shipment of goods. Data collection systems accept data from plastic badges, 80-column cards, data cartridges, and manual entries from keys or dials. Some systems include a clock which automatically records the time of each transaction that enters the system.

Special terminal devices are designed for use in financial institutions such as savings and loan associations and savings or commercial banks. The teller records the transaction directly on the customer's passbook and transmits the transaction to the central computer, which responds and updates the customer's passbook for any unposted interest or transactions. A *split platen* on the terminal allows the passbook or ledger card to move independently of the terminal record tape. Various functional control keys and indicator lights help to make the operation as automatic as possible.

Audio-response units produce prompt voice replies to inquiries which may be initiated from a 12-key touchtone telephone or other inquiry device. The response may be generated in male or female voice from a prerecorded vocabulary which has been created by the user to meet his or her specific needs.

For high-speed data transmission, terminals may consist of a card reader-punch and a line printer. Reading speeds of up to about 400 cards per minute and printing speeds of up to 300 lines per minute are possible with this type of terminal. In remote batch processing, job control cards, programs, and data are read from the card reader and processed by the central computer; results are then returned to the printer.

The ultimate in terminal facilities is a complete computer system, whereby a small system serves as a satellite for transmitting to a larger system. The small computer may be used independently as a stand-alone system, or it may be coupled to the large central computer through transmission lines and used primarily as an input/output device.

A minicomputer at a remote station is often called an *intelligent terminal,* a *line concentrator,* or a *front-end processor.* Its purpose is to perform such functions as editing and verification, data compaction, calculations, and other steps to save work for the central processor and make transmission more efficient. In a distributed network, the minicomputer at the remote station may have its own data base, which may be unique or a copy of part of the data base at the central location.

It is also possible to have line communication between two large-scale, general purpose computer systems to distribute work load or take advantage of special applications or data bases that are housed at one of the locations.

Programming Systems

The software to support a data communications system is made up of three parts: (1) the operating system, (2) the communications control software, and (3) application programs.

Operating system. The supervisor and other features of the computer operating system control and schedule the input/output operations and partitions. The operating system is the interface between the data base and the application programs.

Communications control software. All of the communications functions not provided for in the hardware transmission control units (TCU) must be provided by software. The set of rules that provide that data flows in an orderly manner is called the *line discipline,* or *protocol.*

Basic features of the protocol include:

1. Procedures for determining which network will transmit and which will receive at any given time
2. Procedures for ensuring control of proper recognition and reception of the actual data
3. Provisions for detection of error and requests for retransmission
4. Initiation of polling (inviting terminals to transmit) or calling (directing terminals to receive)
5. Message assembly and disassembly, including conversion from standard internal message form and terminal-oriented message form
6. Other message management functions, such as routing, validation, disposition, and queue management

At the time of this writing, most of these functions must still be provided by software. As technology advances, it is likely that some or all of them will be taken over by hardware or microprogramming.

Application programs. Programs for communications networks must serve the specific objectives of the system. Access of the data base, internal processing or records, calculations and comparisons, editing of input data, formatting of output, and other operations are carried out just as they are for batch applications. The main difference is that the application program must call on the communications control software to carry out all input/output operations involving terminals.

TYPES OF NETWORKS

Terminals, modems, lines, and central processors may be arranged in many different ways. Three such arrangements are (1) star networks, (2) ring networks, and (3) distributed networks.

Star Networks

A star network consists of a central host computer connected to one or more terminals, resembling a star (Figure 12-7). A *pure star network* contains only point-to-point lines between the terminals and the host system. A *modified star network* (Figure 12-8) may provide multipoint lines along with or instead of point-to-point lines.

The central host computer contains all programs and the data base for a star network. Terminals carrying heavy volumes of work can be provided with point-to-point lines, while those with lighter traffic can share lines with a multipoint system.

Ring Networks

Ring networks consist of several computer systems that can communicate with one another. A large mainframe is usually host to the entire system, while mini- or microcomputers are hosts to each cluster of terminals. The smaller hosts can communicate with the central host and perhaps with one another. The data base is at the central site (see Figure 12-9).

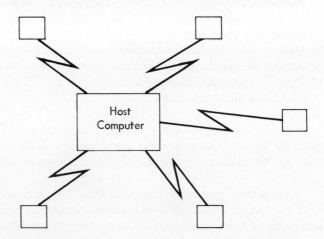

Figure 12-7. A star network has a single line to each terminal. Modems are required as usual at each end of the line but are omitted from this drawing.

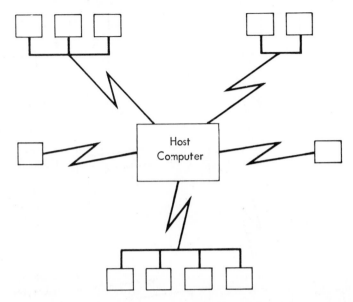

Figure 12-8. The modified star network may use a combination of point-to-point lines to reach the terminals.

Distributed Networks

Distributed networks are extensions of ring networks. They are sometimes called *distributed* or *dispersed* data processing. Each smaller processor in the network not only can communicate with the host processor as any terminal might do but also can perform many functions on a stand-alone basis.

In a true distributed system not only processing functions but portions of the data base itself are located with the smaller processors. Part or all of the distributed data base might be a copy of that available at the central host processor. The data base is distributed wherever it is of most use. The processor at one location has access to data bases at the central station or even at other locations. Figure 12-10 shows a distributed data base.

The smaller processors at remote stations can perform many functions locally and reduce the amount of data that must be transmitted over long distance lines. The large central host can be freed from many tasks in supervising individual terminals and increase total system production.

NETWORK DESIGN CONSIDERATIONS

Certain problems arise in online systems that are not met in batch processing. First, there is no effective way to determine from an inquiry how much information will be required for the answer. Thus a question from a terminal might result in many pages of output data, which are too long to be re-

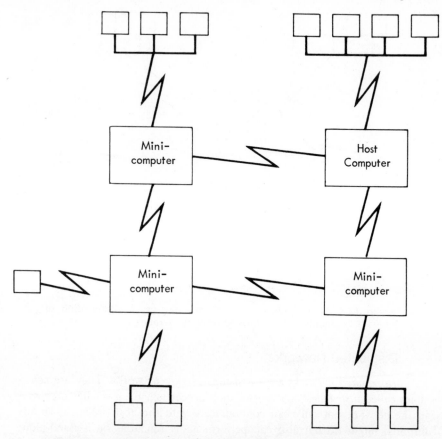

Figure 12-9. The ring network utilizes minicomputers at each remote
location to control a cluster of terminals and take over
certain functions that would otherwise have to be done by
the host computer.

turned over the terminal. One possible solution is to return an estimate of
response time and give the user an option as to whether the answer should
be typed out via terminal or printed out to be sent to the user via messen-
ger or mail. Many users, accustomed to voluminous, detailed printouts, feel
slighted when they receive back only highly concise, digested information.

A second problem concerns the number of online stations that can be
accommodated. It is desirable to make the system serve the maximum number of users, but overloading the system means that some user inevitably
will have to wait for information. The longer she (or he) must wait, the less
likely she will be to use the terminal. After a while the volume of work
waiting in the queue to be processed will be reduced, not because there is
no demand, but because the system is not adequately responsive to the demand.

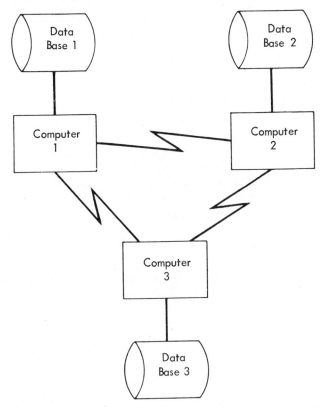

Figure 12-10. The distributed data base provides a separate data base
as well as a separate processor at each remote location.
Ideally, any terminal on the entire network has access to
the resources in any data base at any location.

Even if it were financially possible to have unlimited terminals, the
multiplexing capacity of the systems input channels poses a third problem.
The user may be able to get to a terminal, but if she always receives a busy
signal she will be discouraged from trying to gain access to the system.

A fourth problem arises from the sheer size of the system's auxiliary
storage. If the user must wait for the operator to mount additional tapes or
disk packs before she can access the desired file, she will find the system
less useful and will be more likely to seek her answers in other ways.

CRITICAL FACTORS IN PLANNING

The basic approach to planning a data communications system applies
most of the same steps used in developing other business systems. First the
objectives must be recognized and defined. Then the requirements the sys-

tem must meet are spelled out. Alternative approaches are explored and evaluated, and the most promising one selected. Detailed implementation plans are drawn up, and finally the new system is installed, tested thoroughly, and maintained.

There are seven critical factors which must be carefully considered in all phases of planning for a data communications system:

1. *Function,* or the careful study of the proposed system's objectives
2. *Distribution,* or the geographic locations to be linked by the system, and the flow of information between them
3. *Volume* of data to be transmitted to and from each location
4. *Urgency* in terms of the speed of response
5. *Code* for both the data to be transmitted and the medium on which data is represented
6. *Accuracy,* or the degree of freedom from error that is demanded by the system
7. *Cost* resulting from performing the specified function in the manner selected

Let us examine each of the critical factors in more detail.

Function

It should be clear by this point in our text that no system can be developed until the planner first knows clearly what it is intended to accomplish. Some of the many functions that may be performed by a data communications system are:

1. *Data entry or data collection.* A telecommunications network permits almost instantaneous recording of orders received in branch offices, insurance policies issued, students registered, personnel hired, and dozens of other similar transactions originating in widespread locations.
2. *Inquiry and response.* The system may be intended to make data accessible to many persons who do not have the authority to alter it. Examples include legal decisions, credit ratings, real estate listings, technical and scientific abstracts, and other subjects collected in data banks.
3. *Interactive programming.* Many time-sharing networks, both private and commercial, are designed to solve engineering problems, provide courses of study, or give remedial training whereby the user repeatedly interacts with the computer through a series of entries and responses.
4. *Management information system.* The network may be planned primarily to make highly concentrated and condensed information available quickly for management decision.
5. *Message switching.* Large organizations with many branches often can use the system for rapid and precise communication.

Obviously, the broader the objectives are, the more complex and costly the system is likely to prove. On the other hand, it is good economy to take advantage of the basic terminals, control units, and communication lines that are necessary for any system by using them for as many purposes as may be justified.

Distribution

With respect to location, we must operate in one of two ways: one point to one other point, or one point to many other points. Within either category, information may flow either in one direction only or in both. Distance is not a concern in planning the technical aspects of the system inasmuch as data can as readily be transmitted a thousand miles as a dozen. But distance is certainly a factor affecting the cost involved.

Distribution requires analysis of the relative locations of the various stations. For example, if a network involves three stations on the east coast of the United States and three on the west coast, there normally would be only one transcontinental line and then short branching lines on either end to the individual stations, rather than a spider web of lines directly connecting each station to each other one.

Volume

The work load to be carried by the system must be measured not only in average requirements per day, but also in peak-load figures. Growth must always be anticipated and predicted as accurately as possible.

The volume figures dictate the type of terminal, control unit, line, and even central processing unit that may be selected. If too many stations having too many messages contend for limited time at the central processor, excessive delay may be encountered in response time, rendering the system useless for some purposes. A teletype unit capable of typing 15 characters per second may be adequate for jobs of a certain volume, but totally inadequate for responses involving many lines of data.

Urgency

What might seem the most obvious point in planning a data communications network is all too often the last thing considered: that is, whether the system is needed at all. If orders can be processed satisfactorily within a day or two of their receipt, it may be adequate and far cheaper to batch the orders at the remote location, put them on a reel of tape, and airmail them to the factory. Over shorter distances, the orders might be delivered by automobile or regular mail within allowable time limits.

Urgency also needs to be defined in smaller units than days. For example, a response time of 30 seconds might be adequate for one type of inquiry while in other cases 3 seconds could be too long.

Code

The code chosen for the system imposes restraints on the communications terminals and channels that may be selected. Available codes are:

1. Five-level code (Baudot code). This was the original code used by teletype machines. Because only 5 bits are used to code each character, only 2^5, or 32, different characters may be specified. Since more than 32 characters are needed to accommodate numbers, letters, and special symbols, a special numeric or alphabetic shift character is used to permit the same code to stand for either a number or a letter.
2. Six-level binary coded decimal code (BCD). These codes are similar to those used by some of the more common second-generation computers.
3. Seven-level USASCII code.

A special type of control unit is needed to translate each code to the form carried by the communications line. It is not at all uncommon for large communications networks to have to translate data into a half dozen or more individual codes to accommodate differences among terminals.

Accuracy

The degree of accuracy required by the system determines the amount of verification that must be programmed. Alphabetic text materials to be read by people can tolerate a higher degree of error than numeric information, such as account numbers and amounts, that may be read mainly by machines. To protect against error, many systems do not permit data to be entered directly into the system from remote stations. Instead, the stations are limited to inquiry while connected to the computer. Data to be entered from terminals is first collected on a tape or disk device until a stated time such as the end of the day. Then the input data is subjected to careful editing routines and perhaps merged with input from other stations before it is entered into the permanent files.

The value of accuracy must always be measured against the cost of providing it. The difference between 99 and 100 percent accuracy may be the difference between $2000 and $100,000 in cost.

Cost

We have seen that cost enters into the consideration of most if not all of the preceding six critical factors. Often cost is the controlling element, outweighing any other factor. Sometimes, as when the national security is at stake, cost is secondary to urgency, function, or distribution.

There is always a strong interrelationship between cost and the other factors. It is sometimes difficult, but nevertheless important, to consider value and benefits which accrue to the organization, and not merely the quantity of dollars expended. Improvement of customer service and enhancement of corporate image are valuable returns justifying somewhat larger costs than the bare minimum.

APPLICATIONS

The expansion of data communications applications has been almost beyond belief. Networks now serve not only single organizations, but also multiple users and even the general public. New services are announced almost daily, and new common carriers are devoted exclusively to transmission of data. Five of the more significant applications merit our further attention:

1. Reservations systems, principally those of the airlines and of the hotal and motel industry
2. Financial transactions with customers of commercial banks and savings and loan associations, as well as between banks
3. Educational applications, such as problem solving and computer-assisted instruction (CAI)
4. Law enforcement networks—regional, state, and federal
5. General information services

Reservations Systems

Among the largest and most successful data communications networks are those designed by the airlines to handle their passenger reservations. These systems possess all of the elements necessary for successful use of data communications. Their function is well defined: to provide the maximum carrying capacity for the airplanes and to assure passengers available seats at the desired times. The distribution of the system is enormous. Reservations are received not only from all the airports in the system but from many offices, travel bureaus, and hotels in cities not served by airports. With millions of passengers using the airlines every year, the volume is considerable. The element of urgency is not present to a great extent on an individual reservation, where in most instances a confirmation in several hours would be satisfactory; but for the total requirements of the system there is a tremendous urgency about being sure that the same space has not been sold by more than one ticket agent. Different languages and codes are employed both by the many terminals used in the system and by the variety of central processing units used by the different airlines. Accuracy is critical, for both the passengers and the airlines themselves rely upon prompt and complete reservations. The enormous cost of hundreds of millions of dollars to develop and maintain the reservations system must be justified in terms of increased revenues and passenger satisfaction.

Reservations systems employed by hotels and motels are smaller in scale than those of the airlines. They are employed primarily by chains of hotels, principally those along the interstate highways where a traveler might wish to make a series of stops during a trip. They use inexpensive terminals, such as teletype, and must be very simple because many of the terminal operators are untrained in the technicalities of data processing.

A general reservations system intended to serve both hotels and motels and other events such as sports and concerts on a nationwide scale has not been particularly successful at the time of this writing.

Financial Transactions

The financial institutions of the country comprise one of the major segments of the economy. More than 30 billion checks per year are processed through the commercial banks. Almost every family has banking transactions, makes savings deposits, or pays off mortages or installment loans.

Many of these transactions are processed in batch mode. But others, particularly those regarding savings, are being recorded increasingly over communications networks. Typically, a branch of a bank or savings and loan association receives a payment from a customer and posts the transaction to the customer's passbook, simultaneously recording the data on a terminal. The data is transmitted over the network into a central computer where the customer's account is updated, any accrued interest or unposted transactions are returned to the terminal, and the customer's passbook is posted with his or her current balance.

Automatic teller machines (ATM) offer 24-hour services to bank customers in many locations. After using a magnetic card for identification, the customer keys in a secret password. He or she then may withdraw cash, make deposits, transfer funds between accounts, inquire about balances, or make payments on loans.

The electronic funds transfer system (EFTS) can greatly reduce the need for checks and drafts. Through a terminal at any business establishment on a network, customers can authorize their bank to charge their account and credit the account of the business for the amount of purchase. The EFTS network can also be used for transfer of funds between banks.

After some years of limited experimental use, EFTS is now expanding rapidly. Many technical and political problems are being resolved to make EFTS available in a growing number of business establishments. Cooperation between banks has contributed to effective systems design and control. Users present identification cards encoded with account numbers that can be read magnetically or optically. They then key in secret passwords to guard against misuse and fraud. The full potential of EFTS is just beginning to be realized.

Many banks process transactions over their network for smaller institutions which cannot justify their own computers. Sometimes combinations are made, where a smaller bank will use online facilities tied into a network for posting transactions during the day, and then will post its own specific summary accounts, payrolls, and other accounting applications as a stand-alone computer during the evening.

Education

Most of the major colleges and universities in the country in past years have developed time-sharing systems. These are used primarily for students not only in mathematics, science, and engineering, but in many other disciplines as a tool in solving problems. Most such terminals are of the interactive type, where the student enters statements in a language such as BASIC, FORTRAN, or APL. The central processor receives these statements, compiles them, and executes the programs, returning the results requested. Certain subroutines and some data may be available to the students, but in general, each one is responsible for maintaining his own files and data.

Dartmouth College in Hanover, New Hampshire, was one of the earliest institutions to seize upon this method of making computers available to undergraduates as a problem-solving tool. The system there has been in operation since 1964, serving students not only at Dartmouth but at high schools and colleges as well as other users within the geographic area. It has been estimated that 9 out of 10 Dartmouth students use the time-sharing system.

The Dartmouth system features BASIC, a language for terminals developed by John G. Kemeny and Thomas E. Kurtz. It was designed to be as simple as possible for students to learn and to use. Although developed largely on second-generation equipment with relatively slow cycle time, the Dartmouth system has been an outstanding example of cooperation between manufacturer and user, between faculty and students, and between the computer center and the public.

Some larger universities have developed extensive systems with more sophisticated hardware than that at Dartmouth. It is not uncommon for a single university computer center to process thousands of jobs per day using an intermixture of interactive programming terminals, remote batch job processing, and administrative university applications.

The rapid development of microcomputers starting in the late 1970s has had a profound impact on education. Most microcomputers are used as stand-alone systems with or without disk drives. But some can be formed into small networks to share disk drives or printers among several microcomputers. Others, using an interface such as RS-232, can serve as a terminal to a larger mainframe computer. Many authorities contend that there will soon be computers in every classroom and that every student will become literate in their usage.

The PLATO system, housed at the University of Illinois since the early 1960s, has been expanded until it now serves terminals throughout the United States and even abroad. It contains an enormous library of instructional applications in almost all subjects, ranging from elementary schools to graduate work in universities. Versions of PLATO have been produced for microcomputers.

Computer-assisted instruction (CAI) and computer-assisted learning (CAL) are highly promising educational applications that may use terminals to good advanatage. Beginning with children even younger than six years of age, terminals have been used in teaching numbers, spelling, reading, and other basic skills. Many extremely expensive and sophisticated projects have been funded by public and private sources to develop educational packages. Some such terminals include cathode ray tube screens, with such devices as light pens and keyboards, audio tapes, film strips or slide projectors, and other specialized equipment for presenting the instructional material. The central computer keeps track of the progress of individual students, records responses to the various questions, grades assignments, and directs students to proceed to the next lesson or return to a previous lesson for review as necessary.

Experiments have shown that students learn much of their basic information as well or better from a computer than from a normal classroom environment. The computer is well adapted to presenting material of a repetitive nature to help the student gain skill through drill and exercise. The teacher, thus relieved of the drudgery, can concentrate more upon specific individual problems.

Law Enforcement Networks

Data communications networks have been set up in various parts of the country to enable a quick check to be made of accidents, suspicious characters, or criminal acts. Data banks have been established listing stolen automobiles, persons with known criminal records, patterns of criminal behavior, and other types of data which might be useful in law enforcement and crime prevention.

Quick response is of the essence of a law enforcement network to be effective. A patrolperson on her (or his) beat may telephone her precinct station, which can make an inquiry over a terminal into a central data bank and receive a response within seconds. The response can be relayed to the patrolperson while she is still detaining a suspect. Some terminals are placed in patrol cars to permit direct inquiry and response.

For a number of years the Federal Bureau of Investigation has had on file millions of fingerprints. A large network offers law enforcement officers at all levels assistance in identifying suspects. Other interconnected networks link local police to state, national, and even international sources of information.

Computer analysis makes it possible to predict areas and times of increased criminal activity so that personnel may be assigned accordingly. Analysis of patterns of criminal behavior can help to identify suspects.

General Information Services

A growing number of services offer information via data communications to subscribers on a dial-up basis. Stock market quotations and other financial information are supplied to microcomputers in businesses or private homes around the clock. Educational materials may be transmitted directly to offices or homes. Electronic news is widely available. Electronic mail is becoming commonplace. Specialized information networks, such as real estate offerings or legal precedents, are within the reach of interested users.

LEGAL ASPECTS

Data communications systems permit access to data banks by a wide variety of users who may or may not be employees of the organization responsible for the data in the files. This situation has produced many new legal problems, one of which concerns the authority to construct and use the lines themselves. Telephone and telegraph companies are utilities subject to public regulation. With population growth increasing and demands on telephone systems for voice communication, the additional load of data transmission has at times overtaxed the facilities.

To cope with the enormous growth of the data communications industry, a large number of independent specialized common carriers have been formed in recent years. These specialized common carriers (SCC) intend to concentrate on data communications and not to compete with regular telephone and telegraph services. However, the established carriers, such as American Telephone and Telegraph Company, General Telephone, and Western Union, have considered the SCCs to be a threat.

Unlike the traditional common carriers, the specialized carriers provide only certain wide-band, point-to-point services in certain heavy traffic areas, and only to business users. Various court actions have been taken over the years over the choice of routes, tariffs, and interconnections between companies. The federal government has also been concerned with the questions of monopoly if the present giant carriers try to hinder their competition. There has also been the possibility that computer manufacturers would attempt to enter the communications business, or that the carriers would wish to expand into the computer hardware production.

The technological developments have included the transmission of data via satellite and experiments with glass fibers and lasers as data transmission media.

One of the knottiest problems involved in data communications systems has been the dispersion of responsibility. Frequently, the central processor is made by one manufacturer, the terminal devices by one or more others, and the lines provided by still a third vendor. The user of such a system is involved with contractual arrangements with three or more parties. Pinpointing the responsibility in case of breakdowns, failure of service, or transmission of incorrect information therefore has involved not only systems and control problems, but in some instances legal considerations.

Much concern has been expressed throughout the nation on the question of invasion of individual privacy where personal data is assembled in one place and made available to a large number of outside sources. Credit information, medical history, scholastic records, and court records are highly confidential. Unauthorized release or use of such data can be the basis for lawsuit.

It has even been contended that failure to use a communications system might render a person liable to suit. For example, if programs are readily available to assist in measuring the strength of a bridge and a contractor fails to test his data on the program, he may be liable in the event the bridge fails to hold up to specifications.

In a time-sharing service, if one user gains access to the files of another user through any kind of misfunction of the operating system, the time-sharing service might be held responsible. Furthermore, certain laws require that records be maintained for a minimum number of years. It may be mandatory that such records be in a printed form, for the government has on occasion held that magnetic files alone are not sufficient. A time-sharing service therefore might be obligated to print out the contents of files periodically to meet these requirements.

The safest course of action is for anyone contemplating using a time-sharing service, and certainly anyone planning to develop one and offer it to users, to obtain counsel before making any binding agreements.

AUDITING DATA COMMUNICATIONS SYSTEMS

The rapid growth of real-time systems has complicated the auditor's job. Frequently, there is no source document at all, so that the traditional audit trail which resulted from copying the original document at several stages during processing has tended to disappear. When data is entered almost immediately into the computer, the computer must assume more of the verification and processing steps than formerly. The computer must determine if the transaction was authorized and must safeguard against unauthorized entry. Furthermore, the system still must permit the auditor to trace a transaction back to its source. One common procedure calls for all transactions entering a real-time system to be recorded on a sequential file such as magnetic tape. This technique provides an electronic audit trail, even though the paperwork so highly prized by the conventional auditor may not be present.

Some auditors test real-time systems by creating dummy accounts, processing transactions into the accounts over the normal terminals, verifying results, testing for a variety of exceptions, and finally deleting the dummy accounts. An interesting question arises when auditors follow this procedure: Who audits the auditors? It is conceivable that an auditor could create a dummy account, cash dummy payroll checks, make deposits for his or her own benefit, or perpetrate other frauds.

Data security on real-time systems requires four fundamental safety checks:

1. User identification
2. Authorization to use the system
3. Audit of system usage
4. Preservation of system integrity

The auditing procedure for online systems should check the method for assigning and changing passwords. Passwords are worse than useless if just anyone can learn them, or if operators merely supply them on request to persons who have temporarily forgotten their own. As hardware becomes more sophisticated, it may be possible to use human speech patterns, optical reading of thumbprints, or hand geometry for direct identification of users.

SUMMARY

In this chapter we have examined the elements of a data communications system: central processor, input/output storage, communication control devices, transmission lines, terminal devices, and programming systems.

We have examined each of the seven critical factors in planning: function, distribution, volume, urgency, language, accuracy, and cost. We have seen that while data communications networks are technically possible in almost every case, they are not always economically justified. Where they are needed, they offer service that cannot be matched by any other medium.

We have noted the principal applications of communications systems and have examined some of the more important applications of data communications in the fields of reservations systems, financial transactions, education, and law enforcement.

Finally, we have come to see that data communications networks involve a host of legal issues which must be carefully considered and resolved before embarking upon any ambitious project.

TERMS FOR REVIEW

Asynchronous transmission   Modem
Baud   Multipoint line
Contention system   PLATO
Conversational mode   Polling system
Dial-up system   Protocol
Distributed data base   Ring network
Electronic funds transfer system   Simplex channel
Front-end processor   Star network
Full-duplex channel   Synchronous transmission
Half-duplex channel   Time sharing
Leased line   Voice-grade line

QUESTIONS

1. What are the six essential parts of a data communications system? What elements must be present that are not required for conventional batch processing?
2. What is meant by the term "modem?" What does a modem do?
3. Name the functions of the transmission control unit.
4. What is the difference between a switched network and one that is nonswitched?
5. What categories of communication facilities are available? Classify them as to speed and cost.
6. What are the differences between a contention system and a polling system?
7. What is meant by "remote batch processing?" How does it differ from "interactive computing?"
8. Describe some of the types of devices that may serve as terminals.
9. How do star networks differ from ring networks?
10. In what major respect does a distributed data base differ from a ring network?
11. Name the seven critical factors that must be considered in planning data communications systems. How do the factors compare and contrast between the needs of a network for ordering merchandise and one for serving a law enforcement network?
12. Why should we sometimes be satisfied with less than 100 percent accuracy in data transmission?
13. What are the major differences in function and objectives between reservation systems and education systems?

14. What are some advantages to computer-assisted instruction over conventional classroom teaching? Can you think of any disadvantages?

15. What legal problems are encountered by companies wishing to become common carriers specializing in data communications lines?

16. What legal problems are encountered by suppliers of time-sharing services?

17. What legal problems might be encountered by the user of a data communications network?

18. What are some problems in auditing data communications systems? How may they be overcome?

CASE STUDY
SUNCOAST COMMUNITY COLLEGE

The data communications system at Suncoast is a modified star network. The IBM 4341 computer is the host. Three transmission control units serve 24 terminals each, for a possible total of 72 terminals. There are three terminal printers and 63 CRTs presently installed. Two of the printers and 55 of the CRTS are on the Main Campus. Each of the printers and each cluster of eight CRTs has a separate direct line from the computer center. A special software features permits all terminals to be regarded as local, although the printer and eight CRTs on the South Campus are 30 miles away. A single direct line serves the South Campus. A single control unit at South Campus controls the printer and CRTS there.

The operating system is DOS/VSE, which is capable of running 12 partitions in virtual storage. The Computer Center has recently installed CICS as the communications control software after outgrowing the capabilities of the more limited control software previously in use. The data base management system was written in-house, making use of linked lists to chain together the major divisions of the data base. But the DBMS does not allow full data independence, and programs must define records as they exist physically in the data base.

Only one additional terminal is planned for the alumni application, to be located in the Office of Institutional Advancement. This terminal will require one of the six available ports on the present transmission control units. A user identification code and a secret password are assigned for the new terminal. Only this terminal and the master terminal in the office of Rick Jagsby, Director of Systems Development, will have access to programs and files of the alumni application. In addition, the terminal in the Office of Institutional Advancement is given access to the same online programs that are generally available to terminal users. These include SALP, the student alpha listing; SRDM, student record display; and SNUM, student numeric listing.

The alumni application is not expected to have serious impact on the seven critical factors involved in planning the network. The team reviews the requirements of the system and presents a brief summary below:

1. *Function*: data entry and information retrieval.
2. *Distribution*: local network with maximum 30-mile radius.
3. *Volume*: relatively low volume of work added to existing system.
4. *Urgency*: less urgent than other applications such as student programming projects and registration. Response time of 3 seconds is expected.
5. *Code*: new application fully compatible with existing code.
6. *Accuracy*: assured through visual verification and program editing.
7. *Cost*: terminal lease and maintenance will add $65 per month. Systems costs included in regular payroll.

QUESTIONS AND EXERCISES

1. Draw the modified star network of the Suncoast online system. Do not attempt to draw a separate symbol for each individual terminal.
2. What elements would have to be added to the Suncoast network to make it a complete distributed data base?
3. What advantages would a full data base management system bring to the alumni application? What disadvantages, in addition to cost, can you think of?

13

SYSTEM CONVERSION AND IMPLEMENTATION

OBJECTIVES

At the end of this chapter, you should be able to:

1. Distinguish between the terms *conversion* and *implementation*.
2. Make a workable schedule to convert to the new system.
3. Describe the activities involved in preparing and making the conversion to the new system.
4. Compare and contrast the four implementation plans presented in the chapter.
5. State ways to maintain control of the entire implementation procedure.
6. Name problems that must be anticipated and give ways of dealing with them.
7. Describe the role of the various personnel involved in system implementation.
8. Describe follow-up and evaluation procedures to ensure that the system operates as designed.

Conversion, as a general term, refers to the act of turning from one belief or course to another. In data processing, conversion is more specifically defined as the process of changing (1) from one data processing method to another or (2) from one form of representation to another. In this chapter, we shall be concerned primarily with the process of changing from one data processing system to another. At the same time, we will be involved with converting data from source documents to machine-readable form, converting flowcharts and written procedures into programs, converting people having one set of skills to those having other skills, converting the form and content of input and output documents, and in general changing our entire way of doing things.

To implement means to accomplish, fulfill, complete, carry out, or bring into practical effect by concrete measures. *Implementation* is more specifically defined as the process of installing a computer system. Some writers use this term to cover the entire process of making the systems study, analyzing the existing system, designing a new system, selecting equipment, and other preliminary steps. For our purposes in this chapter, we shall assume that implementation begins when the new system has been approved by top management and the new equipment, if any, has been placed on order. Implementation here will refer to those specific steps needed to make a smooth transition from the old system to the new one.

We will see that there is considerable overlap between the two terms, *conversion* and *implementation*. Where a distinction is made, *conversion* will primarily refer to the relationship between the old and new system whereas *implementation* will refer primarily to the specific means of making the new system operational. For example, designing an inventory file to be processed randomly on disks is a step in implementation. Taking the data from the previous inventory master tapes and combining it with data from other sources to create the new random file is a conversion step.

SCHEDULING THE CONVERSION

Once the design and development phases have been completed on the new system, a definite timetable must be set up to allow sufficient *lead time* for the actual conversion and implementation. The term *lead time* refers to the length of time prior to some due date such as the conversion of the system that some other activity such as placing the order for equipment must be completed. Equipment will usually have been selected and ordered during the development phase. In past years the delivery schedule for equipment has been the controlling factor around which all other aspects of system conversion had to be based. The delivery schedule for some systems has been as long as two years. If it should happen that the delivery time on equipment is shorter than the time necessary for programming and other conversion steps, delivery time may be set back until all other preliminary steps have been completed.

There may be several different types of systems conversions, and each one has its own peculiar combination of scheduling requirements. A few years back, most conversions were from manual systems to punched card or computer systems. Since that time, many changes have been made from unit record to computer, from batch processing to online processing, from tape to disk, from decentralized to centralized systems with remote terminals, from second to third generation, or from one manufacturer to another having different language capability.

Some of the steps that must be scheduled and carried out during implementation are:

1. Staffing
2. File conversion
3. Site preparation
4. Training
5. Test cases and trial runs
6. Final documentation

Each of these phases must be considered in terms of policy, organization, budgets, and time. Estimates of costs and time must be carefully prepared using all available information. Records may be available from regular production or past conversion steps, some of which might be similar to those being employed now. For example, file conversion time is related to volume of records and keyboard strokes.

The extent of the change being implemented has a great deal to do with the length of lead time required and the cost of conversion. For example, no additional site preparation may be required if one computer system is being replaced by another.

Figure 4-18 shows a conversion schedule in the form of a PERT (Program Evaluation and Review Technique) chart. In actual practice the chart would reflect optimistic, most likely, and pessimistic estimates of the time required to complete each of the events shown in circles. The Gantt chart (Figure 13-1) is also widely used as a good graphic device for planning and following the implementation steps.

CONVERSION ACTIVITIES

As in all systems work, the conversion and implementation project can itself be considered a system. It is composed of six steps, or subsystems, named in the preceding section. Each of the six steps should undergo a smaller version of the same analysis, design, and development that the major system did.

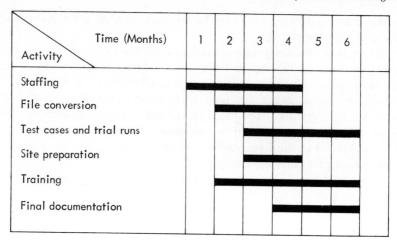

Figure 13-1. Gantt chart showing steps in systems implementation. Steps are listed down the left side of the chart. Time intervals are shown across the top. Solid lines show scheduled time for each step.

Staffing

Let us look in more detail at the points enumerated above. *Staffing* may involve the employment of additional personnel, changes of assignment or duties, or engaging outside help on a temporary basis. Obviously, any conversion experience will require more work than simply continuing with the previous system. This work has to be performed by someone, either on a full-time, part-time, or overtime basis. Where possible, it is desirable to have the people who will be actually operating the new system work on the setup in preparation to implement it.

File Conversion

The time required for *file conversion* will vary greatly according to the type of conversion being made. Converting from a manual to a computer system is the most time-consuming type of conversion, for it requires that all records be keypunched or recorded on magnetic tape for entry into the data processing system. For other conversions, most files can be built largely by the computer and peripheral devices. Records can be combined and consolidated to expand the files. New data may be added to the files through update procedures. Most of the difficult steps of determining lengths of fields, specialized codes, original data entry, verification procedures, and other problems already will have been overcome.

Converting from conventional files to a formal data base can be a highly complex and time-consuming project. As mentioned in Chapter 9, the exact relationship of each data element with specific records must be established, and an elaborate set of pointers to link related fields and records must be provided. In many instances, the files must be completely reorganized and reconstructed to form the data base. Converting to a data base is far more than merely copying the same data from one device or medium to another.

Site Preparation

Site preparation can range all the way from merely repositioning some furniture and equipment to constructing a completely new building. Attention must be given to the demands of the new system for electrical wiring, sound and air conditioning, traffic flow, storage, work space, and telephone or data communications service.

There are at least two features to be considered in preparing the site for a computer installation that are not usually encountered in other facilities. The first is having a raised floor. The large number of cables needed to connect the various control units and input/output devices to the central processing unit can be inconvenient and a hazard to operators if laid along the floor. Special floors with removable squares are available that put all cables out of the way and out of sight. They go through holes in the floor directly under each machine to connect to the next machine.

The second feature is an uninterruptible power supply. Online systems especially are so critical to power fluctuations that the slightest interruption to commercial power can cause possible damage to files and require reinitialization of programs. The uninterruptible power supply is a form of auxiliary device that provides a constant source of power regardless of outside conditions.

Training

Some *training* is necessary at all levels in implementing most systems. Executives and supervisors need orientation to the new format of reports or the new procedures being followed by personnel under their supervision. Clerical personnel and operators must be given both an explanation and actual experience in performing the specific duties they will have under the new system. No system is so good that it will work if operating personnel do not want it to. The training period is invaluable for enlisting the full understanding and support of the persons who actually will operate the new system. Training may be conducted in-house, using members of the systems department, or it may involve sending personnel to special schools conducted by vendors. Training also may be done in a pilot installation where the activies of the new system can be carried out on an experimental basis.

Training for online systems is especially crucial. Often the persons who will be operating the terminals have had little previous data processing training or experience. Yet much of the success of the entire system revolves around the care and accuracy with which they perform data entry and updating.

Terminal instruction can be done effectively with self-instructional units. A well-designed online system will lead the terminal operator through the necessary responses. A short manual with background information and specific directions for each job to be performed can be prepared and distributed to each operator. Then, with an hour or two of practice, most persons, even with no prior experience, can learn the necessary operations.

Test Cases and Trial Runs

In developing *test data* for a new system, it is desirable to use actual information from some previous period. We thus receive a good cross section of the types of transactions that normally occur. It is also important to include exceptions of all types to be sure that errors are recognized and as far as possible corrected. Provision also should be made for having a trial run of information through the entire system, from the point of its original entry until it is finally reported or added into summaries. This includes the various clerical processing steps as well as the processing at the computer center.

Test data generating software is available to simplify the task of testing programs. By making additional entries in the DATA DIVISION of a COBOL program, the software will create data with a variety of ranges and characteristics that can be used in program testing and verification.

Final Documentation

Documentation that began with the analysis phase and continued through design makes up the systems report. During implementation, additional documents are accumulated as programmers do their detailed work and clerical and control procedures are spelled out specifically. The conversion schedule should emphasize the need for keeping all documentation made final.

IMPLEMENTATION PLANS

There are several ways to put the new system into actual effect after all preparations have been accomplished. Four of these are:

1. Direct conversion
2. Pilot installation
3. Parallel operations
4. Phased implementation

Direct Conversion

Direct conversion is sometimes called the "all-at-once" or the "plunge" method. This approach simply says that as of a certain date and time, the new system will be in effect. This approach is recommended if the procedure is fairly simple, does not involve a heavy volume of transactions, and is limited to a single department. Plunging in like this involves a total commitment to the new system and does not provide a ready alternative in case trouble develops. It should not be tried for complex systems involving radical changes or new machines, high volume of transactions, or several far-flung locations. It requires that personnel be completely familiar with and sold on the new system.

Pilot Installation

The *pilot installation* approach is most practical for large, widespread organizations. One branch or department might be selected to implement the new system, using either the all-at-once approach or the parallel method. Any problems to be encountered can be smoothed out in the pilot installation, and the whole system made as nearly error free as possible. Only then is it implemented in the entire organization. The pilot installation has some of the characteristics of the piecemeal method, the major difference being that the segment is one part of the organization rather than one part of the system. The pilot approach is particularly appropriate for such groups as colleges or universities, school systems, governments, chain stores, or other enterprises having a large number of branches which operate in a similar pattern.

Parallel Operations

The *parallel* method probably has more advantages and more disadvantages than any other single approach. It involves continuing the former system for a certain length of time after the new system is put into operation. For large installation projects with intricate processing, it provides an opportunity to compare results with those obtained by the previous method and allows realistic appraisals to be made of time requirements, frequency of error, and operational efficiency. It also eliminates feelings of panic because the old method is still operational. The obvious disadvantage of the parallel operations approach is the duplication of costs, effort, and personnel. Few places can afford to duplicate their work for any extended period of time. It is important, therefore, that the parallel operations be limited to a short term ranging from one week to a maximum of six months.

Phased Implementation

The process of implementing the new system in *phases* is sometimes termed the "piecemeal" approach. However, this term suggests a somewhat random, haphazard process that is nothing like the careful planning that phased implementation entails.

The phased approach is effective for large-volume conversions. In fact, it may be the only way to apply some large, long-range systems. This plan involves installing small segments of the new system individually, seeing that they work properly, and then moving on to the next segment. It allows a gradual, controlled conversion.

This method takes longer and therefore delays any significant dollar savings that might be realized by complete conversion to the new system. It also means that certain daily, weekly, or other short-term reports might be inconsistent during the weeks when only certain segments of the entire system have been converted.

An advantage of this plan is that it can often be carried out with the normal work staff. Working in small steps, one or two applications or programs can be converted, while continuing to operate the old versions of other ones. With online systems, for example, it might be feasible to begin the conversions with programs that merely display the contents of files. This procedure enables programmers to become familiar with the specialized programming needed for online processing and terminal operators to gain experience and confidence without the danger of destroying data within files. Later, the programs that perform the updating and file creation can be introduced.

Figure 13-2 shows a comparison of time and resources required by the four implementation plans.

CONTROL TECHNIQUES

To see that the implementation plan moves forward smoothly and accurately, certain control techniques usually are established. Some of these are:

Resources Required	Time Required		
	Short	Medium	Long
Few	Direct conversion		
Medium		Pilot installation	Phased implementation
Many			Parallel operations

Figure 13-2. Comparison of implementation plans. Direct conversion requires the shortest time and fewest resources but provides no alternative in case of trouble. Parallel operations require duplicate facilities and a long period of time, but, where feasible, offer the safest transition.

1. *Periodic check of progress to date.* Adherence to the schedule is vital if the final conversion is to take place on time.
2. *Accounting control totals.* All accounting procedures have time-tested proofs and balances which should be built into all systems. The use of record counts, proof totals, check digits, and other methods or verifying completeness and accuracy is discussed in detail in Chapter 6.
3. *Paper flow controls.* Log sheets, document counts, transmittal records, acknowledgments, and other methods of controlling document flow should be employed as implementation proceeds.
4. *Task timing.* Careful records of the interval between the arrival and departure times at every station in the system provide the basis for establishing timing standards. The system then must assure that these standards, like all others, are maintained.

Implementation of a new system is a project in itself. In fact it is normally a one-time, unique project of major importance. There are therefore two aspects of control techniques that must be scrupulously employed:

1. *Control of the implementation plan itself.* Adherence to the original plan, maintaining schedules, controlling accuracy of data and files, review of form and card design, and all other phases of the conversion must be ensured.
2. *Control of the new system.* Implementation normally extends over a relatively long period of time. It is therefore possible to make sure that each element of control used in the old system can be adapted to the new one. In addition, new controls which were not a part of the prior system may be incorporated, documented, and tested just like all other parts of the procedure.

Problem Anticipation

From the outset of the systems study every effort has been made to anticipate problem areas, to provide adequate controls, to diagnose difficulties as they develop, and to prescribe remedial action. As the implementation plan progresses, potential trouble spots are likely to emerge. Prompt recognition and treatment of such conditions may well prevent more serious trouble and expense after implementation is complete.

The following questions can aid in anticipating problems during the different stages of implementation.

1. Are the objectives and constraints seen by the designer the same as those perceived by the organization?
2. Have appropriate effectiveness measures been used in the analysis and design of the system?
3. Has the analyst correctly evaluated all available resources?

4. Does the system focus attention and awareness upon the proper critical functions?
5. Has adequate provision been made for updating the system?
6. Are vital system processes protected against danger or failure?
7. Is the system protected against direct falsification or illicit interruption?
8. Will the system accept and act upon signs of impending disaster?
9. Have operating standards been developed for the system?
10. Are operators actually performing according to the system definition and plan?
11. Have potential difficulties between functions, departments, components, or modules been adequately bridged?
12. Is the system big enough?

Role of Personnel

It is important to spell out clearly the role to be played by various personnel involved in an installation. The line supervisor, who will be responsible for conducting the system during day-to-day operations, should assume the prime responsibility from the start: he or she should have been involved in all phases of development and design and should have participated in the development of test data and analysis of results.

The role of the systems person is that of an advisor or consultant during the actual installation. By this time the systems person already should have aided in the training of the participants, provided sufficient documentation, and enlisted support for the new system. He or she should observe all phases of the installation carefully, offering advice and criticism as required. The systems person should respect the responsibility and authority of the line supervisor, and not attempt to usurp the supervisor's role.

The role of each clerk or operator in the new system is to do his or her job as precisely as possible. No one operator has responsiblility for the installation as a whole, but a single flaw at a single station can hamper the entire system. The results of previous planning, training, and orientation will become apprent at this time.

SYSTEM INSTALLATION

The most critical point in the entire conversion process is of course the cutover which puts the new system in actual operation. No matter how careful the planning, organization, and training have been, it is almost certain that some problems will arise. If things have been done correctly, however, the problems will have been anticipated and can be readily corrected. Alternate courses of action usually are provided in case of severe difficulty.

The morale of all personnel involved is put to a crucial test at this time. If management has been well briefed, it will be sympathetic to minor difficulties that may be encountered, realizing that a reasonable amount of time is necessary to achieve smooth operation. But if management has any doubts about the system, it may seize upon any pretext to try to discredit or even reject it. System installation, unlike a political campaign, is not successful if it wins by a vote of 51 to 49. Unless a substantial majority of both management and operating personnel is sold on the system, it will be in serious trouble from the start.

The human factors, which are so important throughout all of systems work, are put to their maximum test at installation time. No amount of planning or briefing can eliminate completely the anxiety, overwork, pressure, and confusion that are so often present at such a time. Advocates of the older system may feel jealously or resentment toward those working with the new one, and some diehards inevitably will tend to gloat over real or imagined inadequacies in the new system. Old habits and procedures must be rearranged and rechanneled. Analysts or programmers who have been so closely involved in the system design are likely to be impatient with those who fail to grasp its functional details.

It is urgent, even critical, that management provide full support and that analysts and supervisors exercise the utmost tact during this period of stress. If respect for individual feelings, recognition of work well done, and good communications and training have been the practice throughout the year, morale will survive periods of stress.

SUMMARY

Implementation begins when the new system has been approved for adoption and when new equipment, if any, has been placed on order. A well-designed and well-documented system goes far toward selling itself to management, but the analyst may have to make a special presentation to management to gain approval. The analyst should tailor his or her presentation to available time, using oral delivery, blackboard, flipcharts, transparencies, slides, or movies to reinforce its appeal.

An implementation schedule should be carefully planned. Staffing, file conversion, test cases and trial runs, site preparation, training, and final documentation should be carefully estimated and scheduled. Some of these activities may be done concurrently, while others must be performed in sequence. A PERT chart or Gantt chart will help to show the proper relationships of these events and their relative time factors.

The new system may be put into effect under one or a combination of four plans: (1) direct conversion, (2) pilot installation, (3) parallel operations, and (4) phased implementation. The size and complexity of the system determine which method will be most effective.

The actual moment of cutover to the new system is a most crucial period. Often time is short, the work load heavy, the personnel fatigued, the costs high, and the management apprehensive. This is a time to exercise human compassion and understanding. Errors should be corrected expeditiously; hard work should be recognized and praised. The art of management and human relations must be at its highest.

TERMS FOR REVIEW

Conversion
Direct conversion
File conversion
Implementation plan
Lead time
Parallel operations
Phased implementation

Pilot installation
Site preparation
Staffing
System installation
Test data
Uninterruptible power supply

QUESTIONS

1. Distinguish between the terms "conversion" and "implementation" as used in this chapter.
2. What activities have been completed before implementation begins?
3. What is meant by lead time? Why is it important in implementing a new system?
4. What activities or events must be provided for in the implementation schedule?
5. What can be done to help gain acceptance for the new system? What are the roles of top management, the line supervisor, and the systems analyst to encourage its support?
6. What additional documentation is produced during the implementation period?
7. What are the four ways described in this chapter for the actual installation of the new system?
8. What human factors need to be considered especially at installation time?
9. What follow-up is made of the new system? Who does it and how?
10. What specific recommendations are made to maintain the system at high efficiency during daily operations?
11. You are convinced that parallel operations are vital to a smooth con-

version. However, your management has stated that it will be utterly impossible to maintain both the old and the new computers in operating condition on your premises for even a few days. What alternative plans can you suggest to give benefits similar to those of parallel operations?

12. As systems manager, after a thorough study you are convinced that you should add disk files to your present card and tape oriented computer system. The addition will increase monthly rentals by $3500, or about 40 percent of your present machine rental. Make an outline of the points you will use in selling your proposal to your management, showing advantages that will offset the additional cost and other objections they may raise.

13. Give specific incentives and suggestions you would make to promote employee cooperation and keep morale high during the time of a systems conversion.

14. Draw a Gantt chart to show a timetable for training activities associated with changing from a magnetic tape to a magnetic disk online computer system. Allow for briefing of top management, orientation of managers in user departments, design of new systems, learning to use new programming software, and training of clerical and control personnel in various departments.

CASE STUDY
SUNCOAST COMMUNITY COLLEGE

The alumni application study team plans to complete implementation by October 15. The system will be installed in phases over a period of several weeks. Target dates are:

September 1: complete documentation.
September 1–20: provide basic terminal training and practice.
September 20: install new terminal.
September 20–October 1: test programs with sample data.
October 1: create alumni master file with Program AMST.
October 1–8: test listing and label programs with actual data sorted in various sequences.
October 8–10: create donor file.
October 10–15: test entire system.

Cash receipts of alumni donors have been retained since the first of the year. The first donor file contains 715 donations, mostly with one donation per alumnus. Three persons have made as many as 10 separate gifts during the year to date. The donor file is created online by Susan Musser, secretary in the Office of Institutional Advancement, who will also be responsible for most of the data entry and information retrieval of the alumni application.

Susan Musser has been given the Terminal Operator's Manual, which covers logging in and off, method of entering passwords, display of the basic menu for selection of programs, and use of special function keys on the terminal. She has also received the Clerical Procedures Manual and applicable portions of the Systems Manual for the alumni application. She has been studying the documentation and practicing basic terminal operation in the nearby Admissions Office for several weeks prior to receiving her own terminal.

Marilyn Woods, Director of Institutional Advancement, has kept Susan Musser informed of developments in the alumni application from the outset. Marilyn also studies terminal procedures and ensures that documentation is complete and understandable in case of possible personnel changes in the future.

No major site preparation is required. The terminal fits into existing space near the secretary's desk in the Office of Institutional Advancement. One additional direct line has been run to that office from the Computer Center, and the line is connected to one of the six remaining ports in the transmission control unit.

Conversion and implementation of the alumni application system are completed on schedule and without serious problems. The actual count of alumni master records, including graduates of the recent spring and summer terms, is 11,768. Gerald Phipps and John Shirley decide to observe the system closely through January 15. This will permit contributions received during the rest of the calendar year to be entered into the donor file, the December graduates to be added to the alumni identification file, summary reports for the calendar year to be prepared, and the donor file for the new year to be started. Thus virtually all aspects of the new system will have been tested with live data.

QUESTIONS AND EXERCISES

1. Compare advantages and disadvantages of each of the following implementation plans with the phased implementation plan that the Suncoast team chose: (a) direct conversion, (b) pilot installation, and (c) parallel operations.
2. Do you think sufficient training was provided for the new alumni application system? What other persons might have been involved?
3. Is there any aspect of the implementation plan that you might have done differently? Give reasons for your answer.

14

SYSTEM
OPERATION
AND EVALUATION

OBJECTIVES

At the end of this chapter, you should be able to:

1. Define system maintenance and name the factors that it includes.
2. State problems that exist in system maintenance and show how they can be alleviated.
3. Give reasons why reprogramming may be desirable or necessary.
4. Describe the steps necessary to create and keep good maintenance documentation.
5. Name the tools that help to smooth job scheduling.
6. Explain the factors that lead to effective machine utilization.
7. Describe documents created by the computer that are valuable in job scheduling.
8. Name and define the four major categories of costs.
9. Name the elements that make up each costing system.
10. Calculate costs of a specific computer job, given a typical formula from a computer center.
11. Describe the role of the systems analyst in the postinstallation audit.
12. Define and illustrate cost-benefit analysis.

Thus far in our text we have been through most of the steps involved in defining, analyzing, designing, developing, and installing a data processing system. Once the new system is functioning, there is a common tendency for systems personnel to heave a great sigh of relief, forget it, and concentrate on the next urgent project.

Such an attitude can be disastrous. In this chapter we shall examine the three critical areas of system maintenance, job scheduling, and determining costs.

When the new system is installed and fully operational, the activities described in previous chapters on analysis, design, testing, programming, and procedures are now put into daily operation. It may be contended that the systems department has finished its task and that the responsibility for smooth day-to-day operations is now with the data processing manager.

In truth, systems personnel are on trial every day that their systems are functioning. The procedures that they have laid out are being tested constantly whenever the programs are being used or forms are being printed and analyzed by various personnel. Indeed, every aspect of the system continuously comes under the full scrutiny of designer, user, and customers.

Let us look at some aspects of system operation and maintenance and see in what respects systems personnel can confirm the job that was done and learn better what to apply to future projects.

SYSTEM MAINTENANCE

To *maintain* means to continue and persevere in or with, or to carry on. The maintenance of a computer system keeps it continuously in tune with the environment of users, data processing operations, associated clerical functions, and external demands from government or other agencies.

No matter how carefully any system is planned, minor changes will be needed during a shakeout period to make it reach maximum efficiency. It is important, however, that these changes do not cause serious deviations from the original plan. After the new system is implemented, the analyst and designer should come back for periodic checks to verify that the procedures being followed are actually those which were outlined.

Some operating personnel undoubtedly will find more efficient ways of doing things than those originally envisioned by the designer. Where such methods are a genuine improvement, they should be incorporated, an amendment made to the system, and documentation brought up to date.

The Attitude toward Maintenance

Often maintenance work on a system is delegated to the least experienced programmers and analysts in an installation. But it would be more effective to establish a regular position of maintenance programmer or a maintenance department for computer operations just as any well-run business organization has its maintenance department to keep its buildings and equipment in top-notch order. Some programmers find that the challenge of a new job is gone once a system is installed. They find the operations of making minor modifications, updating, or attempting to optimize programs less challenging than starting from scratch with something new. This attitude must be discouraged, and the importance of good, continuing maintenance not only should be recognized, but should be rewarded in terms of pay and prestige.

Reprogramming

Every program ever written could be improved. Sometimes combining several hastily written programs into a single, better planned, smooth-running program improves efficiency. On the other hand, occasionally it is desirable to break one large program into smaller segments, especially where main storage is limited or multiprogramming is used.

To make a system operational as rapidly as possible, emulation of the old equipment or languages may have been used. Even after many years, a surprising percentage of the programs still are run under the emulation mode, with resulting loss of efficiency. Rewriting the emulated programs can improve system performance.

One of the major decisions to be made in the maintenance of systems is at what point reprogramming actually becomes desirable. It certainly is not efficient to rewrite all operational programs every time a piece of equipment is changed. Indeed, one of the principal reasons for using high-level languages such as COBOL has been the fact that reprogramming would not be necessary when computer systems were changed. On the other hand, certain deficiencies springing from older machines can be corrected by reprogramming when newer technology and programming systems are available. Some of these are:

1. *Embedded program tables.* Most tabular information of a rapidly changing nature can be read in from files rather than defined as constant information in the program, making it much easier to change as new items are added to the table.
2. *Limited data structures.* It often becomes necessary to increase the size of fields or records to allow for growth unanticipated when the system was designed.
3. *Lack of minimum controls.* Programmers working under the pressure of getting a system on the air may have omitted certain controls which are vital to continued efficient operation.
4. *Lack of programming standards.* During the maintenance period, the programs might be made more uniform, common data names employed, uniform subroutines established, and other devices used to make the system more effective and convenient.

5. *Lack of common data bases.* When first designed, many systems have some duplication of data. If files are reorganized so that each element of data appears only once, updating will be much simpler.

6. *Inadequate or nonexistent test data.* Much of test data used during the initial installation is hastily developed and often not retained. Maintaining the system gives the opportunity to create adequate test data to be used to verify changes made in the system and to compare the results against predetermined output.

7. *Poor documentation.* Almost without exception there will be additional documentation work to be done as the system becomes fully operational. Some documentation was never completed in the last minute rush to get things going; some may have to be changed in light of errors that were discovered; still other changes might spring from general agreement upon more efficient ways of using the system.

8. *Complex and bulky programs.* Often attempts are made to accomplish as much as possible within a single pass of a data file. The resulting large and complex programs may be difficult to modify. Dividing the programs into smaller segments may greatly simplify updating and revising as the inevitable changes do occur.

9. *Program efficiency.* At times, programs may be rewritten to shorten their run time or, in the case of online systems, response time. Even the best system designers cannot always anticipate exactly how long certain types of table searches, sorting methods, or linking techniques through the data base might take. Programs may be rewritten to change a particular algorithm or technique to cause faster operation.

The amount of space required in storage for programs can often be reduced by revising the form in which data is stored, using the same input/output areas for different files, or making loops more efficient.

Interactive dialogue between the terminal operator and the program may be reworked to reduce the number of keystrokes or otherwise simply the operator's job.

Maintenance Documentation

Three steps are necessary for establishing good maintenance procedures:

1. *Document.* Changes should be made in a system only when authorized specifically in writing. The state of the program or file before the change and its condition after the change should be fully spelled out and kept as a part of permanent documentation. Unauthorized changes by anybody who happens to decide that some changes should be made can be disastrous.

2. *Log.* A written record should be kept as maintenance occurs.
3. *Organize.* A regular assignment should be made of the person or group who will be responsible for maintaining programs. A good combination would be to have a senior person working closely with a less skilled programmer, who can learn a great deal from the superior's expertise in analyzing and optimizing programs.

Figure 14-1 shows a document to show proper authorization and verification of each change to be made in a system or program.

Someone has estimated that 40 to 60 percent of all programming effort is directed toward maintenance of existing programs. Certain of these changes are caused by new rates, creation of new departments, correction of errors, and addition or change of equipment. Maintenance programming can be an exciting and challenging task requiring a high level of skill and diagnostic ability. It can be more varied, more professionally demanding, and more important than any other type of programming assignment; hence, it can be highly rewarding. The relatively short time required for any given maintenance assignment, as contrasted with months or years sometimes spent on original programming, can provide variety and immediate satisfaction to the person who relishes this type of work.

SYSTEM OR PROGRAM CHANGE FORM

System Identification: _____

Program Identification: _____

Nature of Change: _____

_____

_____

_____

_____

Requested by: _____   Date: _____

Authorized by: _____   Date: _____

Changed by: _____   Date: _____

Verified by: _____   Date: _____

Figure 14-1. System or program change record. Each change should be fully documented to show the nature of the change, who requested it, who authorized it, who made it, and who confirmed that it was properly made.

JOB SCHEDULING

One of the manager's most important day-to-day activities involves scheduling work in an uninterrupted flow. The purpose of scheduling is to assure that the resources are at hand when and where needed to produce the results on time and in the form desired.

Various tools are useful in helping with the scheduling. For long-range jobs the PERT chart may be used. For day-to-day normal scheduling runs, a blackboard, magnetic board, calendar, or Gantt chart might well be employed. Some organizations publish a daily or weekly schedule to ensure that all persons involved are aware of the requirements.

Scheduling is principally the responsibility of the operations manager. It is basically a production control problem, and its many intricacies are somewhat beyond the scope of the present book. But efficient operation is so closely interwoven with system analysis and design that the analyst also will necessarily be involved in many aspects of scheduling, for it is he or she who must incorporate them into the total systems plan.

Machine Utilization

Virtually all modern computers use multiprogramming. Some have highly complex scheduling programs to establish a job queue. The job control statements are read into a random storage device, assigned priorities, and executed more or less automatically by the operating system. Some systems are able to determine which files are required, which input/output devices are available, the total amount of core storage required, an assigned priority rating, and a number of other factors to determine the sequence in which jobs will be executed.

Where such a complex operating system is not available, the responsibility of much of the scheduling falls upon the manager or chief operator. One common goal is to achieve a high percentage of machine utilization time, but the importance of machine utilization figures has in some instances been grossly overestimated. Almost any manager can keep equipment busy by doing a large number of petty jobs, by making frequent reruns, or by doing other inefficient operations which keep machines running without really yielding productive output.

It is far more important to have a machine that operates a small percent of its clock time, meets the demands of management, and produces reports in the right form at the time they are scheduled than to have one that clocks a higher percentage of utilization if it delivers inaccurate or delayed reports.

Even those systems that commonly operate in a multiprogramming environment occasionally require the use of the entire system. Some systems are dedicated to a single application for certain hours of the day, partitioned for restricted use at other hours, and partitioned in still a third fashion the remaining time.

For example, a savings and loan association or bank system may be operated online during the day, running a limited amount of work in the background while terminals are processing demand deposits, savings, or mortgage payments in the foreground. After normal working hours, the entire system is turned over to a batch mode to update the day's work, produce the necessary summary reports, and do other jobs which can be delayed until the online activities are performed during the daytime.

Computer-Assisted Scheduling

One widely used technique for obtaining maximum scheduling benefits involves *spooling* the output from jobs onto a magnetic disk device. Spooling, sometimes called *buffering,* is the name applied to the diverting of printed output to magnetic devices rather than to printers. This enables the basic job to be finished must faster because nearly all computers read or write from disk much faster than they can print. A program in one small partition may later be used to read the disk and print the reports while other additional work is being performed in the higher-priority partitions.

Input data from terminals, punched cards, or magnetic tape may also be spooled to disk, where it is stored or *queued* until later use by programs. This practice, like spooling output, reduced CPU time and increases total production over a period of time.

Many spooling programs permit the operator to assign priorities to specific jobs or to alter the priority of jobs already in the queue. Jobs may also be grouped in such a way as to reduce the number of setup operations by the operator. For example, if multiple copies of a report are needed, the output queue can be run as many times as desired without having to rerun the entire program that produced the output.

In earlier chapters we have seen how the computer itself can be used as a valuable assistant in flowcharting and in documentation. The computer also can be of great help in providing instructions to the computer operator for the execution of programs. Basic information, job control cards, disk and tape labels, procedural steps, and other necessary information can be stored on magnetic tape or disk. The information can be updated in the same fashion that master files are updated. Job information can be recalled from the file and printed for the use of the operator as needed. Job identification records can be used at the beginning of the day or week to call forth in the desired sequence the schedule of all jobs to be run with all appropriate documentation and labels (see Figure 14-2).

Input/Output Control

Some computer installations have established a position of input/output control clerk, whose duty it is to act as a job scheduler and to keep track of the status of data from input through all processing steps to output. The scheduler must receive the input data, verify control figures,

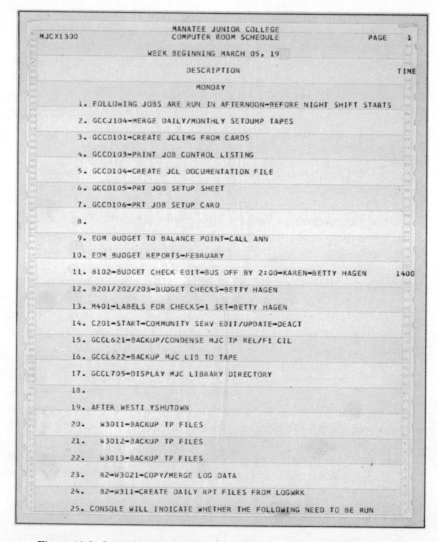

```
                              MANATEE JUNIOR COLLEGE
     MJCX1300                  COMPUTER ROOM SCHEDULE                    PAGE    1

                           WEEK BEGINNING MARCH 05, 19

                                  DESCRIPTION                                  TIME

                                    MONDAY

          1. FOLLOWING JOBS ARE RUN IN AFTERNOON-BEFORE NIGHT SHIFT STARTS

          2. GCCJ104-MERGE DAILY/MONTHLY SETDUMP TAPES

          3. GCCD101-CREATE JCLIMG FROM CARDS

          4. GCCD103-PRINT JOB CONTROL LISTING

          5. GCCD104-CREATE JCL DOCUMENTATION FILE

          6. GCCD105-PRT JOB SETUP SHEET

          7. GCCD106-PRT JOB SETUP CARD

          8.

          9. EOM BUDGET TO BALANCE POINT-CALL ANN

         10. EOM BUDGET REPORTS-FEBRUARY

         11. B102-BUDGET CHECK EDIT-BUS OFF BY 2:00-KAREN-BETTY HAGEN         1400

         12. B201/202/203-BUDGET CHECKS-BETTY HAGEN

         13. M401-LABELS FOR CHECKS-1 SET-BETTY HAGEN

         14. C201-START-COMMUNITY SERV EDIT/UPDATE-DEACT

         15. GCCL621-BACKUP/CONDENSE MJC TP REL/F1 CIL

         16. GCCL622-BACKUP MJC LIB TO TAPE

         17. GCCL705-DISPLAY MJC LIBRARY DIRECTORY

         18.

         19. AFTER WESTI YSHUTDWN

         20.  W3011-BACKUP TP FILES

         21.  W3012-BACKUP TP FILES

         22.  W3013-BACKUP TP FILES

         23.  B2-W3021-COPY/MERGE LOG DATA

         24.  B2-W311-CREATE DAILY RPT FILES FROM LOGWRK

         25. CONSOLE WILL INDICATE WHETHER THE FOLLOWING NEED TO BE RUN
```

Figure 14-2. Job schedule. The schedule may be created, modified, and displayed through use of computer files and regular file processing techniques.

be sure that processing goes according to plan, compare the output results with any preestablished controls, and see that the proper number of copies is distributed to the proper destinations.

The output of one job is often required as input for a succeeding job. The correct sequencing of two such jobs can make a tremendous impact on the total work produced in a day's time.

Another important factor influencing scheduling is the use of similar files by more than one program. For example, if a certain data file on disk can be used simultaneously by programs operating in several different partitions, jobs will be completed faster than they would if the operator had to mount this disk pack several times a day for jobs scheduled at different periods.

Compiling and Testing

Often, insufficient time is scheduled for programmers to compile, debug, and test their program. In some installations, the programming staff is allowed only a few minutes during the day to attempt to do all the necessary compiling and testing. In other places, programmers find that their access to the computer is relegated to the small hours of the night or the weekend. To encourage prompt and efficient results from programmers, the schedule must allow sufficient time for them to test new programs and to modify and maintain existing programs.

Some organizations take the opposite tack and allow programmers principal time on the equipment during the day, running most of the production work during a night shift. However it is done, the important fact is that programmers be allowed enough time to be certain that their programs are as efficient as they can make them.

Scheduling time for testing online programs can be a severe problem. Most systems do not provide the capability for testing new programs that required the data communications handling software at the same time the communications system is operating. Where this is the case, the online system must be brought down temporarily so that testing can be done. Test time should be scheduled so as to cause the least possible disruption to normal operations.

Preventive Maintenance

In working out job scheduling, time for equipment maintenance by the manufacturer or other service agency must not be overlooked. A certain amount of downtime is inevitable, either for preventive maintenance or for correcting errors that may have developed. Where possible, preventive maintenance should be scheduled at a predictable time so that all users will be able to plan their activities around it.

Many larger installations have enough peripheral equipment so that one printer, tape drive, or disk unit can be deactivated for servicing without bringing the entire system to a halt. Some even have parallel processors so that one CPU can be serviced while its work is temporarily shifted to another CPU. Weekend or early morning servicing is fairly common to avoid interfering with normal production schedules.

COSTING AND BUDGETING

In all phases of system development, from the initial request for study through the final installation, cost must be a consideration. It is not always easy to make a clear distinction between *cost* and *value.* For example, what value is assigned to the convenience of having a computer do a job instead of having a person do the same job? Unless it can be shown that the cost to the organization is actually less, or that it receives some other benefit which ultimately can be translated into financial terms, there is no justification for having the computer do the job rather than the person.

The measure of cost must be kept in the foreground during system operation and maintenance. During analysis and planning, most time and cost figures are only estimates, even though based on experience or past records. Only when a system is actually in operation can we determine the true cost of the work being performed.

Collecting Costs

Traditional accounting methods do not lend themselves to the simple and accurate collection of costs. Expenditures traditionally are assembled by department, but departmental costs do not always tell us what a particular procedure or system costs. It is a relatively simple matter to know that the total cost of operating the data processing department is $250,000 per year, but it is much more difficult to find out how much it costs to process the payroll, which involves not only the data processing department but others.

The major categories of costs are (1) *direct* costs, which normally can be determined and applied directly toward the operation in question; (2) *indirect* or *allocated* costs, usually termed overhead; (3) *fixed* costs, such as rent of buildings or equipment, executive salaries, insurance, and other items which do not vary according to the quantity of work done; and (4) *variable* costs, which are proportional to the volume of work done—for example, printed forms tend to be consumed in direct proportion to the length of the job requiring the printing. The true cost of any job then is a combination of fixed and variable costs, which are partly direct and partly allocated.

Unit Costs

We may calculate what it costs to operate each of the devices or to furnish each of the components that make up a job. The total of these unit costs then becomes the total job cost. For example, we may find that our computer rental is $60 per hour. It therefore seems reasonable to charge any computer user $60 for each hour of computer time. The problem is further complicated, however, when we use multiprogramming, where several jobs share the computer during the same hour. To deal with this situation a cost is computed for the amount of core storage used by a job. Thus the program using two-thirds of available storage may be charged $40 per hour, while the one using only one-third is charged $20.

Unit costs may be developed for each individual machine, with the time chargeable to the various jobs recorded on a machine ultiization chart. One approach is to leave one of these sheets on each machine in the installation, so that each operator records whatever time he or she devotes to that machine. Later, records showing the time allocated to each job can be created from each of the sheets each day. The unit costs can be accumulated by job number at the end of the month and charged or allocated to the appropriate user.

The computer center is a service agency. It has no inherent value or purpose of its own. Therefore, the total cost of computer operations can and should be apportioned out among the other using groups. It should be neither a profit-making nor a cost-producing department.

Many operating systems have a job accounting routine as a part of the supervisor. As each job is initiated, the date and time are recorded; when the job is terminated, either normally or abnormally, the elapsed time is recorded and other data, such as the number of lines printed, the number of disk accesses made, the number of instructions executed, the number of bytes of core storage required, and the total number of files opened, may be kept. Standardized job records may be logged out on disk or tape for later summarizing. On the basis of the appropriate unit costs, total job costs may be allocated and charged out at the end of the accounting period. Figure 14-3 shows a monthly summary of online network usage by operator, terminal, and time of day.

Cost Elements

The elements which make up any costing system are:

1. *Equipment.* Included is the rental cost of the equipment or the depreciated cost if the equipment has been purchased.
2. *Environmental cost.* Those costs relating to building modifications, air conditioning, wiring, sound treatment, or other necessary expenditures for creating a proper working condition.
3. *Materials.* This includes both consumable supplies, such as paper, and materials of more permanent nature, such as disk packs and tape reels.
4. *Staff costs.* Salaries are the principal element of cost under this category, but staff benefits, vacations, sick time, recruiting, and other expenses also are included.
5. *Training.* This includes special schools attended by personnel, the duplication and dissemination of training manuals on the premises, apprenticeships, trial periods for new trainees, executive school, and anything else of a training nature.

For a number of years *Datamation Magazine* has made an annual nationwide survey of salaries paid in the data processing industry. Maximum, average, and minimum salaries are presented under a variety of job classifi-

MANATEE JUNIOR COLLEGE
ON-LINE NETWORK
MONTHLY SUMMARY APPLICATION USAGE REPORT

APPL = F-002   FINANCIAL AID UPDATE

01/01/81 THRU 01/31/81

DPR	TERM	SIGNONS	TIME USED	UPDATE	LOGITS	TREAD	TWRITE	ERRORS INIT	OPR	APPL	COMMENT
AHB	044	5	00.09.45	3	4	23	24	0	0	0	
AJR	031	3	00.13.21	1	8	7	9	0	0	0	2 FORCED OFF
CAC	064	2	00.03.39	1	2	5	6	0	0	0	
JEB	037	10	00.24.24	13	31	54	60	0	0	0	1 SECURITY FAIL
JEB	038	71	04.37.24	87	168	392	427	0	0	4	3 FORCED OFF
JEB	044	1	00.01.22	2	3	6	6	0	0	1	
JED	045	4	00.06.47	5	5	13	13	0	0	0	
JED	037	41	36.32.17	5	12	60	65	0	0	0	10 FORCED OFF
JED	038	1	00.28.45	0	0	1	1	0	0	0	1 FORCED OFF
JED	050	1	00.01.45	0	0	2	2	0	0	0	
KTC	037	1	03.01.54	0	4	4	4	0	0	0	
KTC	038	43	06.31.45	74	126	264	278	0	0	2	3 FORCED OFF
KTC	045	2	00.48.24	43	89	95	95	0	0	0	1 FORCED OFF
LGH	037	1	03.01.59	1	2	3	3	0	0	0	
LGH	038	10	00.58.09	8	16	42	47	0	0	0	3 FORCED OFF
LGH	045	100	06.51.42	164	293	513	579	2	0	4	
SLM	037	1	03.12.11	0	0	7	7	2	0	0	1 FORCED OFF
SLM	038	94	12.05.25	86	129	446	478	1	0	2	
SLR	045	2	00.03.56	2	4	9	9	0	0	1	12 FORCED OFF
SLR	058	1	03.02.07	1	1	4	4	0	0	0	
			49.16.48*	495*	893*	1,950*	2,117*				

USAGE COUNT BY HOUR FOR F002 (FROM 01/01/81 THRU 01/31/81)

A.M.	SIGNONS	UPDATES	P.M.	SIGNONS	UPDATES
7:00	0	0	1:00	48	56
8:00	19	57	2:00	73	61
9:00	39	83	3:00	49	71
10:00	65	65	4:00	22	19
11:00	63	75	5:00	5	2
12:00	5	3	6:00	6	3
	191	283		203	212

TOTAL SIGNONS = 394   TOTAL UPDATES = 495

Figure 14-3. Monthly summary of online network usage. The operating system maintains records of equipment utilization by each job. Records may be summarized monthly for review.

cations and geographic areas. The salary survey provides not only a guide against which local salaries may be compared but also valuable information for estimating costs when designing a system.

The entire time during which a system is in operation provides a continuing opportunity to assess and collect costs. When unit costs have been established, it is important to revise them periodically every few months. This is particularly important when users are charged and budgeted according to their share of machine utilization. Many estimates are unrealistic. Most are too favorable because of the tendency of executives or systems analysts to try to make the proposed system appear as desirable as possible. On the other hand, excessive cost estimates tend to discourage the adoption of truly beneficial systems or new devices of much greater capability than those presently being used. Estimates must be based on the best available information, and full costs continuously collected as a basis both for evaluating current performance and for establishing standards for future use.

Intangible Factors

One of the most difficult of all aspects of costing is that of intangible benefits. Suppose a new system permits us to get our customer bills out two days earlier. Does this intangible benefit merit expenditure of additional dollars even if it is not accompanied by increased revenue in the form of quicker payment or a reduction in unpaid accounts? Perhaps our executives like to boast about their fancy new terminals, but do they derive and use more management information to justify the expenditure of several hundred dollars per month?

Do we really need an 1100-line-a-minute printer if printing 600 lines a minute will produce all the work that we need to get out during normal working hours? Would we be better off running our 600-line-a-minute printers two shifts a day rather than our 1100-line-a-minute printer one shift per day? The entire question of costing is one which requires the constant attention of managers of all levels. The important thing is to see that whatever costs are captured are true ones, that all operations are accounted for, and that careful evaluation is made to be certain true benefit is derived for each dollar spent.

Budgeting

A budget is a plan for action translated into financial terms. If we have done a good job of collecting costs, both by individual unit and by project or job, we are in position to project future anticipated costs to cover whatever course of action we choose.

A budget must of course be developed to cover the cost of operating the data processing department for the budget period, normally a year. It must take into account salaries, rental, maintenance, utilities, supplies, furniture and equipment, training, and all the other operational expenses. Unusual or unexpected requirements may cause amendments to be made to the budget, either up or down. The manager must be alert to conditions which may have an effect upon the cost of operating his or her department either before they arise or as they develop. Periodic reports will ensure that the budget is being followed. Figure 14–4 shows a typical monthly budget report for a computer center.

As stated earlier, the data processing department exists mainly to serve others. Its costs, then, ultimately are charged proportionally among the departments that use its services. Hence budgets must be developed showing the costs of the individual services supplied to users.

A large university computer center employs the following scheme to charge the user for only those computer resources which he or she uses in a multiprogramming environment. Each job is charged according to "time," which is defined as

$$\text{TIME} = \text{CPU} + 0.02\ \text{DA} + 0.01\ \text{TA}$$

where CPU = central processing unit time, seconds
DA = number of disk input/output operations
TA = number of tape input/output operations

The total change in dollars for a job would be given by

$$\text{CHARGE} = \frac{(\$200 \times \text{TIME}) + (\text{CORE} \times \text{TIME})}{3600}$$
$$+ \$1.50 \times \text{thousands of cards read}$$
$$+ \$1.00 \times \text{thousands of lines printed}$$
$$+ \$2.00 \times \text{thousands of cards punched}$$

where CORE = amount of core storage allocated to the job in units of 1024 bytes.

In addition, the charges for disk storage would be

Disk = \$0.20/track/month for normal storage
= \$1.00/track/month for procedure library storage

The rates for other services are

Keypunch = \$10.00 per hour
Programming = \$20.00 per hour
Systems analysis = \$30.00 per hour

Using such published rates, each user of the computer center has some basis for projecting the estimated cost of services for the coming year.

Account Title	Acct No.	Annual Budget	Encumbrances	Expenditures to Date	Balance Rest of Year
		MONTHLY BUDGET REPORT FOR DEPARTMENT 1270		COMPUTER CENTER	July 31 19
Supervisors Salaries	550	24,541.00		2,045.00	22,496.00
Programmers Salaries	552	31,200.00		2,560.00	28,640.00
Operators Salaries	554	46,108.00		3,842.00	42,266.00
Travel	601	200.00			200.00
Express and Postage	604	360.00		37.50	322.50
Maintenance on Owned Equipment	616	19,345.00		1,610.00	17,735.00
Equipment Leases and Rentals	622	23,377.00		1,943.00	21,434.00
Office Materials and Supplies	633	14,500.00	248.00	1,157.00	13,095.00
Other Materials and Supplies	649	3,000.00	53.50	44.00	2,902.50
Office Furniture and Equipment	720	5,619.00	135.00	1,240.00	4,244.00
		168,250.00	436.50	14,478.50	153,335.00

Figure 14-4. Typical monthly budget report for a small computer center. The budget is a plan for action shown in financial terms. Encumbrances are amounts committed for purchases that have been ordered but not yet paid for.

The user may then tabulate each quantity of each type of service he or she anticipates using in order to come up with a budget for computer services.

Similar tables of charges customarily are published for time-sharing services, whether provided in-house or by commercial services. Elements of cost include time connected to the system, processor time in seconds, and sectors or tracks of disk storage. The time-sharing user normally pays terminal rental and communication line charges to the vendor or utility, in addition to the charges made by the computer center for processing and storage.

Job accounting data collected for past years by the operating system can provide a useful source for budget planning, both for the data processing department and for users. It does little good to know how long it takes to run 1000 payroll checks unless the accounting department has a good idea of the number of payroll checks it will be running during the coming year. As in all planning, historical records form the basis for making estimates for the coming year. Statistics on the number of transactions of all types; volumes of cards, paper stock, and printer forms; and processing time for different operations are all necessary for effective budget planning.

SYSTEM FOLLOW-UP AND EVALUATION

Too often there is a tendency to feel a tremendous letdown once a new system has been installed. Analysts move on to new assignments, programmers have new projects, operator actions tend to become habitual and routine. It is important to use follow-up in order to consolidate the gains of the new system and to eliminate losses. The line supervisor is of course the most important single person in the follow-up procedure, inasmuch as he or she is in day-to-day contact with the system. However, the analyst also should come back for periodic appraisal and review. In many organizations, the internal auditor will be charged with responsibility for seeing that established procedures and controls are observed. Some of the questions that must be continually reviewed are these:

1. Are costs in line with estimates and established standards?
2. Are the facilities adequate for the job requirement?
3. Do employees give evidence that they accept the new system and perform their duties properly?
4. Is there any evidence of reverting to former practices?
5. Are the various job steps and tasks being performed on schedule and within the specific time allotted?

A badly neglected area in many organizations is that of systems maintenance. Little by little, documentation may be neglected or get out of date. The most able programmers will tend to be assigned to new work rather than to detecting and maintaining problems in existing programs. Operating personnel may tend to disregard established procedures and to fall into poor habit patterns. Supervisors will become preoccupied with more pressing problems and will neglect the routine, ongoing processes.

It is highly desirable to establish a maintenance department within a data processing installation, just a maintenance department is established to keep buildings clean and in good repair. Maintenance programming is a highly skilled, demanding activity. The very best programmers should be assigned to find new ways of improving existing programs. Often it is possible to write more effective algorithms, to cut down on the use of storage, to increase throughput, and to combine steps to make existing programs much more efficient.

As all changes are made and systems maintenance activities are performed, it is imperative that documentation be kept up to date. A library may be established to ensure that all documentation standards are maintained and that only authorized changes are made in either programs or documents.

One final step, often overlooked, is to guard against using the computer for jobs that may be done more effectively some other way. There is a great tendency to try to utilize the computer for clerical jobs, such as preparing address labels or multiple copies of lists. Although information of this type may readily be obtained from a computer, it may be far more efficient to provide master information from the computer, and use other methods for reproducing or duplicating the labels or lists needed. Low-volume jobs requiring elaborate setup are difficult to justify on a computer.

Postinstallation Audit

Even after a newly installed system has been operating normally for a period of time, it is good practice to make a postinstallation audit. The main purposes of an audit at this time are (1) to ensure that the original objectives of the system are being met, (2) verify that prescribed procedures and practices are being followed, (3) measure user satisfaction, and (4) observe quality control for the technical staff.

Role of the Systems Analyst

The postinstallation audit might be conducted by a systems analyst or team of analysts as a special project. In other cases, the internal auditor would conduct the study as part of his or her normal review of operations. Occasionally, an outside auditor or consultant might be brought in.

In any event, the systems analyst should be involved in either making the study itself or in carefully reviewing the findings for any implications that might be found for revision of the system in any way.

The analyst should also be frequently in touch with the data processing manager during the course of normal operations to offer counsel on any questions that may arise or take remedial action when necessary. A close relationship between systems personnel with both operations line personnel and with auditors is essential.

Measurement of Performance against Objectives

The postinstallation audit should include specific measurements to show as precisely as possible the extent to which system objectives are being met. Measurements may be obtained through questionnaires, observation, interviews, document examination, and data collected by the computer system itself.

The measures should include users of all classes, from clerical persons who create input or work with output, to computer center personnel who have to meet production requirements, to top-level management who must act decisively on the basis of information produced.

Each of the objectives that was set forth in the systems study should be evaluated to be sure that it is being met and that it is still relevant in the passage of time and change of circumstances.

Cost-Benefit Analysis

Cost-benefit analysis goes beyond implementation. It is a continuing process that needs to be performed before, during, and after the development of applications. Cost-benefit analysis is designed to measure the system's impact in terms of dollars and to ensure that benefits received equal or exceed costs.

Cost-benefit analysis is complicated by the fact that many of the systems advantages are intangible. The convenience of being able to recall a page of information on a CRT screen versus the need to thumb through a lengthy computer printout to find the same information on a printed page may be difficult to quantify. The savings of time to an individual to do a job one way rather than another is no savings in dollars unless the time saved is put to productive use. But in such terms as are possible, it is precisely the intangible benefits that make or break the value of the system. It can usually be demonstrated that anything that makes employees happier, more responsive, and more productive is good economy in the long run.

Figure 14–5 shows how development costs of a new system may be recovered over time by the benefits of savings in operating costs.

Systems Reviews

The auditor in reviewing online systems must be concerned with far more than mere financial data. The following checklist indicates the wide scope and the thoroughness with which auditors customarily examine the control and management of a computer installation today.

1. *System components.* List personnel, equipment, and applications performed.
2. *Organization*
   2-1. Prepare or obtain an organizational chart of the computer center organization. Determine positions, titles, job descriptions, and name of persons in these positions.
   2-2. Is there a segregation of duties such that:
      a. The functions and duties of system design and programming are separate from computer operation?
      b. Programmers do not operate the computer for regular processing runs?
      c. Computer operators are restricted from access to data and program information not necessary for performing their assigned task?
      d. The employees in data processing are separated from all duties relating to the initiation of transactions and initiation of requests for changes to the master files?
   2-3. Are the operators assigned to individual application runs rotated periodically?
   2-4. Are the computer operators required to take vacations?
   2-5. Is supervision of operators sufficient to verify operators' adherence to prescribed operating procedures?
3. *The control function*
   3-1. Is there a person or group charged with the responsibility for the control function in the data processing department? Obtain description of duties. Do these duties include:

	Current Year	Outyear 1	Outyear 2	Outyear 3	Outyear 4
CURRENT SYSTEM COSTS:					
Personnel	45,000	47,000	49,000	51,300	53,000
Hardware	28,000	30,000	32,000	34,000	35,600
Software	13,000	14,500	16,000	17,800	18,500
Supplies	9,000	10,200	11,800	12,000	13,000
Total	99,300	106,700	114,400	121,100	126,500
NEW SYSTEM COSTS:					
Development Costs:					
Personnel	65,000	10,000			
Hardware	20,000	4,200			
Software	15,000	1,500			
Supplies	3,200	800			
Training	10,400	4,600			
Other	4,100	1,100			
Total Dev. Costs	117,700	22,200			
Operating Costs:					
Personnel		31,100	30,700	31,200	31,500
Hardware		26,000	27,000	27,400	28,000
Software		12,000	14,000	14,200	15,000
Supplies		3,700	4,100	4,200	4,500
Other		2,900	3,000	3,200	3,300
Total Oper. Costs		75,600	78,800	80,200	82,300
NEW SYSTEM BENEFITS:					
Annual Operating Benefits		31,100	35,600	40,900	43,800
Recovery of Development Costs:					
Unrecovered at Start of Year		139,900	108,800	73,200	32,300
Recovered in Benefits		31,100	35,600	40,900	43,800
Unrecovered at End of Year		108,800	73,200	32,300	(11,500)

Figure 14-5. Cost-benefit analysis. This analysis compares operating costs of the old and new systems and indicates that savings of the new system will recover all development costs during the fourth year of operation.

a. Control over receipt of input data and recording of control information?

b. Reconciliation of control information (batch control with computer control totals, run-to-run totals, etc.)?

c. Control over distribution of output?

d. Control over errors to ensure that they are reported, corrected, and reprocessed?

e.   Review of console logs, error listings, and other evidence of error detection and control?

3-2. Is the person or group responsible for control over processing by the data processing department independent from the person or group responsible for the operation of the equipment?

3-3. If there is an internal auditing group, does it perform EDP control activities related to:

   a. Review or audit?

   b. Day-to-day control activity?

   If "Yes," note the nature and extent of these activities.

3-4. Are master file changes or changes in program data factors authorized in writing by initiating department?

3-5. Are departments that initiate changes in master file data or program data factors furnished with notices or a register showing changes actually made? (Example of such changes are changes in pay rate, selling process, credit limits, and commission tables.)

4. *Control over the console*

4-1. Are provisions adequate to prevent unauthorized entry of program changes and/or data through the console? The following questions reflect the types of controls that may be used:

   a. Are adequate machine operation logs being maintained? For each run this should include information covering the run identification, operator, start and stop time, error halts and delays, and details of reruns, idle time, downtime, program testing, etc.

   b. Is there an independent examination of computer logs to check the operator performance and machine efficiency? If "Yes,"

      (1) How often?

      (2) By whom?

      (3) How performed?

   c. If the computer has a typewriter console, is there an independent examination of the console printouts to detect operator problems and unauthorized intervention?

      (1) How often?

      (2) By whom?

      (3) How performed?

5. *Management practices*

5-1. Is there a written plan for future changes to be made to the system?

5-2. Is approval of each application supported by a study of cost and benefits?

5-3. Is a schedule of implementation prepared showing actual versus planned progress?

5-4. Is there a systems and procedures manual for the activities of the installation?

6. *Documentation*
   6-1. Is a run manual prepared for each computer run?
   6-2. Are operator instructions prepared for each run?
   6-3. Are documentation practices adequate? Does the normal documentation for an application include the following:
      a. Problem statement?
      b. System flowchart?
      c. Record layout?
      d. Program flowcharts?
      e. Program listing?
      f. Test data?
      g. Operator instructions?
      h. Summary of controls?
      i. Approval and change records?
   6-4. Is there supervisory review of documentation to ensure that it is adequate?
   6-5. Is documentation kept up to date?
7. *Program revision*
   7-1. Is each program revision authorized by a request for change properly approved by management or supervisory personnel?
      a. Who authorizes?
      b. How evidenced?
   7-2. Are program changes, together with their effective date, documented in a manner that preserves an accurate chronological record of the system?
   7-3. Are program revisions tested in the same manner as new programs?
8. *Hardware controls.* Unless there is evidence of hardware-based processing difficulties, the auditor can usually rely on the hardware. No review is ordinarily required for audit purposes.
9. *Control over input and output data.* Although the control over input and output data must be exercised for each application, general questions regarding these controls may be used to ascertain policy regarding the use of control procedures.
   9-1. Is a schedule maintained of the reports and documents to be produced by the computer center?
   9-2. Are initiating departments required to establish independent control over data submitted for processing (through the use of batch totals, document counts, or otherwise)?
   9-3. Are output reports and documents reviewed before distribution to ascertain the reasonableness of the output?
   9-4. Are there adequate procedures for control over the distribution of reports?
10. *Programmed control over processing.* Programmed control must be evaluated in terms of each application.
11. *Controlling error investigation*

    11-1. Are all error corrections reviewed and approved by persons who are independent of the data processing department?

    11-2. Are records maintained of errors occurring in the data system?

    11-3. Are these error records periodically reviewed by someone independent of data processing?

12. *Physical safeguards over files*

    12-1. Are important computer programs, essential documentation, records, and files kept in fireproof storage?

    12-2. Are copies of important programs, essential documentation, records, and files stored in off-premises locations?

13. *Procedural controls for safeguarding files*

    13-1. Are external labels used on all files?

    13-2. Are internal labels used on all magnetic tape files?

    13-3. Are file header labels checked by programs using the files?

    13-4. Are file protection rings used on all magnetic tape files to be preserved?

    13-5. Is the responsibility for issuing and storing magnetic tape or portable disk packs assigned to a tape librarian, either as a full-time or part-time duty?

14. *Capability for file reconstruction*

    14-1. Are there provisions for the use of alternative facilities in the event of fire or other lengthy interruption?

    14-2. Is there adequate data processing insurance (other than fire coverage)?

    14-3. Are data processing personnel covered by fidelity insurance?

SUMMARY

The responsibility of the systems person is not discharged once the system is installed and operational. He (or she) must review it to see that it is performing according to specifications. He must watch for errors that inevitably occur, incorporate improvements, bring documentation up to date, consolidate, streamline, and simplify. He must coordinate closely with the data processing manager, who has chief responsibility for day-to-day operations.

    Reprogramming of small and occasionally major applications is sometimes indicated. Maintenance programming deserves the attention of qualified, experienced personnel.

    Job scheduling involves a continuing effort to achieve maximum throughput of work. Multiprogramming normally is available to balance rapid internal processing speed with relatively slower input/output operations. Spooling output to a tape or disk for printing at a later time often expedites the flow of jobs.

    Although costs are an important consideration in every phase of system analysis and design, they can most accurately be captured and compared during the period of normal operations. Accurate costs provide the basis for budgeting the future financial plans of the computer center as well as its users in other departments.

The postinstallation audit provides a means of ensuring that the system continues to meet its objectives. The systems analyst should be closely involved with the audit, either as a participant or as a reviewer of the results. Cost-benefit analysis is performed to see that the dollar value of benefits derived from the system exceeds the dollars spent in the cost of producing them. Intangible benefits should be quantified and included in the analysis.

TERMS FOR REVIEW

Budget
Cost-benefit analysis
Direct cost
Embedded program table
Emulation
Fixed cost
Indirect cost
Job scheduling

Machine utilization
Postinstallation audit
Spooling
System follow-up
System maintenance
Unit cost
Variable cost

QUESTIONS

1. Why is maintenance programming often considered less glamorous and less rewarding than creating new programs?
2. Under what conditions is reprogramming justified? What are some alternatives to reprogramming to correct or improve problem conditions?
3. What devices or techniques are used for routine, short-term scheduling of operations that are different from those used for long-term projects?
4. What is spooling? How does it improve job execution time?
5. How can machine utilization percentages give misleading impressions about the real productivity of an installation?
6. Distinguish between cost and value. Which is easier to determine?
7. Which costs of a computer center can be accumulated directly? Which normally have to be allocated or distributed indirectly?

8. Using the figures charged by the large university in this chapter, calculate the cost of a job having the following requirements: two minutes of processing time, 500 disk I/O operations, 1500 cards read, and 1200 lines printed, and 8192 bytes of core storage used.
9. What is postinstallation audit, and who conducts it?
10. What are some of the ways in which performance of a system might be measured against its prescribed objectives?
11. What is cost-benefit analysis? How are intangible factors considered in the analysis?

CASE STUDY
SUNCOAST COMMUNITY COLLEGE

From implementation date of October 15 through January 15, the Suncoast systems team evaluates operation of the new alumni application. As planned, during this interval Susan Musser becomes proficient in all aspects of data entry and production of the desired listings and labels. Gerald Phipps completes the terminal operator's manual and provides copies of it, along with a copy of the complete systems manual, to Marilyn Woods, Director of Institutional Advancement. The programmer's manual and computer operator's manual are retained in the Computer Center.

Two other persons are trained for backup on terminal operations for the alumni application. Sandra Start, Secretary for Community Relations, works in the office next to Institutional Advancement and occasionally fills in when Susan Musser is absent or has a backlog of work. Sally Waters, Data Entry Operator at the Computer Center and a member of the systems study team, who acts as liaison between the center and users in various offices and assists with terminal training, also learns the new system. Both women are eager to learn the new application and help out as needed.

During the period of system evaluation, Arnold Strong, a state auditor, is at Suncoast making a periodic review of accounting and management practices. His services are requested for an postinstallation audit of the alumni application. He determines that procedures outlined during the design and development phases are being followed, all necessary controls are present, and that no changes are necessary.

Gerald Phipps completes a final report on the system. He identifies the following strong points of the system:

1. Maximum use has been made of existing programs, files, and equipment. Programs for the alumni application have been incor-

porated into the regular menu of available programs. Present password procedures, programs to find Social Security numbers for students, standard sort routines, and standard organization for sequential and indexed sequential files have been utilized.

2. The system is relatively simple to understand and to operate. Only two files are required. Virtually no keyboard data entry was required to extract the alumni master file from the student master. Each donor record was created or updated by keying in only five data elements: Social Security number, date, receipt number, purpose, and amount.

3. The system is flexible. Labels and lists can be produced selectively in alphabetic order, by city, by zip code, by degree, by major, and by combinations of these. Donor reports can be produced by year of graduation, by city, and by purpose.

4. The system is inexpensive. It requires only one additional item of hardware—a terminal. Programming has been done by one person working a total of 16 weeks.

Gerald Phipps makes recommendations for further improvements and extensions to the system as the work load and the financial situation permit:

1. The Institutional Advancement Office needs a word processing system to be able to produce individually typed letters and envelopes in both upper- and lowercase. The word processing terminal should be able to serve as a regular communication terminal to the IBM 4341 system.

2. The Suncoast Foundation should develop a complete donor program fully compatible with the alumni application to solicit, record, and report contributions from all sources.

3. The alumni association should be expanded to include a regular newsletter and other publications of interest, and not merely be concerned with fund-raising.

QUESTIONS AND EXERCISES

1. Do you consider three months a long-enough period for follow-up and evaluation of the alumni application? Why or why not?

2. Make a list of points you would examine carefully if you were assigned to make the postinstallation audit.

3. Do you believe that the recommendations for further improvements and extensions to the system should have been incorporated into the system just installed? Give reasons for your answer.

Case Study

MAGNOLIA
MEMORIAL
HOSPITAL

Magnolia Memorial Hospital, containing 500 beds, is a public institution located in a metropolitan area with a population of 140,000. Two years ago, its trustees, on recommendation of Administrator Lane Barclay, decided to computerize its patient billing procedure. The new system would replace a manual system that required hand sorting of 3600 charge slips daily that were prepared in the various departments of the hospital and posting them to patient account cards using a bookkeeping machine.

In the opinion of many observers, the conversion procedure was classic in thorough and precise planning. The first step was to employ Monty Register, an experienced data processing manager who had been an employee of the DATAC computer manufacturer. Register, after thoroughly studying the demands of the new procedure in terms of volume, reporting requirements, and procedures, recommended a BX/180 medium computer system. Register had operated and programmed the BX/180 before going to work for DATAC.

Eighteen months before the target date for converting to the new system, the BX/180 was placed on order. It consisted of 64K of main storage, a 300-line-per-minute card reader, a 600 line-per-minute printer, 30 million bytes of disk storage, and touchtone telephone system attached to a keypunch machine to receive data from various stations throughout the hospital. Monthly rental would be $7800.

Register took full advantage of services offered by the BX/180 manufacturer, obtaining numerous reference manuals and attending several schools. He hired two full-time programmers who were experienced in many aspects of systems design, file layout, and random processing techniques.

Nine months before the scheduled delivery date of the computer, Register employed a computer operator part-time and arranged with a local college to rent up to 20 hours per week of computer time on its BX/180 system for program compiling and testing. The college configuration was almost identical to that ordered by the hospital. Programming and testing continued over the next six months.

Register determined that the payroll could also be implemented initially along with the major patient billing application. He employed two keypunch operators to begin the conversion of files.

Three months before installation of the new system, limited parallel runs were made of the payroll. Sample runs were made of the patient billing using actual data, and the results were compared with those produced from the former system. New custom forms costing $2700 were received and put into operation during these parallel test runs. Day by day the number of patients bills was increased until it approached the number produced under the former system. One month before the scheduled delivery date of the new computer, the two applications were in full operation on the college computer.

Upon delivery of the equipment, only four days were required for the BX/180 engineers to complete the checkout and make it operational. The part-time operator was placed on full-time status, and a second operator was engaged for the night shift. All applications were transferred from the college to the hospital. It appeared that a smooth, gradual, trouble-free conversion had been completed. Visitors from hospitals in various parts of the country came to observe and admire the system.

At the end of the first month of operations, the patient accounts receivable report was out of balance with the control account. The new computer operator had incorrectly used the wrong version of the file for some of the operations; however, this problem was detected and quickly corrected.

The next week it was discovered that some business office personnel had incorrectly coded certain receipts for hospitalization insurance so that numerous patient accounts were credited once for the amount that was to be collected from the insurance and again when the payment was actually received from the company.

At this point Administrator Barclay concluded that the new system was too complex to be learned by the business office employees without a lengthy period of training. He felt that the hospital could not afford the time or expense of providing this training. Without consulting Register and the EDP staff, he recommended to the hospital Board of Trustees that the new system be discontinued at the end of a six-month period, the earliest allowable cancellation date on the computer lease. The board concurred in this recommendation.

Barclay insisted that he had nothing but praise for the work of Register and his data processing staff, for the capability of the equipment, and for the support given by the manufacturer's personnel. He offered to provide jobs in other departments in the hospital for data processing personnel until they were able to find other employment. He contended that the sole reason for his recommendation to discontinue the system was the fact that it was too complicated for the non-data processing personnel who furnished input data to the system and had to interpret the output. He said he had every expectation that a computer system was inevitable and within two or three years he would undoubtedly recommend that one be installed.

QUESTIONS FOR DISCUSSION

1. If you had been a member of the Board of Trustees of the hospital, what questions would you have asked the administrator before considering removal of the computer system?
2. If you had been the data processing manager, what would you have done differently to ensure the smooth implementation of the new system?
3. Whose responsibility was it to ensure that non-data processing personnel were fully acquainted with their duties and that they accepted and supported their new role in providing data and interpreting output?
4. Do you think the new system had a fair trial and enough time to make adjustments and corrections to the problems that occurred?

PROBLEMS AND EXERCISES

1. Draw up a schedule for a training program that should have been carried out for non-data processing personnel of all levels throughout the hospital.
2. Draw a PERT chart for the detailed systems study as conducted and show on it also the training program you designed in Problem 1.

Case Study

INTERCONTINENTAL FOODS

Intercontinental Foods has a worldwide distribution system for food items, grossing over $1 billion per year. Its headquarters are in London, England, and it has major branches in 12 countries. In the United States, company headquarters are in Newark, New Jersey, and regional offices are in Milwaukee, Atlanta, Philadelphia, and Los Angeles.

For processing orders a centralized batch system is used in the Newark office. Three separate departments are involved:

1. The sales department receives the orders and enters them into the computer system through a variety of media. Written orders are keypunched, paper tape is produced as a by-product of typing orders, some documents are scanned optically, and some orders are transmitted from terminals in the regional offices.
2. The distribution group is responsible for inventory control and for forwarding shipping papers to the warehouses.
3. The data processing department creates and mails the invoices. The orders are processed in batches twice a day.

PROBLEM AREAS

The system has been considered adequate, but the error rate has reached 20 percent and is still rising. Robert C. Best, Director of Operations, summarizes the situation for other members of the management team. "We are getting both human and machine errors. Some salespeople are making arithmetic errors or recording the wrong product codes on their order forms. Then we have keypunching errors, or the optical scanner misreads some characters. The paper tape becomes torn or wrinkled, and the holes occasionally are covered and misread. Transmissions from the regional terminals are sometimes garbled."

Best continues, "We can locate and correct these errors, but it costs us time. Under the batch system a lot of our orders are not shipped until the day after they are received. What we need to do is to put the responsibility for the entire order in a single organization as close to the customer as possible. If both the original order and all of the documents we create from it are the responsibility of one branch office, the order can be handled faster and the customer deals with only one organization, instead of with three as at present."

PRELIMINARY STUDY

Best reduces his analysis and recommendations to writing and forwards them to company management at Newark. Donald L. Sellers, Vice President for Systems Engineering, is assigned the task of appointing a team to study the question and make recommendations for improvement. The team, consisting of five persons representing each branch office and the national headquarters, studies the requirements of the system that would provide centralized responsibility and decentralized operational control. They estimate that to develop the system in-house will cost between $2 and $3 million and require 50 to 60 man-years over a period of two to three years.

Instead, the team recommends the employment of Distributed Networks, Inc. (DNI), of Boston, a company that specializes in distributed processing and one that has designed a number of successful similar systems.

The team's report, transmitted through Sellers, is approved by the Intercontinental Foods Executive Committee. A contract is signed with DNI for $500,000 with the stipulation that the work be completed within 15 months.

DETAILED SYSTEMS WORK

Peter Bentley and Catherine Waltham, DNI Vice-Presidents, are assigned to head up the analysis, design, and implementation of the distributed network for Intercontinental Foods. They select three analysts and 10 programmers to work with them full-time. In addition, they are authorized to draw upon other DNI specialists for short periods as needed.

Bentley and Waltham are able to adapt modules they have created for other distribution applications and tailor them to Intercontinental's specific requirements. They also provide a new supporting operating system and an advanced file handling package.

For hardware, they select four DDS-2000 systems for online order entry and inventory update at the four regional offices. The four distributed systems are linked to an IBM 4341 at company headquarters in Newark for centralized order processing. A fifth DDS-2000 is planned for future installation for backup, for program development, and for analysis and control of freight bills.

Applications designed and programmed for the distributed network, in addition to the order entry and inventory control, include:

Transmission of shipping information over communication lines to 27 warehouses, where the shipping documents are printed out on terminals.
Reports of damaged merchandise for each region.
Auditing of expense accounts.
Promotion accounting.
Reports in support of sales.

Procedures

Procedures are developed to permit decentralized order handling but centralized reporting and control. Maximum use is made of evening hours when telephone rates are low. Salespersons telephone their orders each evening to the appropriate regional office, where they are recorded on magnetic tape. Emergency orders may be phoned during the day for direct entry into the system through data terminals. Each order received is acknowledged immediately by the DDS-2000.

If the order cannot be shipped immediately, it is flagged as invalid. Problems such as incomplete information, routing errors, or lack of credit clearance are corrected as quickly as possible and reentered. Orders containing items from more than one warehouse are split into separate orders.

Shipping data for rush orders is prepared immediately at the regional offices and forwarded to the appropriate warehouses for printing on their terminals. Routine orders are verified as to customer name and number and edited for completeness as they are received. Copies of all orders—both rush and routine—are transmitted to the central headquarters CPU the same evening. The central computer generates data for shipping documents for the routine orders and transmits them back to the regional offices. Those offices in turn forward shipping data over the network to the warehouses, where the documents are printed.

Each distributed DDS-2000 produces a number of reports for management, including cash and sales summaries by district, inventory reports, credit reports, and lists of receivables. The central computer produces loading and carrier summaries and a variety of other reports for warehouse management.

Implementation

Development and installation of the entire distributed system requires only 14 months. The total investment by Intercontinental Foods is $500,000 and the time of two persons working in liaison with Distributed Networks, Inc. No structural changes are necessary in any of the offices to accommodate the DDS-2000s. The actual changeover from the batch system to the online distributed system is accomplished in three weeks, taking one branch at a time.

RESULTS

The system meets the most optimistic expectations. Delivery of merchandise is speeded, and accuracy of shipments of orders is greatly improved. The error rate is below 10 percent, and those errors that do occur are readily detected by the online system and corrected fast enough to get all orders to the warehouses for shipment on the same day they are received. No longer is incorrect data transmitted over long-distance lines, as formerly happened on many occasions with the batch system.

The DDS-2000 system handles almost double the previous work load, but actually reduces personnel by two people and helps to free salespeople for better attention to their primary responsibilities. Communication costs are significantly reduced by handling order editing and concentrating at the regional centers.

Further economies are achieved through reducing inventory stocks by several million dollars, as well as by reducing the number of warehouses and distribution centers.

Vice-President Sellers, reporting to the Intercontinental management team at conclusion of the project, summarizes still other benefits: "Besides the money savings and improved order handling time, we have been able to give each regional office greater responsibility for its own business. We anticipate a useful life of 10 years for the present distributed system, and it has the capacity for handling double our present work load. We expect to tie the distribution system into future direct production scheduling and then into advanced market research."

QUESTIONS FOR DISCUSSION

1. Can you propose possible ways to reduce the high error rate at Intercontinental Foods without spending $500,000 for a new distributed processing system?

2. Do you believe this system successfully combined centralized responsibility and decentralized operational control? Why or why not?
3. Do you consider it necessary to transmit all orders from the regional offices to central headquarters and than have the shipping data sent back over the communication lines to the regions and then to the warehouses for printing? Could this procedure be simplified without sacrifice of control and accuracy?
4. Is this case typical in the amount of savings to be expected by using a consulting firm rather than in-house systems development? Give any contrasting cases with which you may be familiar.

PROBLEMS AND EXERCISES

1. Draw a systems flowchart for the procedure for handling both routine and rush orders.
2. Make a list of steps the preliminary study team should take to ensure the competence of Distributed Networks, Inc., before signing the $500,000 systems development contract.

Case Study

BULLDOG INDUSTRIAL SUPPLY COMPANY

Bertrand (Bulldog) Blanchard settled comfortably into the leather chair behind his walnut desk. "Have some coffee, Mike," he said. "Then tell me what you've been doing these last 10 years."

Opposite him, Mike Rivera lifted a coffee cup from the tray the receptionist had brought in. He stirred in a spoonful of sugar and added a dash of cream. "Has it been that long since we graduated from good old Central State? Doesn't seem possible. Well, as you know, my degree at Central State was in electrical engineering. I spent five years designing electronic circuits for computers at Elex International. Then I decided I wanted to get into systems analysis and consulting. I went back to the university to earn an MBA in Management Information Systems. After a couple of years with Micro Services, Inc., I set up my own consulting firm here in the city, concentrating on small business systems."

"That's a coincidence," Blanchard replied. "At our staff meeting this week, my office manager said we really should consider a computer system for our accounting and billing applications. He says our growth will require either additional personnel and another posting machine or a move to computer processing. My secretary is also interesting in a word processor for promotional materials, contracts, and correspondence."

"I'm glad to see your staff is conferring about possible computer usage," responded Rivera. "All too often, I find that decisions to get a computer are based on all the wrong reasons. Some executives merely want to impress their colleagues. Others don't have the slightest idea what a computer can do or how they will use it before they buy it. Last week, one client actually wanted to surprise his staff by getting a computer in just before Christmas with the intention of starting to use it for his accounting and billing on the first of January."

"Well, I don't profess to know much about computers yet," said Blanchard, "but I do know that you have to get expert help and also involve the people who will be programming and operating the equipment. Tell me what we need to do to tell if a computer is practical for us."

Rivera took another sip of coffee and leaned forward. "The traditional steps in analyzing and designing a computer system are pretty straightforward. First, you determine what you want the computer to do for you. Second, you see what system, if any, you are presently using to get the job done and what alternative ways you might use. Third, you select the most likely way and design the reports, files, and programs that are necessary. Fourth, you choose the equipment and write the programs that are needed. Fifth, you install the new system under one of several possible plans. Sixth, you review and evaluate to see that you got what you wanted. If necessary, you make some modifications to fine-tune the system."

"Well, that may be what the book says," observed Blanchard. "But what does that mean in our actual situation? We aren't exactly Exxon or AT&T here."

"True," replied Rivera. "But even a small company usually has one or two bread-and-butter jobs that will justify use of a computer. Then you may be surprised how many additional ways you can utilize the computer as you become more familiar and confident with it. You mentioned your accounting and billing applications. Most companies start there and then move out into other areas. I have installed several accounting software packages that you could probably use without change. But first you need to adopt an overall plan."

"That's where I hope you can help us," said Blanchard. "Could you serve as our consultant to be sure we don't overlook some important steps? I realize that some of our personnel will also have to put some time and effort into our study."

"Right," answered Rivera. "A good decision can only be based on your own needs and preferences. Right now, I can give you a general idea of things you need to do. If you wish to make a formal consultant agreement, I will give you a proposal that you can feel free to accept or reject."

"OK, go ahead. I'm pretty sure that we want to proceed formally, but I would like to hear your suggestions now."

"For starters, how about bringing in your office manager and your secretary? They should hear these preliminary details. They may also have some important suggestions that could determine the direction the study will take later."

Blanchard buzzed his secretary and asked her to call in the office manager. When they arrived, he made the introductions, "Mike, meet Ellen Shirley, my secretary, and Jim Francis, our office manager. This is Mike Rivera, who has some ideas about the use of a computer in our operations. Sit down, everyone."

Rivera outlined his main points. "These are some purely tentative thoughts. Any real decision must be based on a more thorough study of your local situation. Mr. Blanchard has told me you have considered possible use of a computer for accounting, billing, and word processing. These are all valid and common areas of computer usage. Many good programs are available so that you could begin on at least a modest scale without doing additional programming."

After a pause for another taste of coffee, Rivera continued. "The first step is to make a preliminary study to see what sort of detailed study is warranted. If we agree, I think the four of us could make that study. If you can provide some figures for analysis, I could review them and complete a recommendation within two working days. Then if the recommendation is accepted, the full systems study could be completed in about four weeks. I would expect to be on-site for a total of about five working days. Allowing time for equipment delivery, order of forms, and training of personnel, we could begin the first phase of operations within three months."

Francis spoke. "I have been gathering regular figures on the number and dollar value of our transactions. We have about 250 regular customers and average about 3,000 invoices per month. Monthly billings average $240,000. I can get any other figures you might want for analysis."

"Good," said Rivera. "Ms. Shirley, what sort of word processing activity do you envision?"

"I average about 10 letters per day. We have around two contracts per day that are generally a standard form with some variable information. Contracts run about five pages. There are a few office memoranda, several price lists that are revised weekly, and several manuals that are updated periodically."

"Are we talking about one computer for accounting and billing and another for word processing, or can one do both jobs?" asked Blanchard.

"I am tentatively thinking of one microcomputer, using hard disk storage, with two terminals, or workstations, as they are called. The exact configuration will depend on our detailed systems study, but I have a fairly good ballpark estimate of what you are likely to need. Later, another workstation can be added. You will want a letter-quality printer for word processing. It can also be used for invoices, statements, and accounting reports. As the work load expands and other applications are added, you may eventually want to add a matrix printer for the accounting and billing.

It could be practical later to use one computer exclusively for word processing and another for the other applications. It is important to select equipment that can be expanded without having to be replaced as you grow."

"What about programming?" asked Francis.

"I believe we can start entirely with purchased software packages. BASIC, a very popular language, is included with the hardware. You can buy a COBOL compiler later. The local community college has good programming classes that one or more of you can attend. You will undoubtedly find that you will want to add some of your own programs for special purposes as you become more familiar with the computer and its possibilities."

"What is the next step?" asked Blanchard.

"Gather together samples of all the forms you are currently using in your accounting and billing. Collect any written procedures, charts of accounts, or any other documentation you are presently using. I will have a contract proposal in the mail to you tomorrow to help you conduct the preliminary study. It will specify our respective duties and responsibilities and outline a schedule. My standard fee is $250 per day. Since my office is here in the city, there is no per diem or travel. If you decide to accept my proposal, sign the contract and we will set a date to start. After reviewing the report of the preliminary study, we can negotiate a new contract if you want to make a more detailed systems study."

"You've given us a lot to think about," said Blanchard. "We'll be looking for your proposal in the mail."

QUESTIONS FOR DISCUSSION

1. Make a list of positive points illustrated by this case. What, if any, points of possible disagreement or misunderstanding can you identify?
2. Is it realistic to expect to begin to use a computer system entirely with purchased software? Give reasons for your answer.
3. Is it wise to do business with an old friend. Why or why not?
4. What employees other than the office manager and secretary should be involved in the detailed systems study? What should be the role of each one?
5. If you had been Blanchard, what additional questions might you have asked Rivera before you concluded the initial meeting?

PROBLEMS AND EXERCISES

1. Make a list of points that should be included in the contract proposal to be submitted by Rivera for the preliminary study.
2. Draw up what you consider to be a reasonable timetable for conducting the detailed systems study if the parties agree to conduct one.
3. Make a plan for orienting employees to the new system and for training those who will be directly involved in data entry and operations.

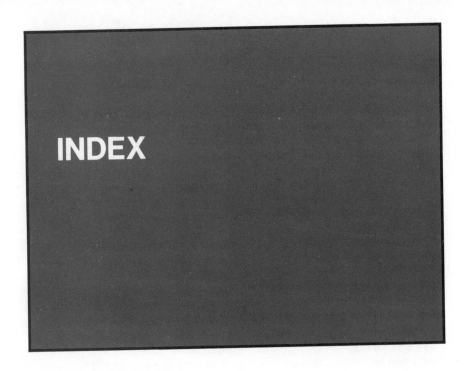

INDEX